*New Directions for Agriculture
and Agricultural Research*

# New Directions
# for Agriculture and
# Agricultural Research

## Neglected Dimensions and
## Emerging Alternatives

*Edited by*

## KENNETH A. DAHLBERG

**ROWMAN & ALLANHELD**
PUBLISHERS

ROWMAN & ALLANHELD

Published in the United States of America in 1986
by Rowman & Allanheld, Publishers
(a division of Littlefield, Adams & Company)
81 Adams Drive, Totowa, New Jersey 07512.

**Library of Congress Cataloging-in-Publication Data**
Main entry under title:

New directions for agriculture and agricultural
research.

Includes index.
1. Agriculture—Research—United States—Congresses.
2. Agriculture—United States—Congresses.  3. Agriculture—Research—Congresses.  4. Agriculture—Congresses. I. Dahlberg, Kenneth A.
S541.N49  1986    630'.72073     85-22046
ISBN 0-8476-7417-7
ISBN 0-8476-7418-5 (pbk.)

86 87 88 / 10 9 8 7 6 5 4 3 2 1
Printed in the United States of America

# Contents

# Tables and Figures

# Preface and Acknowledgments

Ours is a world of specialization. And the dangers of overspecialization—fragmentation, narrowness of vision, and disjointedness—manifest themselves increasingly in events as well as in popular, political, and professional concepts and institutions. Yet the hunger, poverty, energy, resource, and environmental problems of the past decade and a half, by their very interconnectedness, have forced the beginnings of creative rethinkings and restructurings. The process, often stimulated by outside critics or innovators, typically involves painful debate and readjustments in its application to specific fields and institutions. This has certainly been the case with agriculture and agricultural research.

Once we entered a stage where both critics and members of the establishment became less strident and doctrinaire, I felt that an interdisciplinary effort involving both groups as well as outside analysts was needed to take stock of some of the underlying trends and problems. Others agreed and the proposed project that has made this book possible was funded by the Ethics and Values in Science and Technology (EVIST) Program of the National Science Foundation and the National Endowment for the Humanities. Titled "Ethical and Value Choices in the Selection of National Agricultural Research Goals," the project brought the authors together three times—twice for intensive workshops and once for a symposium that presented the papers contained in this book.[1]

The basic questions underlying the project have included: What issues, trends, and phenomena have been neglected in agricultural research and why? How can we better understand the relative importance of these

---

[1] All material is based upon work supported by the National Science Foundation and the National Endowment for the Humanities under NSF Grant No. RII-8309870. Any opinions, findings, and conclusions or recommendations expressed in this publication are those of the authors and do not necessarily reflect the views of the National Science Foundation or the National Endowment for the Humanities.

neglected factors? How do they bear on the debate regarding the sustainability of modern agriculture? What new goals and priorities are emerging from the literature on alternative agriculture? What is the role of ethical and value considerations in the setting of current goals and priorities? Do we obtain new understandings of the nature and importance of agriculture when such factors are included? What are the implications for agriculture and agricultural research?

The project has sought to develop a firmer foundation for addressing such questions by attempting: (a) to make explicit the ethical, value, and goal assumptions and choices contained in current and proposed approaches; (b) to bring together and evaluate data and concepts regarding a number of neglected aspects of agriculture, particularly social, health, resource, and environmental aspects; and (c) to place agriculture in its larger national and global setting by reviewing past and present understandings of the importance of social, political, environmental, and resource factors and trends.

It is also important to stress the things the project has *not* sought to do. A number of important issues, such as world hunger, world trade, food aid, nutritional issues, and consumer issues, were not included as specific project topics because they have already received considerable research and public attention. Nor has the project sought to develop specific policy and organizational recommendations. Rather, it was felt to be more important to focus our efforts on raising and discussing the basic and broader questions facing agriculture and agricultural research. We have sought to do this by providing an overview of what we know and don't know about externalities in agriculture, by reviewing the evolution of agriculture's historic goals into today's goals, by exploring emerging alternatives, and by examining interactions between agriculture and larger societal and global trends, possibilities, and choices.

A complex project such as this has deep and diverse roots. The support and stimulation provided over the years by students and colleagues can be acknowledged only in general terms. My earlier work on the green revolution and the various responses to it provided a basic foundation from which to work. A workshop and conference on "Agriculture, Change and Human Values," held at the University of Florida under the leadership of Richard P. Haynes and Ray Lanier, and the people and ideas I encountered there helped greatly in formulating the ideas for the project. The indispensable financial support of the EVIST Program has already been acknowledged. It is sad to note that NSF recommended the elimination of this innovative program in its 1986 budget—a recommendation recently partly reversed. I owe a great debt to the contributors to this book—properly called the "Core Group" in the project—who through their collaborative efforts have helped to improve and refine the initial overall conceptions of the project. Even so, it should be stressed that while each author has sought to address the common themes and issues of the project, each speaks for him- or herself.

The two workshops, held at the General Accounting Office (GAO), and the Symposium, held at the National Academy of Sciences, were extremely stimulating interdisciplinary colloquia. Among the Core Group, special thanks are due to William Aiken, who, in addition to writing his own chapter, read and offered excellent critical comments on the other chapters. Thanks are also due to John Patrick Jordan, who joined the Core Group before his appointment as Administrator of the Cooperative State Research Service of USDA. After the second workshop, he suggested and then facilitated the participation of Dale L. Stansbury and Jean Lipman-Blumen in the symposium. The issues they address and the perspectives they bring to bear on them complement the initial project topics nicely. Our host for the workshops at GAO, William E. Gahr, also deserves special thanks for his general encouragement of the project and for his assistance in helping to identify the various Washington participants in the project.

My local advisory committee—Jon Bartholic, Charles O. Houston, Maynard Kaufman, Michael Pritchard, and Wayland P. Smith—served as a valuable sounding board and source of constructive criticism and helped in the editorial process by reviewing the chapters at the various stages of their evolution. Special thanks go to Maynard Kaufman for the extra help and creative collaboration he has provided, not only on this project, but over the years. My graduate assistant, Donald Koelb, provided regular and intelligent help in both bibliographic matters and in managing the details of the project. The word processing of the entire manuscript was handled with precision and humor by Krista Cory.

Finally, I would like to dedicate this book to my two daughters, Kirsten and Birgit Dahlberg, whose love and patience have helped to sustain me throughout the whole process. They are my most direct and personal link with that vital repository of hopes and fears, of change and continuity—the next generation. My hope is that this work will contribute to the development of societies and environments for future generations that are more sustainable and regenerative than the threatening and heavily mortgaged ones we inhabit.

Kenneth A. Dahlberg

# 1

# *Introduction: Changing Contexts and Goals and the Need for New Evaluative Approaches*

## Kenneth A. Dahlberg

Over the past century there have been dramatic changes in rural life and agriculture worldwide. These changes have been part of a larger process whereby countries in the temperate zones have moved from being rural and agriculturally based societies to urban and industrial societies. Abundant resources, cheap energy, technological innovations, and cultural factors were all involved—albeit with a different mix in each case. The U.S. case, to be discussed in detail in Chapter 6, involved early and significant government interventions in creating and developing agricultural institutions and research capabilities. An historic pattern of change, criticism, crisis, and adjustment emerged then and continues. Today, however, several new factors bearing upon agriculture and agricultural research place them in a significantly different context.

One factor is that while the agricultural sector in each country has increasingly been incorporated and integrated into a national economy, these national economies have themselves become intertwined in complex international trading patterns (see Chapter 5). Another factor is that population increases, environmental degradation, and potential resource scarcities have raised questions regarding the long-term sustainability of industrial society as currently structured, not to mention the viability of such traditional supporting goals as rapid economic growth and technological progress.

This chapter begins with an overview of the changing global context and how it bears upon problems of international agriculture, Third World development, and U.S. agriculture. Only by appreciating the full dimensions and implications of these larger global and national contexts can the importance and needed redirection of U.S. agriculture and agricultural research be properly evaluated. The main elements and issues involved in developing a new framework for evaluating agriculture and agricultural research are then presented and are addressed in more detail in the succeeding chapters.

## The Changing Global Context

In the burgeoning literature and debates on global problems, which range from threats of nuclear annihilation to limits to growth to world systems of neo-colonialism and dependency, there has been little recognition of the fundamental importance of agriculture, the largest and single most significant interface between natural and human systems. The complex reasons for this neglect tend to cluster around several cultural and disciplinary assumptions and biases. Western cultural assumptions regarding the relationship between man and nature led to a general neglect of environmental factors, including agriculture, until the last twenty-five years. Also, as Western societies industrialized, urban biases increasingly permeated both social and intellectual systems, resulting in lower levels of status and concern for agricultural and rural matters. Finally, most academic disciplines neglected or excluded the informal aspects of society from their analyses—aspects which often represent the major proportion of social and agricultural activity in many non-Western societies and which are still of significance in the industrial world.

### Global Environmental, Resource, and Population Trends

Until recently, resources and the environment have been understood in terms of utilitarian goals and technological mastery. Although there has been concern over rapidly growing populations at least since the time of Malthus, traditional understandings and debates revolved around the different growth rates between food production and population, the predictable consequences, and their moral implications. Concern regarding the "limits to growth" has profoundly altered and broadened this debate; issues of world hunger and the population explosion are still included, but basic questions regarding the physical, biological, and social limits of industrial society are raised in addition. Intertwined are a host of philosophical, ideological, methodological, and ethical issues.

PHYSICAL LIMITS. Debates regarding global physical limits have focused on the work of computer modelers. In contrast to Malthus, they have specifically tried to include estimates of land and resource availability as well as the possibility of technological innovation. In addition, they have included many more elements or sectors and have structured their interactions as dynamic systems involving positive or negative feedback. The resulting models and projects—the most famous being embodied in the *Limits to Growth* (Meadows, *et al.*, 1972), *Mankind at the Turning Point* (Mesarovic and Pestel, 1974), and the *Global 2000 Report to the President* (CEQ, 1980)—have challenged conventional wisdom, technological optimism, as well as disciplinary specialization, and have been the subject of much controversy (see Cole, 1973, and Simon, 1981).

A somewhat different approach to the questions of physical limits has been based upon the laws of thermodynamics, especially the "entropy law." Nicholas Georgescu-Roegen's scientific and philosophical critique of the technological optimism underlying both conventional economic thought and models of industrial growth is most notable (1971). A popularized version which explores the implications of this approach for all sectors of industrial society is found in Rifkin's work (1980). Recently, Georgescu-Roegen has argued that in addition to recognizing the energy limits imposed by the entropy law, we must recognize that matter itself is subject to a similar law and process: *i.e.,* "that matter, like energy, continuously and irrevocably degrades from an available into an unavailable state" (1981). Thus he is doubly skeptical about maintaining an energy-intensive society after "the fossil fuel age" because in addition to limits on easily available energy, the massive energy and material requirements of large-scale energy conversion installations—whether nuclear or solar—make it progressively more difficult and costly to replace each unit as it wears out.

BIOLOGICAL LIMITS. The biological limits of industrial society relate not only to the population explosion, but to the question of how much pollution and environmental destruction the biosphere can endure before its basic biological systems suffer irreparable and irreversible damage. Although usually not thought of in these terms, the most obvious and immediate threat is that of large-scale nuclear war, as the literature on a "nuclear winter" has pointed out (Ehrlich, *et al.*, 1984; London and White, 1984). In addition, a wide range of studies have been conducted to try to estimate the longer-term influence of carbon dioxide and ozone buildups on climate, the effect of acid rain on forests and soils, the problems of desertification and deforestation, water pollution and salinization, pesticide dispersion, and so on—issues which are discussed in more detail in Chapter 4. Perhaps the most fundamental and disturbing indicator of the biological consequences of the spread of industrial society is the increasing loss of species and such biologically important and species-rich habitats as the world's tropical forests. The issues here are basic, whether they are expressed in terms of U.S. national interest (see *The U.S. Strategy Conference on Biological Diversity*, U.S. Dept. of State, 1982), ecologically sound development (see the *World Conservation Strategy*, IUCN, 1980), or of keeping our evolutionary options open (see Dahlberg, 1979).

SOCIAL AND ORGANIZATIONAL LIMITS. Discussion of the social and organizational limits to industrial society can be traced back to the concerns raised by de Tocqueville and elaborated upon by Marx regarding the alienation of workers. Today's concerns are based upon a deep disaffection with industrial society on the part of a much wider range of groups. In addition, and perhaps a major source of this disaffection, are basic questions regarding the nature and rigidity of modern institutions. While productive, the impersonal, large-scale, centralized institutions of industrial society—whether public or private, capitalist or socialist—are slow to adapt to basic changes in their larger environments, whether those changes relate to market changes, social changes, or changes in resource availability. If the capacity to adapt is slower or less than the magnitude of change, there is great risk of collapse.

Three general approaches to dealing with these problems can be seen in the rather meager literature on these topics. Ironically, the dilemmas found within each of these approaches themselves illustrate the social and organizational limits of modern society. First, there is the approach of trying to develop additional organizational and technological capacities in order to control markets, people, and resources. While appealing to some, such increasingly authoritarian approaches not only go against democratic norms, but increase the risks of collapse because of their great rigidity. Second, there are calls for better planning to try to deal with the "lead-time" problems of these large-scale institutions. Such planning suggests much greater dependence upon a technocratic elite, yet the structure of modern institutions is such—witness the U.S. automobile and steel industries—that the planners tend to be insulated from and insensitive to the large changes and trends which they are supposed to anticipate and adapt to. And even if they do identify them, the power and inertia of vested interests makes changes difficult until a "crisis" arrives—often too late for effective action. Third, there are those who argue for greater decentralization. While clearly more compatible with democratic norms and an approach that offers less rigid and more adaptive structures than the other two, the problem here is how to accomplish any significant decentralization.

*Agriculture and the Global Context*

What then is the importance of agriculture in relation to these larger global trends and the instability of industrial society? The various global computer models mentioned earlier give perhaps the best overall picture of the size and significance of agriculture as an interface between natural and human systems. The projections of population trends and of the use and abuse of the land, water, rangeland, forests, and species of the rural regions of the world clearly suggest that in the absence of some catastrophic event such as nuclear war, much of the future of the biosphere will hinge on what happens in rural and agricultural regions. These global studies are important in another regard: that is, they clearly demonstrate that conventional intellectual "maps," which deal largely with the economic, political, and technological aspects of agriculture, cover only a small part of the real territory involved.

Some of the reasons for this are intellectual: as mentioned, the disciplines tend to examine the more visible formal sectors and organizations of society and those physical and social phenomena which are easily measurable. That there are large surrounding "terra incognitae" in the many informal aspects of society and their interactions with natural systems is often not even noted, much less analyzed in comparative terms. In general, the developing countries have much larger informal sectors than the developed countries and much of the agricultural production and exchange is local and non-monetized. Even within the U.S., the USDA has little awareness of the size or importance of the "invisible" produce from family gardens—a "crop" estimated in 1982 to be equal in value to the corn crop of that year (*Newsweek,* July 26)!

There are also the deeper cultural reasons mentioned at the outset: the low status given agriculture, farmers, and rural areas in Western culture, plus the pervasive urban bias in industrial society (see Lipton, 1977, and Blum, 1983). Questions about the stability of industrial society bring out a related dimension. There are few attempts to try to understand the role of agriculture in evolutionary terms. Certainly, anthropologists have contributed much here with their distinctions between hunting and gathering societies, agricultural societies, and industrial societies. Yet much of the literature suffers from either some sort of technological determinism or Western assumptions regarding progress and the spread of urban-industrial civilization. Even so, the examination of industrial society in comparison to societies structured in fundamentally different ways, as well as discussions of how specific societies adapted or collapsed, gives a much needed perspective on modern industrial society and its various intellectual and cultural assumptions and biases (for general discussions, see Bennett, 1976, and Moran, 1979; for an excellent case study of collapse, see Murphey, 1957).

Even though these larger dimensions of agriculture are not included in conventional disciplinary "maps," there has been an increasing awareness of the importance of agriculture in the literature on international relations, international trade, and economic development. International events and the U.N. megaconferences have spurred this expanded awareness. The OPEC oil embargo forced industrial countries to examine carefully their relative resource endowments and trade dependencies. Given the importance of U.S. agricultural exports and trade, it was not long before the U.S. sought their increased use as a foreign policy instrument. For example, at the 1974 World Food Conference, Henry Kissinger pushed for trade-offs with the OPEC countries by seeking from them greater financial commitments for food aid and agricultural development. Later, there was the rather clumsy attempt of the Carter Administration to use food exports as a "weapon" in its grain embargo against the USSR.

In addition, there has been an increase in the literature on agricultural development, rural development, the "green revolution," the role of multinational corporations in these areas, and analyses of how U.S. domestic agriculture is linked to international trade and development. The basic question that emerges out of this literature is: how beneficial or harmful has been the exporting of Western industrial agricultural models and practices? Certainly, there have been dramatic increases in the production of rice, maize, and wheat in various countries (see Wortman and Cummings, 1978). However, the distribution of benefits has been very uneven, there have been nutritional and dietary costs for many groups, and there has been much accompanying social and political dislocation (see Frankel, 1971; Pearse, 1980; and Galli, 1981). Also, since these models and practices are capital- and energy-intensive and are based on temperate zone environmental experience, it is not clear that they are sustainable in the longer-term in very different environments which also suffer from being capital- and energy-poor.

## U.S. Agriculture and Agricultural Research

At the national level, changes, concerns, and debates have emerged which are similar to those at the international level. First, there has been a dramatic change in the basic operating context of U.S. agriculture. The basic resources required—land, water, energy, labor, and capital—have all become more expensive. At the same time, national and international economic conditions and events have led to increased competition and declining prices for major commodities. Politically, the determination of agricultural policy and priorities has been shifting away from farm and rural areas—ironically at a time when the 1980 census confirmed a migration reversal where more people moved to rural areas than away from them. The urban expectations of many of the new rural residents often create new types of conflict with farmers over land use, tax assessments, and farming practices.

Second, the impacts of agriculture and the food system upon environments and people became much more obvious. Soil erosion, declining water tables, salinization, various forms of pollution, and increasing pest resistance to pesticides all became matters of concern as did a range of health, food safety and nutritional issues. These concerns, plus a growing awareness of the dependence of U.S. agriculture on increasingly scarce and expensive fossil fuels (see Chapter 12), have led to a questioning of whether U.S. agriculture, as currently structured and practiced, is sustainable.

Finally, a whole host of equity and distributional issues have emerged from the above changes as well as from the larger social debates about national priorities regarding energy, resources, and the economy. These include the controversies surrounding the increase in unemployment due to increased mechanization, the different regional impacts of rising water and energy costs, the trend towards larger corporate farming and other changes in rural and farming structures, the conflicts between farmers and the new rural residents, and so on.

These challenges and debates—often originating from outside the U.S. agricultural research establishment—and the general failure of the establishment to anticipate and deal with them have led to a number of major reviews of the problems of agricultural research. Some of the more notable include the *World Food and Nutrition Study* (NAS, 1977), the Office of Technology Assessment's *United States Food and Agricultural Research System* (OTA, 1982), the report of a workshop on critical issues in American agricultural research, *Science for Agriculture,* jointly sponsored by the Rockefeller Foundation and the Office of Science and Technology Policy (Rockefeller, 1982), and Vernon Ruttan's thoughtful *Agricultural Research Policy* (1982).

Each of these suggests serious inadequacies in the ability of the U.S. agricultural research system to respond and adapt to the challenges sketched out above. The Rockefeller/OSTP report expresses concern about the parochialism of the system—where regional competition often predominates, about the unevenness in focus and scientific quality of the research done, and about the rigidity of the system. In their view, it is most unfortunate that:

> much of the debate over the future of agricultural research is characterized by interinstitutional and interdiscipline tension, defensiveness, and rigidity at a time when institutional collaboration and flexibility, interdisciplinary efforts, and a focus on scientific and technological problems are essential for progress [Rockefeller, 1982:5].

The various reports—as well as other observers and critics—disagree on the reasons for this rigidity and lack of responsiveness. Even more than the Rockefeller report, an earlier National Academy of Science study, the so-called Pound report (NAS, 1972), stressed the lack of scientific quality in agricultural research. The OTA study largely dismisses this, stressing the productivity of U.S. agriculture and suggesting that "It is generally meaningless for a group of scientists working in basic research to evaluate the quality of those working in the applied area and vice versa" (OTA, 1982:77). The OTA report focuses much more on the institutional and organizational problems currently visible, but concedes that "There is no satisfactory long-term process for evaluating research activities, resource opportunities, and development of research priorities" (OTA, 1982:9). Others argue that the very narrow professional training and the parochial career paths followed by most agricultural scientists greatly influences their research choices and skills (Busch, 1981). Others stress the various ways in which research priorities are easily influenced by external groups and pressures (Hightower, 1973). Finally, there are those who argue that in addition to the above, deeper cultural beliefs and structural forces shape research agendas and the direction of agriculture more generally (Berry, 1977; Dahlberg, 1979).

Proposed remedies tend to be as divergent as the above diagnoses of the underlying reasons for the lack of responsiveness. However, one theme is common to the various proposed remedies: that there is a critical need to develop a set of national goals for agriculture and agricultural research. For example, "The lack of well-defined and agreed-upon national goals for U.S. food and agriculture is a major deterrent in formulating broad food and agricultural policy at the national level" (OTA, 1982:8). Equally, "The lack of a coherent national agricultural policy, relating productivity goals and domestic and international policies with an explicit understanding of the value of agriculture to this country, greatly hampers efforts to establish national goals and priorities for agricultural research" (Rockefeller, 1982:9).

Yet, in spite of a common emphasis on their critical importance, no one—whether in academia, government, or the private sector—has done much systematic thinking about agricultural goals. The changing context of agriculture (described above) as well as the emergence of a number of alternative approaches suggest that it is important to begin this process. Three basic questions would appear to be involved. The first is *What do we want to do?* Even though there are significant differences between the goals of conventional and alternative agriculture, both tend to be broad. Typically, there is little attempt within either group to discuss possible conflicts between goals or to develop a hierarchy of goals (see Chapter 13 for a discussion). Reasons for this include both the difficulty of the intellectual, philosophical, and moral issues involved as well as the high social and political costs of either developing or changing major goals.

Next is the question *Why do we want to do it?* This question relates primarily to the values of the various groups and organizations involved. These values differ considerably both between groups and between levels, as will be shown below. Finally, there is the question *How do we do it?* Several distinct dimensions are involved here. Does this goal conflict with other goals? Do we have the necessary knowledge and technical means? Are both the means chosen and their probable consequences ethically acceptable?

## Developing a New Evaluative Approach

If agriculture is going to be able to deal effectively with the new challenges and problems emerging out of changing global and national contexts, then it is clear that a much broader and systematic approach is required. Not only will goals need to be clarified, but a number of other interacting elements and relationships will need to be evaluated. Figure 1.1 illustrates four major, but often neglected, elements which bear upon the development of national agricultural goals and the setting of research priorities. The following discussion outlines what has and has not been done in terms of analyzing and understanding each of them.

### The Problem of Externalities

The question of what is included and what is excluded in evaluating any substantive field is fundamental. The main evaluative concepts and indices used in agriculture have been economic and have excluded many social, environmental, and health effects. The work of agricultural economists has been primarily concerned with assessing the productivity, efficiency, and the distributional consequences of various policies or technologies (see Arndt, Dalrympl, and Ruttan, 1977; and Fishel, 1971). There is an extensive literature on different approaches and indices, including a National Academy of Sciences study (1975). While this literature is important, greater emphasis needs to be placed on trying to assess more systematically the non-economic externalities. This is in line with Ruttan's argument that while agricultural science needs to continue its commitment to expanding the productive capacity of the resources used in agriculture,

> society should insist that agricultural science embrace a broader agenda that includes a concern for the effects of agricultural technology on the health and safety of agricultural producers, a concern for the nutrition and health of consumers, a concern for the impact of agricultural practices on the aesthetic qualities of both natural and artificial environments, and a concern

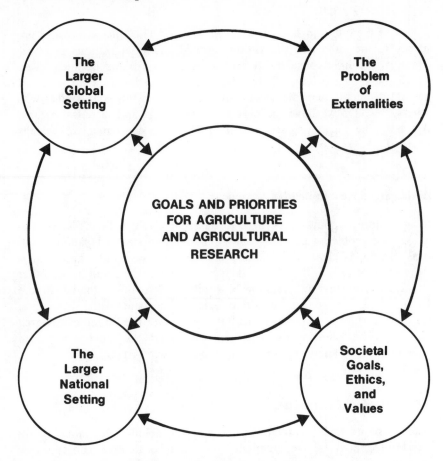

Figure 1.1   Main Elements and Relationships in an Evaluative Framework
for Agriculture and Agricultural Research

for the quality of life in rural communities and that considers the implications of current technical choices on the options that will be available in the future [1982:350–51].

If these concerns are to become an integral part of the agenda for agricultural research, then the research that has been done in each of these areas (usually by researchers outside of agriculture) needs to be assembled, the concepts and indices used made explicit, the underlying assumptions spelled out, and the data availability and data needs assessed. This volume represents an initial step in that direction.

In the health and safety area, there have been traditional concerns with farm equipment accidents. In recent years, there has been controversy over the effects of pesticides and herbicides on farmers and farm workers.

Contamination of food is a matter of increasing concern—whether the contaminants are residues of pesticides (DDT) or fumigants (EDB) or growth hormones given to livestock. Also, there have been systemic accidents such as the PBB disaster in Michigan which contaminated much of the food chain. Chapter 9 gives an overview of these problems.

In the environmental area, concern has been focused on water pollution, salinization, the loss of soil fertility, the increasing resistance of various pests to chemical pesticides, the pollution and health risks of those pesticides and herbicides, the use of genetically similar hybrids, the loss of plant germplasm, and the reduced biological diversity and resiliency of larger ecosystems. These relate directly to the questions of global limits discussed earlier.

In the resource and energy area, major publicity has been given to the loss of soil through erosion and farmland through conversion (Sampson, 1981; USDA, 1981b). The overcommitment and salinization of surface waters have increased pressures on groundwater resources, as have new technological developments such as center-pivot irrigation. The increasing price and scarcity of petroleum has led to a number of studies analyzing agricultural efficiency and productivity in terms of energetics (Steinhart, 1974; Pimentel, 1975; Leach, 1976). These analyses give a very different picture of the efficiency of U.S. agriculture than that viewed through the indices of agricultural economics (and raise basic questions about what one wants to conserve or maximize and why). Chapter 12 gives an updated overview of these matters. Also, the study of energy and resource efficiency rapidly brings one into a discussion of possible alternatives. These may be focused on agriculture (Oelhaf, 1978; Anderson, 1979; Lockeretz, 1981) or may address larger social alternatives (Lovins, 1977; Rifkin, 1980; Henderson, 1981).

When one turns to questions of the quality and importance of rural life, one finds a rich historical tradition of debates and policy battles over alternatives. Our early history involved different views and approaches as to what the destiny and future of the new nation ought to be. The contrasts between the Jeffersonian and the Hamiltonian visions illustrate these and have provided deep cultural roots for various political and social movements. Since World War II, there has been controversy about changes in rural life and in farm size and structure (see USDA, 1981a). The trend towards larger units of production, an aging farm population, declining and decaying small towns, corporate and foreign ownership of land, large migrations first to the urban areas and now away from them, the impacts of larger and more sophisticated farm equipment on both farmer and farm labor—all these have received much publicity and debate, yet there has been no integrated or interdisciplinary attempt on the part of the land grant schools to address this major part of their mandate. Chapter 10 reviews some of the reasons for this. The major thrust of agricultural research and extension has been on increasing production; attempts to assess the technological and social impacts have been secondary and have been done by separate specialists—often rural sociologists. The latter, however, have been torn by self-doubts about their relevance and calls have increased for a new and critical rural sociology (Buttel and Newby, 1980). Certainly, the failure of demographers and rural sociologists to identify the migration turnaround has raised serious questions about both the concepts and indices used to evaluate rural phenomena and changes (see Wardwell, 1982, for a discussion).

A final area that needs further exploration is the informal economy. A consideration of it illustrates the problem that policymakers and the public tend to "see" that which is measured much more than that which is not measured. For example, the annual agricultural census specifically excludes what farmers produce for home consumption, thus restricting statistics and productivity figures to field production for the formal or market economy. However, a recent survey by Gardens for All and The Gallup Organization indicated that in 1982, 44 million of America's estimated 82.4 million households—or 53 percent—had vegetable gardens. The estimated value of this household production was $16 billion (*Newsweek*, July 26, 1982)—an amount roughly equivalent to the value of the entire U.S. corn crop at the depressed prices of 1982. The corn crop is very visible and is a source of much policy and economic debate, legislation, and research. However, these millions of gardens and their billions of dollars worth of produce are, in effect, invisible and have been largely ignored by researchers and policymakers. At a more general level, few philosophers and social critics have stressed basic ethical questions about the increasing size and role of the formal economy and the psychological, practical, and social consequences of the radical separation of production and consumption in modern industrial societies (Ollman, 1976; Illich, 1978 and 1981).

In conclusion, we should note that any more comprehensive assessment of externalities can be expected to suggest different sets of priorities than those currently dominant, and may even suggest different goals. This is because what we "see" to be happening in agriculture and what we understand its "costs" and "benefits" to be also strongly influences (in ways often only secondarily related to ethical and value positions) what we think ought to happen in agriculture and agricultural research.

## Societal Goals, Ethics, and Values

Analyzing the interactions between societal goals, ethics, and values and those found in agriculture is a difficult, but needed task. First, as indicated above, it is important to have as accurate and comprehensive a picture as possible of what is happening in agriculture and its related areas. Next, one must define and categorize national goals for agriculture and ask how such national goals relate to goals currently found within the agricultural sector, including those for agricultural research. *Much of the confusion in agricultural policy and research relates to the simple-minded, and unfounded, assumption that national goals for agriculture are, or should be, the same as the goals of those within the agricultural sector.* The full ramifications of this distinction need to be explored, both ethically and empirically. At a minimum, two levels of research are suggested. One (largely lacking today), would examine the larger functions and importance of agriculture to our society; *i.e.,* how agriculture is basic in some regards, and contributes in others, to the larger health, social, environmental, and economic needs and goals of society, both in the short and long term. The other would involve a re-thinking of the currently dominant level of research—which focuses primarily on meeting the shorter-term economic needs of the major groups within the agricultural sector—to include the externalities outlined above. Still remaining would be the essentially political task for the society of reconciling the differences between the goals at each level, something complicated by differentials of political power among the groups involved.

One example of the confusion between national and sectoral goals is found in the recent Office of Technology Assessment (OTA) study on the U.S. food and agricultural research system (1982). On the one hand, it suggests that:

> With the present structure of USDA, there is some question as to whether USDA has a national research program or merely a series of local and regional activities. Consequently, USDA and SAEA appear to be working on seemingly indistinguishable problems. Many people, including Congress . . . question whether national issues are receiving adequate attention [OTA, 1982:4].

Yet later on in the report, a narrow, production-oriented definition of agricultural research is given, one which would effectively exclude most national issues: "Agricultural research is the systematic search for new ways of improving agricultural production and marketing" (OTA, 1982:29). Typically, no mention is made of the time horizon to be employed in agricultural research and the emphasis is on achievable, shorter-term production goals (an emphasis encouraged by budget cycles and bureaucratic factors). Geographic impacts and issues tend to be discussed more in local, state, and regional terms than national or international terms.

In the literature, one occasionally finds broader definitions, such as that offered in the *World Food and Nutrition Study:* "The role of research is to broaden the range of choices available to all who influence world food supply and nutrition: farmers, consumers, agri-business managers, health service personnel, governmental officials, and politicians" (NAS, 1977:44). Of course, analogous definitions could be given regarding the need for resource and energy conservation, rural development, national and/or global equity, etc. The real question is how to sort out the different levels of goals and priorities and how to evaluate their interacting empirical and ethical dimensions.

To do this, we need: (a) a better categorization of agricultural goals and better descriptions of the actual goals held by all the relevant groups; (b) a better understanding of the types of ethical and value issues involved as well as the actual controversies themselves; and (c) better ways of categorizing and understanding the explicit or implicit evaluation criteria used to set priorities and to choose among goals.

1. GOAL CATEGORIES. The broadest and most systematic set of goal categories appear to be those of D. G. Russell (1975). With some additions and considerable broadening, they are as follows:

## Consumption Category

1. Quantity—including both total production and productivity.
2. Quality—including appeal, nutritive value, reliability, and versatility.
3. Availability—including growth cycle limitations, supply and demand instabilities, and the number of possible substitutes.

## Security Category

4. Health and Safety—including the risk of accidents and disease, as well as food contamination from pesticide residues and hormonal additives.
5. Economic Security—including international concerns such as balance of payments, economic dependence, and such domestic concerns as the economic viability of agriculture and rural regions.
6. Food Sources Security—including traditional concerns such as protecting crops and animals from diseases and pests (and how chemical and IPM approaches compare), plus newer concerns about genetic diversity, plant germplasm conservation, and plant patenting.
7. Conservation—including non-renewable resources and the various threats to renewable resources, such as loss, degradation, pollution, overuse, etc.

## Equity Category

8. Distribution—including production, means of production, wealth and land, as well as costs, risks and losses, and how they are distributed among species, groups, classes, regions, and countries; and on what basis they might be distributed (social utility? some principle of fairness? the free market? individual contribution, merit, or need?).

9. Employment—including matters of free and/or equal access to employment, formal and informal modes of work, and technological impacts upon the nature of work and employment (such as mechanization and computer systems).

10. Individual Rights—including how these conflict with or complement employment and distributional issues as well as how they are and might be handled by social and political structures and institutions. Examples would include civil rights, worker health and safety rights, consumer rights, and, perhaps, animal rights.

This set of goal categories is particularly useful because it includes a much wider range of goals than is typical. Also, it brings out some of the underlying ethical and value issues. However, it neither addresses the issue of how to set priorities among the goals nor how one might choose among alternatives for reaching any given goal. Indeed, given the tendency to emphasize—if not reify—the goals, values, and interests of the dominant groups in society, it is particularly important to try to give genuine consideration to alternative viewpoints, possibilities, and priorities.

An important first step in any such consideration is simply to describe the *goal positions* of both dominant and alternative groups involved with, or concerned about agriculture. Table 1.1 represents an initial attempt at such a description. Two difficulties are involved in deciding which alternatives to include. First, which of a wide range of alternatives is roughly representative? Second, should one try to correct for the urban and homocentric biases found even in much of the literature on alternatives? Unfortunately, little of the "alternative futures" literature has much to say directly about either agriculture or rural life and culture—even though the language generally stresses decentralization and locally adapted, appropriate technologies.

In addition to including alternative positions, the other major feature of Table 1.1 is the breakdown by groups and levels. This is meant to bring out several important points. First, many actual or potential goal conflicts occur between levels as well as between dominant and alternative groups. Second, it helps illustrate how groups at one level may seek to define goals at the next higher (or lower) level for their own advantage. Thus, it

Table 1.1 Goals Held by Dominant and Alternative Groups

| Group/Level Involved | Dominant Positions | | Alternative Positions | |
|---|---|---|---|---|
| | Goals (professed and/or operative) | Underlying ethics and values | Goals (professed and/or operative) | Underlying ethics and values |
| Farmers | Family support<br>Make money, have a high standard of living<br>Produce more through specialization by crop/commodity<br>Stewardship of the land<br>Fighting world hunger | Rural conservatism<br>Individualism<br><br>Love of nature<br>Moral concern | Family and community support<br>Diversified farming/homesteading<br>Conservation of energy, soil, and local species<br>Social justice<br>Having nutritious/healthy food | Family/group self-reliance<br>Rural community<br>Integrated way of life<br>Harmony with nature<br>Moral concern |
| Agriculture as a Sector | Increased production<br>Stable prices & markets domestically<br>Expanding foreign markets<br>Profitable operation<br>Specialization by commodity | Corporate and market economy | Sustainable production<br>More local & regional markets (formal and informal)<br>More small farms<br>Farm & regional diversity<br>Having nutritious/healthy food | Informal & cooperative approaches<br>Regenerative systems<br>Local & regional self-reliance<br>Voluntary simplicity<br>Recycling systems |
| National | Increased production<br>Cheap food<br>Foreign exchange and aid<br>Industrialization of agriculture and urbanization | Economic growth<br>Science and technology linked to progress<br>National power | Rural revival<br>Rural revival and decentralization | Sustainable economic growth<br>Respect of nature and ecosystems<br>Cultural and personal contentment |
| International | Elimination of hunger (through trade and aid)<br>Agricultural development<br>Economic development | National sovereignty & planning<br>Expanding international markets and trade | Elimination of hunger (through local production)<br>Rural & ecodevelopment<br>Cultural development | A globe of villages<br>Greater autarchy |
| Global | Balance between food, population, and resources | Western<br>Anthropocentric | Balance between food, population and resources<br>Conservation of genetic and biological diversity | Recessive Western plus Non-Western<br>Inclusionist |

can be argued that the agricultural sector has been largely successful in having its sectoral goals accepted as U.S. national goals, with the exception of the goal of cheap food and perhaps the use of food and agriculture as an instrument of national power. Finally, such a breakdown also provides a basis for describing how goals are (or are not) related to the basic resource, security, and political needs of groups.

2. TYPES OF ETHICAL AND VALUE ISSUES. To better understand the types of ethical and value issues and the controversies themselves, we must clarify at least five interacting analytic aspects. First, is the problem of *congruence* or consistency. In its simplest form, a lack of congruence or consistency between the goals, values, and means of a particular group can generate ethical and/or value controversies. Next, even if there is internal consistency, conflicts can emerge if these goals, values, and means are not consistent with what is possible in the real world (a question that is complicated by whether one is talking about the "real world" of today, tomorrow, next year, or the next decade). Finally, we must consider whether the answers of one group are compatible or conflict with the goals, values, and means of other groups or the society at large. Here the basic political problem of choosing priorities and making trade-offs emerges once again.

Second, and directly related to this is the matter of *the level and unit of analysis used.* The social sciences are not systematic or consistent here— and confusions abound between economically, socially, and geographically based units and levels (see Dahlberg, 1983b for a discussion). The difficulties are compounded in agriculture because complex interactions of natural, social and technological systems are involved. The natural sciences have their own disciplinary-based typologies. And at present, there are only the barest outlines of a typology of technological systems emerging out of the literature on appropriate technology (see Morrison and Lodwick, 1981). While analytically there is a great need for examining the interactions of these three broad systems at a number of levels, the interdisciplinary approaches required go against the modern academic grain.

Third, there are the *distributional questions.* While the economic impacts of various farm policies are often discussed, typically this is done in general and aggregate terms. Disaggregation is needed to assess the actual distribution of impacts. Little analysis has been done on past, much less potential, impacts of agricultural research (although the California mechanization case is certainly making this a controversial issue). As suggested above, much work is needed to assess non-economic impacts and their distribution. Finally, this is an area where different ethics, values, and theories of justice become visible, particularly when one consciously addresses such important questions as: (a) What groups are to be included in our assessments (only individuals? only groups? only present generations? or also future generations? only our own nation? or all nations?

only humans? or other animals and species?)? (b) What sorts of causal chains, risks, and responsibilities do we accept or not accept as reasonable in our assessment? (c) Over what time horizon? (d) How do different social systems influence distribution? does ideology (capitalist or socialist) or do infrastructural patterns (large-scale, centralized, industrial infrastructures vs. small-scale, decentralized, non- or post-industrial infrastructures) have more influence in shaping the distribution of a society's costs, benefits, and risks—however defined?

Fourth, and already mentioned, is the matter of *the time horizon* employed (consciously, or more often, unconsciously). The time horizon one chooses influences both the level and the scope of analysis. The natural sciences consciously employ many time horizons; for example, biology has one set of concepts related to the multi-century theory of evolution, a different set associated with the theory of succession (approximately a century), and other concepts linked to ecosystem theory (short term). Not only are the concepts different, but the scope and degree of detail which can be captured are different. Evolutionary theory can speak only of species, not of individuals; at the other end of the spectrum, specific ecosystem studies are very detailed, but tell us little about evolution. Among the social sciences, only anthropology has dealt much with evolutionary theory and different time horizons. In ethical terms, there is not only the question of intergenerational justice, but whether it is ethical or right for one species to increasingly threaten and destroy other species which have evolved on our shared biosphere over the millenia.

Finally, there is the matter of *different cultural values, settings, and perceptions.* While dominant cultures have always tended to assume that their values and practices were superior—and consequently tended to impose them on others—modern techniques have increased the capability to do so. Some of the problems involved can be seen in the transfer of that mega-technology called the "green revolution." While some might see this as an example of adaptation since the new high yielding varieties were adapted to tropical photoperiods and seasons, all of the larger characteristics of modern industrial agriculture were simply transferred. Simple goals of greater productivity were accepted and transferred (the assumption evidently being that increased productivity would increase welfare). Definitions of efficiency (that which is to be saved) based on the factor proportions in the U.S. were transferred without questioning whether one should seek to substitute energy and capital (machinery) for labor in the developing countries, where both energy, capital, and natural resources are typically scarce and labor plentiful (for a full analysis, see Dahlberg, 1979). In addition, many fundamental differences between temperature zone and tropical or semi-arid zone agriculture were ignored, not to mention differences in social structure, land tenure, etc.

EVALUATION CRITERIA. The question of how one evaluates such matters brings us to our third task: trying to find better ways of categorizing and understanding the explicit or implicit criteria that are used to set priorities and choose among goals (Chapter 2 contains a detailed discussion of this). As with ethical and value issues, evaluation criteria can range from the general to the contextually specific. General criteria may be based on customary practices, religious beliefs, legal and/or political doctrines, philosophical systems, or scientific theories. Any of these goes well beyond the agricultural sector, and consequently the determination of agricultural priorities in their terms is only one part of a much larger evaluation or balancing process. Selecting a specific set of criteria by which to evaluate agricultural priorities has its own difficulties. This is because goals and values are dynamic and interact with the development of new knowledge as well as with basic changes in technologies and production systems, social structures, resource availability, and/or environmental conditions. Also involved is the relative merit of the claims and needs of different groups at different levels.

Some of these dimensions are captured in Aiken's discussion (1984) of the criteria against which agriculture should be evaluated: profitability, sustainability, environmental soundness, the satisfaction of human needs, and compatibility with a just social order. Even here, each such criterion needs much further specification and clarification if it is to offer a clear guide for choice and judgment. Let us examine in some detail one of the "newer" criterion used extensively in both conventional and alternative agricultural literature: *substainability*. Gordon Douglass (1984) argues that the term is given three major meanings; (a) sustainability as food sufficiency, a conventional and primarily economic definition that adds a bit to the time horizon employed; (b) sustainability as stewardship, a definition emerging from the literature on organic farming and stressing the use of renewable resources; (c) sustainability as community, a much more socially oriented definition stressing the justness or fairness of social structures and the need for participation in decision making.

Douglass finds certain problems with each of these and proposes his own composite definition (1984:25): "Agriculture will be found to be sustainable when ways are discovered to meet future demands for foodstuffs without imposing on society real increases in the social costs of production and without causing the distribution of opportunities or incomes to worsen." This definition, cast primarily in individualistic (and Rawlsian) terms, takes account of, but does not stress either the ecological or community aspects of the other definitions. More importantly, it appears to accept uncritically whatever demand may exist for foodstuffs and, unlike the other definitions, offers no guidance as to either why one would want to pursue sustainable systems or how one might do it. Finally, like all of the other definitions, it appears to be based on concepts of homeostasis and/or balanced linear change over time.

This is where the term "regenerative agriculture" may offer some potential advantages (for a useful overview, see Rodale, 1984). It strongly points to the fundamental problem of all living systems: regeneration or reproduction. Yet it does not directly point to other needed and complementary concepts: mutation, adaptation, succession, and evolution. These concepts involve a profoundly different understanding of change than linear or even general systems models; they seek to describe systems with constantly shifting parameters—or one might say, systems with constantly evolving patterns of change and continuity. Thus, to draw one implication, the problems and approaches to "regenerative food provisioning" were, and are, very different between hunting and gathering societies, agricultural societies, and industrial societies. [Note that we cannot even use the term "agriculture" when we employ an evolutionary time-frame and its concomitant concepts.]

We also need to think through the different levels or systems that need to be regenerated or reproduced. As indicated above, contemporary agriculture involves complex interactions between natural, social, and technological systems. In terms of natural systems, there is concern regarding the reproduction of the basic seeds and plantstocks needed in agriculture. As is being increasingly recognized, this requires the preservation of genetic and biological diversity. The storage of foodplant germplasm in seed banks is important, but not enough, and the development of a system for preserving genetic resources in their natural habits is crucial (see Dahlberg, 1983a for a discussion). The same need exists for livestock and fisheries. There has been somewhat more discussion of how one regenerates soils, grasslands, and forests, but typically for smaller scale systems, rather than on a global basis. As yet, few people have asked how we regenerate the other critical living component of contemporary agriculture: farmers and their families. This is partly because Western culture tends to define humans as outside the world of nature and partly because of our technological optimism. Yet as soon as one asks how one regenerates farmers and their families, one moves into a wide range of social and institutional issues. What kind of educational system is needed? What kind of farm structure? What kind of economic system and incentives? What kind of inheritance system?

There has been virtually no discussion of how one might regenerate various technological systems—whether agricultural or otherwise. Granted, there has been much debate and analysis of how we might "reindustrialize America." Yet, such discussions are based on linear models of change and industrial assumptions. Those exploring alternative and appropriate technologies are more concerned with the shifting parameters of industrial society (the depletion of non-renewable resources, especially fossil fuels, and the need to base technologies more on renewable resources). Yet there remain problems of understanding what the maintenance requirements of "renewable" resources are as well as of appreciating the longer-term dimensions of the entropy process—in both its energetic and material terms (see Georgescu-Roegen, 1981). And, of course, technologies and technological systems involve knowledge and skill—and thus humans—so that once again, questions of education, institutions, incentives, etc. emerge. In any case, the whole area of technological systems, their cultural and environmental underpinnings, their inherent structural tendencies, and their interactions with social and natural systems needs considerable study, especially in agriculture. Such broader concerns bring us to the final two elements which need to be considered in developing an evaluative framework for agriculture and agricultural research.

## The Larger National and Global Settings

Obviously, there is a need to examine at the national and global levels the same sorts of interactions between natural, social, and technological systems that have been discussed in terms of agriculture. Here too, a much longer time horizon than is typical helps to identify deeper structural trends as well as to reduce various cultural biases. Let us begin by reviewing some of the broad cultural and historical issues and themes that have shaped our understandings of agriculture and industrial society. Western conceptions and values regarding nature have been particularly influential. In both science and religion, two broad approaches are found. One stresses the separation of humankind from nature, mind from body, material from spiritual. This tradition may encourage the exploitation of nature (either as an act of dominance or defense), particularly if there are facilitating technological developments. The other approach stresses that humankind is an integral part of nature, that mind is intertwined with body, and that matter often can be seen to embody values—intrinsic as well as imparted. This tradition—which has been a recessive strand the past few centuries—may encourage more respect and care for nature, although the example of the degradation of traditional Chinese forests and landscapes in spite of a strong cultural reverence for nature suggests that such respect may be a necessary, but not sufficient condition for effective conservation of nature.

Other contrasting cultural themes relate to the views that Western civilization has had of the ideal social life. While Mumford (1967) overstates the way in which utopias—from Plato onwards—have been visualized in terms of cities, there clearly has been a stress on urban social groups. The contrasting cultural tradition—arcadianism—has also been found since the time of the ancient world (see Meeker's discussion [1974] of Theocritis and Virgil). Obviously, the type and extent of technology in a society may strongly affect the desires and ability of different groups to try to establish one or the other of these social orders. Elements of these two themes are found in the Jeffersonian and Hamiltonian visions of what the new nation should strive to become (see Lipset, 1967, and White and White, 1977). The Jeffersonian vision of a rural and largely self-governing democracy based on small-scale farmers and artisans was a strong one in the nineteenth century and was complemented by arguments that small farms also ensured freedom of occupational choice and that they offered competitive markets as guides to rational economic behavior (Raup, 1972). The rhetorical bows which policymakers today make to the importance of the family farm are either rituals of nostalgia or attempts to divert attention away from basic structural changes in agriculture (Vogeler, 1981).

Current discussions of rural and/or agricultural alternatives is curiously divided between an almost purely intellectual and academic discussion conducted by various humanists and the discussions emerging out of the actions and concerns of the environmental and appropriate technology movements. Academic interest in arcadianism and the pastoral ideal has continued (see Frye, 1967; Marx, 1969; and White and White, 1977). Discussion emerging out of the women's movement—at least that part emphasizing feminist spirituality—has stressed radically different views of nature and humankind's place in it (see Gray, 1981; and Spretnak, 1982), while largely ignoring the practical implications of these ideas for rural and farm women. The interest of environmentalists in rural and agricultural issues focuses on finding less energy intensive and less environmentally damaging approaches to agriculture (see Anderson, 1979; and Jackson, 1980). Appropriate technologists have stressed the virtues of decentralization—both urban and rural—as well as local self-reliance in their search for smaller scale, more localized, and less destructive technologies (for somewhat different perspectives on the appropriate technology movement, see Long and Oleson, 1980, and Morrison and Lodwick, 1981). Unfortunately, most futurist literature ignores these issues and concerns and—much like classical utopian writings—sees agriculture as a secondary and uninteresting sector.

The concerns expressed by these groups and movements are largely domestic. However, there are echoes at the international level, implicitly calling for a transformation of society and the place of agriculture in it. Some of these derive from analyses of the global environmental, resource, and population trends discussed at the outset. Others are based more on equity concerns and how global trends may affect their local accomplishment. Particularly notable here is the extensive literature criticizing conventional approaches to development (see Farvar and Milton, 1972;

Griffin, 1974; and Diwan and Livingston, 1979). Also, concern has been expressed about the consequences of the increasing internationalization of agriculture, its increasing commoditization, and its increasing incorporation in the agribusiness chain (de Janvry, 1983). This can be seen as part of a larger trend, whereby economic factors have been progressively abstracted and removed from their social and environmental matrices (Polanyi, 1957). Equally, there is concern that over the longer-term, modern industrial agriculture may not be sustainable either at home or abroad, and may be reducing—along with other industrial processes—the evolutionary options of the biosphere, and thus of humankind (Dahlberg, 1979).

In a certain sense, these writers, analysts, and movements may be seeking to "assess" in broad cultural and environmental terms the "externalities" occasioned by the transformation of agriculture over the past centuries and to envision what their "internationalization" would mean to society, particularly if combined with some set of neo-arcadian values. Their "wishful thinking" becomes more practical in rough proposition to the degree that resource depletion, non-monetary externalities, and the social entropy of large-scale organizations turn out to be truly significant factors over the coming decades.

It may be a difficult challenge to trace out these various themes at the national and global levels; yet it should be clear that we need a more comprehensive understanding of the various forces and values at play. Only by stretching our imagination—by more carefully examining the richness of our cultural roots and history as well as by reviewing the literature on alternatives—can we adequately understand and evaluate the changing interactions between society-wide trends and goals and those more specific to agriculture.

## Summary and Conclusions

In this chapter, we have tried to place the changes and challenges facing U.S. agriculture and agricultural research into their larger national and global contexts. Doing this makes clear that conventional understandings of agriculture need to be informed with a much greater awareness of global environmental, resource, population, and structural trends. Equally, as argued in the final section, we need to explore more systematically the different cultural and intellectual roots of Western understandings of nature, the environment, agriculture, and the "ideal society." The various urban and industrial biases in our thinking that derive from the utopian tradition—as contrasted to the more rural-oriented arcadian tradition— were stressed. The undervaluing and neglect of rural and agricultural matters is an integral part of this larger cultural context. However, public uneasiness with the costs and impacts of industrial systems, shifts in visions of the "good life," and the possibility of fundamental shifts in the resource base of industrial society—essentially away from dependence on non-renewable resources—all suggest that currently dominant urban-industrial ideals may be obsolete or at a minimum in need of reinterpretation.

The main thrust of the chapter and the book is on the implications of these various changes, challenges, and trends for U.S. agriculture and agricultural research. Many of these are expressed (although often implicitly) in the various reports and critiques that have appeared in the past decade. Reviewing them in the light of the larger global trends makes clear the need for a much broader and comprehensive framework for evaluating the goals, priorities, and direction of U.S. agriculture and agricultural research.

The broad outlines of such a framework were presented, along with a discussion of the main elements involved. These all relate to matters which have been neglected or have received insufficient attention or research within current approaches: (a) the social, environmental, and health externalities of agriculture; (b) the ethical, value, and goal dimensions; (c) the larger national setting; and (d) the larger global setting. In addition to summarizing the major externalities (as a prelude to the more detailed analyses presented in the chapters that follow), some of the intellectual, methodological, and sociological sources of their neglect were sketched. Finally, emphasis was placed on a detailed examination of ethical, value, and goal dimensions, particularly as they relate to the various goals and values held by dominant and alternative groups. Different concepts of sustainable and regenerative agriculture were also reviewed. As with conventional agriculture, a basic weakness identified here is that few analysts understand agriculture as a complex interaction of natural, social, and technological systems.

All of these things have a great bearing upon what researchers and policymakers "see" or do not "see" as important matters—that is to say, they have a strong bearing upon goals and priorities, not to mention upon our ability to imagine or envision adaptive alternatives and changes to present approaches, systems, and institutions. It is hoped that the chapters which follow will help to clarify what we know and what we need to know in each of these broad areas. In this way, it is hoped that the basic importance of agriculture (at all levels) will be more clearly demonstrated; that the new approaches, concepts, and data suggested for better evaluating agriculture and agricultural research will encourage others; and that all of this will help provide a basis for developing more regenerative and sustainable agricultural systems that are (and are understood to be) integral parts of larger natural and social systems.

# References

Aiken, William. 1983. "The Goals of Agriculture." In *Agriculture, Change, and Human Values,* ed. Richard P. Haynes and Ray Lanier. Vol. I, pp. 29–54. Gainesville: University of Florida Humanities and Agriculture Program.

Anderson, Russell E. 1979. *Biological Paths to Self-Reliance.* New York: Van Nostrand Reinhold.

Arndt, Thomas G.; Dana G. Dalrymple; and Vernon W. Ruttan, eds. 1977. *Resource Allocation and Productivity in National and International Agricultural Research.* Minneapolis: University of Minnesota Press.

Bennett, John W. 1976. *The Ecological Transition.* London: Pergamon Press.

Berry, Wendell. 1977. *The Unsettling of America: Culture and Agriculture.* San Francisco: Sierra Club Books.

Blum, Jerome, ed. 1983. *Our Forgotten Past.* London: Thames and Hudson.

Busch, Lawrence, ed. 1981. *Science and Agricultural Development.* Montclair, New Jersey: Allanheld, Osmun.

Buttel, Frederick H., and Howard Newby, ed. 1980. *The Rural Sociology of the Advanced Societies: Critical Perspectives.* Montclair, New Jersey: Allanheld, Osmun.

Cole, H. D. S., *et al.,* eds. 1973. *Models of Doom.* New York: Universe.

Council on Environmental Quality (CEQ). 1980. *The Global 2000 Report to the President.* Washington, D.C.: U.S. Government Printing Office.

Dahlberg, Kenneth A. 1979. *Beyond the Green Revolution: The Ecology and Politics of Global Agricultural Development.* New York and London: Plenum.

_____. 1983a. "Plant Germplasm Conservation: Emerging Issues and Problems." *Mazingira* 7:14–25.

_____. 1983b. "Contextual Analysis: Taking Space, Time, and Place Seriously." *International Studies Quarterly* 27:257–266.

de Janvry, Alain. 1983. "Historical Forces That Have Shaped World Agriculture: A Structuralist Perspective." In *Agriculture, Change, and Human Values,* ed. Richard P. Haynes and Ray Lanier. Vol. I, pp. 14–28. Gainesville: University of Florida Humanities and Agriculture Program.

Diwan, Romesh, and Dennis Livingston. 1979. *Alternative Development Strategies and Appropriate Technologies.* Oxford: Pergamon Press.

Douglass, Gordan K. 1984. "The Meanings of Agricultural Sustainability." In *Agricultural Sustainability in a Changing World Order,* ed. G. K. Douglass, pp. 3–29. Boulder, Colorado: Westview Press.

Ehrlich, Paul R.; Carl Sagan; Donald Kennedy; and Walter Orr Roberts. 1984. *The Cold and the Dark: The World after Nuclear War.* New York: Norton.

Farvar, M. Taghi, and John P. Milton, eds. 1972. *The Careless Technology: Ecology and International Development.* New York: Natural History Press.

Fishel, Walter L., ed. 1971. *Resource Allocation in Agricultural Research.* Minneapolis: University of Minnesota Press.

Frankel, Francine. 1971. *India's Green Revolution: Economic Gains and Political Costs.* Princeton, New Jersey: Princeton University Press.

Frye, Northrop. 1967. "Varieties of Literary Utopias." In *Utopias and Utopian Thought,* ed. Frank P. Manuel, pp. 25–34. Boston: Beacon Press.

Galli, Rosemary E., ed. 1981. *The Political Economy of Rural Development.* Albany: State University of New York Press.

Georgescu-Roegen, Nicholas. 1971. *The Entropy Law and the Economic Process.* Cambridge: Harvard University Press.

_____. 1981. "The Crisis of Resources: Its Nature and Its Unfolding." In *Energy, Economics, and the Environment,* ed. G.A. Daneke, pp. 9–24. Lexington, Massachusetts: D. C. Heath.

Gray, Elizabeth Dodson. 1981. *Green Paradise Lost.* Wellesley, Massachusetts: Roundtable Press.

Griffin, Keith. 1974. *The Political Economy of Agrarian Change.* Cambridge: Harvard University Press.

Henderson, Hazel. 1981. *The Politics of the Solar Age: Alternatives to Economics.* Garden City, New York: Anchor Books.

Hightower, Jim. 1973. *Hard Tomatoes, Hard Times.* Cambridge, Massachusetts: Schenkman.

Illich, Ivan. 1978. *Toward a History of Needs.* New York: Pantheon Books.

_____. 1981. *Shadow Work.* Boston: Marion Boyars.

International Union for the Conservation of Nature and Natural Resources (IUCN). 1981. *World Conservation Strategy.* New York: UNIPUB.

Jackson, Wes. 1980. *New Roots for Agriculture.* San Francisco: Friends of the Earth.

Leach, Gerald. 1976. *Energy and Food Production.* Surrey, England: IPC Sciences and Technology Press.

Lipset, Seymour Martin. 1967. *The First New Nation.* Garden City, New York: Doubleday.

Lipton, Michael. 1977. *Why Poor People Stay Poor: Urban Bias in World Development.* Cambridge: Harvard University Press.

Lockeretz, William, *et al.* 1981. "Organic Farming in the Corn Belt." *Science* 211:540–547.

London, Julius, and Gilbert F. White, eds. 1984. *The Environmental Effects of Nuclear War.* Boulder, Colorado: Westview Press.

Long, Franklin A., and Alexandria Oleson. 1980. *Appropriate Technology and Social Values: A Critical Appraisal.* Cambridge, Massachusetts: Ballinger.

Lovins, Amory B. 1977. *Soft Energy Paths: Toward a Durable Peace.* New York: Harper and Row.

Marx, Leo. 1969. *The Machine in the Garden: Technology and the Pastoral Ideal in America.* New York: Oxford University Press.

Meadows, Donella H., *et al.* 1972. *The Limits to Growth.* New York: Universe.

Mesarovic, Mihajla, and Edward Pestel. 1974. *Mankind at the Turning Point.* New York: Dutton.

Moran, Emilio F. 1979. *Human Adaptability.* Belmont, California: Wadsworth.

Morrison, Denton E., and Dora G. Lodwick. 1981. "The Social Impacts of Soft and Hard Energy Systems: The Lovins' Claims as a Social Science Challenge." *Annual Review of Energy.* Volume 6. Palo Alto, California: Annual Reviews.

Murphey, Rhoads. 1957. "The Ruin of Ancient Ceylon." *Journal of Asian Studies* 16:181–200.

National Academy of Sciences (NAS). 1972. *Report of the Committee on Research Advisory to the U.S. Department of Agriculture.* Washington, D.C.: National Academy of Sciences.

_____. 1975. *Agricultural Production Efficiency.* Washington, D.C.: National Academy of Sciences.

_____. 1977. *World Food and Nutrition Study.* Washington, D.C.: National Academy of Sciences.

Oelhaf, Robert. 1978. *Organic Agriculture: Economic and Ecological Comparisons with Conventional Methods.* Montclair, New Jersey: Allanheld, Osmun.

Ollman, Bartell. 1976. *Alienation.* New York: Cambridge University Press.

Office of Technology Assessment (OTA). 1982. *An Assessment of the United States Food and Agricultural Research System.* Washington, D.C.: Office of Technology Assessment.

Pearse, Andrew. 1980. *Seeds of Plenty, Seeds of Want.* New York: Oxford University Press.

Pimentel, David, William Dritschilo, John Krummel, and John Kutzman. 1975. "Energy and Land Constraints in Food Protein Production." *Science* 190:754–761.

Polanyi, Karl. 1957. *The Great Transformation.* Boston: Beacon Press.

Raup, Phillip M. 1971. "Societal Goals in Farm Size." In *Size, Structure, and Future of Farms,* ed. A. B. Ball and E. O. Heady, pp. 3–18. Ames: Iowa State University Press.

Rifkin, Jeremy. 1980. *Entropy: A New World View.* New York: Viking Press.

Rockefeller Foundation. 1982. *Science for Agriculture: Report of a Workshop on Critical Issues in American Agricultural Research.* New York: The Rockefeller Foundation.

Rodale, Robert. 1983. "Breaking New Ground: The Search for a Sustainable Agriculture." *The Futurist* 17:15–20.

Russell, D. G. 1975. "Resource Allocation in Agricultural Research Using Socio-Economic Evaluation and Mathematical Models." *Canadian Journal of Agricultural Economics* 23:29–52.

Ruttan, Vernon W. 1982. *Agricultural Research Policy.* Minneapolis: University of Minnesota Press.

Sampson, R. Neil. 1981. *Farmland or Wasteland.* Emmaus, Pennsylvania: Rodale Press.

Simon, Julian L. 1981. *The Ultimate Resource.* Princeton: Princeton University Press.

Spretnak, Charlene, ed. 1982. *The Politics of Women's Spirituality.* Garden City, New York: Doubleday Anchor Books.

Steinhart, John, and Carol Steinhart. 1974. "Energy Use in the United States Food System." *Science* 184:307–316.

U.S. Department of Agriculture (USDA). 1981a. *A Time to Choose: Summary Report on the Structure of Agriculture.* Washington, D.C.: Department of Agriculture.

_____. 1981b. *National Agricultural Lands Study. Final Report.* Washington, D.C.: Department of Agriculture.

U.S. Department of State. 1982. *Proceedings of the U.S. Strategy Conference on Biological Diversity.* Washington, D.C.: U.S. Department of State.

Vogeler, Ingolf. 1981. *The Myth of the Family Farm.* Boulder, Colorado: Westview Press.

Wardwell, John M. 1982. "The Reversal of Nonmetropolitan Migration Loss." In *Rural Society in the U.S.: Issues for the 1980s,* ed. Don A. Dillman and Daryl J. Hobbs, pp. 22–33. Boulder, Colorado: Westview Press.

White, Morton, and Lucia White. 1977. *Intellectuals Versus the City: From Thomas Jefferson to Frank Lloyd Wright.* Oxford: Oxford University Press.

Wortman, Sterling, and Ralph W. Cummings, Jr. 1978. *To Feed This World: The Challenge and the Strategy.* Baltimore: Johns Hopkins University Press.

# Part I

# Ethical and Value Issues

# 2

# On Evaluating
# Agricultural Research

## William H. Aiken

There is no question that the American agricultural research system has produced some wonderous results. Who could deny that this research has yielded benefits that have generally improved the quality of life for millions of people? And who could seriously argue that we would have been better off without any of the results of this activity? But, on the other hand, the activity created by the agricultural research system, just like any other sustained, cooperative human activity, has had some negative effects on people. To maintain that it has produced only good seems just as out of touch with reality as to deny that it has produced any good whatsoever. So let us grant that there have been some negative effects and that we can generally agree on what these are.

But this does not get us very far in understanding the value controversies that have arisen over the results of agricultural research. We want to know why some rational, informed, and responsible people find these negative effects acceptable and judge the system that caused them to be justified—while other rational, informed, and responsible people find these effects intolerable and judge the system that caused them to be morally blameworthy. How can such differences of opinion be explained? How

I wish to acknowledge, with sincere gratitude, my debt to several people whose comments on an earlier draft of this paper helped to shape my thinking on these matters. Glenn L. Johnson stimulated my thoughts on combining these views. Sara Ebenreck suggested the holistic approach. Rachelle Hollander suggested the first "compatiblist" step in the final approach. And, of course, Kenneth A. Dahlberg initiated and inspired the process and provided valuable guidance to the project which led to the writing of this paper.

can these negative effects be evaluated so differently?  In this essay, I am proposing that the way we evaluate these negative effects greatly depends upon our assumptions about the way that values are related.  Many differences of opinion arise because the parties to the conflict hold fundamentally different views about values.  I will describe four different views about values and will show how each results in a different way of evaluating the negative effects of agricultural research.  These views are:  the priority view, the trade-off view, the constraint view, and the holistic view.  After constructing this "conceptual map" as an aid to understanding, I will briefly discuss some of the problems which arise for policy makers in light of this plurality of views about values.[1]

## The Priority View

This view sees values predominantly as goals which are ranked in a hierarchy from the most important to the least important.  Decisions are to be made in accordance with the ranking.  So the prime goal is advanced first, or if it is inappropriate, the secondary one is advanced and so on down the line.  More than one goal may be advanced at the same time if the subsidiary goals are compatible with the higher priority goal.  But if in advancing the higher order goal, a lower one can not be advanced, one still should advance the higher goal. Negative effects are due to this neglecting of the lower order goals.  They are unfortunate, but unavoidable, by-products of acting appropriately; that is, in following the priority ranking.

For instance, if "increased productivity" is placed as a higher goal for research than "protecting environmental quality," then it is right to pursue an innovation which increases productivity even if it erodes environmental quality.  The negative effects to the environment are unintentional and unfortunate by-products of pursuing the higher goal.  They do not need to be justified any further than to point out the proper ranking and to demonstrate that the lower order goal is incompatible with the higher order one in this particular instance (that is, that you can not do both on this project).

Many defenders of the agricultural research system's success in increasing productivity or total production output evoke this view of values to offer reasons why the negative side effects are acceptable.  So too, many critics of the system adopt this view when they claim that the system has its priorities confused; that is, that it has either adopted the wrong set of goals or it has ranked them incorrectly.  For instance, critics say that the set of goals should be expanded to include non-economic values, or they suggest that the ranking should be altered to give highest priority to different goals such as "long-term sustainability," or "energy efficiency," or "human health and safety," or "traditional rural lifestyles." For defenders to point out that this re-ranking may have the negative result of decreasing total production would be beside the point since such a negative result would be treated by the re-rankers as an unfortunate side-effect of acting on the appropriate priority of goals.

The battle then is really over the identification of the appropriate set of goals for agricultural research and the correct ranking of those goals. The set and ranking determine which by-products are tolerable and thus what negative consequences are acceptable.

### The Trade-Off View

The trade-off view does not see values as a ranked set of goals. Rather, they are seen as a set of goods which are often incompatible (pursuing one precludes pursuing another) and conflictual (advancing one diminishes another). Since an a priori index of priorities is not available, determination of what to do (or what policy to adopt) requires a decision. The trade-off view uses a "balancing" method in which potential "good" results are balanced on a common scale with potential "bad" results. Thus, negative effects are treated as "costs" and positive effects as "benefits." If promoting a particular good will yield a higher net gain than available alternatives, then we should promote it. One good is thus "traded-off" for another and the negative effects resulting from neglecting the lost good are justified because they are "outweighed" in the overall balance. Negative effects are not merely by-products; they are costs which may or may not be outweighed.

This view of values and negative effects is so common that some may have a hard time imagining any alternative perspective. The problems it raises are well know but since they are the source of many of the battles between defenders and critics of the research system, I will briefly recite the litany of relevant questions:

- What is the ultimate criterion being used to determine what is a benefit and what is a cost (is it "human well being" or some other standard) and how is it justified?
- How do you find a common measure to weigh diverse goods (such as farmworker safety vs. consumer preference for unblemished vegetables)?
- How do you assign a weight to intangible things (like quality of life, rural community, wilderness, and a non-polluted environment)?
- How do you determine the scope of the consequences to be considered both in terms of time span (are future generations to be included) and breadth (are distant peoples, non-human animals, or things like institutions, species, and systems to be included)?

- And finally, how do you deal with the distribution of costs and benefits (who pays and who benefits) or does distribution not matter?

All of these questions deserve careful discussion, but I will defer to my colleagues on this project who have raised and addressed many of these questions from within this trade-off perspective on values.

### The Constraint View

This view divides value issues into two types: goods (that may serve as goals which may or may not be ranked) and constraints (which proscribe *types* of actions). Goods may be advanced only within the parameters set by the constraints. If the negative effects of an action violate the constraints they are not seen merely as by-products or even as "costs" to be balanced, but as "harms" and thus as *prima facie* wrongs (that is, in need of a justification other than the cost-benefit type). Harms are not neutral, open to be assigned a weighting. They are *types* of acts which are not permitted.

Legal constraints are the most familiar example of this type of norm, and though some prefer to restrict constraints to legal proscriptions (so that any action which is not illegal is permissible), others advocate including ethical proscriptions which are not currently protected by law. The very process of making law is subject to disputes between the constraint view and the trade-off view as the debates over acceptable standards of risk, wilderness preservation, and toxic chemical regulations demonstrate.

It is important to see how this view differs from the trade-off view. Since causing harm is seen as a wrong (it abrogates the duty of non-maleficence or violates the right not to be harmed) it will not do to merely offer a demonstration of the "net gain" in benefits which can be achieved by doing the "harm". Much to the frustration of the trade-off advocates, the constraint advocates resist this reduction of "harms" to "costs." It is not that they are assigning too much weight to these negative effects. Rather, they resist assigning any weight at all to them. Some types of acts, they claim, have no price tag and some things simply cannot be sold for gain.

Many critics of the agricultural research system take this view and argue that the activities sponsored by the system cause unjustifiable harm. A variety of harms can be listed: harm to fieldworkers' health and safety, harm to consumers' health or autonomy, harm to rural communities, to family farmers, to future generations, to wild and domestic animals, to wild species and ecosystems, and harm to the poor in this and other lands. Just as there were numerous problems with the trade-off view, so too there are many serious conceptual problems to be solved to make this perspective a coherent normative theory. I will once again simply cite a litany of pertinent questions:

- What is a harm and when is it a wrong (must the harm be directly caused?, must it be severe?, does it always involve violating a right?)?
- When can someone be held accountable for committing a wrong (must it be intended or foreseen, or not? can an institution be held accountable?)?
- Who or what can be harmed (only individuals?, only humans?, can collective groups, such as communities, species, generations, or systems be harmed?)?
- Can wrongs ever be justified (if not by cost/benefit, then how?, what happens when two constraints conflict and one or the other must be violated?, when overridden is compensation always due?)?

It is not necessary to decide whether all of these questions can be satisfactorily answered here. What is important to see is how this perspective could be made into a coherent normative theory. The implications for the agricultural research system of such a theory would be at least two. First, all alternative policies and projects that could avoid violating the specified constraints would have to be explored and found to be ineffective *before* one could justifiably consider a project with probable harmful (wrongful) effects. And second, the burden of proof would be placed on those proposing such a harmful policy or project to provide in advance the reasons why the constraint must be overridden. These reasons must be strong enough either: (a) to justify the wrong sufficiently to those against whom it is being committed so that they give their consent: or, (b) if consent is not obtainable, to convince a thoroughly impartial and disinterested observer that the wrong, even so, is justified. I would suggest that direction and evaluation of projects by the research system would be quite different if it were held accountable to such standards. The "net gain" standard and the "top priority" standard do not appear to be nearly as demanding.

**The Holistic View**

Though similar to the priority view, this increasingly popular perspective is different enough to warrant separate attention. The holistic view does not see values as a set of goals, goods, or constraints that can be known non-contextually. Values are not "external" factors which we import into our deliberations. Rather, they are derived contextually. By understanding the dynamics and internal properties of a system's functioning we can empirically determine the types of things which are conducive to that functioning and the types of things which are disruptive to it. That which will preserve, maintain, or enhance the system's functioning (or "stability," or "growth," or "health," or "integrity") is of value. That which threatens it is disvaluable.

Such a view is "holistic" because it sees the whole picture and not just the parts. Actions which affect the system are good or bad relative to their total, long term impact on the system. Consequences which flow from the system are positive or negative only with reference to the whole. So what may be judged to be a "negative effect" (by some external criterion) because it is detrimental to some part of the system, may not be negative to the whole. On the contrary, it may be positive. So in this view, many of the alleged negative effects of a subsystem are not considered to be negative at all. They are only *prima facie* negative. Further consideration shows them to be positive effects since they are beneficial to the whole. This view differs from the priority view in that the effects are not seen as undesirable by-products. They are often seen as important means of promoting the whole. Nor are they treated as "costs" or "harms" since from the broader perspective, they are not in any way negative or in need of justification.

The agricultural research system has been criticized by two camps adopting this view: those advocating ecosphere holism and those advocating global economic holism. The former call for a new ethics and criticize agriculture policy and research on the grounds that they are not leading to practices conducive to environmental health or integrity. To reply that adopting alternative, ecologically-benign agricultural methods may have the effect of decreasing the human population (by starvation) would not rebut a pure advocate of this view (even if this consequence would follow, which is arguable). This is because human population reduction can be seen as desirable from a long-term ecological point of view. Though unpleasant, this effect is not really negative.

Global economic holism seeks to expand the socioeconomic "system" which is served by the research community to include all the peoples of the world and not just those in the advanced industrial countries. From this global perspective acts which may adversely affect a part of the total system (for instance, American farmers) may be beneficial from the perspective of the whole. Agricultural research which serves the exclusive interest of a part of the system may be neglecting the long run dynamic interactions between parts of the system and thus may be jeopardizing the stability of the whole, which is disvaluable.

The same kind of argument can be used to defend research which is oriented toward national economic goals rather than peculiarly regional ones. For instance, when using research to enhance a greater concentration in production, one could appeal to the national economic system to explain why the elimination of small "non-competitive" local operators is not a negative effect, since the bankruptcies promote the effectiveness of the system.

As with the other perspectives of values, we need to ask some questions of the holistic view.

- Which system should we enhance? (is there any non-arbitrary way to determine the proper scope of a system: that is, regional, national, continental, global?, why should we choose an ecological system over an economic one or vice versa?, can some "supersystem" that encompasses all lesser ones be constructed and would this be desirable?)
- What counts as enhancing or preserving a system? (is there some optimal equilibrium state or only various phases and points of relative stability?, if a system can embody more than one point of equilibrium why would one be preferable to another?)
- How can we avoid being stymied in action when such great demands are placed on foreknowledge before an action can be justifiably undertaken?

To the same degree that the agricultural research system is scrutinized from this perspective, it will also be expected to do more extensive planning and more careful assessments of the projected impacts of its projects upon the total network of economic and ecological relationships. The holistic perspective creates a more demanding standard than the "top priority" and the "net gain" standards. Perhaps it is even more demanding than the "constraint" standard.

### Discussion

Now that I have run through these distinctions, what do we do with them? What good are they? For one thing, they may let you identify, if you did not already know, what type of critic or defender you are and thus who your allies and enemies are likely to be. Furthermore, they may help you to appreciate that there are four distinct types of battles over values going on and that they are being fought on very different battle grounds. Without this awareness, one is tempted to simply reduce or restructure the other perspectives to fit your own and then dismiss the debate (which, of course, will merely stifle debate rather than resolve it). Without this awareness, one is also tempted to make simplistic appeals based on the "self-evident" superiority of your own evaluative perspective (such as "holistic," "net gain," or "justice") without providing arguments. Since your evaluative framework will not be shared by advocates of other perspectives, they will not accept your appeals. But beyond these meager

results, what good is this type of "perspectives" analysis?  How can understanding these perspectives help in the process of making policy involving
the future direction of agricultural research?

There are several approaches we could take.  First, we could argue for
one of these perspectives as the exclusive guide for policy.  For instance,
we could maintain the traditional priorities view and continue to pursue
"increased productivity."  Or we could adopt a holistic view and call for a
totally new research agenda.  Adopting this approach of choosing a single
perspective is probably the least taxing approach to take since each of
these perspectives has a fairly well worked-out program and is at least
coherent and consistent—even if not complete.

But there are some problems with such an approach.  First, it is not
likely to resolve the value controversies which have arisen over the future
directions of agricultural research.  This has both theoretical and political
implications.  Theoretically, this approach assumes that one perspective
can be defended as the best and only appropriate one.  Although I do not
want to rule out the possibility of making such a case, I am dubious about
limiting the variety and richness of moral reflection on right and wrong
actions by narrowing the range of pertinent moral insights so as to
exclude those from diverse perspectives.[2]  Also, adoption of one perspective will tend to cut off open and sincere dialogue, leaving differences
between advocates to be solved by power rather than by reason.  The political implications are equally unsettling.  If I am right in assuming that
each of these perspectives is represented by a constituency with a
significant power base, then an effective political solution to the controversies over the future of agricultural research would seem to require some
effort at balancing between these various groups.  I am doubtful that this
can be done without some recognition of the at least partial legitimacy of
the value frameworks of those constituencies.

Rather than adopt a single perspective as the exclusive one for policy
we could try another approach which would somehow combine the various perspectives.  But in combining them some conflicts will arise.  So we
must develop a means of relating them and arbitrating conflict between
them.  One way to combine them would be to construct a "supertheory"
of value which would not only encompass each individual perspective on
value but would fully capture its unique significance.  By assuming that
each is but a limited view of the "elephant" we could set out to accurately
describe him in his entirety.  Another way to combine the theories is to
establish a priority ranking among them.  For example, one could argue
that first the parameters for legitimate action must be set, then the effect
on the whole system predicted, then particular costs and benefits be made

within the context of the constraints and the systemic prescriptions, and then the highest priority be chosen given the limitations placed by the other three considerations.

It should be obvious what is happening here. To create a workable combination we are adopting one of the particular views of the relations between values to account for the relations between the different theories of values. We have simply moved up to a higher level of analysis. Instead of talking about the relation between individual values we are talking about the relation between theories of value. But we are assuming one of those theories to adjudicate between theories. The "supertheory" suggestion uses the holistic view, and the ranking suggestion uses the priorities view. A similar position could be developed by using the trade-off view. When we try to combine these theories, we want to know why we should use a holistic rather than a ranking procedure. Why should we choose one "combination" over another? The only way that we can answer that question is to go to a still higher level of analysis so that we could see how to properly "combine" the "combinations". You can see how this can lead to an infinite regress. I do not know if this problem of finding a firm basis for combining theories can ultimately be solved. Maybe there are limits to our ability to give rational justifications for our theories of value.[3]

But let us come down from these flights of contemplation and return to the knotty problem of setting policy. Some actions must be taken and some decisions must be made. If adopting one perspective as the exclusive guide to policy is undesirable, and constructing an adequate combination of theories is problematic, is there no other way of proceeding?

It seems to me that there is one other approach which we could take which though not very elegant, may be quite workable in practice. This approach focuses upon actual proposals for policy and actual decisions and tries to avoid conflicts between the various perspectives. The first step then would be to adopt as a working assumption that a given policy or proposal will be seen as either acceptable or unacceptable by all four value perspectives. It is at least possible that a policy would be acceptable to all four perspectives and the negative effects anticipated would be seen as justifiable regardless of how each view describes them (as by-products, costs, harms, or as only *prima facie* negative). And it is possible that all four would judge a decision to be wrong (wrong priority, cost too high, causes unjustifiable harm, disrupts systemic functioning). Of course, to be able to make such a judgement would require that the proposed policy be carefully assessed from each different perspective. The best way to accomplish this would be to create a space in the decision making process for input from representatives of the divergent perspectives. This would insure that the implications of the proposal as seen from each perspective would be thoroughly understood. In the happy event that the proposal satisfied proponents of all four perspectives (at least to the degree of being seen as acceptable even if not preferable) then this policy could be adopted without having to settle the question of how to "combine" these views.

Even though this concurrence should be sought as a first step, it is not very likely that complete unanimity among perspectives will be common, and thus some kind of "combination" will have to be formulated. A procedure that may work out to be useful, would be to try to adopt the perspective which seems most germaine to the problem at hand. To do this requires being able to judge when a perspective's peculiar domain is likely to be affected by a given policy. For instance, the constraint view is especially concerned with human health, safety, and welfare. Policies which will have direct effects in this area should not be decided without giving extra weight to the constraint view. A decision which will especially affect an ecosystem's viability should not be made without giving extra weight to the holistic view. It may be the case that each perspective has staked out a specific territory in which its understanding of the relation of values is most appropriate. And it will defend this territory adamantly, but will be willing to make concessions on policies that only marginally affect it. If we could determine which perspective is the most suitable one to adopt for a given policy problem, then it might be possible to advance the goals of that perspective with the acceptance, even if not the endorsement of the other perspectives. We would not have to decide in advance how to rank or how to combine these various views on values. Rather, we would carefully examine the nature of the problem about which we are trying to make policy, and then make a judgement about which perspective seems most suited to this problem. Experience with this procedure should lead to the development of some mutually-agreed-upon criteria which could serve as guidelines for judging when a particular perspective is most suitable.

Taking this approach may not yield a very consistent record of decision-making across the broad range of areas which the agricultural research system affects. But it may be more flexible and actually more satisfactory to the many constituencies which this system serves than would be the exclusive adoption of one perspective or one particular combination of perspectives decided on in advance and abstracted from the concrete particulars of a given policy decision. It requires responsible judgments by wise and attentive decision-makers who must be held accountable for their decisions to the various advocates of these divergent views. But perhaps relying upon the art of statesmanship is the only way to reach an effective political resolution on such divisive issues as adjudicating between fundamentally different perspectives on the way that values are related.

## Notes

1. Although I will be treating these views descriptively (that is, as givens that groups of people happen to hold), I do not mean to imply that the normative grounding of these views is unimportant. There are good theoretical reasons why each of these views has been put forth as an appropriate model for evaluation. And each model has been associated with a tradition of normative ethics ("priority" with various hierarchical deontologies, "trade-off" with utilitarianism, "constraint" with natural rights theory, and "holism" with Hegelianism).

2. Of course, only an examination of the arguments for the superiority of one of the views can settle this issue.

3. This observation should not be construed as recommending that such meta-theoretical investigations are worthless. In fact, I would argue that confusion on these theoretical matters is significantly hampering progress in the application of ethical theories to real-world social problems.

# 3

# Exquisite Decisions in a Global Village

## Jean Lipman-Blumen

As we stand in the foothills of the 21st century, mountainous issues confront our Third World neighbors. Despite three decades of development activity, intransigent problems loom ominously for all citizens of the geo-political and ecological global village in which we now live. Many observers of the developing nations sense a growing disquietude, a profound humility, and even an existential despair about the prospects of helping the Third World gain "First World Parity."[1]

### Macroeconomic "Success"

Development efforts emerged in the wake of World War II, sparked by a complex set of mixed motives. These initiatives met with initial "success," if we narrowly define "success" to mean economic growth measured in macroeconomic terms. From 1950 to 1980, the Gross Domestic Product (GDP), as well as the GDP per capita, of the Third World (excluding China) increased at a dramatic rate, despite some deceleration after the 1974–75 recession.[2] For the 1970–80 decade alone, the Third World's average annual growth rate was 5.5 percent, double that of the now-developed nations at a comparable period in their own development.[3] In addition, in these last thirty years, the GDP per capita of developing nations (again, excluding China) grew only 0.2 percent less than that of

This is a revised and expanded version of a speech, "Third World Development in a Time of Global Instability," presented at The President's Forum, Claremont Graduate School, Claremont, California, May 10, 1984.

the developed world (3.0 vs. 3.2 percent). Most remarkably, all this occurred in the face of unprecedented population growth in the Third World.[4]

At first glance, these statistics are rather impressive. If we look more closely, however, at the condition of developing nations relative to the developed world, our disquietude stirs. To begin, a slight increase in the *relative* gap (i.e., ratio of the average GDP's per capita) between the GDP per capita has occurred in tandem with a significant rise in the *absolute* gap (i.e., difference of these average GDP's per capita measured in constant prices, that is, controlling for inflation)(Loup, 1980:8). From 1950 to 1975, the absolute gap between the GDP per capita of the developing and the developed nations (measured in dollars, constant 1974 prices) more than doubled, increasing from $2,200 to $4,800. Among the developing nations, only Libya was able to decrease the absolute gap with the developed world. Economists warn that a reduction of the absolute gap is unlikely during the next several decades and, therefore, should be abandoned as an inappropriate development goal.

It is also important to examine internal trends and to recognize the inadequacies of the GDP per capita and other comparable aggregative indicators, which tend to ignore or distort various aspects of the countries they seek to describe. First, the process of averaging prevents any clear reading of how benefits actually are distributed regionally and/or across the various socioeconomic strata. Second, such measures provide only an overall measure of economic activity, without sorting the environmentally, institutionally, and sociologically positive and negative components of economic activity (Schultze, 1974; Boulding, 1978). Third, such measures fail to capture the so-called "hidden economy," including "home and family economics, non-market activities of small communities and small-scale social networks, voluntary activities within associations, as well as unaccounted for illegal or fraudulent monetary activities, or simply any activity which the administration can hardly control" (Schiray, 1984:1). Although commonly ignored by economic analysis or national accounting, these activities assume considerable importance in the Third World, as well as within developed nations.[5]

Serious methodological problems notwithstanding, the widening economic gap between the developing and the developed world is not the only disparity we must confront. The economic differences between nations *within* the developing world increase as diverse groups of developing countries grow at different rates and experience distinctive problems. Measured in terms of per capita income, middle-income countries grew more rapidly than low-income countries in a pattern described by Alain Barrère (1978) as "divergent development." For example, within the Third World, the oil-exporting countries faced spectacularly different problems from the non-industrialized, non-oil exporting countries.

Here our disquietude and humility deepen, as we begin to recognize the problems we have failed to ameliorate—perhaps even exacerbated—by our inability to differentiate the important variation among and within Third World countries. The result: we fall into the trap of dealing with the Third World as a monolith. This monolithic approach has characterized much of the developed world's strategies in the first three decades of development activity. It emanated from a complex set of factors, not the least of which was the cultural and psychological distance we maintained from our neighbors in this global village. As we recognize the myopic inadequacies of this monolithic development approach, we also begin to perceive the necessity of formulating a multiciplicity of development models and strategies. More formidably yet, these models and strategies must be simultaneously developed and coordinated.

An holistic strategic planning approach is essential if we are to come to grips with the fact that the Third World, in all its splendored variety, is an interlinked social, geopolitical, economic, and ecological system. To complicate the task, the developed nations—capitalist and socialist alike—are also critical parts of this unevenly interdependent system.

## Imperfect Interdependence

The imperfect interdependence among nations in this global village has many sources. This uneven interdependence emanates from differential degrees of dependence, power, responsibility, wealth, and well-being, which so complicate the relations among these global neighbors. Immense differences in natural resources alone give rise to many of these differences, including industrial and agricultural strength.

In this imperfectly interdependent world, accelerating economic growth and liberalized trade have brought the developed and developing nations into expanded trade relations. The developed market economies' capacity to export depends upon other nations' willingness and ability to import—wheat or arms, the exporting countries often do not seem to care. Two-thirds of the developing nations' imports come from the developed countries with market economies.[6] They represent 22–24 percent of the total exports of these developed market economies. Despite its unevenness, our interdependence is unmistakable.

The Third World's dependence upon the developed world encompasses food, technology, and other goods. It also relies upon the developed world's capacity (a) to buy their raw materials and manufactured goods, and (b) not insignificantly, to offer financial assistance. Our disquietude is stirred again by what some might interpret as a new form of Colonialism. For example, in the agricultural sector, the assistance packages (and I emphasize "packages" because loans, seeds, fertilizer, and loan repayment commonly are wrapped into a single agreement) conjure up images of the company store in the company town. Now, however, the operation is on a much grander scale: the company nation. The indebtedness, the poverty, the powerlessness seem uncomfortably familiar.

Some observers suggest that a partial answer lies in helping the developing nations to become self-sustaining, possibly in interdependent regional groupings. Still others argue that the bonds of international trade and indebtedness are too intertwined to untangle without generating monumental world-wide economic perturbations.

## Beyond Macroeconomics to People

These are complex macroeconomic issues, so complex they often mask a crucial sociological question: what does all this mean for concrete living conditions in developing nations? After three decades of feverish development activity, how should we characterize the social fabric of Third World life? What does this imply about the conditions for different socioeconomic strata within Third World nations and from one developing country to the next? The answers, once again, are profoundly depressing.

The actual living conditions for the vast majority of Third World inhabitants have not improved markedly. In fact, living conditions for some groups actually have deteriorated, since relatively little development aid has reached those who need it most. There is little evidence that the profits of growth have been automatically and evenly diffused (i.e., that they have trickled down) among all social strata within the developing world. The World Bank, acknowledging that it still does not have a firm handle on the criteria for poverty (I call this the "How Poor is Poor?" game), estimates that 800 million people currently live in *absolute* poverty (i.e., $50 to $75 per capita in 1970 dollars)(The World Bank, 1983). By the year 2000, the World Bank predicts the figure will not have fallen much below 600 million.[7]

Additional indicators point to the stagnation of the lowest income nations. For example, over a 30-year period, more than a billion people in 40 countries have seen their average annual incomes edge up ever so slowly from $170 to $250 (in 1980 dollars). Moreover, some Third World nations are demonstrably worse off than their developing neighbors. Sub-Saharan Africa and the Indian subcontinent represent a bedrock of poverty. By all measures, they lag behind the remainder of the Third World in every economic sector.

### Other Indices of Poverty

Still other indices of poverty besides income (i.e., education, employment, assets, nutrition, health, class or caste, access to public services, etc.) confront us. The picture is less sharp than we would like, owing to the methodological complexity of the poverty concept and the poor quality of the data (Loup, 1980). Even so, we see unmistakably the haggard face of destitution staring through the statistics on malnutrition, other health problems, education (including literacy), employment, energy, landlessness, and housing.

Poverty is particularly marked in the rural areas. By most counts, approximately 85 percent of the poor live in the countryside, where per capita incomes are below urban incomes (even considering differential rural/urban purchasing power). Although the crowding in Third World cities makes urban poverty more visible to visitors, the pervasiveness and depth of rural poverty is even greater. The Brandt Commission (1980) noted that the continuing migration to urban centers was evidence of the desperate poverty rural dwellers were seeking to escape.

Agriculture is the primary employment of the poorest strata. With few exceptions, rural residents are largely dependent upon agriculture for their living. According to available, if less than satisfactory, data, the very poorest rely even more heavily on agriculture for their sustenance. Self-employment characterizes the most poverty stricken, with relatively few wage earners in this category. Most of the poorest rural residents derive their income "in kind" from their work as tenants, sharecroppers, and landowners.

Land ownership is highly concentrated in most Third World countries. Although data here, too, leave much to be desired, in Asia and Latin America, particularly, a relatively large proportion of small farms (i.e., under one hectare) account for a very small percent of the total land area. The concentration of land among the small remaining proportion of the population increases the poverty of the many. Also, the poorest strata tend to have the highest fertility rates. As a result, even when the very poor manage to own a hectare on which to raise crops for their own use, the land is fragmented through inheritance in the next generation. This land distribution pattern, an indirect measure of capital distribution, is a serious problem in most Third World countries, one which incremental measures are unlikely to ameliorate.

High birth rates, low wages of the unskilled (a problem exacerbated by a large labor pool linked to population growth), low literacy rates, and inequitable land distribution together contribute to the diminished economic viability of the very poorest. The poorest strata require help both to maintain what self-sufficiency they have and to increase their productivity and, therefore, their cash incomes. Otherwise, the most poverty-stricken groups still will not benefit from any overall economic growth their countries might enjoy. They will remain poor while the small affluent elite will continue to prosper, in fact, grow even more affluent. This is an area where advances have come exceedingly slowly.

Even where advances have been made, such as in literacy, much remains to be done. For example, in the three decades between 1950 and 1980, the proportion of the adult population enumerated as literate rose from one-third to one-half. Nonetheless, the literacy rate in low-income countries was 34 percent, in lower-middle income countries 59 percent, and in upper-middle income nations 66 percent. Within the low-income group, Mali had a 5 percent literacy rate, Bangladesh 22 percent, and India 34 percent. These figures stand in sharp contrast to the 97 percent literacy rate among high-income countries (Overseas Development Council, 1979). Given the direct relationship between education and health, not to mention all the cross-cutting relationships among these component indices of poverty, the poverty picture is very bleak. It remains discouraging despite macroeconomic advances in the first three decades of development activity.

Only a very thin layer of Third World elites have benefited from the billions of dollars in development aid that have been channeled to the developing nations. Government-to-government assistance almost invariably involves bureaucratic, landed, and industrial elites, but little of this aid trickles down to those who need it most and for whom it is ostensibly intended.[8] Ironically, the major share of assistance funds goes to technical experts, many from developed countries. The World Bank acknowledges that "more than half the estimated $7 billion to $8 billion spent annually by donors on technical assistance goes to finance expatriate personnel," who are imported to help implement assistance programs (The World Bank, 1983).

Women and girls, traditionally undervalued, face special problems. They receive less of everything: food, education, health care, housing, and employment. A recent FAO nutritional study in Bangladesh (*Los Angeles Times,* May 9, 1984) revealed serious disparities in food distribution within households, with women and girls receiving substantially less food than men and boys. This food distribution pattern is associated with a higher incidence of malnutrition among women and girls and increased female infant mortality.

## Inappropriate Technologies

Earlier decades of development activity were characterized by the transfer of an array of technologies heralded as near-panaceas for Third World problems. Despite and often because of the developed world's expertise and near obsession with technology, overly-sophisticated, expensive, and inappropriate technologies have been introduced in Third World settings. In many instances, smaller and less costly methods would have sufficed.

*Effects Upon Women*

Here, too, females have been seriously affected. In 1970, Ester Boserup's landmark work on women in development demonstrated that the introduction of new technology actually tends to worsen women's economic status. This paradoxical result occurs because the mechanized tools of technology generally are given to men, thereby depriving women of their previous, more simply-supported occupational roles.

A measure of how little progress Third World women have made since then may be taken from a United Nations Food and Agricultural Organization report on women in Africa. According to this study, the "typical African woman walks from her village to the fields before dawn and works for nine to ten hours hoeing, planting, weeding, or harvesting" (*Los Angeles Times,* May 9, 1984:2). The study reports that the African woman walks several miles for water and firewood and returns carrying 40 pounds of water. Her other duties include grinding and pounding grain, cleaning house, cooking, nursing an infant, washing dishes and clothes, as well as caring for other children and the elderly. If that were not enough, she also cures meat and fish, besides processing and storing other food. She carries her surplus food to market, walking for miles, in order to exchange or sell her produce for different goods.

> She may make beer or handicrafts or run some other cottage industry to provide what is usually her family's only cash income. She is pregnant most of the time. . . . Yet, when mechanized equipment is introduced to grow cash crops . . . it is the men who get it—-lured . . . by the novelty of the machinery and the promise of more money with a minimum of effort. The women are thus not only deprived of a new source of income, they are also forced to continue raising their family's food with outdated tools and methods while at the same time performing additional chores related to the new cash crops—-such as weeding, hoeing and planting:  all tasks considered 'too easy' for men [*Los Angeles Times,* May 9, 1984:2].

The report goes on to suggest that women need improved hand tools. Hoes, which serve as extremely versatile agricultural implements in the Third World, are particularly vital.

*Factors Promoting Inappropriate Technology*

Imported technology, then, has been far from an unalloyed benefit in Third World countries. Expensive mechanized equipment has helped mostly large land owners, rather than small farmers. Farm laborers have found themselves replaced by costly mechanization. This pattern of inappropriate technology adoption also characterizes the industrialized sector, where policies have favored capital-intensive, labor-saving devices. As

Loup (1980:175–178) suggests, one need not be an economist to appreciate that in developing countries, with scarce capital and plentiful labor, technologies that are capital-intensive and labor-saving are patently inappropriate. Nonetheless, in the industrial sector, particularly, several factors converge to encourage the selection of these inappropriate technologies.

First among these factors is the higher cost of industrial labor compared to its opportunity cost (a result of trade union and government guidelines and regulations). Second, and quite the reverse, the cost of capital commonly is below that of its opportunity cost. In large part, this is the result of preferential exchange rates, tariffs, and tax regulations, as well as subsidized interest rates offered by banking institutions. Third, the glamour and status of modern Western technology are seductive to Third World bureaucrats, bankers, and business people. Fourth, technology and equipment suppliers, as well as Western consultants, tend to recommend those technologies and equipment with which they are most familiar and/or from which they make the most profit. Fifth, regulations for assistance packages frequently restrict financial aid to the import costs or foreign exchange components of projects (Tendler, 1975; Loup, 1980; Ramsay and Lipman-Blumen, 1984).

*Inappropriate Technology and the Land*

The use of inappropriate technology is particularly evident with regard to land use. Large dam projects, designed to increase power supplies and irrigate land, initially were heralded as miraculous answers to Third World prayers for higher yields. Only more recently have the long-term negative sequelae of this technology become apparent. Egypt's Aswan High Dam has increased soil salinity, reduced soil fertility, and spread bilharziasis. Some agriculturists now think that big-dam schemes harbor the seeds of their own destruction over the long term. Nevertheless, the inappropriateness of this technology was far from apparent in the earlier days of the Green Revolution.

Not inconsequentially, the extended period of time required to build large dams often leads to cost over-runs. In 1970, Sri Lanka initiated a 30-year project to dam the 207-mile Mahaweli River in an effort to "triple the nation's generating supply and irrigate 900,000 acres of new land, where 1.5 million people were to be resettled" (*Development Forum*, April 1984:7). Subsequently, Sri Lanka decided to scale down the project but accelerate the completion time to six years. During those six years, the cost of the project tripled.

Resettlement brought its own problems. Planners failed to include in their project design the replanting of bare hillsides to prevent heavy rains from washing silt into the riverbed.  As a result, the silt blocked dams and flowed downstream where it damaged irrigation canals.  Nor was transportation for the resettlement area incorporated into the original plan.  As a result, insufficient roads left the new settlers isolated.

To add to Sri Lanka's problems, local talent to maintain the dam was not available, reflecting poor implementation planning at the initial design stage.  Foreign consultants brought in to plan and build the dam had little understanding of local customs and conditions that would have provided for a more enthusiastic reception by local inhabitants.  The need for dam construction companies to find new territories beyond Europe and North America provides a powerful impetus for those companies to build dams that will require their continuing service.

Even if we set aside all these problems, we are just beginning to recognize what are perhaps the most serious long-term consequences of irrigation: salinization of the soil, water logging, deforestation, erosion, and eventually desertification.  Desertification is a significant problem in all three continents of the Third World.  The annual loss of soil attributable to desertification in the Third World is estimated at 0.3 percent, an area double the size of Belgium.  An additional annual loss of 0.2 percent of irrigated lands is caused by high levels of soil salinity or alkalinity resulting from long-term irrigation (Loup, 1980; UN Environment Program, International Union for Conservation of Nature, and the World Wildlife Fund, 1980).  The World Bank estimates that approximately half of the world's nearly 200 million hectares of irrigated land suffer from salinization or inadequate draining.  As a result, each year between two and three percent of that land becomes totally unusable (The World Bank, 1983).

Irrigation is a major cause of deforestation.  Ironically, however, dams themselves often are impaired by deforestation and the resulting floods, landslides, and silt build-up.  Deforestation is increased by the demand for firewood, especially in higher, more arid areas, where tree growth is very slow.  The World Bank estimates that 1.3 billion people "must cut firewood faster than it can be replaced by natural growth" in order to meet their daily energy needs (The World Bank, 1984).

Lost and degraded land, diminishing fuel supplies (i.e., charcoal and firewood), contaminated water, rising energy costs, and increasing population create a downward spiral from which it will take the most ingenious and knowledgeable minds to map an escape route.  A broad spectrum of factors—effective family planning programs; serious land reform; greater emphasis upon agriculture, traditional crops and livestock, as well as increased respect for agricultural workers; appropriate and affordable technology in both the agricultural and new industrial sectors; understanding the long-term consequences of new technology (from irrigation to genetic engineering); improving the productivity and thereby the welfare of the poorest socioeconomic strata; small-scale rural industries close to energy sources; alternative renewable local energy sources (traditional and commercial); rural development projects; and foreign trade—are key interconnected points along that route. This, however, is just the beginning.

**Toward More Appropriate Technology: The "Barefoot Microchip"**

A growing disillusionment with large-scale and capital-intensive technology has spawned a nascent interest in appropriate technology. There is considerable debate among international planners regarding the appropriateness of decentralized, but high technology approaches. Much attention has been focused on microcomputers—the "barefoot microchip"—and their potential for helping or harming the Third World.

Some analysts argue that "user-friendly" microcomputers could do much to help. If they are introduced in areas where the literacy level is sufficient to permit individuals to "log on" and read simple instructions, "menu-driven" programs could direct users to perform a variety of tasks. For example, "user friendly" microcomputers could help farmers to correct the mixture of soil, water, seed, and tillage, as well as to conduct a host of other tasks. Plant pathology, as well as human symptoms, could be diagnosed by computer. Literacy, itself, could be improved. Eventually, communication nets among rural areas could be established. Even the use of appropriate alternative energy sources could be monitored by computer. Solar, hydro, wind, and photovoltaic cell energy projects are just the start.

Other analysts argue that the real value of microcomputers depends heavily upon detailed local knowledge and scientific research available on water, soils, micro-climates, predator-prey relationships, and symbiotic relationships among soils, plants, and animals (Dahlberg, 1985). Still others suggest that priority should be given to recording available "folk knowledge" before it is irrevocably lost with the passing of the current generation.

*Caveats for New Technology and Scientific Advances*

The eventual uses of technology and science undoubtedly are far beyond anything we have yet imagined. Entering the land of the "barefoot microchip" and genetic engineering has *Alice in Wonderland* qualities, perhaps too much so. While often appropriate and even life-saving in some contexts, the developed world's love affair with science-driven technology frequently has costly, sometimes ruinous, side effects—in the developed, as well as the developing, world. Hazardous waste, acid precipitation, and polluted water are vivid examples. We are just beginning to recognize the profound and potentially enduring impacts these by-products of miracle-bringing technology and scientific advances can shower upon the entire global village.

Let me emphasize that I am *not* arguing against technology per se, but rather for the intelligent, thoughtful use of *appropriate* technology. Initial euphoria over the Green Revolution in agriculture obscured the need to consider and study the possible longer-term negative effects on people and the environment. We must not repeat this serious error with the newer technologies, including genetic engineering, that promise both spectacular benefits and uncertain sequelae. At the same time, we should not allow ourselves to become immobilized by unsophisticated predictors of technological doomsday, who see the shadow of disaster looming ominously behind every genetic experiment. If we must exercise caution in our own developed environments, we should be even more circumspect in introducing these technologies to the Third World, about whose environment, institutions, and culture we are less knowledgeable.

Several caveats are in order with regard to "appropriate" technology. First, the definition of "appropriate" varies from culture to culture. Cultural beliefs regarding the neutrality of technology are more characteristic of developed than developing societies. Evaluation of the "appropriateness" of a specific technology for a particular socio-ecological context requires serious attention to (a) the technology's environmental and social history, as well as to its organizational and resource demands; (b) the receiving environment's natural ecosystem, its institutional and power structures, as well as its cultural landscape (including all factors that bear upon the environment's capacity to accept and benefit from the technology); and (c) the intended goals to be achieved through introducing a particular technology (such as reinforcing or changing certain institutions and/or enhancing or undermining specific groups within the society).

The last few decades of development work have demonstrated the developed nations' tendencies to offer or impose First World solutions on Third World problems. Admittedly, Third World nations have participated—often willingly, occasionally reluctantly—in this process. More often than not, the developed world has pursued such a course without any significant understanding of the culture, values, history, even the language, of their Third World neighbors.

This process is unwittingly facilitated by another form of inappropriate technology, this time "inappropriate education." More specifically, when we bring foreign nationals to our universities, we are acting irresponsibly if the curriculum (a) includes only First World issues and problems, and (b) presents only technological and policy solutions appropriate to post-industrialized societies. Such First World solutions cannot simply be miniaturized or otherwise directly adapted to Third World problems. Solutions to agricultural and industrial problems formulated for developed nations do not necessarily work in smaller, poorer, Third World countries. We need to examine our methods, our misconceptions, and our motives.

## Ten Exquisite Decisions

To be responsible citizens and good neighbors in this global village, we must confront and resolve, or at least learn to live with, a growing set of painful truths, contradictions, and complexities. In the coming years, we are going to face some exquisitely difficult and delicate decisions. Let me briefly sketch the ten most crucial issues as I see them.

1. At the very outset, we shall have to confront a double-barreled grim reality. First, economic growth does not necessarily mean development, particularly when growth measured by macroeconomic indicators may reflect primarily the improvement of life for a very small, local elite. We must recognize the discomforting reality that within every Third World nation there is a small First World subnation, whose sustenance and support we assist, while ignoring the larger population of poverty-stricken Third World inhabitants.

Second, there is no escaping the need to reconcile economic growth and social justice. Is economic growth to be purchased at the price of increasing poverty for the millions living in remote rural areas and urban ghettos of the Third World? Or must we finally force both the developing and developed worlds' elites to face up to the necessity of reducing inequitable distributions of wealth, improving the productivity, and thus ultimately increasing the incomes and welfare of the most poverty-stricken groups?

Several difficult strategies are possible routes for addressing these twin problems. They focus primarily on rural areas, where the poverty is greatest. First, a program of land reform must be the cornerstone of any effort to relieve the abject poverty of the most deprived groups. In countries where agriculture represents a major source of livelihood for vast numbers of people, there can be no denying the need to distribute land in a more equitable fashion. Nor can we avoid recognizing that such an initiative will encounter enormous obstacles.

A second and related strategy focuses on strengthening the agricultural sector, which would provide the most destitute with both food and income to purchase their other needs. Until recently, most development models emphasized the industrial sector to the neglect of agriculture. They failed to recognize that a well-developed agricultural sector can promote industry by its demands for equipment and supplies. Small rural industry programs should be designed to complement agricultural development, and rural development projects should be encouraged to strengthen rural economic development. In this way, the desperately poor in the countryside would be given the opportunity to develop their own sustainable economic base. Such an approach offers a longer-term solution than uncertain annual economic aid that meets only the immediate pressing need.

This strategy addresses the concern of those who argue that we face a very difficult choice between economic growth, as currently defined in materialistic and macroeconomic terms, and a new type of development that joins human growth and self-sustaining individual economic productivity with community and rural growth. This revised definition of development would include areas within the developed world that still require "development assistance."

2. Within every First World society is a Third World subnation, whose problems we have yet to eradicate. This alone should give us pause. The persistent existence of our own internal Third World subnation should increase our humility regarding our capacity to solve the problems facing geographically more distant Third World neighbors. The basic question here is: Will our own economic growth, as well as our desire to help developing nations, be bought at the price of social injustice at home for the poor living in urban ghettoes, on city grates, and in rural ghost-towns?

3. A third exquisite decision concerns values, particularly values associated with power. If we boldly choose social justice and the eradication of poverty and powerlessness, then we must align ourselves with those in developing nations and at home who recognize that the bottom-line issue is control over resources. Control over resources lies at the very heart of all power relationships—between nations, races, socioeconomic and ethnic groups, generations, and individuals—most particularly between women and men. In fact, as we have discussed elsewhere, the power relationship between women and men, with their differential control over resources, provides the basic blueprint for all power relationships (Lipman-Blumen, 1984).

The paradigmatic power relationship between women and men, with its intransigent inequality mapped on all other relationships, across all nations, is the most crucial and fundamental issue underlying social justice. Both macro- and micro-indicators suggest that women and girls are the most powerless, the most poverty-stricken, the most malnourished, the most poorly educated Third World inhabitants. And, as we have seen, current patterns of technology transfer tend to weaken the already precarious economic and social position of Third World women. In developed nations, too, women's status, relative to that of men in their own countries, is consistently less favorable, despite recent gains (Lipman-Blumen and Bernard, 1979).

Without changing this template of power relationships—the inequality between women and men—we cannot hope to restructure power relationships and the institutional structures built upon this model. Without addressing this painful issue, we cannot hope to ameliorate, much less eradicate, inequality among nations. As a result, relationships among all groups, within and between developed and developing nations, are at grave risk.

The reconciliation of power is a monumental task. Perhaps, in the short term, we can only hope to restructure power relationships. To make this choice requires formulating foreign aid policies that inevitably challenge the interests of the elites who control most governments and private sector institutions, with their massive resources. Such a formulation would affect elites in developed and developing nations. Land reform, alone, intrudes on a long-standing paradigm of power. But, as noted above, this is a crucial problem that cannot be ignored. Undoubtedly, such attempts to change the status quo will ignite the powerful engines of resistance among established interests, particularly the multinational corporations, but other special interest groups as well. And so on. And so on.

Reconceptualizing and restructuring power relationships inevitably will draw in their wake additional choices. At a minimum, this wrenching task will force us to review our entire repertoire of values. Our task will be neither easy nor quick. In fact, it will be exquisitely delicate and difficult.

4. Once we rethink our values, the related problem of priorities remains. To which shall we give primacy: economic security or world peace? agriculture or arms? health or productivity? At present, we quietly collude with Third World nations in a secondary international arms race. Small, impoverished nations, which can ill afford to buy food and medicine, still spend substantial amounts on defense, primarily in developed nations. The manufacture and sale of armaments bind the developed and Third World economies more closely than we choose to acknowledge.

The increasingly insane arms race, in which we spend $1.4 billion a day, causes an economic hemorrhage that bleeds through the thinning social fabric of our global village. Our problem with priorities is evident when we compare this figure to the $80 million a day that in ten years would provide the world with uncontaminated drinking water and healthy sanitation, as Barbara Ward (1982) reminds us. Clearly our priorities need serious attention. We must decide whether the world needs grain or guns, technology or tanks, medicine or MX missiles.

It seems unlikely, however, that we can resolve our values and priorities problems unless we address the deeper social and psychological conflicts to which we are heir. These conflicts have serious consequences. For example, they prompt our oil "habit," as well as our search for security through technology and weapons rather than through nurturing and building community.

5. A related series of exquisite decisions must be made under the rubric of "international trade" and "foreign markets." For example, should we continue to provide so-called "foreign aid" and "private support" that lock Third World nations into an endless round of debt and virtual insolvency? Is overproducing on our own land the best strategy for dealing with world hunger and domestic agricultural problems? Should we jeopardize the long-term renewability of our own natural resources in order to function as the "bread basket" of the world? Is this the correct course, or should we, instead, help developing nations create their own sustainable agriculture? Will a strengthened agricultural sector foster an expanding industrial sector, and vice versa?

A comparable set of questions could be raised about every economic sector. If the developing nations become more self-reliant, will important foreign markets for our goods disappear? Will developing nations become our competitors rather than our customers in foreign trade? How will the United States' recent transition into a net debtor status, for the first time since 1914, influence our perceived alternatives and choices? How will the continuing strength of the dollar, as well as the escalating U.S. deficit, affect these choices? Some observers think time ran out long ago for making these decisions.

6. Our decisions concerning the transfer of technologies pose another set of related and equally complex problems. At first glance, questions such as "what kind?," how much?," and "under what conditions shall we transfer?" technology appear to be rather innocuous; however, they represent a set of exquisitely concatenated dilemmas and contradictions, as suggested earlier. At a minimum, the need to examine our cultural belief in the neutrality of technology is fundamental. Until we confront this cultural myopia, we shall be unable to evaluate meaningfully the appropriateness or inappropriateness of any given technological solution for any specific problem.

7. Next, given the economic constraints the U.S. currently faces, can we really afford to formulate the multiple development models and strategies that a less monolithic view of the developing world seems to dictate? As economically distressed countries, do the developed nations have the resources, the experience, the will, and the understanding to create alternative development strategies for a differentiated Third World? Fast- and slow-growing, oil-rich and oil-poor, low-, lower middle-, and upper middle-income countries need different kinds of assistance, often on distinctive timetables. From what other domestic problems are we willing to redirect human, technical, and budgetary resources to tackle this complex set of issues?

8. We must acknowledge another embarrassing truth: foreign aid, more often than not, is foreign policy in thinnest disguise. Those countries we

wish to keep or sweep into our orbit are courted by handsome foreign assistance packages. Others, equally needy but perceived as less "strategic" or "friendly" from a foreign policy perspective, are ignored. Nor is our foreign aid strategy uncolored by military considerations and the influence of multinational corporations. Moreover, although the Percy Amendment attempts to prevent foreign aid from undercutting the welfare of Third World women, it is honored more in the breach than in practice. Until we recognize and deal directly, ethically, and realistically with the unacknowledged influences on foreign assistance, neither our foreign policy, nor our foreign aid programs, will be effective.

9. As educators, we must also concede a persistent lack of rigorous curricula that could offer useful concepts and methodologies to address Third World problems. Nonetheless, we profess to educate Third World nationals whom we welcome to our universities, research centers, and policy institutes. Yet, we still lack sufficient understanding of the cultures, the institutions, the power structures, the languages, the values of these countries, as well as their pressing problems, to offer appropriate solutions. Perhaps, the exquisite issue we confront here is the immense complexity of translating and adapting knowledge developed under one set of circumstances for the multiplicity of circumstances that represent the Third World experience.

It is not unusual for Third World policy makers to propose solutions to their national problems that are identical to the policy formulations designed for the developed world, particularly if they have studied at universities and research centers in developed nations. Solutions designed for the developed world have been miniaturized or recut to fit problems in countries vastly different in size, economic structure, demography, and history. Such retailoring will not create a useful suit for developing nations, despite the "designer label" of the developed world. Reworked First World policies are unlikely to provide "First World parity" for developing nations. Rather, we must join with our Third World neighbors to construct more useful educational programs and institutional arrangements to prepare both Third and First World future policy makers to address realistically the problems they will confront in the global village.

Several strategies are possible. One involves engaging Third World leaders and experts in the development of more useful curricula to teach students from both developed and developing countries about Third World problems and potential solutions. A second strategy might focus on strengthening Third World home-base, on-site educational programs, assisted by experts from developed nations. The critical ingredient here would be experts or advisers who have a substantial understanding of the indigenous culture, values, history, and language, in addition to substantive expertise relative to the problems at hand. I am not suggesting that we close our educational doors to foreign nationals. Rather, we should improve our curricular offerings here so that the U.S. education Third World nationals receive will prove more useful at home. In addition, we should collaborate with our Third World neighbors to help strengthen their own on-site educational programs.

There are some obvious drawbacks that such a home-based strategy would have to overcome. First, learning in their home environments may seem less glamorous, less status-conferring to some Third World students. Second, universities, research institutes, and policy centers in the developed world would have to forego some intellectual and financial resources supplied by Third World students and researchers. Third, the possibility of Third World nationals developing a reciprocal understanding of the culture, the values, the languages, and the institutions of developed nations would be seriously diminished, at least during their student years. Fourth, the potential for developing in one's student years individual cross-national bonds of friendship that transcend time and intergovernmental dialogs would be regrettably reduced. There are serious drawbacks, but not entirely insurmountable.

A third strategy envisions a "Global Development Corps," designed to help our Third World neighbors develop their own indigenous policies, projects, and technologies, as well as needed cadres of experts and skilled workers. Such a mechanism would be a collaborative effort, engaging both First and Third World nationals, who would exchange information and skills. Problems would be defined by indigenous individuals, who request technical, social, and scientific help from other members of the Corps. Such an effort would initiate a dialogue, in which professional experts would be able to suggest, where appropriate, redefinitions of the problem for consideration by the indigenous members.

Corps members would work for and be responsible to local individuals, who are most familiar with the problem and the environmental context. Nor would the Global Development Corps be a one-way street. Third World nationals would be invited to work with their First World colleagues on problems in the developed world conducive to Third World solutions.

Although the exact structure and mandate of a Global Development Corps require more elaboration than is possible in this context, a coalition of academia, the corporate world, and the public sector could spearhead this effort. Most crucial, of course, is the need to avoid the mistakes of past paternalism and elitism. For example, extended periods of time in the host country would enable visiting Corps members to learn the language, customs, values, ecology, economics, politics, institutions, geography, and critical problems in their new environment. Corps members would return repeatedly in subsequent years, so that, eventually, they would become knowledgable, culturally-sensitive, accepted members of the community. Armed with this in-depth knowledge and understanding of their host countries, Corps members, when invited, could offer their services on a collaborative basis. These collaborative projects would be supervised and approved by local members. Perhaps recurrent tours of duty in nations requesting the Corps' help would develop a cadre of "intermittent citizens," who could work effectively on both First and Third World problems. Many issues would have to be addressed in formulating such a program; however, such a mechanism could go far toward reconceptualizing and implementing a new thrust in development activity.

In some respects, this Global Development Corps is reminiscent of the Peace Corps, only with a higher level of expertise. Perhaps individuals who served in the Peace Corps as young, not particularly skilled, but enthusiastic and dedicated, helpers would lead the way. With the advantage of their previous knowledge of particular Third World communities, they could return. This time, they would also be bringing the substantive expertise they had developed since their Peace Corps days. Now, they would represent the cutting edge. This integration of former Peace Corps workers and new Global Development Corps members from academia, the corporate world, and the public domain from both First and Third World nations would provide the beginning for a new strategy.

This is a bare-bones idea with many obvious rough edges. I present it simply as a prototype of one possible strategy for developing indigenous solutions, local cadres of skilled inhabitants, appropriate technologies, and external assistance for Third World nations. Such a strategy also would enable the First World to benefit from the knowledge and skills of their Third World colleagues.

10. Finally, all the exquisite decisions that we ponder on the cusp of the 21st century involve complexity, paradox, risk, ambiguity, and contradiction. They demand leaders who can reorder and reconceptualize the problems and priorities we confront in this inescapably interdependent world. Leaders who understand every international exchange—cultural, scientific, economic, or athletic—only as a foreign policy contest bring us closer to Armageddon. Here the key question is: how shall we develop leaders who can handle complex, paradoxical decisions laced with moral imperatives?

There is a desperate need for such leaders who can forge new institutions and bold policies mindful of the need to prevail over cultural biases and national differences. This new breed of leadership has become a matter of the greatest urgency as science and technology, as well as complex international economic patterns, propel us into unique situations without useful precedents. M.I.T. Professor Emeritus Elting E. Morison suggests that the "novel situations created by technology are a determining characteristic of [post-industrialized] society" (Morison, 1981). There is every reason to believe that this will continue into the 21st century. We need leaders who can confront these unprecedented situations and reconceptualize meaningful, equitable, and effective priorities for our socioeconomic, geopolitical, and environmental global village. These must be leaders who can weld intelligence, creativity, ethics, and imagination (Lipman-Blumen, 1985).

Before we can produce such bold and visionary leaders, we need a better understanding of the dynamics of leadership—political, corporate, religious, entrepreneurial, legal, educational, moral, and military. We need to understand these different modes of leadership. It is critical to articulate the underlying factors and processes that enable one individual, but not another, to confront paradox, uncertainty, risk, and complexity. It is critical to identify those capacities, trained or innate, that empower certain individuals to make exquisite choices for the imperfectly interdependent good of this global village.

We should place a high priority on establishing international "Institutes for Leadership Studies." Such institutes could study and develop new forms of leadership that can flourish in and help create an interdependent, peaceful world. Through such institutions we might learn to develop, or at least identify and nurture, effective leaders who can transcend cultural boundaries, visualize new directions, meaningful goals, and new pathways to solving the unprecedented problems of a rapidly changing world.

Perhaps, in this way, we shall evoke leaders who understand that the needs of multiple constituencies, within and beyond their own national borders, must be addressed. Leaders who can communicate with large-scale publics, who can effectively use (but not abuse) the media in the process of projecting a new vision are sorely needed. There is a vacuum to be filled by leaders who can reconcile the needs of the masses and the small constituencies, without resorting to false hopes and forced consensus.

Perhaps, in this way, we shall foster leaders who understand that there are no leaders whose authenticity is not willingly legitimated by their followers (Barnard, 1964). Such leaders' creativity and strength of purpose should enable them to invite their followers into the policy process at the outset, when problems are being defined and alternative solutions considered. For without involving in these critical early stages those whom we would help to help themselves, both in the Third World and at home, all is lost. For without the so-called "beneficiaries'" early involvement, there can be no acceptance, no viable implementation of the leader's most creative vision.

Where do we start to accept these challenges? Despite and because of the bewildering multitude of issues begging solution, we must begin in an holistic way, taking into account every level of society, every group, every institution, every individual. We must take bold steps, real and symbolic, to achieve not simply "First World," but *"Global Parity,"* for all nations. Male and female policy makers, corporate leaders, and academicians must make their own unique contributions to the global village. Scientists, electricians, artists, gardeners, poets, nurses, philosophers, homemakers, and athletes must join efforts to define and ponder the possibilities for the future. We must draw on the wisdom and experience of all racial, ethnic, and religious groups. Somehow we must integrate the wisdom and creativity of the generations. As neighbors in the global village, we each must contribute to the solutions so sorely needed. If we meet this momentous challenge, we may yet conquer those mountains we now watch so anxiously from the foothills.

## Notes

1. Given the resource limits that have garnered world-wide concern, First World Parity is regarded by some analysts as an unrealistic goal. Nor is the term, "First World Parity," in the current context, meant to imply that our own consumption and conservation patterns are necessarily models for emulation.

2. Between 1950 and 1980, the Gross Domestic Product (GDP) for the Third World (excluding China) increased at an annual rate of approximately 5.3 percent and the GDP per capita at almost 3 percent. From 1970 to 1974, annual growth was approximately 5.9 percent, but overall growth decelerated after the 1974–75 recession. For the 1970–80 decade, the average annual growth rate was 5.5 percent.

3. At the beginning of their industrialization periods in the nineteenth century, the now-developed European nations and the U.S.A. experienced average annual growth rates of GDP's ranging from 2.0 to 2.5 percent, and GDP's per capita from 1.2 to 1.7 percent (Bairoch as cited in Loup, 1983:6).

4. Between 1950 and 1975, the less developed nations of the world experienced a 74.9 percent population increase, compared to the more developed nations' figure of 31.4 percent (*World Population Trends and Prospects by Country,* 1950–2000: Summary Report of the 1978 Assessment, United Nations publication, ST/ESA/SER.R/33).

5. The unobserved economy has recently begun to capture the attention of economists. For example, an "International Conference on the Unobserved Economy," held at the Netherlands Institute for Advanced Study in Wassenaar, the Netherlands, June 3–6, 1982, focused on the evaluation and macro economic aspects of the hidden economy. Besides economists, an increasing number of other social and behavioral scientists are beginning to address the distinctive contributions of the official economy, the unofficial monetary economy, and the non-monetary household economy (Rose, 1983). Still other analysts have suggested that the Physical Quality of Life Index offers a more appropriate measure of development. The PQLI, however, is not without its own methodological problems (Overseas Development Council, 1979).

6. Since most Third World countries produce 90 to 95 percent of their own food, they look to developed nations to assist, primarily in times of droughts and famines. Imports from developed countries are also used to compensate for inadequate rural development programs.

7. Here, too, of course, the commonly used measures, as well as the data, are regrettably crude.

8. For an analysis of the impact of the organizational environment and bureaucratic constraints upon this aspect of development assistance programs, see Judith Tendler, 1974. For an analysis of various external donor agency, institutional, and interorganizational strategies and constraints on Third World biomass energy programs, see Ramsay and Lipman-Blumen, 1984.

## References

Bairoch, Paul. 1975. *The Economic Development of the Third World since 1900.* London: Methuen.

Barnard, Chester I. 1964. *The Functions of the Executive.* Cambridge, Mass.: Harvard University Press.

Barrère, Alain. 1978. *Le Développement Divergent: Essai sur la Richesse et la Pauvreté des Nations.* Paris: Economica.

Boserup, Ester. 1970. *Woman's Role in Economic Development.* London: George Allen and Unwin Ltd.

Boulding, Kenneth E. 1978. *Ecodynamics: A New Theory of Societal Evolution.* Beverly Hills, Cal.: Sage Publications, Inc.

Dahlberg, Kenneth A. 1985. Private Communication.

*Development Forum.* April, 1984.

Lipman-Blumen, Jean. 1984. *Gender Roles and Power.* Englewood Cliffs, N.J.: Prentice-Hall.

_____. 1985. "The Creative Tension between Liberal Arts and Specialization," *Liberal Education 71(1): 17–26.*

Lipman-Blumen, Jean, and Jessie Bernard. 1979. *Sex Roles and Social Policy.* Beverly Hills, Cal.: Sage Publications, Inc.

*Los Angeles Times,* May 9, 1984.

Loup, Jacques. 1980. *Can the Third World Survive?* Baltimore, Md.: Johns Hopkins Press.

Morison, Elting E. 1981. "The New Liberal Arts: Response I." In *The New Liberal Arts: An Exchange of Views,* ed. James D. Koerner. New York: Alfred P. Sloan Foundation.

Overseas Development Council. 1979. *The United States and World Development: Agenda 1979.* New York: Praeger.

Ramsay, William, and Jean Lipman-Blumen. 1984. "Institutional Issues in Biomass Energy Policy: The No-Man's Land Between Agricultural, Forestry, and Energy Policies in Developing Nations." Paper presented at the Annual Meeting of the International Association of Energy Economists, New Delhi, January 4–6, 1984. Forthcoming in *Third World Energy Policy,* ed. William Ramsay, *et al.* Boulder, Colo.: Westview Press.

Rose, Richard. 1983. *Getting by in Three Economies: The Resources of the Official, Unofficial, and Domestic Economies.* Glasgow, Scotland: Centre for the Study of Public Policy, University of Strathclyde.

Schiray, Michel. 1984. "The Hidden Economy and the Structures of Daily Life." *Ecodevelopment News 28–29:1–5.*

Schultze, Charles L. 1974. *National Income Analysis.* 3rd Edition. Englewood Cliffs, N.J.: Prentice-Hall.

Tendler, Judith. 1974. *Inside Foreign Aid.* Baltimore, Md.: The Johns Hopkins University Press.

United Nations. 1978. *World Population Trends and Prospects by Country, 1950–2000: Summary Report of the 1978 Assessment.* New York: United Nations ST/ESA/SER.R/33.

United Nations Environment Program, the International Union for Conservation of Nature, and the World Wildlife Fund. 1980. *World Conservation Strategy.* Geneva, Switzerland: United Nations.

Ward, Barbara. 1982. "Foreword." In *Down to Earth.,* ed. Erik P. Eckholm, New York: W.W. Norton.

World Bank. 1983. *World Development Report 1983.* New York: Oxford University Press.

_____. 1984 *World Development Report 1984.* New York: Oxford University Press.

# Part II

# The Global Setting:
# Resource, Environmental, and
# Socio-Economic Trends

# 4

# American Agriculture and the World Community

## Charles F. Cooper

## Introduction

American agriculture and agricultural research are inextricably linked to the global biosphere and the global economy. Agriculture in the U.S. is subject to global trends in such essential factors of production as climate, atmospheric carbon dioxide, and genetic diversity. The economic base of American agriculture today is sale of American surpluses to the rest of the world. Attainment of food self-sufficiency everywhere, a goal of many national and international development programs including our own, would significantly affect American farmers.

America is one of the world's principal food producers for two chief reasons: a natural endowment of soil and climate, and a capital-intensive production system backed by extensive public and private research and effective information dissemination. The agricultural potential of, say, Jordan can never equal that of Illinois, but much can be done to improve production in the poorer countries. What is the proper role of American agriculture and agricultural research in a global context? How can our own self-interest be reconciled with the needs of the rest of the world, particularly in the developing countries? These questions are basic to any examination of ethics and values in American agricultural research.

## The Global Atmosphere

The earth's atmosphere is truly global; it circulates worldwide in days or months, touching every land plant. It carries lifegiving carbon dioxide and damaging pollutants. It transports the heat and moisture that make local weather, and its long term state defines the regional climates that make agriculture possible.

Man affects the atmosphere primarily through release of chemicals and particulate matter, and through land use practices that alter the reflectivity (albedo) and heat budget of the surface. Chemical additions include long-lived compounds such as carbon dioxide and chlorofluorocarbons (Freon), and more reactive substances such as ozone and oxides of sulfur and nitrogen. The impact of the long-lived components is pervasive, touching the entire globe. Shorter-lived components are confined to regions reached by air masses containing them before they are washed out. Sources of many of these short-lived pollutants are so widely dispersed, however, that their combined effects are equally pervasive.

### Weather and Climate:   Control and Prediction

Farmers have always been at the mercy of the weather. An international workshop on interactions of food and climate (Bach, *et al.*, 1981) identified fluctuations in yearly weather as the principal threat to world food supplies, now and in the future. Control of these fluctuations is a next to impossible dream. Ever since Vincent Schaefer's 1947 discovery that small amounts of Dry Ice (and later other substances such as silver iodide) could initiate condensation in supercooled clouds and sometimes stimulate precipitation, efforts have been underway to develop a scientific technology for deliberate weather modification. The results are mixed at best (Hsu and Changnon 1983). Almost four decades of serious effort have still not demonstrated that deliberate weather modification can make more than a marginal contribution to agriculture.

If we cannot control the weather (or even modify it to any significant degree), the next best thing is to predict it. Satellite technology and improved understanding of atmospheric processes have combined to greatly improve meteorologists' abilities to predict weather ten days or so ahead. But what really concerns a farmer is the weather next season or next year. The prognosis for such long term forecasting is less certain.

Several groups—at the National Weather Service, Scripps Institution of Oceanography, and elsewhere—have had some success in predicting deviations from normal regional temperature and precipitation several months in advance. The results are generally somewhat better than chance; that is, the forecasts are right 55 to 60 percent of the time. There are prospects that this score can eventually be improved enough to aid in planning. Drought in northeastern Brazil has periodically led to great deprivation through crop failure. Statistical methods have been developed which would apparently have made it possible to predict, for instance, the severe drought of 1958 (Hastenrath, 1984). Such prediction would not have averted hardship, but might have alleviated it.

It will probably never be possible, though, to make accurate long term predictions of the time and size of individual storms—information of great value in planting and harvest decisions. The inherent irregularity of atmospheric turbulence seemingly rules out long term prediction of anything more precise than broad seasonal trends (Lorenz, 1984). For many purposes, though, it is less important to hit the right day or week of a storm than to predict a monthly amount of precipitation reasonably closely. Predictions of the general magnitude of precipitation one to two years ahead would allow reservoirs to be operated more efficiently, making more water available for irrigation (Changnon, 1982).

The ability to predict major global events such as El Niño, the warming of the waters off Peru and Ecuador that occurs sporadically around the Christmas season, would be of great importance to agriculture and fisheries. The 1982–83 El Niño was the strongest in this century. In addition to its impact on South American fisheries, it brought unprecedented flooding in Ecuador and Peru. The severe coastal storms of March 1983 spread across the continent to wreak destruction in the Amazonian lowlands of Bolivia, which have not yet recovered. The Bolivian highlands were plagued by three years of drought which caused great deprivation, if not actual starvation. Local residents firmly attribute the drought to El Niño, but no causal link has been clearly shown. El Niño seems more definitely to have been associated with abnormal weather in North America during 1982–83.

To an oceanographer, El Niño is the ocean's response to anomalies in atmospheric circulation collectively called the Southern Oscillation (Cane, 1983). To a meteorologist, the Southern Oscillation is a periodic change in atmospheric circulation driven by changes in sea surface temperature (Rasmusson and Wallace, 1983). This unsatisfactorily circular explanation has nevertheless led to better understanding of both phenomena, which in turn permits improved prediction. It is now thought possible to detect, mostly through satellite observation of sea level and temperature anomalies, an incipient El Niño. The 1982 event was not detected until several months after it is now known to have begun. Information gained in 1982 and 1983 makes possible more reliable prediction of the course, severity, and duration of a new El Niño. What cannot yet be predicted, pending a scientific breakthrough, is the start of a new event. These typically occur at intervals of about four years, but the range is from two to ten. Until the causes of the linked atmospheric and oceanic responses are unraveled, forecasting the advent of a new El Niño cannot be much improved.

If science and technology can provide better long range weather forecasts, who really benefits? For the foreseeable future, forecasts will be far from deterministic and foolproof. They will be probabilistic and couched in quite general terms. Those who can best take advantage of such incremental improvements in knowledge are seemingly those with the greatest ability to shift resources and with large enough capital reserves to be able to play the odds over the longer term: multinational corporations, operators of multipurpose water storage systems, and similar large enterprises. A major challenge for agricultural research is to assist the small farmer in making more effective use of forecasts that are uncertain but still better than chance.

*Air Pollutants*

Farmers are at the mercy not only of the weather but of a variety of substances injected into the atmosphere by human activities. Many atmospheric pollutants are known to reduce agricultural production. Sulfur dioxide and acid precipitation have received the biggest press and the most political attention, but strong oxidants, principally ozone ($O_3$), are thought to be more important contributors to current crop losses and forest damage. Oxidants, however, are probably not as responsible as acidic compounds for long term deterioration of poorly buffered soils.

Normal background levels of ozone in the lower atmosphere are in the range of 0.02–0.03 parts per million (ppm). Ambient levels as high as 0.10 ppm are regularly detected in urban and industrial regions. The principal mechanism of ozone formation is a photochemical reaction involving oxides of nitrogen formed during high temperature combustion in industrial boilers and gasoline engines. Relatively little is produced through low temperature cooking or space heating. Ozone damage is thus a disease of industrialization.

As part of the National Crop Loss Assessment, Heck, *et al.* (1982) developed estimates of the loss in yield of 19 species and varieties of crop plants for each 0.01 ppm increase in atmospheric ozone concentration over background. These losses range from about 1 percent for each 0.01 ppm in corn to 7 percent in peanuts (Table 4.1). Taking a somewhat different approach, Loucks and Armentano (1982) estimated crop losses for the six-state Ohio River Basin, based on ambient ozone measurements in the major crop areas of the basin. For 1976, the last year for which data were available, they concluded that the most probable decrease in soybean yield was 14 percent in the basin as a whole when compared with the yield that would have been obtained without ozone contamination. The upper bound of the loss estimate was 26 percent, and the lower bound 5 percent (Table 4.2). Corn and wheat were deemed somewhat less sensitive to ozone, with probable loss estimates of 8 percent and 6 percent respectively. Loss due to the additive effect of sulfur dioxide ($SO_2$) exposure at levels encountered in the Ohio River Basin was much less (Table 4.2). $SO_2$ emissions are usually confined to areas of less than 100 square miles surrounding a source, whereas elevated $O_3$ is more widely disseminated in regional air masses. Because of the lower sensitivity of crops to $SO_2$ and its spatially restricted occurrence, loss in yield due to this pollutant was judged to be minor in the Ohio River Basin.

Full abatement of oxidant emissions, an unlikely outcome, would increase U.S. agricultural output by several percent, enough to have a direct effect on surpluses and on national agricultural policy. Increased industrialization in agricultural zones of developing countries could lead to locally diminished food production, particularly in the absence of pollution control measures.

### Carbon Dioxide and Trace Gases

Progressive increases in the burning of fossil fuels and the clearing of forests have been significantly increasing atmospheric carbon dioxide ($CO_2$) for more than a century. The rate of increase is now somewhat more than 0.04 percent per year. (For a general account of knowledge about effects of increasing $CO_2$ see Clark, 1982, and National Academy of Sciences, 1983.) Since $CO_2$ is transparent to the wavelengths of incoming solar radiation but largely opaque to the longer wavelengths radiated back to space by Earth, the gas traps some of the outgoing heat and makes

---

Table 4.1    Percentage Reduction in Yield of Selected Crops for each 0.01 ppm Increase over "Normal" (0.025 ppm) in Ozone Exposure

| Crop | Yield reduction (percent) |
|------|---------------------------|
| Soybeans | 4.7 |
| Winter wheat | 3.1 |
| Corn | 1.1 |
| Peanuts | 7.1 |
| Lettuce, spinach, kidney beans, turnips | 5.2 |

*Source:*    Heck *et al.,* 1982.

**Table 4.2    Estimated Crop Loss Coefficients for Chronic $O_3$ and $So_2$ Exposure in Ohio River Basin**

|  | Reduction in yield (percent) | | |
|---|---|---|---|
|  | Minimum | Probable | Maximum |
| Ozone |  |  |  |
|    Soybeans | 5 | 14 | 26 |
|    Corn | 4 | 8 | 15 |
|    Wheat | 3 | 6 | 10 |
| Sulfur dioxide (0.05–0.10 ppm) |  |  |  |
|    Soybeans | 1 | 3 | 4 |
|    Corn | 0 | 0 | 2 |
|    Wheat | 1 | 2 | 3 |

*Source:*  Loucks and Armentano, 1982.

Earth warmer than it would otherwise be.  The increase in $CO_2$ is expected to result in global warming in the next decades, although some qualified atmospheric scientists (Elsaesser, 1984) believe that the warming will be long delayed.  Majority opinion is however converging on an estimate that a doubling of $CO_2$ from its levels in the 1890's—expected sometime near the middle of the next century—will increase global mean temperature by about 3°C.  The increase will not be uniformly distributed, though; feedback mechanisms will result in substantially greater warming near the poles—perhaps 8–12°C—than at the equator, where the change may be less than a degree.  Expected to accompany the temperature change are shifts in the earth's major precipitation belts.

This asymmetry has significant implications for agriculture in the United States and throughout the world.  The northward movement of the subtropical dry zone could leave the fertile soils of the American Midwest, which even now lack enough precipitation for optimal production, dangerously short.  Some agronomists (Wittwer, 1980) believe that impacts of climatic change represent no more than "interesting technical challenges" which agricultural research can easily meet.  Others feel the problem will be more difficult.

If the prognostications are correct, developing countries in the tropics are likely to feel little direct impact of climatic change except perhaps for some increase in precipitation at the semiarid margins of the equatorial tropics. There the effect would be largely beneficial.

Increasing atmospheric $CO_2$ could also have a significant non-climatic effect on plant growth.  It has long been known that added $CO_2$ stimulates growth of well-watered and fertilized greenhouse plants.  Whether this is true in the field, where many other growth factors are in short supply, is unknown. The increase in atmospheric $CO_2$ since the beginning of the industrial era has been about 20 percent. If this has translated into only a 5 percent increase in photosynthesis, it would suggest a significant agronomic effect, even though the harvestable yield of current crop varieties may not be directly proportional to photosynthesis. Since the physiological response to $CO_2$ is relatively subtle, plant breeding programs designed to take advantage of increased $CO_2$ are likely to be more sophisticated than those designed to improve disease resistance or response to fertilizer and water. Thus, the benefits may accrue chiefly to technically advanced nations, accentuating the imbalance between them and the poorer nations.

Other trace gases—chloroflourocarbons (Freon), methane, oxides of nitrogen, and others, are also increasing in the atmosphere and may likewise affect both global climate and the earth's protective ozone layer. Whereas ozone at the surface is clearly detrimental to plants, in the stratosphere it is essential to shield Earth from harmful ultraviolet radiation. A widespread hypothesis suggests the possibility of stratospheric ozone depletion due to photochemical reactions involving nitrous oxide emitted by heavily fertilized agricultural soils. Increasing knowledge of atmospheric chemistry over the last 10 years has left these predictions in flux. A recent assessment (NASA, 1984) of responsible predictions of potential changes in stratospheric ozone, made at various times in the decade 1974–1984, shows a range of $-19$ to $+4$ percent, with no consistent trend (assuming the same future increase in nitrogen compounds). This is not to say that agricultural emissions are not potentially troublesome, but rather indicates the need for research to establish a consensus before policy decisions are promulgated.

### Environmental Impacts in Developing Countries

The popular image of the sturdy farmer zealously guarding his land for future generations, whatever its truth, masks the fact that agriculture often has significant adverse environmental consequences. Environmental degradation from modern high technology farming is dealt with elsewhere in this book. Perhaps even more serious in the long run, though, are environmental consequences of more traditional forms of cultivation in the poorer countries. Soil erosion, loss of nutrients, degradation of pastures, are each responsible for enormous losses of potential food production every year.

The *Global 2000 Report* (Council on Environmental Quality, 1980) concluded that the environmental problems associated with increased food production are manageable in theory, but are unlikely to be well-managed in reality. The authors of that report identified two broad classes of agro-environmental problems: those related to expanded and intensified use of land resources, and those brought about by increased use of external inputs. In the first category are such likely consequences as soil erosion and loss of fertility due to improper cultivation, decline of grazing lands, and salinization and waterlogging of irrigated soils. The second includes eutrophication of lakes and rivers and nitrate poisoning of ground water by fertilizer runoff, and the external effects of chemical control of diseases and pests.

An important contributor to resource degradation is that measures to reduce it are seldom cost-effective for the individual farmer (Brown, 1981). Given typical socio-economic conditions, reducing erosion is more costly in terms of time, energy, and loss of current production than is justified by the prospect of long term gains.

There is hope, though, that the decline in the resource base may be arrested through properly channeled agricultural development buttressed by research. "Develop without destroying" is the exhortation to the people of Bolivia by the noted German ecologist Heinz Ellenberg (1981). He offers workable prescriptions for incorporating ecological principles into development planning in the climatically different regions of that poverty-stricken land. He recognizes nevertheless that improving the life of the Bolivian *campesinos* depends mostly on socio-economic and political factors beyond their control.

An environmental problem of increasing concern is the conversion of semiarid farm and pasture land to virtual deserts. A hypothesis relating land use, surface albedo and drought through a biophysical feedback mechanism (Charney, 1975) has gained wide currency as an explanation of the persistence of drought in regions such as the African Sahel. It is that drought and overgrazing diminish vegetation cover and expose light-colored soil. The energy reflected by increased albedo is replaced in part by heat drawn from the atmosphere. Descending air warms and dries, reducing precipitation, so the system feeds on itself. Analysis of satellite data now fails to confirm the hypothesis, however. The albedo of the Sahel as a whole increased to a peak in 1973, at the worst of the drought; but although drought still persists, regional albedo decreased by nearly a third between 1973 and 1979 (Courel, *et al.,* 1984). This does not disprove the Charney hypothesis, but does cast doubt on its importance.

Estimates of the loss of potential food production in the developing countries from environmental deterioration vary widely, and are somewhat beside the point. What matters is to ensure that intensification of agriculture in the developing world is not accompanied by equal degradation of its biological and soil base, negating the effects of the agricultural improvement. Prevention and alleviation of environmental deterioration has not generally been a high priority of agricultural aid and technology transfer programs. The gloomy conclusion of the *Global 2000 Report* is that the perceived urgency of food deficiencies and calorie gaps is likely to outweigh environmental degradation in the eyes of developing countries and international assistance agencies.

*Genetic and Biological Diversity*

Worldwide loss of genetic and biological diversity is attracting increased attention (Dahlberg, 1983). Gene banks have been established to preserve local crop varieties displaced by modern high-yielding selections. This may not be enough, though. The best gene banks are native ecosystems, cultivated and non-cultivated, with their continuing genetic exchange between wild and domesticated plants, facilitated by native pollinators.

Few of the world's major food plants have their centers of origin in the industrialized world. It is therefore in the developing countries that these ecosystem gene banks must be maintained. Insistence on preservation in a relatively undeveloped state of much of their national territory is seen, not unreasonably, by these countries as arrogance and elitism. It should be possible, though, to devise mechanisms for effective conservation of ecosystems which include people. Maintenance of subsistence cultivation communities, perhaps through external subsidies, could have substantial value for tourism as well as for protection of biological resources.

Much lowland tropical forest has been converted to pasture in Honduras, Brazil, and elsewhere in Latin American (Myers, 1984). The process has been aided by national governments, multilateral development banks, and international development organizations. Little of the meat produced serves local markets. Most is low-grade beef for export, primarily to the North American fast food trade. Because of poor, quickly depleted soils and rapid reestablishment of forest undergrowth, many of these pastures will not long remain profitable for beef production. In Honduras, pastures created from former forest supports one animal per hectare in the first year. Within five to ten years, 5 to 7 hectares per head are required. Production usually ends after about 10 years (Nations and Komer, 1983). Much scarce tropical forest habitat and its biological diversity has been sacrificed for a few years of meat production to satisfy our voracious national appetite for a cheap hamburger.

I suspect that reliable data from the private sector would show that the great preponderance of American agricultural research and consultation expenditures in countries such as Honduras has been in support of beef production ventures. I know of American rangeland development consultants who refused to participate after viewing the extent of ecosystem destruction already accomplished in that country. Beef production is so firmly entrenched in the economics and politics of the region, however, that abandonment is not a realistic solution. The key is intensification of production through better breeds, better disease control, and above all better management of both pastures and animals (Nations and Komer, 1983). As in so much of tropical agriculture, the problems are more political and financial than technical.

What is occurring in Honduras is symptomatic of a process long established in tropical agriculture. European colonial administrators in the nineteenth and early twentieth centuries devised plantation systems to produce raw materials for manufacture at home at the expense of indigenous food production. Scientific agriculture in the tropics was long confined to export crops with a high return on investment. Food and fiber have often not been produced in adequate quantities for the local market, and economies have become dependent on fluctuations in commodity prices in the developed countries. That subsistence farming is commonly women's work makes the problem worse. Local extension workers, mostly male, aim their advice at men and at men's activities and crops. This bias may depress production of food, grown by women, in favor of increased production of the cash crops produced by men, so that family nutrition suffers (FAO, 1981).

It is not only in developing countries that loss of genetic and biological diversity is a problem. Similar losses in the U.S. are almost inevitable if projected export goals are to be met. Intensive high-yield forest practices will only make the matter worse. This is a question that the research establishment has so far shown little willingness to face.

But beyond the practical issue of preserving genes for future economic use is evolutionary ethics. Should man, the dominant species, "accept the prospect that few species will remain which are not either of actual or potential value to man, or which for the time being he is unable to subdue or exterminate?" (Frankel, 1970). We may someday be able to engineer living organisms to our specifications, but it is inconceivable that we can recreate the incredibly complex and adapted communities that have arisen through time. Sir Otto Frankel says that because of our dominance over the rest of nature, "We have acquired evolutionary responsibility." How to reconcile this responsibility with the immediate needs of impoverished people who inhabit regions of great ecological diversity and genetic importance is a fundamental ethical issue.

## Food and People

Despite a few strong dissenting views (Simon, 1982), growth of world population is widely perceived as one of humanity's pressing problems. American agriculture is expected by many to play a major role in feeding this burgeoning population.

Projections of future population and economic growth are notoriously unreliable. Nevertheless, general trends in global population and in agricultural production are evident, barring major catastrophe or worldwide social upheaval. United Nations projections are that the population of all developing countries will double between 1980 and 2025, even though the rate of population increase in those countries has been declining for a decade. The increase for Latin America alone is estimated at 130 percent. Even if each family has fewer children, the great number of young people born in the last quarter century means many more families of child-bearing age. A falling birthrate will be accompanied by rapidly rising absolute numbers of people at least into the third decade of the next century.

Adequate food for all depends more on economic conditions and on jobs than on the earth's ability to grow food. If some go hungry, it is because of inadequate distribution among nations and among people within nations, not because of an absolute shortage of food. All developed countries are adequately fed overall. The developing countries are unable as a group to satisfy the calorie requirements of their people fully, but the situation has distinctly improved during the 1960s and '70s (Table 4.3). Contrary to general belief, the percentage increase in food production in the low income countries has averaged a bit higher than in the developed world over the last 25 years, although per capita increase has not (Murdoch, 1980). Globally, there is enough food to provide an adequate intake of calories for all (Parikh and Rabar, 1981), although protein deficiencies remain.

Distribution within developing countries is, however, markedly uneven. For instance, Kenya has only a marginal nationwide calorie deficit, yet the diet of 40 percent of the urban population falls short of daily requirements by an average of one-sixth. Hunger is also widespread among the landless in rural areas of Kenya (Parikh and Rabar, 1981). It is not clear

Table 4.3  Per Capita Daily Supply of Calories

| Region | Calories per capita (kcal) | | Supply as percentage of requirement (percent) | |
|---|---|---|---|---|
| | 1961–63 | 1972–74 | 1961–63 | 1972–74 |
| Developed market economies | 3130 | 3340 | 123 | 131 |
| Eastern Europe and USSR | 3240 | 3460 | 126 | 135 |
| Developing market economies | 2110 | 2180 | 92 | 95 |
| Asian centrally planned economies | 1960 | 2290 | 83 | 97 |
| All developing countries | 2060 | 2210 | 89 | 96 |
| World | 2410 | 2550 | 101 | 107 |

*Source:*  Parikh and Rabar, 1981, from FAO, *Fourth World Food Survey*, 1977.

that agricultural research, even if it leads to substantially enhanced production, can by itself do much to alleviate the plight of the urban poor in developing countries. The United States has not wholly solved the problem of local malnutrition despite our food surpluses. The basic cause of hunger in both urban and rural areas of the developing world is poverty and maldistribution of food. Nevertheless, increased local food production would surely be of some help to the rural population.

Losses to spoilage and animals (including insects) after harvest account for up to 40 percent of total food production in tropical developing countries (Council on Environmental Quality, 1980). As with food availability, this problem is more social and economic than technological. Inadequate roads hinder movement of food from farm to market, so it spoils. Where food is abundant, there are too few consumers with sufficient disposable income to absorb it before it spoils. Nevertheless, much can be done to reduce post-harvest losses and to make the food conserved available for human use. Intermediate or "appropriate" technologies are of great value in providing methods of food processing and preservation that are both simple and effective. Unfortunately, few of these technologies are commercially attractive to the private sector, even though their use may bring benefits far out of proportion to their costs (Robinson, 1983). This is a fertile area both for research and for dissemination of information.

A little noted source of food loss is the high seed requirements of inefficient agriculture. Four percent of U.S. wheat production is retained for seed; in the Soviet Union, 16.5 percent (Johnson, 1983). In many developing countries even more is needed. Although part of the reason for high seed retention is losses due to variable weather, much can be done through research and demonstration to increase seeding efficiency.

Even if enough food could be produced to feed the world today, what of the more distant future? What happens in the next century, when the 390 million people of Latin America become 800 million (Fox, 1983), and similar increases are recorded in other developing regions? Until a few years ago many thought that not enough could be grown to feed the expanding populations of the poorer countries. More recent studies of potentially cultivable land and its productive capacity have convinced many people that the global food problem is mainly social, economic and political, not biological or technological.

Several global models have incorporated assessments of the world food situation. Those with the most reliable data bases include the World Food Problem Study of the President's Science Advisory Committee (PSAC, 1967), the model developed by Fundacion Bariloche in Argentina (Herrera, et al., 1976), the MOIRA model from the Netherlands (Linnemann, et al., 1979) and the Global 2000 Model (Council on Environmental Quality, 1980). These studies all show that much more food could be produced than today. The *Global 2000 Report* says that the world has the capacity to produce enough food to meet substantial increases in demand, and that this finding is compatible with other studies which suggest a world food potential several times higher than current production levels. Another authoritative report agrees: "over the next two decades the developing countries could double their food and agricultural production" (FAO, 1981). There is grave doubt, though, that this potential will actually be realized in time.

Sufficient food cannot be produced solely by labor-oriented agriculture, defined as systems in which no chemical fertilizers or machinery are used, and almost all work is done by hand labor and animal traction (Buringh and van Heemst, 1977). If this form of agriculture were applied everywhere, even where modern technology now governs, it would be impossible to feed today's world population. Soil conservation activities would be impossible because of the low income of farmers, so soil erosion, degradation, and desertification would be even more disastrous than now. This study from the Netherlands concludes that "From a point of view of living conditions, natural resources, ecology and conservation of the environment it seems to be much wiser to introduce on a large scale modern systems of farming in those parts of the various countries where productive land is already cultivated, but where productivity is still very low. . . . Reclamation of new land [should] be restricted" (Buringh and van Heemst, 1977). "Modern systems of farming" need not, however, imply the energy-intensive methods used in North America, with their heavy machinery and advanced technology. Light gasoline tractors and hand operated power cultivators have greatly augmented Japanese rice production. Agroforestry and other mixed cropping systems can reduce the need for pesticides and fertilizers. The important point is that greater gains can be achieved by improving yields from the best land rather than breaking new land for cultivation. This is now happening in many of the more advanced tropical countries such as Costa Rica. Research is needed to accelerate the process. Success could benefit the U.S. economy through export of small-scale machinery and technology. Unfortunately, such exports are not likely to be thought of as being as profitable as the high technology alternative.

## U.S. Exports and Developing Country Imports

Agricultural exports of $28 billion in 1981 paid for a large share of that year's $42 billion of oil imports. The United States' merchandise balance of trade is now seemingly permanently negative for the first time since 1917. Economists and money managers consider expansion of agricultural exports essential to a healthy U.S. economy.

Four key crops—wheat, feedgrains, cotton, and soybeans—account for three-fourths of all harvested land in the U.S., and are the agricultural products in greatest demand for export. A study by Resources for the Future (RFF) projects a substantial increase in U.S. production of these four crops to the year 2010, achieved through use of land not now in cultivation and through greater yield per acre, although the yield increases of the past two decades will surely not be matched. The fraction of total production which is exported will also increase from roughly 50 percent to about 60 percent (Crosson and Brubaker, 1982).

The developing countries are the principal future targets of crop exporters. Import demands in western Europe, the USSR, and Japan for crops other than soybeans are expected to increase at little more than the rate of population growth, and in some cases to decrease as a result of improved local production. Not only are the developing countries expected to increase their imports, but at least in the case of feedgrains a larger fraction of total consumption will be imported (Crosson and Brubaker, 1982).

Will the developing countries be able to afford the projected levels of imports? The RFF researchers think so, but others have serious doubts. Nevertheless, American agricultural policy is now strongly oriented toward export. American agriculture would be far different if it had to depend only on a national market. So would be conditions in the importing countries if they had to grow their own food instead of relying heavily on grain produced by American farmers. This implies an important ethical dilemma for American agricultural research: are we justified in continuing to emphasize high production, with its attendant environmental problems, when that production may inhibit rural development in the importing countries?

## Conclusions

There is a spectrum of prevailing views about long term availability of resources and sustainability of food production. At one end is the infinite resources argument, typified by Goeller and Zucker (1984). They contend that projections of global population and demand for nonrenewable resources make it unlikely that the world will run short of any needed element before about 2050. This gives ample time to develop technology for exploiting lower grade ores and for using some 30 elements in "essentially infinite supply" to provide substitute products for satisfaction of society's needs. They conclude that "[A] strategy of infinite resources . . . would mean that future shortages will be at most only transient events and that a stable population of 8.5 billion people will not be imperiled or impoverished by lack of materials required for civilized life." They wholly omit the energy required to process lower grade ores and less efficient substitutes, nor do they consider food supplies or threats to renewable resources more generally.

At the other end of the spectrum are the various doomsday prophets. Less extreme but still pessimistic are the views of Meadows, *et al.*, (1972) in *The Limits to Growth* and of the authors of the *Global 2000 Report to the President* (Council on Environmental Quality, 1980). Meadows, *et al.*, concluded that behavior of the world system would be characterized by overshoot and collapse, brought about by depletion of nonrenewable resources and increasing pollution of air, water, and land. They were probably the first since Malthus to present such conclusions forcefully and effectively enough to bring them to wide public attention. Even if resources are assumed to be "infinite", as in Goeller and Zucker's projection, the Meadows model predicts a stoppage of growth by devastating pollution.

If the more pessimistic scenarios are to be avoided, an important task for agricultural research is to build more resilience into the world's food production and distribution system. The distinction between resilience and stability is gaining increasing currency as a framework for ecological analysis (Holling, 1973). It is equally applicable to world agriculture.

Agricultural policies, in the U.S. and elsewhere, have mostly been built around a paradigm of ecological stability. A perturbed system that is globally stable will always return to its initial state after removal of the stress. The stability view emphasizes equilibrium, the maintenance of a predictable world, and the harvesting of Nature's surplus with as little fluctuation as possible. It assumes an infinitely forgiving Nature. That this assumption has been at least partially true is shown by the relative success until now of the trial-and-error approach that has historically characterized agricultural development. If one approach didn't work, try something else—or move on.

The resilience view, on the other hand, recognizes that a system may have several stable states. It will return to the initial state after relatively minor perturbations, but a still greater impact may move it into a new, albeit perhaps impermanent stable state to which it will again return after other minor perturbations.

If the system has several regions of stability rather than one, Nature can seem to play the practical joker rather than the forgiving benefactor. Policies will seemingly operate effectively so long as the system remains within existing stability domains. However, if the system moves close to a stability boundary, incremental disturbances can precipitate radically altered behavior (Holling, 1983).

The history of pest control in high technology agriculture offers a vivid example. Policies and practices succeeded in the short run, only to make the system more vulnerable in the long run to the very problem they were meant to control. Insects and other pests developed resistance to formerly effective agents at the same time that their natural enemies, unintended targets of the same pesticides, were decimated. In some instances, farmers find that return to earlier, less efficient but still reasonably effective forms of pest control is virtually impossible, at least in the short run. They are locked in a new stable state requiring ever more intensive application of pesticides.

Corn growers in the early 1970's had a production system that effectively withstood assaults from southern corn blight until an altered form of the fungus flipped the system without warning into a new stable state—crop failure. The system had lost resilience. In that instance, resilience has been regained by introduction of several resistant genes instead of just one.

More dangerous, though, than these simple examples are instances in which changes accumulate slowly and virtually undetected until they ultimately produce sharply altered behavior. The system evolves to become less and less resilient and threatens larger and more extensive failures. Once resilience is lost, the system can be sustained only by increasing external subsidies of energy and resources, increasing knowledge, and increasingly error-free control. It is no longer well matched to human and institutional frailties (Holling, 1983).

Loss of resilience is already well advanced in American agriculture and its relations with the rest of the world. A major task of agricultural research must be to find ways to increase the resilience of the agricultural system and thereby to assure its sustainability in a world of increasing population and demands for resources.

### References

Bach, Wilfrid; Jurgen Pankrath; and Stephen H. Schneider, eds. 1981. *Food-Climate Interactions.* Dordrecht: Reidel.

Brown, Lester R. 1981. "World Population Growth, Soil Erosion, and Food Security." *Science* 214:995–1002.

Buringh, Pieter, and H. D. J. van Heemst. 1977. *An Estimation of World Food Production Based on Labour-oriented Agriculture.* Wageningen, The Netherlands: The Agricultural University.

Cane, Mark A. 1983. "Oceanographic Events during El Niño." *Science* 222:1189–1195.

Changnon, Stanley A., Jr. 1982. "Possible Uses of Long-range Weather Outlooks in Water Resources." In *International Symposium on Hydrometeorology,* pp. 231–234. Bethesda, Maryland: American Water Resources Association.

Charney, Jule G. 1975. "Dynamics of Deserts and Drought in the Sahel." *Quarterly Journal Royal Meteorological Society* 101:193–202.

Clark, W. C. 1982. *Carbon Dioxide Review: 1982.* New York: Oxford University Press.

Council on Environmental Quality. 1980. *Global 2000: Report to the President.* Washington, D.C.: Government Printing Office.

Courel, M. F., R. S. Kandel, and S. I. Rasool. 1984. "Surface Albedo and the Sahel Drought." *Nature* 307:528–531.

Crosson, Pierre R., and Stuart Brubaker. 1982. *Resource and Environmental Effects of U.S. Agriculture.* Washington, D.C.: Resources for the Future.

Dahlberg, Kenneth A. 1983. "Plant Germplasm Conservation: Emerging Problems and Issues." *Mazingira* 7:14–25.

Ellenberg, Heinz. 1981. "Desarrollar sin Destruir: Repuestas de un Ecólogo a 15 Preguntas de Agrónomas y Planificadores Bolivianos." Cochabamba, Bolivia: Centro Pedagógogico y Cultural de Portales.

Elsaesser, H. W. 1984. "The Climatic Effect of $CO_2$: A Different View." *Atmospheric Environment* 18:421–434.

FAO. 1981. *Agriculture: Toward 2000.* Rome: Food and Agriculture Organization of the United Nations.

Fox, R. 1983. "The Challenge of Numbers." *Inter-American Development Bank News* 10(10):6–7.

Frankel, Otto H. 1970. "Variation—the Essence of Life. Sir William Macleay Memorial Lecture." *Proceedings Linnean Society of New South Wales* 95:158–169.

Goeller, H. E., and A. Zucker. 1984. "Infinite Resources: The Ultimate Strategy." *Science* 223:456–462.

Hastenrath, S. 1984. "Predictability of North-east Brazil Droughts." *Nature* 307:531–533.

Heck, W.H.; O.C. Taylor; R. Adams; G. Bingham; J. Miller; E. Preston; and L. Weinstein. 1982. "Assessment of Crop Losses from Ozone." *Air Pollution Control Federation Journal* 32:353–361.

Herrera, A. D., *et al.* 1976. *Catastrophe or New Society?: A Latin American World Model.* Ottawa, Ontario: International Development Center.

Holling, C. S. 1973. "Resilience and Stability of Ecological Systems." *Annual Review of Ecology and Systematics* 4:1–23.

_____. 1983. "Director's Corner: Suprise!" *Options* (International Institute for Applied Systems Analysis) 4:16

Hsu, C-F., and S. A. Changnon, Jr. 1983. "On the Evaluation of Operational Cloud Seeding Projects." *Water Resources Bulletin* 19:563–569.

Johnson, D. G. 1983. The Soviet Union: Agriculture—Management and Performance. *Bulletin of Atomic Scientists* 39(2):16–22.

Linneman, H.; J. De Hoogh; M. Keyser; and H. Van Heemst. 1979. *MOIRA—Model of International Relations in Agriculture.* Amsterdam: North-Holland.

Lorenz, Edward N. 1984. "Irregularity: A Fundamental Property of the Atmosphere." *Tellus* 36A:98–110.

Loucks, Orie L., and T. V. Armentano. 1982. "Estimating Crop Yield Effects from Ambient Air Pollutants in the Ohio River Valley." *Air Pollution Control Federation Journal* 32:147–150.

Meadows, Donella H.; D. L. Meadows; J. Randers; and W. H. Behrens III. 1972. *The Limits to Growth.* New York: Universe Books.

Murdoch, William. 1980. *The Poverty of Nations.* Baltimore: John Hopkins University Press.

Myers, Norman. 1984. *The Primary Source: Tropical Forests and Our Future.* New York: Norton.

NASA. 1984. *Present State of Knowledge of the Upper Atmosphere.* Washington, D.C.: National Aeronautics and Space Administration.

National Academy of Sciences. 1983. *Changing Climate: Report of the Carbon Dioxide Assessment Committee.* Washington, D.C.: National Academy Press.

Nations, James D., and Daniel I. Komer, 1983. "Central America's Tropical Rainforests: Positive Steps for Survival." *Ambio* 12:232–238.

Parikh, K., and P. Rabar. 1981. *Food for All in a Sustainable World.* Laxenburg, Austria: International Institurte for Applied Systems Analysis.

PSAC. 1967. *The World Food Problem.* Volume II. Report of the Panel on the World Food Situation. Washington, D.C.: The White House.

Rasmusson, Eugene M., and John M. Wallace. 1983. "Meteorological Aspects of the El Niño/Southern Oscillation." *Science* 222:1195–1202.

Robinson, R. K. 1983. *The Vanishing Harvest: A Study of Food and its Conservation.* Oxford: Oxford Universtiy Press.

Simon, Julian L. 1981. *The Ultimate Resource.* Princeton, N.J.: Princton University Press.
Wittwer, Sylvan H. 1980. "Environmental and Societal Consequences of a Possible $CO_2$ Induced Climate Change on Agriculture." Paper presented at Annual Meeting of American Association for Advancement of Science, San Francisco, January 5, 1980.

# 5

# Historical Forces That Have Shaped World Agriculture: A Structural Perspective

## Alain de Janvry and E. Phillip LeVeen

The organization of world agriculture is currently undergoing profound changes that are transforming both the capacity of nations to insure their food security and the welfare of their rural populations. These changes are not random occurrences or natural phenomena but the product of a set of socially defined historical forces. Even though these forces are highly complex and assume great geographical specificity, they acquire consistency when located within the logic of particular social systems. To limit the scope of the analysis, we will consider here only First and Third World nations where markets exist for products, labor, land, capital, and technology. Socialist economies will be referred to only inasmuch as their participation in the world market influences agriculture in the First and Third Worlds; an analysis of agriculture and other domestic forces within socialist economies will not be made here.*

---

*Reviewers of previous drafts have objected to the exclusion of socialist agriculture from the scope of this analysis. More than one reviewer suggested that our analysis addresses the consequences of "industrial" rather than "capitalist" agricultural development, and hence the problems we identify are supposedly inherent in both socialist and capitalist systems. While we acknowledge that both types of agriculture have become increasingly dependent on productivity-increasing, industrial technologies, our position is that the nature of agricultural development is determined much more by prevailing economic, political, and social relations than by the requirements of these technologies. We focus on capitalist agrarian development because it is the dominant force that underlies many of the world's food problems, and because it is within this context that United States' policies have their broadest

The backdrop against which these historical forces must be judged is one of chronic and substantial malnutrition for many, even in the face of improving food status for the majority of the world's population and increasing evidence of improved agricultural productivity in many Third World nations. While the percentage of the population below critical nutritional levels probably has dropped somewhat during the last ten years, it remains as high as 25 percent in many Third World nations, and the absolute number of malnourished and hungry is definitely increasing (UN, 1974). Even in the U.S., the issue of hunger has resurfaced, with national attention focused on inadequate nutrition, especially of children in poor families. Not only is the emerging international food system unable to provide basic nutrition for a large segment of the world's population, but also it is marked by short-run instability in food availability and prices which contribute to a broad array of economic problems for all nations alike. And finally, while the historical record indicates that modern agricultural technologies have made possible the productivity that is a precondition for adequate world food supplies, there are increasing questions as to whether rates of productivity growth and even current levels of productivity can be sustained in the face of resource and environmental constraints.

In this chapter, we are interested primarily in explaining the social and economic consequences that arise in the transformation from pre-capitalist to capitalist forms of agriculture throughout the world. We analyze this process in terms of three fundamental processes: (a) the commodification of agriculture, (b) the integration of farming into and its submission to the agribusiness chain, and (c) the internationalization of capital and its consequences for the place of agriculture in the emerging international division of labor.

We shall review the key aspects of each of these three processes and derive from them the patterns that the development of capitalism in agriculture is currently generating. From this analysis, we will identify a number of key contradictions that characterize the current status of world agriculture, and suggest how they are responsible for the persistence of malnutrition and poverty, even in the face of improved agricultural productivity. In the concluding section, we will explore some of the implications our analysis for the issues raised in this book.

---

impacts. We do not contend, however, that socialist development has resolved all of the problems plaguing the capitalist approach to transforming agrarian societies into modern industrial and agricultural ones. A full analysis of socialist development raises different questions that cannot be addressed within the framework of this chapter.

## I.   The Commodification of Agriculture

A condition for the capitalist development of agriculture is the commodification of the product and of the means of production. Thus, agricultural products, land and other natural resources, labor, capital, and technology all become commodities—which means that they can be sold and bought in markets where they acquire a price.

### *Formation of the Product Market*

The commodification of agriculture is marked by the shift away from production for home use toward production for the market and for the sake of profit making. This shift occurs in response to the development of an effective demand for agricultural products which itself is associated with the rise of the urban economy and the opening of long-distance trade. The orientation toward production for a market is a necessary condition for profits to be realized and, hence, for investment to occur and for growth and social differentiation.

The way in which the market develops, in terms of location and type of products demanded, is important in conditioning the social structure of agriculture. Thus, opening of long-distance trade tends to bias production toward agroexports (which often are not staple foods) and to submit the peasants to the intermediation of landlords and merchants. This was the case in eastern Europe in the 18th and 19th centuries (Kay, 1974) as well as in the colonial plantation economies of Latin America and Africa. The outcome has generally been "socially disarticulated" growth based on cheap labor and cheap food, where farmers' incomes and wages are not an important source of effective demand to the other sectors of the economy (de Janvry, 1981).

By contrast, the development of local markets allows direct access for peasants to effective demand, tends to orient agriculture toward the production of staple foods, and allows peasants to differentiate by incorporating the activities of merchant capital as an additional source of accumulation. This pattern characterized western Europe in the 17th and 18th centuries as well as the United States; it tends to result in "socially articulated" growth whereby the production of wage-goods is the key economic activity. The rise in wages and farmers' incomes in relation to productivity growth is necessary to expand the size of the domestic market, which, in turn, is the basis of further industrial development. Because socially articulated growth demands some degree of "parity" between farm and non-farm income, it is not surprising to find agricultural price policies in First World nations aimed at protecting farm incomes.

We advance the hypothesis that these contrasting patterns of overvalued agricultural commodities in First World nations and undervalued commodities in Third World nations—which have been widely decried by Schultz (1978); Lutz and Scandizzo (1980); and others—is, to a significant extent, the outcome of the contrasting historical forces that defined the geographical extent and social location of the ultimate markets for agricultural products. These patterns have, in turn, resulted in articulated growth in the former and extractivist, disarticulated growth in the latter. A present-day manifestation of these same processes is increasing staple food surpluses in many First World nations and growing deficits in most Third World nations.

### Privatization of the Land

An important early undertaking of the capitalist state is the privatization of the land. This requires the development of a legal system of property rights, the registration of land titles, and the subsequent enforcement of these rights. For instance, in Latin America, starting in the 1850s, but mainly between 1900 and 1940, semifeudal rights over land were transformed into modern property rights. In the United States, various land distribution policies, the most important of which were the Land Grant Act of 1850, which granted 150 million acres to subsidize railroad development, and the Homestead Act of 1862, helped to establish a pattern of owner-occupied, family farms as the principal form of land tenure throughout much of the Midwest and West. Plantation agriculture, based on the institution of slavery, dominated the South. In Africa, privatization of the land held in communal forms occurred rapidly after decolonization and is still an ongoing phenomenon in many countries.

The process of privatization of land is commonly fraught with serious social conflicts, abuses of the law, and violence (Brabdy, 1975; Rey, 1976). Examples are the expropriation of Indian communal lands under the Porfirrato in Mexico; the dispossession of the *colonos* in the Brazilian Amazon; the *violencia* period in Columbia that led to a massive exodus of squatters, sharecroppers, and tenants; civil wars that broke out between settlers and railroads in the western U.S., such as occurred in 1871 at Mussel Slough in California (McWilliams, 1971); and the systematic violation of the 160-acre limitation for federal Reclamation projects in the western United States in the 20th century.

Once private property over the land has been established, the structural conditions are set for a process of concentration-expropriation to occur through the continued operation of market forces and further state interventions. Land ownership tends to become concentrated, eventually well beyond the labor capacity of the farm household, while others are dispossessed of access to the land and forced to turn to wage work as a means of subsistence or to migrate to the cities or abroad.

Privatization of the land is thus the essence of the formation of capitalist social relations in agriculture. The subsequent process of social differentiation is accelerated by favorable income opportunities in the rest of the economy and by unfavorable natural or economic conditions in agriculture as well as by periods of intense technological change. It is also conditioned by continued state intervention. Thus, the massive elimination of small family farms in the United States has been accelerated by a set of farm income policies introduced in the name of protecting the family farm but which, in fact, have benefited larger farms at the expense of smaller units (Vogeler, 1981). Elsewhere, land reform programs in Mexico, Peru, Egypt, India, and the Philippines have eliminated large-scale estates and remnants of feudal social relations in agriculture.

## Formation of the Labor Market

The commodification of labor is another precondition for the emergence of capitalist social relations in agriculture and the subsequent process of social differentiation. There are several key steps—in which the state is typically directly involved. One is the emergence of surplus labor which within traditional systems cancels the rationality of holding labor bonded in agriculture. The state can engineer an emergence of surplus labor (a) by its land policy—essentially by closing the frontier and canceling free access to land, such as occurred during the Enclosure Movements beginning in the 15th century in England; (b) by policies influencing labor mobility and immigration, as, for example, in the management of apartheid in South Africa (Wolpe, 1972), or by encouraging immigration of foreign workers, such as with Chinese, Japanese, Filipino, and Mexican workers in California; and (c) by technological policies, especially the promotion of labor-saving mechanization. Surplus labor is also created by the very process of the development of capitalism in agriculture, whereby there is usually a wholesale expropriation of sharecroppers and tenants. Another step for the formation of a labor market involves the state taking responsibility for, and assuming political control over the labor force, thereby replacing landlords' traditional extra-economic rights over labor (Garrett, 1978).

The emergence of surplus labor in agriculture in the Third World nations since World War II has been under conditions where the rest of the economy lacks absorptive capacity and where the outlet of large-scale international migration is no longer available. This surplus labor leads to overcrowding in agriculture, a deepening dualism between subsistence and capitalist farm sectors, an increase in the number of semi-proletarian households (where family members are both agriculturalists and wage workers), seasonal migration, and extensive rural poverty. The result is a severe conflict between agricultural and rural development, i.e., between increased productivity and rural welfare—a conflict that did not exist (at least not in the same relative magnitude) in the history of most First World nations.

Partial mechanization and increased specialization of production on farms leads to the bunching of labor demands in specific time periods, and hence to an increase in the seasonality of labor needs. Thus, the development of capitalist social relations in agriculture fosters an increasingly mobile labor force, often with labor contractors mediating between workers and employers. Family labor then becomes increasingly confined to managerial and maintenance tasks (da Silva, 1981). In First World nations, where agriculture must compete with the industrial economy for wage workers, pressures created by specialization and partial mechanization lead to still greater incentives for additional mechanization—something which permits the development of a smaller, but more stable and productive labor force that justifies higher (and more competitive) wages.

*Formation of the Markets for Financial Capital and Technology*

The formation of a capital market is important in stimulating investment, but typically results in accelerating social differentiation in agriculture owing to unequal access to credit arising out of differential social positions in the political economy. This is particularly the case in Third World nations where capital is scarce and where it is consequently allocated less by market rules than by social forces. Numerous studies have shown that access to institutional credit may well be an important source of agricultural growth but that such access produces highly regressive agricultural income distributions (Berry and Cline, 1979).

With the possibilities of expanding areas under cultivation increasingly limited by the exhaustion of virgin land, technological change has become an essential source of agricultural growth. However, the unleashing of a technological treadmill (Owen, 1966; Cochrane, 1979) has profound consequences on the structure of world agriculture since it (a) selectively favors specific commodities, areas, and types of farms; (b) transforms the labor process and the farm structure; (c) affects the pace and direction of social differentiation; and (d) redefines international comparative advantages. Both public and private sectors have had important roles in the generation and diffusion of the technologies which fuel the treadmill. Public-sector innovations tend to be biased not only toward saving the "scarce" factors of production (Hayami and Ruttan, 1971), but also to satisfy the demands of the most powerful interest groups in society (de Janvry, 1977). Even technologies that are neutral to scale at the farm level, for example the seed-chemical advances of the Green Revolution, accelerate social differentiation if there is unequal access to the institutions that determine the adoption and productivity of technological advances (e.g., extension, credit, and infrastructure).

Increasingly, technology has become a commodity produced for profit by the private sector. Traditionally, the private sector has underwritten the production of mechanical innovations (which can be easily patented and transferred internationally), but only recently has this sector taken an interest in biological innovations (other than hybridization). This new interest results both from recent legislative developments permitting the patenting of genetic innovations and from the possibility of reducing the time period for development through new techniques of manipulating DNA in the laboratory (Mooney, 1979). Not only does the sale of technology become a source of royalties, but it also becomes an instrument of control over farming and a source of profits for the agribusiness sectors. Private research is, however, not a substitute for public research as it is oriented toward relatively short-run solutions for commodities enjoying expanding effective demand. The result is that in the Third World, private research is strongly biased toward technologies favoring large-scale farming of commodities for export or for industrial uses.

## II. Integration of Farming Into and Submission to the Agribusiness Chain

Historically, the rise of industry was made possible by the rise of labor productivity in agriculture, something which both released labor for urban employment and provided a surplus for investment in industry (Owen, 1966). Thus, Bairoch (1973) showed that the industrial revolutions of all western countries as well as Japan followed agricultural revolutions with a lag of some 50 years. However, another 50 years or so later, it was industry that revolutionized agriculture anew by supplying modern industrial inputs such as machinery, fertilizers, and insecticides. The second agricultural revolution has integrated farming into the agribusiness chain. Forward and backward linkages with industry developed as the importance of production for home consumption declined, the technification of production led to increasing use of purchased inputs, and specialization and deepening in the division of labor led to externalization from the farm of many activities previously performed on the farm. By 1979, for example, of the total value of domestically produced and consumed food in the United States, 26 percent went to input supply firms, taxes, interest, and hired labor costs, 68 percent to processing, distribution and marketing of food, leaving only 4 percent for net farm income (Wessel, 1983).

This integration of farming into the agribusiness chain also made it easier for agribusinesses to gain control over farming. This control has been used to force dramatic technological changes and agricultural growth and has provided a mechanism which has introduced specific biases into the production process and has transformed the class structure in agriculture.

Agribusiness dominance over farming occurs, in particular, through vertical integration and contract farming, which allows agribusiness firms to monitor closely the production process through technological specifications, production standards, timing of delivery, etc. In the United States, as of 1970, approximately 80 percent of seed crops, 85 percent of processed vegetables, and 90 percent of broilers were produced under contractual arrangements (Harshbarger and Stahl, 1974). Control need not be exercised directly through contracts; for example, the extensive development of hybrid seeds requires farmers to purchase seeds from agribusiness firms rather than retaining a portion of their crop for seed purposes. Similarly, technological innovations frequently come in "packages" of inputs. Once a farmer decides to adopt mechanical harvesting in crops like cotton and tomatoes, he then also must adopt certain cultural practices that require the use of various chemicals for defoliation or for stimulating uniform crop maturation.

The profitable market opportunities which agribusiness offers commercial farms in the Third World have led to dramatic expansion of specific crops. Thus, the demands of the animal industry, especially the broiler sector, have led to a massive expansion in feed grain production in the Bajio, Mexico, and the Valle del Cauca, Colombia (Kalmanowitz, 1981; Rama and Rello, 1981). The demand for agroexports has greatly stimulated the production of fruits and vegetables under contract in Mexico, that of soybeans in Brazil (Burbach and Flinn, 1980), tropical fruits for export in Thailand, etc.

The influence of agribusiness over farming has gone beyond the choice of products, the level of yields, and the quality and uniformity of products. It has also profoundly transformed the labor process in agriculture. In some cases, agribusiness has been directly involved in the production of its own raw materials, such as Hershey's cocoa plantations and del Monte's fruit and vegetable ranches. But, in general, production and the risks associated with it are left to independent producers while agribusiness defines the labor process from above. A salient example is that of the broiler industry in the United States which was integrated by the feed firms that gained monopolistic control over the new technology; as a result, these firms were able to impose the technology on individual producers, and at the same time, reduce them to the status of employees (Roy, 1971). The broiler industry has been reorganized along similar lines in Mexico (Rama and Rello, 1981), Colombia (Medrano, 1981), and Peru

(Vigil *et al.*, 1981). Large U.S. meat packing firms are now in the process of establishing similar kinds of control over domestic feed lot operators.

With the rising role of the private sector in agricultural research, agribusiness has become a dynamic source of new technologies which have implications for the labor process. Pushed by the profit motive, the technological thrust of private research necessarily tends to focus on the large farmers and on those commodities that are experiencing rapid increases in demand. The case of machinery is particularly revealing. Mechanization of tomato harvesting in California followed immediately upon the termination of the *Bracero* program, under which Mexican workers had been allowed to work on a temporary basis in agriculture throughout the western United States. Without this source of cheap labor, and spurred by premium prices processors paid to growers who mechanized their harvest, the entire processed tomato crop was mechanized within a four year period. Under the new regime, a grower needed no less than 100 acres to utilize efficiently the new harvest technology. However, 65 percent of the growers producing processing tomatoes had less than 100 acres in production just prior to the transformation of the harvest. The majority of these smaller producers were thus forced to give up the crop. New technological advances redefined the minimum farm size to 150 acres by 1970 and to 200 acres by 1973, further accelerating the process of farm consolidation (de Janvry, LeVeen, Runsten, 1980). Labor demands were reduced, bunched in time (because of the one-shot method of mechanical harvesting), and deskilled as male pickers were replaced by lower paid, and less easily organized women, who sorted tomatoes on the machines. Even these sorters have started to be eliminated by electric-eye sorters (Friedland and Barton, 1975).

### III. Internationalization of Capital and the Place of Agriculture in the International Division of Labor

Capital is an expansionist force which is driven into new geographical areas under the double rationale of the quest for new sources of profits and for new markets. Which of these related purposes propels the internationalization of capital at a particular point in time is very much determined by the particular crises of the moment in the advanced economies; i.e., at one time profitability crises and the need to counteract falling rates of profit or, at another time, underconsumption crises and the need to capture new sources of effective demand. In agriculture, the internationalization of capital has correspondingly taken the form of (a) First World investments in plantations or agribusiness contracts with Third World producers; (b) investments by First World food processors and distributors in retail marketing in Third World nations in an effort to expand world consumption of processed foods, thereby attempting to overcome the inherent limits to further expansion in the demand for food characteristic of First World nations; and (c) the opening of new markets for agriculture exports, in particular for U.S. cereals, through the dramatic shift from food aid in the 1960s—which created patterns of food dependency—to trade for hard currency in the 1970s.

With the massive development of trade in agricultural commodities, nations and individuals across the world have acquired the possibility—whenever purchasing power exists—of overcoming local production short-falls and their consequent reductions in consumption and famines. Thus, today, malnutrition and hunger are mainly income and not production problems. Farming systems worldwide have become integrated in a division of labor based on both natural and acquired comparative advantages, the latter due to differential advances in productivity resulting from infrastructure investments and technological change as well as to trade and monetary policies. The result is that the logic of particular farming systems can no longer be understood in isolation from world market forces and international political forces. In this new international division of labor, the advanced economies, (e.g., United States, Canada, France, and Australia) tend to specialize in the production of staple food and feed grains, while the Third World nations export primary meat, commodities for animal feed, and speciality crops.

## Consequences for Third World Food Systems

For the Third World, the most dramatic impact arising from the insertion of agriculture in the international division of labor has been the end of food self-sufficiency (Barkin and Suarez, 1982). The combination of the commodification of agriculture, the insertion of farming into the agribusiness chain (which facilitates access to markets), and the internationalization of capital is diverting agricultural production away from basic needs and toward what is profitable on either the domestic or international markets. A widening income gap between the First and Third World nations, as well as increasingly regressive patterns in the distribution of income within most Third World nations, means that the opportunities for profits in farming are increasingly found in catering to the effective demand of the advanced nations and of the rich in the poor countries.

In Mexico, for example, this has meant the abandonment of large tracts of rain-fed land traditionally devoted to production of staple foods, the rapid increase in food dependency on corn and wheat, and expansion of the area dedicated to export products (fruits, vegetables, and meat) and to the production of luxury foods and agroindustrial inputs (sorghum for chicken feed). Imposition of the law of comparative advantage, while rational in terms of a short-term global economic calculus, has had the high social cost of bankrupting the peasant economy and forcing large numbers in the rural population to migrate prematurely toward the cities and the United States.

Aggravating the problems of the already strained food systems of Third World nations is the increasing role played by agribusiness processors in their domestic food systems. Because the demand for food grows mainly with the rate of population growth in First World nations, processors are faced with natural limits on their ability to expand markets. A successful past strategy for offsetting this constraint has been to encourage consumers to substitute processed for nonprocessed foods. This allows food manufacturers to capture a larger portion of the relatively fixed food dollar and thus to expand more rapidly than overall food consumption in the First World. Nonetheless, food manufacturers have also sought out the higher income consumers of Third World nations to further expand their markets.

Most of the processed food products sold in Third World nations are produced locally (not exported from First World nations) by subsidiaries of the multinational firms. For example, in 1975 sales of subsidiaries of U.S. food manufacturing firms in Third World nations amounted to $4 billion, almost $3.5 billion of which was in Latin America (U.S. Dept. of Commerce, 1976:31).

The major food products sold by these U.S. corporations in Latin America are not staple foods, but highly processed and advertised products, including breakfast cereals, instant coffee, canned soups, baby foods, processed cheeses, frozen and canned vegetables, mayonnaise and salad dressing, chewing gum, and most importantly, soft drinks (Horst, 1974). Such investments do nothing to reduce malnutrition; indeed, to the extent that food processors depend on locally-produced raw commodities, they introduce a new element of competition for local agricultural resources and further exaggerate the tendencies noted above. The nutritional problems associated with the introduction of infant formulae are well documented and are related to this expansionist tendency of capital, but nutritional problems are not confined to infant formulas. Equally adverse impacts on nutrition result from the promotion of products such as soft drinks. There is even some evidence that the poor will sell the more nutritious products they produce locally, such as oranges, in order to earn enough money to buy a soft drink (Ledogar, 1976).

*Implications for First World Economies*

The internationalization of capital has also profoundly changed the orientation of First World agriculture; the world grain trade has grown dramatically over the past decade, in part because of the inability of many Third World nations to maintain food self-sufficiency, and also because of changing diets in many wealthier nations toward greater consumption of meat. This trend has been observed in both the USSR and the Eastern European nations as well as in Japan and Middle Eastern nations. The growth of the grain trade has been particularly important for the United States—which has become the world's foremost grain trader over the past decade.

The implications for the United States of the expanded grain trade are widespread and go far beyond the welfare of its farmers. Since 1972, when U.S. commercial farm exports began their rapid rise, the net surplus on the agricultural trade account has been about $200 billion while the deficit on the nonagricultural trade account has been about $500 billion. Thus, agricultural exports have become essential to moderate increasingly adverse balance of payments and have been relied upon to offset the effects of failing industrial exports and to counteract stagnant industrial productivity, runaway industries, high wage costs, overvaluation of the dollar and the high costs of oil imports. This role is somewhat diminished today, in part because the growth in the value of agricultural exports has been slowed dramatically by the strong dollar, and in part because of a dramatic increase in nonagricultural imports (and thus, trade account deficits) for the same reason.

U.S. farm exports have also come to be seen as a possible weapon to be used in international diplomacy on issues having nothing to do with food. Finally, these exports are looked upon as a way of simultaneously solving the chronic oversupply crisis in agriculture (one third of all crop production is now exported), the crisis in farm incomes (depressed by overproduction in the face of inelastic demand and escalating input costs), and the high public costs of conventional agricultural policies aimed at supporting farm incomes.

The strategy of encouraging commercial exports evolved in the late 1960s in reaction to two decades of supply management and price support policies that were perceived to be inefficient and inequitable. The restructured and more successful supply management programs of the late 1960s that virtually eliminated public grain stocks, the devaluation of the dollar beginning in 1971, detente, and modest crop shortfalls in the early 1970s all contributed to dramatic increases in commercial exports for all of the major grain exporting nations, particularly the United States. The initial success of the strategy led to much higher farm incomes, the elimination of public price support subsidies, and the beneficial trade surpluses mentioned above.

The increasing dependence of the U.S. on agricultural exports, however, has some serious adverse consequences, for both farmers and the U.S.

economy more generally, that are not widely discussed or openly debated, especially by those who design agricultural policy. The initial predictions were that the internationalization of U.S. agriculture would lead to a steady increase in the consumption of U.S. commodities, much higher farm incomes, and perhaps even insufficient capacity to meet the antici- pated demand (Schuh, 1976). In reality, grain exports have proven very unstable over the past decade, because (a) protectionist trade policies abroad have served to intensify the effects of changes in world production and trade for the U.S.; (b) erratic U.S. monetary and fiscal policies have caused sudden changes in exchange rates and, hence, in the prices of grain to foreign buyers; (c) attempts by the U.S. to use food as an instru- ment of foreign policy (such as the embargo imposed against the USSR when it invaded Afghanistan) have contributed to short-term swings in demand for U.S. exports. Instability is further encouraged on the supply side because increased agricultural exports have led U.S. farmers to expand into more marginal lands with their greater vulnerability to varia- tions in the weather (compounding this is the possibility that weather pat- terns have become more unstable and extreme).

This instability has given rise to a series of booms (1972–74; 1979–80) and busts (1975–77; 1981–82) in farm incomes, the net effect of which is that farmers are probably worse off today than they were under the non- export oriented policies of the 1950s and 60s (Wessel, 1983). Not only must farmers continue to cope with the rigors of a competitive race to keep up with the technologically driven treadmill, but also they must now deal with the new sources of uncertainty and risk associated with sudden changes in prices and incomes. These latter risks affected farmers of all sizes and they compounded the problems posed by the treadmill. The overall result has been that farm bankruptcy rates have reached levels unknown since the Depression Era.

One important consequence of the increased economic difficulties experienced in agriculture was the re-imposition in 1977 of traditional price/income, supply management, and support policies, the costs of which soon rose to new levels. The combined costs of federal agricultural subsidy programs in 1983, including the ill-conceived Payments in Kind Program which idled more than 80 million acres, amounted to more than $54 billion (*Wall Street Journal,* 1983), more than double actual net farm income. These figures suggest first that government farm income support programs are very inefficient in their provision of benefits, and second, that the internationalization of U.S. agriculture has not achieved one of its major objectives—which was to eliminate the need for government inter- vention and to place commercial agriculture on a firm "market-oriented" basis. During the pre-export period of the 1960s, total government subsi- dies to agriculture never exceeded $7 billion in any year while the 1983

PIK program alone cost in excess of $20 billion; thus, even after allowing for inflation, it is apparent that the instability generated by the internationalization of agriculture has increased, not decreased the need for government intervention.

The costs of the export strategy affect the entire economy; as a consequence of the boom periods, consumer food prices have risen dramatically. For example, food prices rose almost 30 percent between 1972 and 1974; substantial increases again occurred in 1979 and 1980, largely because of increases in commodity prices and the effects of higher grain prices on the cattle and hog cycles. Higher food prices were important contributors to the high general inflation rates observed during these same time periods (Kaldor, 1965; Hopkins, 1982). The effort over the past decade to control double digit inflation led to restrictive monetary and fiscal policies that produced two of the deepest recessions experienced since the 1930s. At least some of the very high costs associated with the lost productivity and unemployment attributable to these episodes can be assigned to the food price instability and thus to the export strategy.

Notwithstanding the accumulation of evidence against the desirability of maintaining its export strategy, the U.S. continues to pursue both a conventional policy of supporting farm incomes through direct subsidy and land retirement (mainly because of pressure from the traditional farm interests) *and* a policy of expanding agricultural exports (mainly because of pressure from large grain corporations that have come to enjoy a powerful role in shaping agricultural policy over the past decade). These latter efforts take the form of negotiations to reduce world trade barriers for agricultural products and credit subsidies for foreign buyers. Trade negotiations have yielded very little additional trade liberalization, mainly because the protectionist policies of other First World nations have powerful political support. The Common Market nations are experiencing most of the same problems of overproduction as the U.S., and are therefore also attempting to solve their internal problems by finding foreign outlets for their surpluses.

A further obstacle to U.S. success in developing additional foreign markets is the overvaluation of the dollar, a condition that reflects large government deficits and related high real rates of interest. At least part of the reason for the deficits is the failure of the U.S. economy to grow rapidly over the past decade. This stagnation of the economy, is, in part, related to high rates of inflation and the subsequent anti-growth policies used to reduce it. The inflation of the 1970s was largely a product of external "shocks" created by increased energy prices and periodic food shortages. Thus, we come full circle. Today's problems in agriculture are largely the consequence of the rapid internationalization of U.S. agriculture.

At the same time that the world grain economy has moved from a condition of scarcity and high prices to one of surplus and low prices, there is evidence that the additional output has been purchased at a high cost, not only in terms of lower farm welfare, but also in terms of resource depletion, as farmers have sought to get the most of their resources in order to avoid bankruptcy. Soil erosion (Mayer, 1982) and water depletion (Wessel, 1983) are but two of the indications that current levels of productivity will not be sustained in the future. There is also evidence of a slowing in the overall rate of land productivity, perhaps because of inherent limits in the biological/chemical technologies that underly such productivity.

The instability of the past decade and the costly government efforts to cope with its consequences, both within and outside of the agricultural economy, are guaranteed to be a part of the future as long as the U.S. continues its policy of giving exports the highest priority. This instability may become even stronger if the current lull in energy price rises is broken, if exchange-rate fluctuations continue (which, given the complex connection between deficits, interest rates, and the value of the dollar, seems certain), and if productivity in agriculture does not keep pace with labor and land prices. In the event that the current period of surpluses and low prices again gives way to shortages and high commodity prices, world inflation levels will again rise sharply and rising food prices will again threaten the welfare of the poor, no matter whether they reside in the First or Third World.

### IV. Patterns of Development in Capitalist Agriculture: Social Class Formation and Rural Welfare

In the context of the commodification-integration-internationalization of agriculture outlined above, the development of capitalism progresses along a number of alternative roads, each of which results in a particular social class structure. Some of these roads have been analyzed in the classics of political economy, such as Lenin (1964) and Kautsky (1976), while others are specific to the modern forms of capitalist development.

One classical pattern of social differentiation involves small-scale farms. Along this "American" road family farms are transformed into commercial farms managed by families, something which necessitates the use of increased amounts of hired labor. This road can originate in homesteading programs, as in the United States; in colonization schemes, as in northern Argentina and in the Venezuelan Amazon; or in redistributive land reforms, as in Taiwan and South Korea.

In the United States the total number of farms declined from a peak of 6.8 million during the 1930s to less than 2.4 million at the present time, while the percentage of farmland held in farms exceeding 1,000 acres increased from 28 percent to about 60 percent. Absentee landownership is also increasing in the U.S. where today more than half of all cropland is rented. The share of hired labor in the total labor force has increased more slowly—from about 24 percent in 1940 to about 33 percent today; the rest is "family" labor. However, 75 percent of the largest farms (7 percent of all farms) hire labor. Since these farms also produce more than 56 percent of all output, it is clear that capitalist social relations increasingly dominate agricultural production in the United States.

Another classical pattern is the *Junker* road where feudal estates modernize into farms with capitalist social relations without significant redefinition of the boundaries of the estates. The former feudal lords become the capitalist entrepreneurs, and the bonded laborers and sharecroppers are expelled or retained as wage workers. Transition out of feudalism is often induced by the prohibition of serfdom or the threat of land reforms. Such was the underlying purpose of many of the Latin American land reforms in the 1960s as in Ecuador, Colombia, and Venezuela. New Deal cotton programs have been credited with forcing the transition from plantation to capitalist agriculture in the U.S. South (James, 1981).

The transition to capitalist agriculture has been speeded up by the growing insertion of agriculture into the agribusiness chain, into the international division of labor, and with the movements of capital across sectors and countries. Today, the welfare of agrarian classes can no longer be understood in isolation from domestic and foreign social groups external to agriculture. Under either corporate or direct ownership, much land has been acquired by urban and foreign capitalists, particularly in Latin America. Under these forms of tenure, land is not held, like in semifeudal times, by absentee landlords for the sake of social status or the sheltering of wealth in land values. Here the purpose of absentee capital is purely profit seeking. It manifests itself in a class of domestic supervisors of the production process, under the domination of absentee capital. Decisions regarding borrowing, technological choices, cropping patterns, and marketing are made externally to the farm. Alternatively, urban-industrial capital contracts production with independent producers (usually on medium and large farms) without assuming ownership of the land. In this case, too, managerial decisions are largely made outside of agriculture and specified in the contracts.

The common features of all these roads are the dispossession of peasants, the dominance of a capitalist class with concentrated ownership of land, the rise of landlessness and the formation of a class of rural wage workers, and the expulsion of populations from agriculture. When there exists a strong labor absorption capacity in the rest of the economic system (as was the case in the United States) or where the opportunity for international migrations exist, this transformation occurs without long-term welfare losses for most of the rural migrants. There is, of course, a large short-term social cost associated with dislocation and the disruption of the traditional rural economy. And for many unable to adjust to the new conditions, the quality of residual rural life is deeply transformed, and minority sectors like the U.S. black sharecropping population are net losers.

As great as these transformation costs are in a nation that can absorb most of the dispossessed, they are small in comparison to the problems created when there is no place for the landless to go, as is true of most Third World nations. Agricultural labor in such nations finds itself cornered between the expansion of larger-scale, more mechanized farming and the lack of labor absorption capacity in the domestic and international economy, and consequently many workers remain attached to small plots of land in an association with capitalist farms—something which is both functional in delivering cheap labor and highly contradictory in terms of insuring the reproduction of peasant farms. The result is that the peasantry may well increase in numbers, but its social function is increasingly transformed from that of providing cheap food for the domestic market to that of serving as a cheap labor reserve.

It is this "cornered peasantry" that experiences the worst forms of poverty. While there are serious empirical difficulties with the measurement of poverty, the World Bank (IBRD, 1975) estimated that in 1969 about 55 percent of the world's rural population fell below a poverty line of $75 per capita and 86 percent of the world's poor were rural inhabitants. International Labor Organization data for seven Asian countries showed a clear increase in the population of the rural population falling below the poverty line between 1960 and 1970 as well as increases in absolute poverty in several cases (ILO, 1977). Similar trends appear to hold for Africa and Latin America (Klein, 1978; Ghai, Lee, and Radwan, 1979). Such poverty is strongly related to the concentration of land ownership or control, increasing landlessness, unfavorable terms of trade for agriculture, and falling or stagnant real rural wages in several countries such as the Philippines and many Indian states. In many cases, particularly Latin America and India, this dramatic rise in rural poverty has occurred in the context of strong agricultural growth, contradicting the theoretical expectation of beneficial trickle-down effects from economic growth.

### Conclusions

The commodification-integration-internationalization of agriculture has taken divergent forms throughout the First and Third World nations; yet in all areas it has led to the emergence of new social classes, and it has redefined the role of agriculture in economic development. In order to define new policies which are effective in promoting economic development, it is important to understand these new social relations for what they are and to define political programs that properly account for them.

In the United States, for example, much of the debate over agrarian policy misses the importance of the newly emerging social relations, on the one hand, and the important forces shaping U.S. agriculture that arise from the internationalization of the food economy, on the other. With regard to the former, there is wide agreement on the fact that landownership is increasingly concentrated among a minority of large farms and on the related roles that agricultural policy and technology have had in accelerating this concentration. Yet, at the level of political debate this recognition has led to two contrasting positions, neither of which takes into account the essential structural changes that we have described above.

One of these positions is that in spite of the trends in landownership, the family farm (now highly capitalized) is still the most important component of U.S. agriculture, and that continuing its growth and increasing its capitalization poses no threat to the future of this fundamental agrarian institution. Under this interpretation, agricultural policy should remain targeted, as it has since the 1930s, to the income and productivity needs of the family farmer (Gardner and Pope, 1978; Cochrane, 1979).

Contrasting with this position is one that seeks to show that the family farm is undergoing rapid collapse; it denounces as "myth" the family farm ideology that is generally used to rationalize the continuation of existing income and price support programs. It argues that it is these very programs which help to destroy the family farm (Rodefeld et al., 1978; Vogeler, 1981). Instead of continuing the old policies, advocates of this position call for an active defense of the family farm and rural communities through what Vogeler calls "a new populism in our lifetime." This neopopulist position has characterized most of the recent progressive writings in U.S. agricultural economics and rural sociology.

To us, both of these positions contain serious errors in their neglect of the new social relations which are emerging within agriculture and between agriculture and the agribusiness food chain. On the one hand, we see no support for the contention that the family farm will remain unchanged by the forces of technology and the increasing submission of farmers to powerful agribusiness firms. On the other hand, however, we agree with Buttel's skepticism (1981) that a comprehensive policy package can be implemented for a renaissance of the family farm. Such a set of reforms is unrealistic because it ignores the existence of economies of scale in agriculture (which arise principally in institutional forces external to the farm) and the importance of the integration of farming into a larger system of control, and because it contradicts the basic political reality that those within agriculture with political influence who "speak" for the "family farm" are in fact either large-scale family producers or larger-than-family producers; neither of these groups share the vision of those who would preserve the small family farmer.

We also find that most of those interested in the agrarian structure of the U.S. have failed to recognize the other important political reality that has fundamentally changed the politics of agriculture over the past decade, and that is the insertion into the policy-making process of a new set of actors and interests having no direct interest in farming. The most important of these interests, according to Hathaway (1981), are (a) the "cooperator" groups organized to facilitate foreign market development, and (b) the agribusiness-exporter firms which have benefited most from the internationalization of the food economy. The cooperator groups are the private representatives organized by the USDA and its Foreign Agricultural Service to carry out the goals of U.S. agricultural market development overseas. These groups are similar in form to the older Agricultural Stabilization Commodity Service committees that implemented agricultural policies at the local level. The agribusiness-exporter groups included, in addition to the well-publicized grain merchants, specialty-crop cooperatives and cotton and rice exporters, which Hathaway describes as exercising immense power on issues relevant to their export business. As these groups gain power and influence over the development of future agricultural policy, the resulting policies will reflect all the more the needs of agribusiness rather than those of the farmer. At present, farmers fully support policies to facilitate the further development of foreign markets and exports, and thus possible conflicts between farmers and exporters have not yet materialized.

Perhaps the most important impending contradiction for the U.S. arising out of the internationalization of the food economy is how the needs of commodity exporters can be harmonized with the overall need for economic stability and growth. While the conflict between increased food exports and domestic economy price stability is not yet a matter of debate (mainly because the overall interest for economic stability has no strong political representative, while the interests for exports do), as we have indicated above, the costs to the U.S of internationalizing its food system may be much greater than commonly recognized. We expect that future debates over food policy will not be in terms of whether to preserve the family farm but, rather, how to reconcile the conflicting interests of consumers, taxpayers, exporters, and farmers. A related issue that will also arise will be how to reconcile the needs of the present generation relative to future generations, for the internationalization of agriculture also poses significant potential threats to the long-term sustainability of the resource base.

In the past, policies that increased the capitalization of farms were perceived to be in the interests of all—they were, in fact, the basis of "articulated" growth. Today, the internationalization of agriculture threatens to introduce a new pattern of "disarticulated" development in the U.S.

In the Third World, similarly, the development of new social relations in the context of the processes described above make many of the demands for redistributive land reform and community development programs increasingly anachronistic. This is because there are few countries where this process of social transformation has been barely initiated, where land is used extensively through traditional social relations. In such situations, there is no question that programs of redistributive land reform and rural development are essential for economic development. This has been demonstrated by the experiences of Japan, Taiwan, and South Korea. However, when capitalist social relations in agriculture are well advanced, the more typical case today, political programs for agriculture have to be defined in terms of the conflicting demands of capitalists versus workers and of the insertion of agriculture in the domestic and international divisions of labor. Like neopopulist programs in the United States, extensive redistributive programs in the Third World are both economically fragile and politically audacious. It is more important to question the social control over the labor process and over the surplus generated by agriculture.

## References

Bairoch, Peter. 1973. "Agriculture and the Industrial Revolution, 1700–1914." In *The Fontana Economic History of Europe: The Industrial Revolution,* ed. C. Cipolla, pp. 452–506. London: Fontana Books.

Barkin, David, and B. Suarez. 1982. *El Fin de la Autosuficiencia Alimentaria.* Mexico: Editorial Nueva Imagen.

Berry, R. Albert, and W. Cline. 1979. *Agrarian Structure and Productivity in Developing Countries.* Baltimore: The Johns Hopkins University Press.

Brabdy, Barbara. 1975. "The Destruction of Natural Economy." *Economy and Society* 4:127–161.

Burbach, Roger, and P. Flinn. 1980. *Agribusiness in the Americas.* New York: Monthly Review Press.

Buttel, Frederick H. 1981. *American Agriculture and Rural America: Challenges for Progressive Politics.* Ithaca, N.Y.: Cornell University, Department of Rural Sociology, Bulletin No. 120.

Cochrane, Willard W. 1979. *The Development of American Agriculture.* Minneapolis: University of Minnesota Press.

da Silva, J. Graziano. 1981. *Progresso Technico e Relacoes de Trabalho na Agricultura.* Sao Paulo, Brazil: Editoria Huirtec.

de Janvry, Alain. 1981. *The Agrarian Question and Reformism in Latin America.* Baltimore: The Johns Hopkins University Press.

_____. 1977. "Inducement of Technological and Institutional Innovations: An Interpretative Framework." In *Resource Allocation and Productivity of National and International Agricultural Research,* ed. T. Arndt; D. Dalrymple; and V. Ruttan, pp. 551–563. Minneapolis: University of Minnesota Press.

de Janvry, Alain; P. LeVeen; and D. Runsten. 1980. *Mechanization in California Agriculture: The Case of Canning Tomatoes.* Costa Rica: IICA.

Friedland, William, and A. Barton. 1975. *Destalking the Wily Tomato.* Davis: University of California, Department of Applied Behaviorial Sciences, Research Monograph No. 15.

Gardner, Delworth, and R. Pope. 1978. "How is Scale and Structure Determined in Agriculture?" *American Journal of Agricultural Economics* 60:235–302.

Garrett, Patricia. 1978. "Some Economic and Political Aspects of Subsistence Production: The Landlord's Perspective." Paper presented at the Society for the Study of Social Problems. San Francisco, 1978.

Ghai, Dharam; E. Lee; and S. Radwan. 1979. "Rural Poverty in the Third World: Trends, Causes, and Policy Reorientation." Geneva: International Labor Organization, ILO Working Paper, World Employment Program Research.

Harshbarger, C., and S. Stahl. 1974. "Economic Concentration in Agriculture: Trends and Developments." *Monthly Review.* Kansas City: Federal Reserve Bank, April, 1974.

Hathaway, Dale. 1981. "Government and Agriculture Revisited: A Review of Two Decades of Change." *American Journal of Agricultural Economics* 63:779–787.

Hayami, Yujiro, and Vernon Ruttan. 1971. *Agricultural Development: An International Perspective.* Baltimore: The Johns Hopkins University Press.

Hopkins, Ray. 1982. "Food Policymaking." In *Food Policy and Farm Programs,* ed. Don F. Hadwiger and Ross Talbot, pp. 12–24. New York: The Academy of Political Science.

Horst, Thomas. 1974. *At Home Abroad.* Cambridge, Mass.: Ballinger.

International Bank for Reconstruction and Development (IBRD). 1975. *Rural Development: Sector Policy Paper.* Washington, D.C.: IBRD.

International Labor Organization (ILO). 1977. *Poverty and Landlessness in Rural Asia.* Geneva: ILO.

James, D. 1981. "The State, Rural Class Structure and the Adoption of Innovation in Cotton Agriculture." Paper presented at the annual meeting of the Rural Sociological Society, Guelph, Ontario, August, 1981.

Kaldor, Nicholas. 1976. "Inflation and Recession in the World Economy." *Economic Journal* 86:703–714.

Kalmonovitz, Salomon. "La Inversion Extranjera en la Agroindustria en Colombia." In *El Dessarrollo Agroindustrial y la Economia Latino-Americana,* pp. 107–128. Mexico: CODAI, SARAH.

Kautsky, Karl. 1976. *La Question Agraria.* Bogota: Editorial Latina.

Kay, C. 1974. "Comparative Development of the European Manorial System and the Latin American Hacienda System." *Journal of Peasant Studies* 2:69–98.

Klein, E. 1978. *Employment in Peasant Economies.* Santiago: PREALC.

Ledogar, Robert. 1976. *Hungry for Profits: U.S. Food and Drug Multinations in Latin America.* New York: IDOC.

Lenin, V. I. 1964. "The Development of Capitalism in Russia." In *Collected Works,* Vol. 3. Moscow: Progress Public Press.

Lutz, Ernst, and P. Scandizzo. 1980. "Price Distortions in Developing Countries: A Bias Against Agriculture." *European Review of Agricultural Economics* 7:5–27.

McWilliams, Carey. 1971. *Factories in the Field.* Santa Barbara, Calif.: Peregrine Publishers.

Mayer, Leo. 1982. "Farm Exports and Soil Conservation." In *Food Policy and Farm Programs,* ed. Don F. Hadwinger and Ross Talbot, pp. 99–111. New York: The Academy of Political Science.

Medrano, D. 1981. "El Caso de la Ralston Purina en Colombia." In *El Dessarrollo Agroindustrial y la Economia Latino Americana.* Mexico: CODAI, SARAH.

Mooney, Pat. 1979. *Seeds of the Earth.* Ottawa, Canada: Inter Pares.

Owen, Wyn. 1966. "The Double Developmental Squeeze on Agriculture." *American Economic Review* 56:43–70.

Rama, Ruth, and T. Rello. 1981. *Alimentos Balanceados en Mexico.* Mexico: UNAM.

Rey, Pierre Philippe. 1976. *Les Alliances de Classes.* Paris: Maspero.

Rodefeld, Richard, *et al.* 1978. *Change in Rural America.* St. Louis: C.V. Mosby.

Roy, Ewell P. 1971. *Contract Farming and Economic Integration.* Danville, Illinois: Interstate.

Schuh, Edward. 1976. "The New Macroeconomics of Agriculture." *American Journal of Agricultural Economics* 58:802–811.

Schultz, Theodore W. 1978. *Distortions of Agricultural Incentives.* Bloomington: Indiana University Press.

United Nations (UN). 1974. *Assessment of the World Food Situation, Present and Future.* Rome: Food and Agriculture Organization.

United States Department of Commerce. 1976. *Survey of Current Business.* August, 1976, p. 31.

Vigil, *et al.* 1981. *Alimentos y Transnacionales.* Mexico: DESCO, 1981.

Vogeler, Ingolf. 1981. *The Myth of the Family Farm: Agribusiness Dominance of U.S. Agriculture.* Boulder, Colorado: Westview Press.

*Wall Street Journal.* 1983. "U.S. Farm Programs Come Under Attack as Their Costs Soar." Nov. 10, 1983

Wessel, James. 1983. *Trading the Future: Farm Exports and the Concentration of Economic Power in Our Food System.* San Francisco, Calif.: Institute for Food and Development Policy.

Wolpe, Howard. 1972. "Capitalism and Cheap Labour Power in South Africa: From Segregation to Apartheid." *Economy and Society* 1:923–956.

# Part III

# The National Setting: Past and Present Goals and Priorities

# 6

# Publicly Sponsored Agricultural Research in the United States from an Historical Perspective

## David B. Danbom

Public policies regarding agriculture during the early decades of our existence as a republic were shaped by the dominant view of farmers and rural life held by most statesmen and social thinkers. This viewpoint, usually referred to by scholars as "agrarianism" or "Jeffersonianism" or some hybrid of the two, came close to being a national secular faith at a time when rural life was generally assumed to embody and support a variety of republican virtues. Its tenets linger on even today, though they are seldom specifically enunciated and though they have little practical relevance to the nation or to modern agriculture and rural life.

The American agrarianism of the early republic is justly associated with Thomas Jefferson, one of its most gifted articulators. Certainly, Jefferson's remark that "those who labor in the earth are the chosen people of God, if ever he had a chosen people, whose breasts he has made his peculiar deposit for substantial and genuine virtue," remains the strongest and clearest historical expression of the agrarian faith (Jefferson, 1955:164–165). Agrarianism was rooted in 18th century European popular and philosophical thought, but it was appropriated by Americans and modified by them because it appeared to explain American exceptionalism in an especially flattering way and because it seemed particularly appropriate for the world's first modern republic.

The essence of American agrarianism was the notion that farmers and rural life formed the safest basis for a free society and a republican political system. Agrarians believed that farming was the most legitimate, elevated, and moral occupation because farmers produced basic foods and fibers which everybody needed. Moreover, agrarians believed that, because they were "natural" people, living in and shaped by nature, rural people were more moral and wise than urban people. Agrarians also argued that farming and natural life, along with property ownership and the management of farm enterprises, made agriculturalists independent, conservative, patriotic, and freedom-loving. Because rural people embodied these traits they were crucial for the survival of the republic, which was based on the risky and generally untried idea of popular self-government. Increasing the importance of rural people to the survival of the republic, in agrarians' eyes, was the belief that they formed a stable middle class which could balance and control the vicious and selfish upper and lower classes. "The proportion which the aggregate of the other classes of citizens bears in any state to that of its husbandmen, is the proportion of its unsound to its healthy parts. . . . The mobs of great cities add just so much to the support of pure government, as sores do to the strength of the human body," wrote Jefferson (1955:165).

In retrospect, these agrarian expressions seem excessively romantic and idealistic. To be sure, there was always a mythic quality to agrarianism, but its congruence with reality at a time when most white adult males were relatively self-sufficient farmers was closer than it later became. It is also important to remember that Jefferson and other agrarians had a practical view of the economic importance of agriculture to the nation (see Appleby, 1982). Jefferson, his supposed opposite Alexander Hamilton, and every other political leader of note agreed that agriculture had to be sustained at least in part because it was the key element of the American economy and the engine of national progress. What has become so apparent in this century—that a highly productive agriculture and a vibrant and broadly based rural life might be contradictory goals—did not occur to the Founding Fathers.

Pursuing the practical and idealistic motives which they unconsciously tangled in their minds, the Founding Fathers and their successors did what they could to encourage agriculture. They expanded boundaries of the country, removed Indians from potentially valuable lands, made land progressively easier to acquire, searched for foreign markets, encouraged invention, cleared rivers, improved harbors, built canals, and so forth. In short, they helped farmers to help themselves, to some extent anticipating the actions of those who later created the research system.

What the statesmen of the young republic failed to do was to provide systematic support for agricultural science. The Patent Office collected and distributed seed from other lands, but most early agricultural experimentation was carried out by farmers, often under the auspices of or in response to the stimulation of local agricultural societies (see Rossiter,

1976). The work consisted mainly of tinkering by elite farmers, it was usually in the natural-science tradition of observation, and the "experimentation" carried on fell far short even of the standards of the time. The formal agricultural sciences really did not exist in the United States until about 1850, when the first professional soil chemists made their appearance in this country. These first scientists were trained in Germany, which Justus Liebig made the world leader in soil chemistry, and they sought simply to apply at home the lessons they learned overseas. Even with this promising development in professional agricultural science, the trained people and the scientific knowledge necessary for the foundation of a scientific establishment worthy of the name simply did not exist in ante-bellum America (see Rossiter, 1975).

In the early 1860s the Federal government initiated what has proved to be a very enduring and fruitful program of support for agricultural science. In 1862 Congress created the United States Department of Agriculture and placed the few agriculturally related scientific activities carried on by the Federal government under the control of the Commissioner of Agriculture. In that same year Congress passed the Morrill Land-Grant College Act, providing land which could be sold by the states for the creation of colleges which would teach the scientific principles of agriculture. It was by no means fortuitous that these two measures were passed in 1862. Both reflected what might be termed the "Whig-Republican" view that government could and should take steps to direct and encourage economic development. The secession of the traditionally obstructionist South allowed the legislative expression of this attitude in these and other measures.

A quarter century later another spasm of Congressional activity in support of agricultural science took place. In 1887 Federal funds were provided for state agricultural experiment stations under the Hatch Act. These experiment stations were modeled on similar German institutions, though their expansion of functions made them uniquely American within a few years. Two years later the Secretary of Agriculture was accorded cabinet rank, elevating the USDA. In 1890, more Federal money was appropriated to the land-grant colleges, including funds for the support of the "1890 colleges," black agricultural schools in the segregated South.

This high level of public support for science in agriculture was something of an anomaly in the late 19th century, a period of *laissez-faire* in which government avoided involvement in many economic activities. The fact that it was often justified in agrarian rhetoric as aid to nature's noblemen, the independent, patriotic, and moral farmers, obscured more than it revealed. Why farmers, celebrated for their independence, should enjoy special government attention was an apparent contradiction which was never clarified, though there were precedents for this type of activity in the public agricultural policies of the early republic.

The fact is that farmers were not strongly interested in these measures, nor were agriculturalists uppermost in the minds of policy makers. A. Hunter Dupree (1957:149) identified "journalists, professional consultants, gentlemen farmers, enthusiasts for manual-labor farm schools, and a few chemists," at "the core of the pressure groups agitating for . . . agricultural measures." The concerns of these people were not parochial and farm-centered. They were concerned about the future of the nation and its economic strength in the face of static productivity, declining fertility, and unprecedented challenges to agriculture in the nation's last reserve of virgin lands. They spoke of doing something for the farmer, but their main goal was a productive agriculture which would strengthen the nation.

Another remarkable aspect of this activity was that the scientific and personnel base necessary for the creation of the contemplated establishment simply did not exist. Aside from chemistry and botany there were no coherent disciplines and, consequently, no specifically trained experts in most areas of agricultural science. As a result, the early years of the system witnessed what Margaret Rossiter (1979:212) calls "'force-fed' specialization—in which the outside funding agency and the pressing social and economic problems it sought to solve directed the course of research and helped create new branches of science, perhaps before they would have emerged on their own." The people in these areas of study received what could be most accurately described as on-the-job training. "We were suddenly called upon to do something," one experiment station veteran recollected, "and in doing it we have have been receiving the necessary training" (Jordan, 1901:46). Congress, so often damned for shortsightedness, was in this instance creating institutions *before* they could function adequately.

However much it contradicted the accepted practices of times, and however little it reflected contemporary scientific reality, this Federal aid did indicate some things about how the country was changing. The United States was becoming a modern industrial nation, and one which saw education and science as engines of progress. Increasingly, American policy makers believed science and technology, rather than republicanism or Christianity, were the means of individual elevation and social advancement. Certainly that was the attitude of the scientists, publicists, educators, and others who created the elements of the agricultural research system.

Just as the creation of the system indicated an emerging view of the relationship of science to society and social progress, it also reflected a shifting attitude toward farmers. Supporters of agricultural science often spoke in romantic Jeffersonian terms, but they were amending agrarianism in subtle ways. In addition to being viewed as sturdy and independent yeomen, farmers were now being seen as people who had problems which demanded special social attention. Suddenly, they seemed to need the help of trained professionals. Paralleling this unarticulated assumption was another—that current farming practices posed a threat to society so grave as to demand public attention. Governmental aid for agricultural science was supported as a means of maintaining a vital yeomanry on the land, and it is reasonable to surmise that Jefferson himself, with his interest in science in farming, and his concern with declining productivity, might have approved this public activity (for his concerns regarding farm practices, see Jefferson, 1955:85). Still, there is no question that government support for agricultural research implied a failure in practice, if not in character, in the farming population.

Behind the subtle, tentative alterations in the image of the farmer were shifting social perceptions of the nature of virtue and the means of attaining it. To the agrarians of the early republic, farmers were virtuous simply because they were farmers. Living close to nature and pursuing the most legitimate occupation made farmers virtuous. By the late 19th century it was no longer sufficient for farmers simply to *be* in order to achieve virtue, now they had to *do* something. And what they had to do was to become trained professionals who would demonstrate their expertise by increasing their productivity, which would serve society. What was essentially an urban and industrial judgment of virtue, which measured it in terms of technique and skill and scientific expertise was now being applied to people who had previously been awarded virtue on another, less demanding and more intrinsic basis.

The growing celebration of professionalism and the increasing emphasis on technical expertise was but one indication of urban cultural hegemony in 19th century America. As cities grew and became centers of learning and wealth and power, urban attitudes and opinions assumed dominance in the United States. As that occurred, the image of the farmer increasingly became an unflattering, urban one. From the sturdy yeoman of Jefferson's day, the farmer was subtly transformed into a benighted hick, yokel, or rube, who did work requiring brawn but precious little brain. The farm came to be seen a a place to escape from, not a place to return to. Andrew Jackson followed the examples of Washington and Jefferson when he retired to his country estate following his term of public service. Barely a generation later Abraham Lincoln yearned to return to his law office in Springfield.

The people who created the agricultural research system reflected urban cultural hegemony, even while they resisted some of its implications. Clearly, professionalism was an important force in the creation of the system. As Barton Bledstein has indicated, the second half of the 19th century was the time when new professions arose, when old occupations were transformed into professions, and when professional status became an acceptable way in which members of an egalitarian society set themselves above their fellows (Bledstein, 1976). The experience of agricultural scientists themselves provided classic examples of professional self-creation, of the search for status, and the erection of institutions under professional control. Their professional status received further underpinning as coherent disciplines based on special bodies of knowledge developed, and as professional societies were founded in the agricultural sciences (Rossiter, 1979).

Moreover, the supporters of agricultural research hoped to elevate the farmer by professionalizing him, thereby countering the unflattering urban image of farming and those engaged in it. As Charles Rosenberg (1977:403) has pointed out, "The application of science to agriculture promised to raise the American farmer's moral and intellectual status. . . . The successful infusion of 'scientific' procedures and ideas . . . would make the ordinary farmer a man of learning . . . a professional like . . . lawyers and physicians." According to one of his eulogists at the 1899 convention of the Association of American Agricultural Colleges and Experiment Stations, the great Justin Morrill himself undertook to create scientific and educational institutions so that agriculture would be "lifted to the plane of the other professions" and farmers would enjoy "equal respectability" with other professionals (Buckham, 1900:34).

The professionalization of agriculture was a circular process. As farmers, with professional help, became more intelligent and expert, the status of those who aided them would in turn be enhanced. But this fact should not detract from the idealism of the supporters of and participants in the system, nor besmirch the dignity of their goal for farmers. They sought nothing less than the elevation of farmers in accordance with changing social standards of value. The idealism of that effort was reflected in their statements throughout the early years of publicly sponsored agricultural research. In a remark typical of those made by supporters of the system, farm editor Clarence Poe (1905:5951) wrote that the alteration of farming "from an industry requiring only physical strength to one requiring skill and trained intelligence means that it has now acquired a dignity which it has never had before."

Those currently within the agricultural research system who have reflected on its past have usually shared Poe's one-dimensional view of its purposes. In a statement typical of those made many times before and since, one champion of the establishment (Tweeten, 1971:54–55) argued that "The purpose of this system was to improve the welfare of farmers." Remarks of this sort are as unexceptionable as they are uninformative. The system was supposed to improve the welfare of farmers, but in one way only, by helping them become more professional. And for most supporters of the system greater and more efficient production were the indices of professionalism. This was not the only potential means of improving farmers' welfare in the latter part of the 19th century. Organizations such as the Grange, the Farmers' Alliance, and the Populist Party argued that the farmer's problems lay not with himself and his own shortcomings, but with the bankers, railroads, and middlemen which oppressed him. The creators and supporters of the research system held a sharply different attitude. To them, the farmer's problems lay in himself, and self-improvement through scientific advancement was the only way to solve them which would elevate the farmer and serve the nation. Those who believed otherwise were wrongheaded cranks or dangerous radicals whose "extreme ideas should be cleared away" (Harwood, 1893:141).

The thoroughgoing professionalism embodied in the agricultural research system from the beginning imparted a conservative cast to it, in both narrow and broad senses of the word. Their assumption that the farmer's problems were internal rather than external set the researchers against a substantial portion of the agricultural community and a fluctuating number of social and economic reformers outside of agriculture. This professional orientation and its innate conservatism remain vibrant attitudes within the system today.

The creation of publicly supported research institutions in agriculture did not insure their success, and many had to follow a rocky road in the late 19th century. The agricultural colleges squandered their grants. They attracted mere handfuls of students, almost none of real college caliber. More established colleges held them in contempt. Agriculture was not taught elsewhere, and few knew how to teach it or what it should entail. Promising scientists were difficult to attract and harder to keep. Schools suffered from political interference. College missions were murky, and futures were anything but bright. By every standard, the land-grant schools were the ugly ducklings of American higher education.

The experiment stations fared little better. The impoverished land-grant colleges struggled to control the new institutions and thus turn their staffs and monies to college purposes. In state after state, long wrangles ensued over where the stations should be located and who should control them, disputes which were often intensified by factional political divisions. Once established, the stations suffered from problems of self-definition. Were they to teach students, experiment, generate revenue, conduct model farms, carry on extension activities, or what? What was the experimentation to entail, and who would determine plans of work? Were experiments to be of a pure or applied nature, and how much of each? Moreover, the creation of new institutions merely worsened the shortage of trained scientists, and states competed with one another for personnel. As one observer noted in 1890, "from seventeen the number of experiment stations suddenly increased to fifty, with nothing like a proportional increase in men who were capable at the onset of filling the places to which they were appointed" (Parsons, 1890:353). Small wonder that leaders in the field could see little scientific progress in the early years of the stations (see, for example, Henry, 1894:39–45).

The Federal establishment did better. The national government could pay more to scientists, buffer them more completely from immediate political pressures, and help to create the critical intellectual mass which is of such importance in scientific development. Under James Wilson, whose sixteen-year secretaryship began in 1897, scientific activities in the USDA were vastly expanded and were better coordinated than had been the case in the past. Unfortunately, USDA successes seemed mainly to intensify the difficulties under which the state stations labored. Shortages of quality personnel and the difficulties of doing the more prestigious "pure" work were exacerbated by the expansion of the USDA and its functions. The state establishments often disliked the situation, and sometimes their resentments became public (see, for example, Davenport, 1913).

In retrospect, it appears that the infant scientific establishment had two serious basic problems, in addition to the more transitory difficulties incidental to any new endeavor. The first of these problems was an internal one—the weakness of the scientific foundation on which the institutions had to build. With the exception of agricultural chemistry, bodies of knowledge were primitive or insufficient in the new disciplines. Moreover, there was a shortage of trained people in all fields, and the facilities for filling the demand simply did not exist. In this situation, true scientific advancement could not take place. The best the scientists could reasonably expect to do was to grasp and communicate to farmers the best standards of contemporary farm practice. "To be frank with you," admitted Association of American Agricultural Colleges and Experiment Stations President W.A. Henry to his colleagues in 1893, "I believe that our station workers have . . . accomplished more good for the cause of advanced agriculture through their efforts at instruction than through all they may have discovered" (Henry, 1893:41). As Henry implied, the improvement of current practices was no mean task, and it did increase productive efficiency and address particular production problems. But it did not involve true scientific work, even by the standards of the time.

The second problem faced by the new institutions, and an especially intense one on the state level, was external—there was little support for or even interest in agricultural science among farmers. Despite the rhetoric of the supporters of scientific agriculture, few farmers desired the institutions, the aid they offered, or, apparently, the professionalism they promised. Many farmers viewed "book farming" with contempt and the scientific institutions as wastes of tax money.

Taken together, the weakness of the scientific foundations and the lack of external support pushed the research institutions to do things in the early years which they had wanted to avoid—specifically, to emphasize practical, or applied research, and to build relationships with supportive client groups. On the state level especially, the new research agencies emphasized the practical, because directly applicable work would prove the institutions' utility, gain public support, and cover failures of training or knowledge. In the new states of the west, pressures for immediate solutions to the problems of farming under difficult conditions were particularly intense and unrealistic, pushing research institutions to emphasize practical, short-term gains. Consequently, the land grant schools and the experiment stations devoted disproportionate resources to such activities as testing fertilizer, feed, and seed, analyzing food and drug products, and maintaining "model" farms which used the best current methods in order to demonstrate maximum productive potential. Although these activities seemed necessary, and much political pressure was generated for them, there was significant opposition to this emphasis from within the research community itself. Major scientific developments would never take place, and quality scientists would never be developed internally or attracted from outside as long as agricultural researchers appeared to be little more than master farmers (for an early, but cogent, criticism of the practical orientation, see Bolley, 1898). Still, the political realities in most places dictated a heavily practical emphasis to most research, and in many cases that early tendency has never really been reversed.

The practical emphasis of many institutions was dictated by political realities. Within the research community, many hoped to avoid entangling the new institutions with politics. "Politics . . . or anything pertaining to politics should have no place in the college or its management," argued the president of the AACES in 1898, "either in legislature, board of control, board of trustees, or faculty" (White, 1899:41). However attractive this ideal might have been to scientists, it was never approximated in the agricultural research system. As is true with all public agencies in the United States, the agricultural research organizations were political creations, and their maintenance and direction depended largely on political decisions. All of the component parts of the system were intimately involved in politics from the beginning on, though many scientists were unwilling or unable to recognize that reality. Legislative and Congressional appropriations, issues of governance, site selection, and even programs of work were political questions, and the perceptive pioneers in the research establishment recognized that the health and even the survival of their institutions was tied to their political acumen and the political alliances they made. The "research entrepreneurs" about whom Charles Rosenberg (1971) has written, men such as Eugene Davenport, W.E. Henry, and Eugene Hilgard, were able to build substantial state research establishments *and* create respectable scientific institutions through alliances with powerful groups. Others were not as fortunate. In some states, powerful commodity groups, railroads, and business associations bent on attracting new settlers exercised disproportionate power. Everywhere, chambers of commerce and bankers' associations provided substantial support and exercised considerable influence.

As might be expected, the research institutions were most likely to attract support from and make alliances with groups which already shared their outlook and sympathized with their work. Businessmen, bankers, and highly specialized, market-oriented farmers were all likely to agree that the problems of agriculture were mainly problems of production, and that these could be solved within agriculture if farmers became more professional. Still, even though they allied with ideologically congenial people, the researchers paid a price. While the alliance helped the institutions survive, it also limited their freedom of action. As Charles Rosenberg (1977:407–408) has pointed out, "dependence on influential laymen often meant an active role for such men in the planning and even execution of research."

Their relationship with market-oriented, productivity-conscious, commodity-based farmers had other effects on the researchers as well. It narrowed their focus and their interest, leading them unconsciously to identify the problems of agriculture with particular production problems of relatively small groups of commercial farmers. Hog cholera, or the Hessian fly, or raising butterfat content in milk were production problems, but to identify each as *the* problem of farmers was to lose sight of the forest for the trees. Along with disciplinization, which became more pronounced as agricultural science matured, this narrow problem focus made it hard for researchers to develop a comprehensive understanding either of agricultural problems or of the broad effects of their own research.

Finally, the alliances it made and the directions it took led the research establishment to burn whatever bridges it had to a substantial portion of the agricultural community—those farmers, often small, poorly educated, undercapitalized, and inefficient, who believed that their problems derived mainly from an unfavorable social and economic situation rather than from their own shortcomings. The researchers and their professionally oriented supporters in business and farming simply did not accept these definitions of agricultural problems, and were unwilling to address them. At best, the research system was becoming irrelevant to much of the rural community.

With their emphasis on greater productivity, enhanced by their alliance with groups which shared their modern views, the researchers potentially threatened many farmers. This was something which few of the scientists realized. Most researchers at the turn of this century, as well as most other forward-looking Americans, had a simplistic, one-dimensional view of science. To them, science was the search for truth and the means of progress in a modern society. Scientists supposedly searched for truth in an autonomous, untrammeled fashion, and the results of their search were "undiluted good" (Busch and Lacy, 1983:34). If science could help men fly, or devise perfect governmental mechanisms, or determine the cause of insanity, or double the corn crop, all would benefit and none would be harmed. In the case of agriculture, increased productivity could easily be seen as universally beneficial at a time when world demand grew faster than supply. It is not surprising that researchers "never considered the possibility that insofar as their work proved successful it might help enrich the rich, impoverishing and ultimately forcing many worthy if less entrepreneurial farmers from the land" (Rosenberg, 1977:402).

On those occasions when farmers complained that the products of agricultural research were harming some in agriculture, driving them from the land, research spokesmen treated them with the sort of contempt urbanites demonstrated for untutored rustics. Cornell's I.P. Roberts (1897:81) held little sympathy for backward and unprofessional producers: "There are many who now occupy the land who must, of necessity, leave it, since neither by nature nor by training are they adapted to their vocation," he told his colleagues, "and the sooner they leave . . . the better it will be for all concerned."

By 1900, then, the agricultural research establishment had developed a habit of mind which made critical self-analysis difficult. Concentrating on increasing production, researchers failed to see the potential validity of other goals, or to recognize that their efforts might harm some in the agricultural community. Nor could they see that their support groups might be self-interested, and might be directing research for their own ends. Self-conscious seekers of truth who wanted to benefit society, they could not fail to see their critics as backward, reactionary impediments to social progress.

The early years of the 20th century witnessed a slow and incomplete alleviation of the problems from which the research system had suffered in the late 19th century. Static productivity in agriculture and the steady rise of food prices reminded policy makers of the apparent necessity of changing farm practices. Those agencies which were devoted to professionalizing farmers and to improving agricultural productivity consequently enjoyed a higher status and rising appropriations (Danbom, 1979). Two pieces of legislation—the Adams Act of 1906 and the Smith-Lever Act of 1914—had a major impact on the research establishment at the state level. The first provided for an annual Federal appropriation to encourage research at the state experiment stations. This appropriation provided a higher level of financial stability to the stations than they had enjoyed previously, allowed a greater concentration on "pure" rather than applied research, facilitated the undertaking of projects of long duration, and freed researchers from classroom duties. The Smith-Lever Act provided Federal support for agricultural extension, facilitating the dissemination of scientific knowledge and freeing state researchers from their extension chores. It was also eventuated in the creation of the American Farm Bureau Federation, a nationwide support organization for publicly sponsored research.[1]

Despite this generally favorable situation, the system still suffered from some difficulties. The relationship between the Federal and state organizations remained tense, and the latter generally distrusted the rapid expansion of the former under Secretary Wilson, seeing it as an aggressive effort to dominate research. Federal expansion and the growth of most of the state establishments meant that the demand for quality researchers continued to exceed the supply, even though more were being trained than had previously been the case. The shortage was particularly acute, of course, in areas where pay was low and where the climate—social as well as meteorological—was unattractive.[2] This was one factor which led many schools to emphasize training their own researchers, a practice which contributed to the in-bred condition some of state research establishments today. Another continuing problem was the weakness of the scientific base in many disciplines, though great strides were made in several areas early in the century. Weak science and the emphasis on application, which remained prominent despite the largese of the Adams Act, meant that agricultural researchers continued to be second-class citizens in the scientific community as a whole. The Carnegie Institute's exclusion of land-grant colleges from its professorial retirement plan in 1908 "on the grounds that they were not really collegiate-level institutions" was only the most blatant example of this attitude (Porter, 1979:87).

As long as policy makers perceived low agricultural productivity as a national problem, the research establishment enjoyed a relatively favorable position. Beginning in 1920, overproduction rather than underproduction appeared to be the major agricultural problem, and in that situation publicly sponsored, productivity-oriented agricultural research faced a serious challenge. In the early 1920's the scientific establishment was widely blamed for rising agricultural production and the consequent deflation of prices. The system was put on the defensive, and angry farmers demanded that agricultural science be redirected, with productivity-oriented research de-emphasized or even ended. These demands became especially strident during the thirties, when institutions which encouraged production seemed irrelevant to national problems at best and destructive at worst.

Negative attitudes toward the system were reflected in Congress and in the state legislatures. Financial support was cut, particularly in the early thirties. In part this was due to the fact that governmental revenues declined, but the apparent pointlessness of production-stimulation meant that appropriations for agricultural research suffered disproportionately. Moreover, in many states and in the Federal government there was more sympathy than previously for the small farmers who traditionally criticized the research system. As a result of these factors, the scientific agricultural establishment found itself in serious fiscal trouble.

In addition to the more precarious position of the system as a whole, the research establishment faced demands that it redirect its attention from the stimulation of production to marketing and even to studying the social consequences of agricultural change. These demands were acknowledged by Congress in 1925 when the Purnell Act, providing funds for state experiment station research in economics and sociology, as well as home economics, was passed. During the Roosevelt Administration the USDA also broadened its research emphasis, expanding the Bureau of Agricultural Economics and undertaking more economic and sociological investigation.

Secretary of Agriculture Henry A. Wallace was a crucial figure in attempting to save the old research system while infusing it with a new, broader perspective. A researcher in hybrid corn, Wallace had little patience with those who argued that over-abundance dictated an end to agricultural science: "We might just as well command the sun to stand still as to say that science should take a holiday," he wrote in 1934. "Science has turned scarcity into plenty. Merely because it has served us well is no reason why we should charge science with the responsibility for our failure to apportion production to need and to distribute the fruits of plenty equitably" (Wallace, 1934a:2). But he also recognized the shortcomings of a science which did not consider larger social goals or recognize the purposes to which it was being put. He complained of scientists who felt that "as long as they could get enough money to pursue their researches, why should they care how someone else handled the social and economic power derived from these researches?" And he warned that science "has been creating another world and another civilization that simply must be motivated by some conscious social purpose, if civilization is to endure" (Wallace, 1934b:3–4). Wallace favored a stronger role for economists and other social scientists in helping to develop such a "conscious social purpose."

The agricultural research establishment listened to Wallace and accepted the necessity of a partial shift in emphasis, but it was not converted. Within the system, there was almost no sympathy with social scientists, particularly when their investigations resulted in implicit or explicit criticism of the nature and direction of agricultural research. The historian of the Virginia Agricultural Experiment Station has noted that, during the Depression, rural sociology at the station "was not popular. . . .

The major contribution of the rural sociology research program before 1946 was perhaps its influence on the conscience of Virginia with respect to the obligation of society to the underprivileged, the unfortunate, the ill, and the poorly nourished" (Young, 1975:126). Although this scholar does not say as much, the "major contribution" was probably the main cause of unpopularity, not only in the station but also with traditional support groups of agricultural research—the professionally-oriented farmers, chambers of commerce, bankers' associations, and agribusiness corporations. The position of most of the establishment was similar to that of the director of the experiment station in Kansas in 1934. Although he was willing to "acknowledge" the new emphases, "he indicated that the college had no intention of dropping its old emphasis on efficiency in production" (cited in Jones, 1968:292).

The traditional orientation of the system was too deeply embedded in its very purpose, too habitual, and too heavily reinforced by support groups to be changed quickly or easily. The institutions broadened their activities as a tactical adjustment, but the soul of the system and its accustomed pattern was not altered. Eventually, the research establishment emerged from the twenties and thirties in a position of strength, its traditional direction unchanged. On the Federal level, Wallace's patronage stimulated the growth of the established agricultural sciences along with the social sciences. Everywhere, new developments, the most striking of which was hybrid corn, increased the prestige of the scientists, and with the beginning of World War II productivity again became something to be celebrated rather than regretted. Just when production became important again agricultural science began paying off on research investments of forty or more years duration.

The forties and fifties were bright times for the publicly supported agricultural research system. Hybridization and pesticide development brought the scientists respect they had not enjoyed previously. Agricultural researchers came to be viewed as real scientists, and this at a time when science enjoyed more respect and even awe than in any previous period of American history. One enthusiast, for example, fell just short of crediting the developers of hybrid corn with the defeat of the Axis. "It became necessary to pit our total strength against a coalition of ruthless, lawless aggressor nations in a life-and-death struggle," wrote Richard Crabb (1947:12) in what was surely one of the most dramatic passages ever penned about corn. "Immediately, American corn was projected into unprecedented importance around the world." In *Two Blades of Grass*, a celebration of the research system, T. Swann Harding (1947:319) suggested that nobody was likely again to question the pure science done by agricultural researchers when he compared it favorably with the pure research which resulted in the creation of the atomic bomb. "When such research can . . . develop a relatively small bomb capable of destroying a city of a quarter of a million persons, who can say that pure research is of dubious value?" Few other champions of the system cared to compare its work to the creation of horrible destructive devices, but they did not doubt that science benefited society greatly. Moreover, the new glamour of science produced tangible benefits, not the least of which was a flood of young, well-trained Ph.Ds into the research system.

The confidence of the champions of the system seemed well placed in the forties and fifties. Agricultural productivity leaped ahead, tripling in the 25 years after the end of World War II. Much of this increase was due to mechanization and the increased reliance on chemicals of all kinds, two developments for which agribusiness corporations were largely responsible. But the publicly supported scientific institutions deserved some credit for the growth in productivity through applications studies and research on hybrids and cultivation practices. The rise in productivity was so striking and so rapid as to hold out the vision of banishing hunger from the world, through the exportation either of American food or American technology, thus regenerating the idealistic component of agricultural research.

Another benefit for the system was a decline in criticism of the nature and direction of agricultural research. Many of the traditional critics of the system, the small, marginal producers, migrated to urban areas. The resulting proportionate increase in large, commercially-oriented producers also meant that the traditional argument that the research system served farmers (which in practice meant the larger farmers), became more accurate. Finally, the postwar period was not a congenial time for the radical social critics of agricultural research, who came to be viewed as cranks at best and communists at worst.[3]

Yet even in the golden age all was not auspicious for the system of agricultural research. One major problem was the slow erosion of interest in and support for the system. As the number of farmers declined, both absolutely and relatively, the size of the actual and potential client group for agricultural research diminished. Moreover, the largest and most efficient farmers, who traditionally supported the system, turned increasingly to chemical, seed, and machinery companies for at least some advice and information. State-level research establishments often tried to compensate for this loss of clients by doing contract work for agribusiness corporations, but the future of that was dubious given the increasing corporate emphasis on internal research and development. Moreover, research for agribusiness reopened old debates about whether the system benefited farmers. The search for new clients also led research spokesmen to emphasize how much consumers had benefited from their efforts. However true this may have been, consumers do not compose the sort of permanent, self-conscious client group on which a public agency can comfortably depend. It was also the case, ironically, that the system suffered because it had apparently succeeded. Public agencies which solve the problems they address are rewarded with de-emphasis at best and destruction at worst. In this case, the system had apparently succeeded so well in stimulating production that surpluses were once again a problem. As during the twenties and thirties, "general doubts were raised about the wisdom of appropriating public funds for agricultural research, especially that focused on enhanced production" (National Research Council, 1975). The system compensated to some extent by placing greater emphasis on marketing research, but throughout the fifties and sixties researchers complained that funding failed to increase adequately to meet the challenges of the future or even to maintain existing levels of activity.

Perhaps the major problem of the golden age, with its celebration of science and scientists, was the effect it had on the self-consciousness and self-image of the people in the system. Nothing happened in the immediate postwar years to encourage any critical self-analysis among agricultural scientists. Charles Rosenberg (1977:401) has noted that "American agricultural research has been marked . . . by an inability to predict, evaluate, and contend with the social and economic consequences of innovation." This had been Wallace's complaint, and he had suggested more socially conscious scientists and more social scientists in the system. Ironically, the influx of highly trained young researchers after World War II intensified the narrow disciplinary specialization which had always limited broad social consciousness, even while it improved the quality of science. And the social scientists were either purged out by the early fifties or were working in non-controversial areas, such as innovation-adoption research. As a result, most agricultural scientists continued to see what they did as unquestionably good by nature, ignored the normative dimensions of their work, and acknowledged no ills flowing from it. There were those within the system who expressed some doubts. For example, Iowa State University President James H. Hilton argued in 1961 that, in addition to production, "the land-grant colleges . . . must *also* deal with the complex problems of economic and social adjustments. . . . Increasingly, the orientation of our research must be more around people and their welfare" (Hilton, 1961:41–42). But Hilton and other internal critics were voices in the wilderness during the golden age. When substantial criticism of the system arose in the 1960's, it can mainly from outside the agricultural research establishment.

The sixties and seventies witnessed a rising level of criticism of the purposes and direction of the agricultural research system from outside of the establishment. Defenders of the system date their travails with outside critics from the publication of Rachel Carson's *Silent Spring* in 1962 (see, for example, Whitten, 1966).  Certainly, Carson's book helped stimulate and galvanize the inchoate environmental movement, and before long agricultural research was under fire—not always justly—for its over-reliance on chemicals, its relative disinterest in food quality, safety, and nutrition, and its general emphasis on short-term economic gains at the expense of long-term ecological considerations.  The energy and food crises of the mid-seventies led many ecologically oriented critics to question whether American agriculture, energy- and chemical-intensive and careless of conservation as it was, could even be sustained.  To these critics, the research establishment was a major part of the problem rather than part of a solution.  Instead of preparing for a smaller scale, more environmentally sound, less energy- and chemical-intensive, "postindustrial" agriculture, the research establishment seemed merely to be encouraging and building on the destructive methods and technologies of the past (see, for example, Merrill, 1976).  Many concluded that agricultural science had delivered more—and worse—than it had promised. Abundance had come, but it was achieved through practices which seemed even to threaten human survival.  Perhaps a Frankenstein had been created, attractive in prospect but horrible in reality.  Even the promise that world hunger could be banished by the application of American know-how and techniques seemed hollow when failures were recognized and costs were reckoned.

Most of this criticism reflected a shift in social attitudes apparent during the sixties and seventies.  No longer were science and technology widely accepted in a one-dimensional fashion as handmaidens of goodness and progress.  The implications of atomic warfare, the dissatisfactions of material affluence, the discovery of environmental degradation, fears of new developments such as genetic engineering, and revulsion at the military for the highly technological war in Vietnam rapidly removed the bloom from the rose of science, and those identified with it were put on the defensive.  Other social changes in the sixties and seventies also led to questioning of the agricultural research establishment.  The poor were rediscovered, and social and racial injustice briefly became priority problems in the United States.  Radicalism revived in the country, stimulated by the Civil Rights and Vietnam controversies, spawning critics both of American economic arrangements and conventional lifestyles and values.

The new radicalism contributed another strain of external criticism of the agricultural research system.  The most telling blow was struck by Jim Hightower's *Hard Tomatoes, Hard Times* (1973).  Hightower's thesis (1973:xxvi) was "that the tax-paid, land grant complex has come to serve an elite of private, corporate interests in rural America, while ignoring those who have the most urgent needs and the most legitimate claims for assistance."  Hightower, who based his indictment largely on the activities of publicly-sponsored researchers in California, argued that large farmers and agribusiness corporations had been well-served by the system, while small farmers, sharecroppers, farm laborers, and ultimately consumers had been harmed. The impact of Hightower's criticism was intensified not because it was new—for it was not—but because critical self-analysis in the system had been stifled for so long (a point made by Olson, 1978:253).

Other radical critics, more concerned with lifestyle than economics, scored the system for helping make agriculture more of a business and less of a way of life. Wendell Berry (1977), an eloquent, modern-day pastoralist, argued that agriculture had lost its dignity, its uniqueness, its satisfaction, and its ability to contribute to the larger culture as farming became more of a business. Because agricultural scientists have continually admonished farmers to become more efficient, businesslike, and professional, and have helped create an environment in which those characteristics are rewarded, they have received much criticism. "The most telling critique of agricultural science . . . has been its emphasis on efficiency . . . ," argued one writer recently. "The quest for the illusive goal of efficiency permits practitioners to avoid considering values. Human values are reduced to economic 'value'" (Busch, 1981:3).

Hightower, Berry, and other critics of modern farming, though viewed as radicals by the agricultural establishment, were actually rooting their analyses in traditional agrarian thought. They implied that agriculture had special value, and that its value diminished as farmers became more businesslike and professional. The critics believed that the research system had betrayed farmers. While it had been created ostensibly to preserve a special and valuable lifestyle, the system had in practice undermined that lifestyle, making farmers more like the urbanites Jefferson abhorred. Whether the critics have accurately represented the true purposes of the system or even traditional American agrarian attitudes is questionable. What cannot be questioned is that the research system has traditionally claimed to be engaged in preserving the rural lifestyle, saving the family farm, and so forth. The system's undermining of what it claims to be saving reflects a basic and long-standing contradiction between the stated aims of American agricultural policies and their effects—a contradiction which transcends the research system per se. Insofar as the system continues to claim these traditional goals, it is either hypocritical or unable to analyze itself.

Some people in the research establishment have showed a willingness to acknowledge the justice of some criticisms by outside observers, though this response has not been universal by any means. Initially, there was rather a defensive, circle-up-the-wagons reaction, if the critics were recognized at all. In his history of agricultural research in California, for example, George Wells (1969:5) lambasted environmentalists and those concerned with agricultural laborers for standing in the way of the "miracle a day" offered by science. Wells (1969:43) praised the very tomato research on which Hightower later focused for relieving hard-pressed growers from having to pay "wetbacks" doing "stoop labor" at "executive-level salaries." Seven years later, the director of the Connecticut Experiment Station dismissed the criticisms of the sixties and seventies as mere "hard knocks" which the system would surmount (Waggoner, 1976:236). This sort of attitude has faded somewhat from public expression in recent years, though the basically conservative biases of many people in the system suggest that it is still widely held.

More remarkable than the continuation of negative attitudes toward critics is the willingness seriously to consider some of what they have to say. Spokesmen for the system now regularly, and publicly, acknowledge that research policies and developments have effects beyond the farm, and that sometimes these effects are bad. Increased rural and urban unemployment, economic concentration, environmental deterioration, disintegration of country towns and other unintended results now receive acknowledgement (See, for example, Heady and Whiting, 1975). In his recent, thoughtful exploration of agricultural research policy, Vernon Ruttan (1983:81) went so far as to credit Rachel Carson and Jim Hightower for pointing out "a major limitation of the agricultural research system—that it was too narrowly focused on plants, animals, and soils and inadequately oriented toward the problems of rural communities and consumers." Ruttan (1983:333) also noted that agricultural scientists "have wanted to revolutionize technology but have preferred to neglect the revolutionary impact of technology on society . . . . Because of their beliefs, they have often failed to recognize the link between the technical changes in which they took pride and the institutional changes that they either failed to perceive or feared to accept." Attitudes such as Ruttan's cannot fail to give hope to those who would like to see more flexibility in the system.

There has also been another strain of criticism of the system which has appeared in the last fifteen years, this one largely internal. Since 1969, the system has been rocked by criticism based not on what it does, but on how well it does it. In 1972, a National Research Council committee on agricultural research formed in 1969 issued a scathing report on the research system. The "Pound" Committee, nicknamed for Chairman Glenn S. Pound of the University of Wisconsin, acknowledged the responsibility of the system for environmental degradation, ignorance of nutrition, and social and economic externalities, but it concentrated on the system's failures from a conventional scientific point of view. The committee found "much . . . agricultural research . . . outmoded, pedestrian, and inefficient." It argued that support for the basic sciences in the system was "grossly inadequate," that the system suffered from "an unwarranted duplication of effort in some areas and thus a wastage of resources," and that it was stultified by a rigid bureaucracy, particularly at the USDA level (National Research Council, 1972:11–18). In 1975, another National Research Council group studied the system. Again, the investigators noted the importance of the "environmental and social consequences" of research, but they focused on the ability of the system to increase productive efficiency. The energy and food crises of 1973–74 indicated to this group that productive efficiency would have to be increased, but there were doubts about the ability of the system to undertake that task successfully. Like the Pound Committee, these researchers pointed to duplication and inflexibility as problems in the system (National Research Council, 1975). In 1981, the Congressional Office of Technology Assessment studied the system. Its report repeated the formula of recognizing social and economic externalities, but it concentrated on the organizational efficiency of the system. The lack of "overall planning and coordination of research," inadequate attention to "national problems," and "duplication" were areas of special concern (OTA, 1981:4).

Whether external or internal, the criticism of the last two decades has generally been healthy, though not always fair. It is important to note that the problems internal and external critics perceive and the direction they would like to see agricultural research take are very different. The criticisms of the system from internal critics, such as those brought together by the National Research Council, are telling ones, and they undoubtedly sting and threaten many within the system, not least because they reflect the tradition of elite scientific derogation of agricultural researchers. But the internal critics share the assumptions of those in the system, they value what the researchers have tried to do, and they are mainly interested in seeing it done better. Many of the external critics, however, see problems which are fundamental and systemic, and they favor a radical redirection of agricultural research. The internalists are willing to acknowledge what the externalists have said, but they are unwilling to follow the implications of external criticism to a fundamental restructuring. Clearly, they believe that more good than ill has come from the system. "From the primary objectives of research flow secondary benefits," the OTA argued, "which include improved human nutrition, improved food quality and safety, an international trade balance, expansionary impacts on other sectors of society, and increased leisure time" (OTA, 1981:62). Indeed, the internalists fear the implications for the system of increased attention to the demands of external critics, even while they recognize some justice in those demands. "Public demand . . . has in recent years caused shifts toward an increased emphasis on environment and health protection problems and on efforts to improve the quality of human life," noted the National Research Council group (1975:191), adding that this attention raised the question "whether production research is being neglected to the extent that our food supply will lag for lack of new discoveries." "New issues are being funded at the expense of traditional agricultural interests," added the OTA. "Concern exists within the agricultural research establishment that all areas will be increasingly underfunded as the research base continues to expand" (OTA, 1981:139). This reaction to the minimal concessions made to external criticism provides some indication of how the people in the system would respond to a fundamental restructuring.

The past does not predict the future, but the character and the dynamics of institutions help determine how they are likely to react in given situations, just as human personality helps determine human reaction. The agricultural research system has a personality—character, values, beliefs, and dynamics established over a long period—which provides indications of how it will respond to pressures for change.

These are public institutions, the people in them view themselves as public servants, and they have a strong strain of idealism, however much they might shun that word. Institutions always aim first to survive, and public institutions do so by filling the needs of, and establishing relationships with some, or all sectors of the public. The remarkable durability and heath of the agricultural research system indicates how successful it has been in that endeavor. In recent years the traditional clients of the agricultural research institutions have dwindled away, to the acute consternation of spokesmen for the system. Obviously, this creates the possibility that "new agenda" groups—concerned with such areas as nutrition, food and farmer safety, the environment, farm workers, rural community development, and a number of others—can influence the system to some extent, especially if they show an ability to survive over the long term. Certainly, many agricultural spokesmen now recognize the validity of these groups' concerns and the legitimacy of their having an input in the policy making process (see, for example, Paarlberg, 1980; and USDA, 1981).

There are other positive aspects as well for those who hope to see a redirection of agricultural research. The variety, complexity, and decentralization of the system, while damned by internal critics for impeding efficiency, lends flexibility to it. As Lawrence Busch and William Lacy (1983) recently pointed out in an extensive survey of the system, every discipline, every region, and even, I might add, every state differs slightly from every other one in its research emphases, client relationships, and openness to change. This creates numerous possibilities for redirection, albeit on a local and limited scale. Another promising development for those seeking redirection of the system lies in the increasing commitment of agribusiness firms to production-oriented research and development. For example, the financial and manpower commitment of private firms and non-land-grant public institutions to biotechnical research is effectively closing this new area to the traditional publicly supported research agencies. This extends the possibility that these public agencies might turn more attention to "new agenda" research areas, such as alternative agricultural systems or small-farmer-oriented technologies.

At the same time, other institutional dynamics limit the degree to which change can be expected to occur. The system would like to broaden its base of support, but it does not want to lose its traditional client groups. Moreover, the very variety, complexity, and localism of the system which makes some change possible limits the extent of that change. It is also important to remember that the system will not easily alter its traditional orientation toward increasing productivity. The policy makers who created the system were interested primarily in raising production, and the system has worked mainly toward that goal. The costs of achieving greater productivity have been high for marginal farmers, agricultural workers, and rural communities, but it is unreasonable to deny that society as a whole has benefited from the cheap and abundant production we enjoy for home consumption and exportation. Nor can we assume that problems of production have or will cease, or that research directed to solving these problems should be ended. The system was created to address production problems, it has done so effectively, and it should not be expected to stop doing so. This is related to a final important point. The people in the system are tightly bound together, and they share values and attitudes shaped by what they do and where they do it. They want to see the system maintained, of course, but they will have much influence on what sort of a system it is.

In conclusion, then, while there is potential for changes in the system, these are likely to be limited in kind and degree by realities which have been more than a century in the making.

## Notes

1. For the relationship between the American Farm Bureau Federation and the public research agencies see Grant McConnell, *The Decline of Agrarian Democracy*, Berkeley: University of California, 1953.

2. For the unattractiveness of stations in some areas see Jane M. Porter, "Experiment Stations in the South, 1877–1940," *Agricultural History* 53:84–101.

3. Critics did, however, continue to exist. See, for example Ralph Borsodi, "The Case Against Farming as a Big Business," *The Land* 6:446–451.

## References

Appleby, Joyce. 1982. "Commercial Farming and the 'Agrarian Myth' in the Early Republic," *The Journal of American History* 68:833–849.

Berry, Wendell. 1977. *The Unsettling of America: Culture and Agriculture.* San Francisco: Sierra Club Books.

Bledstein, Barton. 1976. *The Culture of Professionalism: The Middle Class and the Development of Higher Education in America.* New York: Norton.

Bolley, H.L. 1898. "An Experiment: Its Conception and Methods of Procedure." In *Proceedings of the Eleventh Annual Convention of the Association of American Agricultural Colleges and Experiment Stations, Held at Minneapolis, Minnesota, July 13–15, 1897,* pp. 47–51. USDA Office of Experiment Stations Bulletin No. 49. Washington, D.C.: Government Printing Office.

Borsodi, Ralph. 1947. "The Case Against Farming As a Big Business." *The Land* 6:446-451.

Buckham, M.H. 1900. In *Proceedings of the Thirteenth Annual Convention of the Association of American Agricultural Colleges and Experiment Stations, Held at San Francisco, California, July 5–7, 1899,* pp. 30–36. USDA Office of Experiment Stations Bulletin No. 76. Washington, D.C.: Government Printing Office.

Busch, Lawrence. 1981. "Introduction." In *Science and Agricultural Development,* ed. Lawrence Busch, pp. 1–5. Montclair, New Jersey: Allanheld, Osmun.

Busch, Lawrence, and William B. Lacy. 1983. *Science, Agriculture, and the Politics of Research.* Boulder: Westview.

Carson, Rachel. 1962. *Silent Spring.* Boston: Houghton Mifflin Company.

Crabb, Richard. 1947. *The Hybrid-Corn Makers: Prophets of Plenty.* New Brunswick: Rutgers University.

Danbom, David B. 1979. *The Resisted Revolution: Urban America and the Industrialization of Agriculture, 1900–1930.* Ames: Iowa State University Press.

Davenport, Eugene. 1913. "The Relations Between the Federal Department of Agriculture and the Agricultural Colleges and Experiment Stations." Urbana, Illinois.

Dupree, A. Hunter. 1957. *Science in the Federal Government: A History of Policies and Activities to 1940.* Cambridge: Harvard University Press.

Harding, T. Swann. 1947. *Two Blades of Grass: A History of Scientific Development in the U.S. Department of Agriculture.* Norman: University of Oklahoma Press.

Harwood, P.M. 1893. "What Shall the Professor of Agriculture Teach?" In *Proceedings of the Sixth Annual Convention of the Association of American Agricultural Colleges and Experiment Stations, Held at New Orleans, Louisiana, November 15–19, 1892,* pp. 139–142. USDA Office of Experiment Stations Bulletin No. 16. Washington, D.C.: Government Printing Office.

Heady, Earl O., and Larry R. Whiting, eds. 1975. *Externalities in the Transformation of Agriculture: Distribution of Benefits and Costs from Development.* Ames: Iowa State University Press.

Henry, W.A. 1894. "President's Address." In *Proceedings of the Seventh Annual Convention of the Association of American Agricultural Colleges and Experiment Stations, Held at Chicago, Illinois, October 17–19, 1893,* pp. 39–45. USDA Office of Experiment Stations Bulletin No. 20. Washington, D.C.: Government Printing Office.

Hightower, Jim. 1973. *Hard Tomatoes, Hard Times: A Report of the Agribusiness Accountability Project on the Failure of America's Land Grant College Complex.* Cambridge, Mass.: Schenkman.

Hilton, James H. 1961. "The Land-Grant College: Past and Present." In *Lecture Series in Honor of the United States Department of Agriculture Centennial Year,* ed. Wayne D. Rasmussen, pp. 33–45. Washington, D.C.: U.S. Dept. of Agriculture Graduate School.

Jefferson, Thomas. 1955. *Notes on the State of Virginia.* Chapel Hill: University of North Carolina.

Jones, C. Clyde. 1968. "An Agricultural College's Response to a Changing World." *Agricultural History* 42:283-295.

Jordan, W.H. 1901. "American Agricultural Experiment Stations." In *Proceedings of the Fourteenth Annual Convention of the Association of American Agricultural Colleges and Experiment Stations Held at New Haven and Middletown, Connecticut, November 13–15, 1900,* pp. 42-51. USDA Office of Experiment Stations Bulletin No. 99. Washington, D.C.: Government Printing Office.

McConnell, Grant. 1953. *The Decline of Agrarian Democracy.* Berkeley: University of California Press.

Merrill, Richard. ed. 1976. *Radical Agriculture.* New York: Harper and Row.

National Research Council. 1972. *Report of the Committee on Research Advisory to the U.S. Department of Agriculture.* Washington, D.C.: National Academy of Sciences.

National Research Council. 1975. *Agricultural Production Efficiency.* Washington, D.C.: National Academy of Sciences.

Olson, Philip. 1978. "Social Research and Public Policy: The Case of American Agriculture." In *The New Politics of Food,* ed. Don F. Hadwiger and William P. Brown, pp. 247–255. Lexington, Mass.: D.C. Heath.

Office of Technology Assessment. 1981. *An Assessment of the United States Food and Agricultural Research System.* Washington, D.C.: U.S. Government Printing Office.

Paarlberg, Don. 1980. *Farm and Food Policy: Issues of the 1980s.* Lincoln: University of Nebraska Press.

Parsons, Charles Lathrop. 1890. "Our Agricultural Experiment Stations." *Popular Science Monthly* 39:348–358.

Poe, Clarence. 1905. "The Government and the New Farmer." *The World's Work* 9:5951–5964.

Porter, Jane M. 1979. "Experiment Stations in the South, 1877–1940." *Agricultural History* 53:84–101.

Roberts, I.P. 1897. "The Exodus From the Farm: What Are Its Causes and What Can the Colleges of Agriculture Do to Nourish a Hearty Sentiment for Rural Life?" In *Proceedings of the Tenth Annual Convention of the Association of American Agricultural Colleges and Experiment Stations, Held at Washington, D.C., November 10–12, 1896,* pp. 80–87. USDA Office of Experiment Stations, Bulletin No. 41. Washington, D.C.: Government Printing Office.

Rosenberg, Charles. 1971. "Science, Technology, and Economic Growth: The Case of the Agricultural Experiment Station Scientist, 1875–1914." *Agricultural History* 45:1–20.

————. 1977. "Rationalization and Reality in the Shaping of American Agricultural Research." *Social Studies of Science* 7:401–422.

Rossiter, Margaret W. 1975. *The Emergence of Agricultural Science: Justis Liebig and the Americans, 1840–1880.* New Haven: Yale University Press.

————. 1976. "The Organization of Agricultural Improvement in the United States, 1785–1865." In *The Pursuit of Knowledge in the Early American Republic: American Scientific and Learned Societies from Colonial Times to the Civil War,* ed. Alexandra Oleson and Sanborn C. Brown, pp. 279–298. Baltimore: Johns Hopkins University Press.

————. 1979. "The Organization of the Agricultural Sciences." In *The Organization of Knowledge in Modern America, 1860–1920,* ed. Alexandra Oleson and John Voss, pp. 211–248. Baltimore: Johns Hopkins.

Ruttan, Vernon. 1983. *Agricultural Research Policy.* Minneapolis: University of Minnesota Press.

Tweeten, Luther G. 1971. "The Search for a Theory and Methodology of Research Resource Allocation." In *Resource Allocation in Agricultural Research,* ed. Walter L. Fishel, pp. 25–61. Minneapolis: University of Minnesota Press.

U.S. Department of Agriculture. 1981. *A Time to Choose: Summary Report on the Structure of Agriculture.* Washington, D.C.: U.S. Dept. of Agriculture.

Waggoner, Paul E. 1976. "Research and Education in American Agriculture." *Agricultural History* 50:230–247.

Wallace, Henry A. 1934a. "Research and Adjustment March Together." USDA Agricultural Adjustment Administration. Washington, D.C.: United States Government Printing Office.

————. 1934b. "The Social Advantages and Disadvantages of the Engineering-Scientific Approach to Civilization." *Science* 79:1–5.

Wells, George. 1969. *Garden in the West: A Dramatic Account of Science in Agriculture.* New York: Dodd, Mead.

White, H.C. 1899. "President's Address." In *Proceedings of the Twelfth Annual Convention of the Association of American Agricultural Colleges and Experiment Stations, Held at Washington, D.C., November 15–17, 1898,* pp. 34–42. USDA Office of Experiment Stations Bulletin No. 65. Washington, D.C.: Government Printing Office.

Whitten, Jamie L. 1966. *That We May Live.* Princeton, N.J.: D. Van Nostrand.
Young, Harold N. 1975. *The Virginia Agricultural Experiment Station, 1886–1966.* Charlottesville: University Press of Virginia.

# 7

# The Context and Implications of the National Agricultural Research, Extension, and Teaching Act of 1977

## Dale L. Stansbury

The fishing report for the Chesapeake Bay is a regular summer feature of the *Washington Post*. These reports describe fishing in the world's largest estuary at a few selected points of reference such as "buoy 52," "the Bay Bridge," or "Point no Point." The fishing could be equal or superior in a thousand other spots in the Bay but for the lack of a reference point they go unreported.

Agricultural research, extension, and teaching legislation—like the Bay—has relatively few reference points. The legislation stretches over 120 years, fills hundreds of pages of the U.S. code and touches on nearly every imaginable issue from apples to zygotes, but most of it is generally uncharted or unknown except for those historical reference points like "Morrill," "Hatch," and "Smith-Lever." The National Agricultural Research, Extension, and Teaching Act of 1977, commonly known as the 1977 Farm Bill, is a current and prominent reference point, particularly its Title XIV. It has become almost equal to Morrill, Hatch and Smith-Lever in discussions on agricultural research. How important is Title XIV and what are its continuing implications for the future of agricultural research, extension, and teaching?

The only way to assess the importance and implications of Title XIV of the 1977 Farm Bill is to put it in the social, economic, scientific, and political context of that time. It did not result from a single event or interest group, nor is it a concensus statement of objectives. Rather, it is the amalgamation of several decades of thought, hope, and debate by a complex group of interests—many of which held conflicting views regarding agricultural research and the objectives of Title XIV.

## The Social Context

Socially, American agriculture, and especially agricultural science, enjoyed blissful inattention during the 1950s and 1960s. The long struggle of man to break free of the spectre of hunger seemed to come to the United States most unexpectedly with World War II. Many of the food rationing programs proved to be unnecessary or of limited importance as the war mobilization effort drew upon a stockpile of technology and resources to provide both guns and butter. The remarkable story of the agricultural war effort is detailed in the composite USDA "yearbook" of agriculture for 1943–1947, entitled *Science in Farming* (USDA, 1947).

As a nation we asked one question of agriculture in that period—how much can you produce? With this new demand, new technologies, and new zeal, agriculture exceeded anyone's expectations.

The happy days of the 50s were even less demanding in social accounting of agriculture than the War period. Nationally, we were enjoying the recent victories over the economic depression and world dictators. We did make a gesture to help with world hunger through passage of P.L. 480 (the Food for Peace Program). While many have suggested the only objective of P.L. 480 was to dump our surpluses, it was an honest gesture of good will. We were happy and had surpluses and we were glad to share. We may have been naïve to a fault, but we were definitely not malicious.

During the 60s our national focus switched to major issues of civil rights for our citizens. While this concern did result in the beginning of major domestic food programs, it overwhelmed emerging issues like environmental degradation. Moreover, the mounting debate of the Viet Nam War distracted attention from virtually all other issues including agricultural research.

However, the early 70s brought social and environmental issues to the forefront and with them a sudden and intense criticism of agricultural research that totally shocked the system. The system had had significant doubts about many of the miracle technologies for decades. Secretary Anderson in his 1947 foreword to *Science in Farming* (USDA, 1947), expressed concern that DDT killed honey bees as well as Japanese Beetles and about acquired resistance. The concerns were increased by the haunting questions that Rachel Carson raised. However, the system responded with the standard scientific rationalization—we cannot fear the unknown.

The sudden proclamations that the system—USDA, land-grant colleges, state experiment stations, extension, and agri-business—was evil or at least maliciously negligent were not comprehensible to men and women who had devoted their lives to doing what they believed was good.

Their reaction was predictably defensive. They circled the wagons and began shooting back.

## Economic Context

Since the early 1900s, except for brief interludes with high war-related demand, agriculture has had one economic condition—surplus production and depressed prices. Most of the nation has had little interest in the economic problems of agriculture. There were several "high food price" periods when consumers expressed discontent, but the actual criticism was limited. In the early 70s, however, several dramatic events caused significant economic shifts and new public awareness of agriculture.

Demand for animal products, especially beef, increased due to general increases in income levels and a sharp expansion of food stamp programs. The consequent increased demand for feed resulted in upward price pressure. This was further stimulated by production problems, such as the corn blight in 1970, the floods, drought, and early frost in 1974, and similar problems around the world. The worldwide problems resulted in the world food crisis. Massive Soviet grain purchases and a general opening of world markets caused a quantum change in U.S. and world markets.

Monetary and fiscal policy changes, such as the decision to let the dollar float, improved national money markets, and large federal deficits all combined to shatter the long term economic stability of the United States. The so called energy crisis that was precipitated by OPEC not only shook the economy, it brought into question the sustainability of a petroleum-based agriculture. A direct effect of the economic changes was a tightening of available funds for universities and university research. Researchers who faced budget cuts quickly identified the funds in agricultural research as a prime replacement source. However, agriculture research was also enduring real declines in federal funding. The agricultural research community was therefore actively working to protect its base and to get expanded funds.

## Scientific Context

The agricultural research system, with a Federal Charter in the 1887 Hatch Act, was the first federal research effort. It predates centralized planning, priority setting, and management. Major concerns at that time were states' rights and public purpose. This meant that the states decided on the specifics of the research and extension programs within the legislative parameters. The states rights position was very clearly stated by Representative Lever in the House Report (1914) for the Smith-Lever Act:

> The principles involved are those of cooperation, the Federal Government aiding by advice and assistance in coordinating effort and the States performing the more important details of the local work. This bill places the responsibility for the actual conduct of the work proposed in the agricultural college and provides specifically for the adjustment of work to local conditions through a cooperative relationship established between the college of agriculture and the Secretary of Agriculture. There is thus avoided any possibility of developing a centralized and dominating agency, as is also avoided any possibility of forcing upon the States types or kinds of work not readily adapted to the needs of the people.

The public purpose doctrine grew out of the 19th century "land granting" tendencies of the Congress. Congressional land grants to private companies to encourage development of railroads were challenged in court as unconstitutional, but were generally upheld on the basis of sufficient public purpose. The same debate slowed the original passage of the Morrill Act and resulted in the 1858 veto by President Buchanan. This public purpose focus is clearly evident in Section I of the Bankhead-Jones Act of 1935 (7 U.S.C. 427) which states:

> It is hereby declared to be the policy of the Congress to promote the efficient production and utilization of products of the soil as essential to the health and welfare of our people and to promote a sound and prosperous agriculture and rural life as indispensable to the maintenance of maximum employment and national prosperity. . . . for the attainment of these objectives, the Secretary of Agriculture is authorized and directed to conduct and to stimulate research into the laws and principles underlying the basic problems of agriculture in its broadest aspects.

The decentralized and applied nature of the agricultural research and extension system is an anomaly among modern Federal science programs and is the antithesis to "modern" OMB organizational concepts.

In the 1970s, these organizational "flaws" provided a hungry research community every justification to demand access to the cloistered funds of agricultural research. Whether the motives were old fashioned greed or high principle, the arguments quickly fell into a subjective debate of whether the nonagricultural research deities (basic research, competitive grants and peer review) were more holy than the agricultural research deities (applied research, formula funds, and public purpose).

A debate also developed about the nature of agricultural research and the implications of this research for the structure, environment, and sustainability of agriculture.  In essence, agricultural research was being accused of engaging in science to the detriment of society rather than in the service of society.  CAST, the Council on Agricultural Science and Technology, along with other establishment representatives, set forth to correct these "foolish" thoughts.

## The Political Context

The political context reflected all of the above.  In Congress, the agriculture committees were viewed by most members during the 50s and 60s as being relatively unattractive.  The committees were dominated by senior members from agricultural states primarily in the South and Midwest. Most of the committees' legislative calendars dealt with agricultural surpluses and low farm incomes.  The party caucuses had difficulty recruiting members to serve on the Agriculture Committees and at times "forced" junior members onto the committees.

In the early 70s, the Russian grain purchases, the world food crisis, the expansion of the food stamp program, the revision of the Federal Insecticide, Fungicide and Rodenticide Act (FIFRA), and the volatility in the economy reversed this attitude.  Agriculture became front page news in the *New York Times* as well as the *Des Moines Register.*  Members, including urban members, clamored to get on the committees.  The House Agriculture Committee was nearly doubled in size and the Senate Committee was increased by a half.  Hearings before the committees became national media events with long witness lists.  Environmental, poverty, and religious interest groups joined the traditional agricultural groups in attempts to set "farm policy."  Their agendas were frequently in sharp conflict.

The emotional nature of these issues stimulated sharp philosophical differences and turf battles between congressional committees.  In the House, The Committee on Science and Technology and the Agriculture Committee developed alternative views of "good research."  In the Senate, the Agriculture Committee and the Commerce Committee had an extended skirmish over FIFRA.  In this latter case, the committees reflected the position of their respective interest groups.  For instance, the environmentalists had relatively more influence with the Senate Commerce Committee and agri-business interests had more support in the Senate Agriculture Committee.

These same political factors affected the executive branch.  USDA, EPA, OSHA, State, Interior, and HEW experienced significant conflicts among themselves in the 70s.  For example, State and USDA were in significant disagreement about the propriety of using food as a diplomatic weapon.  EPA and USDA were played against each other on the pesticide issue by their respective clientele.

## The Confluence of the Cross Currents

In the mid-70s, the many cross currents of perceptions about agricultural research were channeled into a common arena. Nearly all the interest groups came to see legislation as the key to correct the problem, even though there was no agreement about what the problem was. There were, however, a multitude of panaceas offered. The difficulty was that no two agreed and all were based on perceptions of the system that were less than accurate.

For example, the *New York Times* reported that an answer to the world hunger crisis was to be found in high lysine corn—a high-protein corn. The article suggested that the agricultural research community had neglected research on this valuable crop variety. The accusation of neglect was, in fact, wrong. The University of Illinois, for example, had done six decades of research on high lysine corn. This research demonstrated there were, and are, real limits to this panacea for hunger. Yields and total food production per acre of high lysine varieties tend to be lower than other varieties. High lysine corn also has a higher moisture content which results in various storage and handling problems.

The hunger lobby accused American agriculture of devoting too much time to animal agriculture. They offered the panacea of not eating hamburger as a solution to world hunger. In fact, about twice as much crop research is funded as animal research. They also overlooked the value of animal transformation of inedible cellulose to high value foods, especially protein. (This idea was not limited to non-agricultural groups. An Iowa State agronomist testified before the Senate Agriculture Committee that the world food crisis was due to too much animal research and too little *agronomic* research!)

Agricultural addiction to nonrenewable energy sources—petro-chemical products—was denounced. The research system was accused of perpetuating this addiction. Some saw the ultimate solution in solar energy or renewable biomass energy sources. In fact, passive as well as active solar and biomass energy systems had been research projects of many experiment stations for decades. However, then prevailing economic circumstances precluded application of these technologies. In addition, actual agricultural production uses a relatively small share of the total U.S. energy budget. Air conditioning uses more and the energy used in homes to refrigerate and cook food matches the energy used on farms to produce food.

Use of chemical fertilizers and pesticides, varietal development to meet marketing problems, as well as food processing were denounced as creating inferior quality products and unsafe foods. Contrasting arguments pointed to the "facts" of lower rates of food-borne diseases, lower rates of chronic food related deficiencies, plus universal and continuous supplies of a broad variety of foods. These same technologies are accused of being environmentally destructive and unnecessary. There is little question that pesticides and fertilizers have resulted in environmental problems. However, it is not clear that they are unnecessary. Mother Nature does not discriminate. Weeds are equal to humans in her plan.

Agricultural technology, and thus agricultural research, was perceived by some as dictating agricultural structure. In its simplist form, the argument was that agriculture research was destroying the family farm. In these discussions family farms are equated with small farms. The economic viability of "smallness" is enhanced by USDA studies that state all economies of scale are achieved with relatively small production units. The agricultural research community argued that the technologies they developed were size neutral. Regardless of the correctness of this latter argument, research was responding to effective demand.

The small farm fans and simple economic analyses tend to overlook the natural inclination of farm producers to achieve income levels that permit more than subsistence and that scale economics are constant over a wide range of production unit sizes. "Family farmers" have little tolerance for $50,000 bureaucrats who feel producers should be happy with five or ten thousand dollar net incomes. The small farm debate also fails to recognize the *only* justification in having state and national food and farm policies is to produce food for people. Clearly, an essential requirement for food production is a viable production sector. The overall goal does require consideration of the quality of the production sector. However, Ken Boulding's question "What is the difference between family farmers and family dry cleaners?" is thought-provoking.

Nonagricultural scientists perceived agricultural scientists as pedestrian and behind the plow. They either ignored the frequent successes of agricultural scientists in the general grant fields or argued that these "exceptions" were very few and only proved their case: that the good scientists in agriculture had to go outside to get funding for "meaningful" research.

Agricultural scientists accused the other side of a lack of relevance and real social contributions. The "other" research system as embodied in NIH and NSF has been characterized by Daniel Yankelovich (1984) as a social contract where scientists say: "leave us to do our own work in our own way. Support us and give us the resources we need. Have patience and faith. Do not demand quick, utilitarian payoffs. Do these things and you will be amply rewarded. They also say with great regularity, 'If you don't do it my way, it's inferior.'"

The land-grant system also held a number of misconceptions. A major problem in their minds was the "unequal" treatment of the Agricultural Research Service (ARS) of USDA cooperative state research funding.

The principal factor in this belief was the supplemental appropriations opportunities available to ARS and their inclusion in federally mandated pay raises. Recognizing that statistics are third after lies and damned lies, the statistics suggest that changes in funding rates for each were almost exactly the same over the period of perceived difference. Between 1970 and 1980, Hatch funding increased by 114 percent and ARS funding went up 131 percent. ARS did better, right? Maybe, but if you adjust the ARS budget for the special human nutrition research initiative of Congress, the ARS increase is 113 percent. So they did equally well, right? Maybe, but if you adjust the state funding for special grant funding, their increase from 1970 to 1980 was 132 percent.

It was in this wonderful climate of "concensus" that Congress began to work on legislation to address the real and perceived problems of agricultural research.

### The Legislative Response

The legislative response was initiated in 1976 in the House. The House Agriculture Committee bill was passed by the House and included the following purposes:

1. to emphasize agricultural research and education as distinct missions of the United States Department of Agriculture;
2. to encourage and facilitate the development and implementation of more efficient and environmentally sound methods of producing, processing, marketing, and utilizing food, fiber, and wood products;
3. to provide for research on human nutrition in order to maximize the health and vitality of the people of the United States; and
4. to provide a mechanism for identifying the Nation's highest priorities for agricultural research, to assure that high priority research is effectively implemented, and to be certain that all research related to agriculture is effectively planned, coordinated, and evaluated.

In addition, the bill would have established a national agricultural research policy advisory board, ostensibly to provide new authority for competitive grants, and to assure adequate funding for mission oriented research.

This effort stalled in the Senate for several reasons. First, the need for more authorization was not clear. Every purported new authority already existed somewhere in the more than 50 research authorizations already in the books. The research and education mission was included in the Organic Act of 1862; items 2. and 3. were included in the Bankhead-Jones Act of 1935 as amended in 1946; and item 4. is implicitly included in these acts as well as others. Competitive grants were provided for in PL

89–106, passed in 1965. Second, there were questions about the function, membership, and cost of the policy board. The most important factor was the desire of the Senate Committee to have time to analyze the proposal more fully. Thus, the Senate Committee decided to hold the issue until the 1977 Farm Bill.

### The '77 Farm Bill

The 1977 Farm Bill was initiated by the Senate as S 275. The research title was originally Title XIII, which seemed appropriate given the tensions between the various interest groups. While there were many differences between the House and Senate versions of what became Title XIV, they were more differences of tone than of substance. The Senate version was more general in approach and stressed communications. The House version had greater specificity and stressed coordination and planning. It should be noted, however, that neither expected nor called for centralized control.

At the risk of bruising the self-esteem of the research community, it must be noted that Title XIV was not the primary focus of the two committees during the consideration of the '77 Farm Bill. In fact, resolution of the differences was delegated to staff while the members dealt with commodity programs and food stamp issues.

The final version incorporated the major items of both the House and Senate titles and the legitimacy of every concern was ultimately recognized. The result was a voluminous document that "found" that each concern expressed should receive "appropriate" attention. It called for new initiatives in fifteen areas, authorized a variety of grant programs to address the needs, and created a system of coordination and planning. (See Appendix A for the "findings and purposes.")

A reflection of the process is that the verbiage went from four pages of legislative style language in the 1976 House bill to 41 pages of language in Title XIV of P.L. 95–113. The perception of virtually everyone involved with agricultural research outside of Congress was "now it will work right." The only problem with this concensus was that the term "right" was defined differently by each observer. In addition, as an authorization bill, the language, especially in the findings and purpose sections, had and continues to have little or no direct effect on the point of greatest interest—appropriations.

### Implementation of Title XIV

Title XIV was implemented by the Department of Agriculture under Secretary Bergland. The Department at that time had several top administrators who had questions about the existing research system, including Secretary Bergland, Assistant Secretary Foreman, and Assistant Secretary Hjort. Their first concrete efforts to implement Title XIV—a $22 million competitive grants program with an "unrelated" $22 million cut in Hatch funding, plus the appointment of anti-establishment people to the Users Advisory Board (UAB)—amounted to a declaration of war. This adversarial situation was worsened by organizational decisions. The creation of the Science and Education Administration not only reduced extension and cooperative research to sub-agency levels, it took away their parking spaces in the executive parking lot at USDA.

The planning and coordination process, especially the Joint Council, became mired in a preoccupation with form rather than substance. The matrix of geographic, institutional and program representation for regional councils rivaled national input/output charts. This problem was aggravated by the fact that this process excluded the existing planning systems. This period was less than peaceful; in fact, "guerrilla warfare" would be a reasonable description.

Congress bears part of the responsibility for these problems. The willingness to declare everything important is a poor guide. Further, the Senate Committee was too precise in its planning scheme for the UAB, Joint Council, and the Federal Subcommittee in the White House science office. The committee's idea had been to differentiate and assign responsibilities to appropriate groups. The UAB was to be an early warning system to bring to the surface perceived problems that users were confronting. The Joint Council was to be a science court which would determine the legitimacy of these perceived issues. It was also to be a federal information forum composed of representatives from USDA and other federal agencies with only limited representation from the states. The Subcommittee was to be the executive branch policy forum.

In practice, the form was maintained but the responsibilities were merged. In essence everyone became policy spokesmen. In addition, the Conference Committee deleted the other federal representatives from the Joint Council in a final compromise as they were walking out the door because one conferee didn't want OSHA or EPA messing around in agriculture. This seriously damaged the idea of a government-wide federal communications effort and left the Joint Council as a bilateral council of USDA and the states (but one heavily weighted toward USDA). Given the personalities and climate of the time these factors predicated the early ineffectiveness of the Joint Council. The problems were not resolved until amendments were made in the 1981 Farm Bill and a shift in leadership had taken place at the USDA. These amendments did not address the federal interagency communications issue. Interagency communications are now being developed; however, this is almost exclusively the result of personal dedication by individual administrators at USDA and other agencies.

## An Evaluation of Title XIV

My most critical assessment of Title XIV is that from a legislative perspective it was unnecessary. It resulted in severe acrimony and delayed progress in cooperation and communications. In addition, it caused a preoccupation with form rather than substance.

My positive assessment is that it has fully brought out critical issues of conflict. The diatribes have become dialogue. The dialogue has resulted in broader appreciation of the system, is expanding the compass of research within the system, and is reducing interagency tensions. Overall, I would suggest that it is enhancing the responsiveness and performance level of agricultural research. It has not, however, caused an absolute metamorphosis of the system, nor should it.

The structure of the agricultural research system is uniquely adapted to the needs of our country. This point is made by Nelson and Langlois (1983:11):

> The federal-state system of agricultural experiment stations evolved in a way that took advantage of the market structure in agriculture, marshaling the support of farmers and giving them an important position in the evaluation and selection of projects. Coupled with the regional nature of agricultural technology, this led to a system in which farmers see it as advantageous to them to advance even very specific technologies as quickly as possible. As a model for the administration of a government-supported applied R&D program, the agricultural system is quite instructive. It is highly decentralized, and specific resource allocation decisions are made at state and county levels. Those decisions respond with some sensitivity to the demands of two constituencies: farmers (given voice through state legislatures) and the agricultural science community.

In the language of the social scientist, we might call this a "captured" system, in much the same sense that transportation, communication, and other industries are said to have captured their regulators. Capture of this sort is not very often congruent with the general interest of consumers; but in the case of agriculture the system seems to have evolved in a salutary fashion.

Agriculture is a remarkably complex subject. The variations of commodities, climates, and markets exceed that of any other research field. The entire system is dynamic with the problems changing in many cases as fast as the solutions are found. While perfection can be hoped for, it is unrealistic to expect any system to significantly exceed the social and economic standards of the nation. Nor can any human institution be expected to know in advance every effect—positive and negative—of its activities. As a general rule, a problem must be defined before it can be solved. No one can require solutions before we know what we are trying to solve. Nor can we stop all inquiry because discovery and change bring mixed blessings. The system has demonstrated honest responsiveness and is becoming increasingly proactive.

The single issue before us is not structure, priority setting, or focus of research; it is control. Each interest group wants control ostensibly because it wants to do good.

A democracy is a frustrating experience for individuals who seek change and improvement. But as Churchill suggested, it is the least worst system. A market economy is equally frustrating for people who have values different than those expressed in the market place. It is easy to declare that the people and the market are being manipulated. However, I don't believe this rationalization will justify dictatorship by the benevolent elitist, much less the greedy egotist.

For agricultural research to meet the challenges of the future and to make its maximum contribution in the future, it must remain flexible, responsive and relevant. A constant battle against the despotism of tradition must be waged. The status quo of departments, disciplines, and budgets must constantly be challenged. This is what the Title XIV experience has done, is doing, and is its greatest contribution. There is no doubt that the system has flaws; however, it has performed remarkable feats. It is not static. It is constantly changing and usually identifies and solves problems with neither fan-fare nor public awareness. It has a strategic capacity in that its structure fits the problem. Further, the system is not a monolithic entity. Its breadth of research focus and the philosophic breadth of the system's individual scientists assure its ultimate responsiveness.

**Appendix A: Findings and Purposes of The National Agricultural Research, Extension, and Teaching Act of 1977.**

*Findings (Section 1402)*

Congress finds that-

1. the Federal Government of the United States has provided funding support for agricultural research and extension for many years in order to promote and protect the general health and welfare of the people of the United States, and this support has significantly contributed to the development of the Nation's agricultural system;

2. the agencies conducting such federally supported research were established at different times in response to different and specific needs and their work is not fully coordinated;
3. these agencies have only been partially successful in responding to the needs of all persons affected by their research, and useful information produced through such federally supported research is not being efficiently transferred to the people of the United States;
4. expanded agricultural research and extension are needed to meet the rising demand for food and fiber caused by increases in world-wide population and food shortages due to short-term localized, and adverse climatic conditions;
5. increased research is necessary to alleviate inadequacies of the marketing system (including storage, transportation, and distribution of agricultural and forest products) which have impaired United States agricultural production and utilization;
6. advances in food and agricultural sciences and technology have become increasingly limited by the concentration upon the thorough development and exploitation of currently known scientific principles and technological approaches at the expense of more fundamental research, and a strong research effort in the basic sciences is necessary to achieve breakthroughs in knowledge that can support new and innovative food and agricultural technologies;
7. Federal funding levels for agricultural research and extension in recent years have not been commensurate with needs stemming from changes in United States agricultural practices and the world food and agricultural situation;
8. new Federal initiatives are needed in the areas of
   A. research to find alternatives to technologies based on fossil fuels;
   B. research and extension on human nutrition and food consumption patterns in order to improve the health and vitality of the people of the United States;
   C. research to find solutions to environmental problems caused by technological changes in food and agricultural production;
   D. aquacultural research and extension;
   E. research and extension directed toward improving the management and use of the Nation's natural and renewable resources, in order to meet the increased demand for forest products, conserve water resources (through irrigation management, tail water reuse, desalinization, crop conversion, and other water conservation techniques), conserve soil resources, and properly manage rangelands;
   F. improving and expanding the research and extension programs in home economics;

G. extension programs in energy conservation;

H. extension programs in forestry and natural resources, with special emphasis to be given to improving the productivity of small private woodlands, modernizing wood harvesting and utilization, developing and disseminating reliable multiple-use resource management information to all landowners and consumers, and the general public, wildlife, watershed, and recreational management, and cultural practices including reforestation, protection, and related matters);

I. research on climate, drought, and weather modification as factors in food and agricultural production;

J. more intensive agricultural research and extension programs oriented to the needs of small farmers and their families and the family farm system, which is a vital component of the agricultural production capacity of this country;

K. research to expand export markets for agricultural commodities;

L. development and implementation, through research, of more efficient, less wasteful, and environmentally sound methods of producing, processing, marketing, and utilizing food, fiber, waste products, other nonfood agricultural products, and forest and rangeland products;

M. expanded programs of animal disease and health care research and extension;

N. research to develop new crops, in order to expand our use of varied soils and increase the choice of nutritional and economically viable crops available for cultivation; and

O. investigation and analysis of the practicability, desirability, and feasibility of using organic waste materials to improve soil tilth and fertility, and extension programs to disseminate practical information resulting from such investigations and analyses; and

9. the existing agricultural research system consisting of the Federal Government, the land-grant colleges and universities, other colleges and universities engaged in agricultural research, the agricultural experiment stations, and the private sector constitute an essential national resource which must serve as the foundation for any further strengthening of agricultural research in the United States.

*Purposes (Section 1403)*

The purposes of this title are to-

1. establish firmly the Department of Agriculture as the lead agency in the Federal Government for the food and agricultural sciences, and to emphasize that agricultural research, extension, and teaching are distinct missions of the Department of Agriculture;

2. undertake the special measures set forth in this title to improve the coordination and planning of agricultural research, identify needs and establish priorities for such research, assure that high priority research is given adequate funding, assure that national agricultural research, extension, and teaching objectives are fully achieved, and assure that the results of agricultural research are effectively communicated and demonstrated to farmers, processors, handlers, consumers, and all other users who can benefit therefrom;

3. increase cooperation and coordination in the performance of agricultural research by Federal departments and agencies, the States, State agricultural experiment stations, colleges and universities, and user groups;

4. enable the Federal Government, the States, colleges and universities, and others to implement needed agricultural research, extension, and teaching programs, including the initiatives specified in section 1402(8) of this title, through the establishment of new programs and the improvement of existing programs, as provided for in this title;

5. establish a new program of grants for high-priority agricultural research to be awarded on the basis of competition among scientific research workers and all colleges and universities;

6. establish a new program of grants for facilities and instrumentation used in agricultural research; and

7. establish a new program of education grants and fellowships to strengthen training and research programs in the food and agricultural sciences, to be awarded on the basis of competition.

## References

Nelson, Richard R., and Richard N. Langlois. 1983. "Industrial Innovation Policy: Lessons from American History." *Science* 210:814–818.

U.S. Department of Agriculture. 1947. *Science in Farming; Yearbook of Agriculture 1943–1947.* Washington, D.C.: U.S. Government Printing Office.

U.S. Congress. House. 1914. *Cooperative Agricultural Extension Work: Report to Accompany H.R. 7951.* 63d Cong., 2d Sess., House Rpt. 110.

Yankelovich, Daniel. 1984. "Science and the Public Process: Why the Gap Must Close." *Issues in Science and Technology* 1:6–12.

# 8

# Historical Evolution of the State Agricultural Experiment Station System

## John Patrick Jordan, Paul F. O'Connell, and Roland R. Robinson

### Introduction

The publicly supported agricultural research system has two major components. One is the U.S. Department of Agriculture (USDA) component consisting of the research agencies of the Agricultural Research Service (ARS), the Economic Research Service (ERS), the Forest Service (FS), etc. The other is the state research system—which is supported by both state and federal funds, the latter being administered by the Cooperative State Research Service (CSRS). There are also several subsystems within this total system, but we will confine our attention to the State Agricultural Experiment Stations that are associated with Land-Grant Universities, hereafter referred to as SAES.

Initially this chapter highlights the legislative actions that institutionalized the SAES, including some of the major forces involved. The next section discusses the key differences between the federal and state

The authors wish to acknowledge the assistance of Dr. Eldon E. Weeks (Cooperative State Research Service, USDA) in formulating the concepts and in gathering data during the early part of manuscript development.

partners. The third section addresses accomplishments of the system and the last section provides a short description of future challenges.

## Legislative Actions

In 1796, President George Washington recommended the establishment of an agricultural branch of the national government. In 1841 the president of Norwich University proposed to Congress that it appropriate funds from land sales to be distributed to the states for establishing institutions to teach agriculture. During the 1840s and 1850s, state legislatures, farm leaders, the editors of agricultural periodicals, and farm organizations (particularly the United States Agriculture Society) urged Congress to act on both of these proposals.

In 1839, Congress appropriated $1,000 of Patent Office funds for collecting agricultural statistics, conducting agricultural investigations, and distributing seeds. These efforts were continued, even though they were opposed by some groups as being inadequate or as representing federal intervention. The matter was settled by the establishment of the Department of Agriculture and the land-grant colleges in 1862 as part of an agrarian reform package offered to the voters by the Republican Party (Rasmussen and Hildreth, 1983).

### Establishment of the Land-Grant System

The Morrill Act of 1862 was the foundation legislation for the land-grant colleges. The primary focus of this act was not research but to provide an opportunity for higher education by all citizens of the United States, especially those identified as the working classes. The legislation states that these colleges should: "teach such branches of learning as are related to agriculture and the mechanical arts, in such manner as the legislatures of the States may respectively prescribe, in order to promote the liberal and practical education of the industrial classes in the several pursuits and professions in life."

According to Knoblauch et al. (1962), the indistinct nature of the research authority in the Morrill Act, compared to the emphatic assignment of a teaching mission, prompted the first generation of college administrators to doubt that the act authorized the colleges to experiment, except as an aid in the instruction of students.

At the 1871 convention of agriculture educators,* President John M. Gregory, from the University of Illinois, called attention to the seemingly

---

*Convention of Friends of Agriculture Education, 1872. Meeting held at Chicago on the 24th and 25th of August, 1871.

incidental role the Morrill Act had allotted to research. A tone of urgency sounded in Gregory's words when he observed that the need for a well-developed system of research had become a very serious practical question. Farmers, beset with problems they could not solve, were bringing to the college staff questions that could be answered only by astute, continuous, and productive experimentation. The infant colleges, depending for their existence on the public purse and public confidence, could not afford to ignore the public need; neither could they afford to mislead the farm population by giving it incorrect advice lest the potent suspicion of "book-farmers" would deepen into scorn (Knoblauch *et al.*, 1962).

After considerable discussion in the press and at public meetings about state versus federal responsibilities, the science and education leaders of the time were able to convince Congress of the need for federal funding of agricultural research. A forceful voice in causing this action to occur was Professor Eugene Hilgard, Director of the California Station at Berkeley.

In an 1882 *Atlantic Monthly* article Hilgard argued that the federal government should recognize an unfortunate situation of nationwide dimension—namely, that states most in need of improved technology did not have the resources and collective will to provide the necessary support. The federal government, then should follow a corrective policy of enlightened intervention and supply substantial aid to each land-grant college for the specific purpose of operating a station.

The precedents for federal action, Hilgard pointed out, lay immediately at hand. Congress could follow the principle of the Morrill Act and provide additional endowments, or it could increase its annual appropriation to the Department of Agriculture, which by direct cooperation with the land-grant colleges would operate a station in each state. Hilgard preferred the latter alternative because it would enable the linkage of two great potentials: the scientific capacity of a federal research center at the nation's capital, and the existing collection of talents awaiting formal organization at the agricultural college in each state. This combination of resources, Hilgard declared, would produce a "radiating network" of scientific research.

The result of all this discussion was the Hatch Act of 1887. Its purpose was to establish agricultural experiment stations in connection with the land-grant colleges that were authorized in 1862. These experiment stations were to conduct scientific investigations and experiments that would provide practical and useful information for the people of the United States. The act specifically mentioned original research and verified experiments. Research topics included:

- the physiology of plants and animals,
- the diseases of plants and animals,

- crop rotation advantages,
- the chemical composition of plants at different stages of growth,
- analysis of soil and water,
- chemical composition of manures,
- the digestibility of different kinds of foods for animals,
- the scientific and economic questions involved in the production of butter and cheese, and
- other such research or experiments bearing directly on U.S. agriculture.

The 1887 act also indicated the need for publishing bulletins or reports of progress.


### Follow-up Legislation

Under the Morrill Act, the federal government was unable to gain state cooperation in the provision of support for separate black institutions. To overcome this problem, a second Morrill Act was passed in 1890 specifically to support black land-grant institutions. These sixteen institutions, plus the Tuskegee Institute, are called the 1890 Institutions. Subsequent lack of federal and state financial support generally constrained the 1890 Institutions to teaching roles until the 1960s when the civil rights movements resulted in sufficient funding for these institutions to begin establishment of research and extension programs (Mayberry, 1976).

The primary purpose of the Adams Act of 1906 and the Purnell Act of 1925 was to provide for additional federal investment in state experiment station research. In the Purnell Act, two additional research topics (or goals) were added: the establishment and maintenance of a permanent and efficient agricultural industry, and the development and improvement of the rural home and rural life.

The various research areas described in the legislation for the achievement of the first goal included the production, manufacturing, preparation, use, distribution, and marketing of agricultural products. Since considerable emphasis was given to agricultural industry problems encountered beyond the farm gate, it was obviously assumed that the research to be supported was not only to advance the farm sector of the agricultural industry but the market sector as well.

Sociological and economic investigations were to be conducted to achieve the second goal. The post–World War I depression in agriculture, surplus production and depressed farm income, the beginning of the exodus of farmers from agriculture and the migration of rural people to urban areas probably had an influence on including "the development and improvement of the rural home and rural life" as a research goal in the Purnell legislation. Apparently it was beginning to be realized at the time that research to generate new production technology was not adequate by itself and that economic and sociological investigations were also needed to produce the information and knowledge required to achieve this people-oriented goal.

Cooperative Agricultural Extension work was established by the Smith-Lever Act of 1914. The legislation authorized the U.S. Department of Agriculture to provide, through the land-grant colleges, instruction and practical demonstrations in agriculture and home economics and related subjects and to encourage the application of such information by demonstrations, publications, and other means to persons not attending or resident in the colleges. The system thus established is a grassroots one with local people, land-grant universities, and USDA sharing the responsibility of determining educational needs and program design. The basic job of Cooperative Extension is to help people identify and solve their farm, home, and community problems.

The Bankhead-Jones Act of 1935 increased support for research into basic laws and principles relating to agriculture and for extension and teaching activities. This legislation set a new direction in terms of funding processes. Until the passage of the act, all federal funds had been distributed equally among the experiment stations. Also, the three earlier acts (Hatch, Adam, and Purnell) provided funds for the support of experiment station research with no requirement that the state in which the station was located provide any matching funds. The Bankhead-Jones Act modifed these two principles. First, federal funds appropriated under this act were allocated to each station in relation to the relative importance of the rural population (both farm and non-farm) of the state.

Secondly the states were required to match the level of federal funds received to support experiment station research. The allocation of federal funds to the experiment station on the basis of rural population made it legitimate to expend federal funds to advance the welfare of both segments of the rural population–farm and non-farm. The research agenda of the experiment station could therefore expand accordingly to encompass the problems confronting farmers and rural non-farmers alike.

The amended Bankhead-Jones Act of 1946 provided additional support for research into basic laws and principles of agriculture production and funds were specifically designated for research to improve and facilitate the marketing and distribution of agricultural products. It provides for the establishment of a national advisory committee to consult with the Secretary and the Department in making recommendations on the research and service work authorized by the act and in obtaining the cooperation of producers, farm organizations, industry groups and federal and state agencies in the development of these research and service programs. The act also authorized funding of regional research. This amendment allocated 25 percent of the increase in Hatch funding to SAES to a regional research fund to support cooperative research on problems of concern to more than one state. The legislation established a Committee of Nine, elected by and representing experiment station directors, to review and approve regional research projects.

The amended Hatch Act of 1955 consolidated the several laws providing federal funds to support SAES research. It did not significantly alter the intent or direction of earlier acts. Language and funding mechanisms were standardized and clarified.

## Recent Legislation Activities

The most recent federal legislation having a significant impact on state Agricultural Experiment Stations was the National Agricultural Research, Extension, and Teaching Policy Act of 1977, as amended in 1981. Highlights of this legislation include the following:

- It firmly established that the Department of Agriculture is the lead federal agency for the food and agricultural sciences.
- It established an Assistant Secretary of Agriculture for Science and Education to carry out the responsibilities of the 1977 Act as amended in 1981.
- It provided for better cooperation and coordination in the performance of agricultural research by federal departments and agencies, the states, state agricultural experiment stations, colleges and universities, and user groups.
- It recognized that the food and agricultural sciences need extra effort in the basic sciences to achieve breakthroughs in knowledge that can support innovative food and agricultural technologies.
- It established a program of grants for high-priority agricultural research, to be awarded on the basis of competition among scientific research workers at universities, federal agencies, private organizations, and individuals not associated with any institution.
- It established a program of education grants and fellowships to strengthen training and research programs in the food and agricultural sciences.

Action has been taken on all these legislative requirements.

To provide for better cooperation and coordination a Joint Council on Food and Agricultural Sciences was established. To carry out its assignment the Council recently completed four planning documents—a Needs Assessment; a 5-Year Plan; a Priorities Report; and an Accomplishments Report. These documents are being used extensively by those planning and conducting programs of research and education.

To incorporate views of users, a National Agricultural Research and Extension Users Advisory Board was established. The board makes annual recommendations on budgets, program priorities, and agency operations.

Another area of considerable activity is the competitive grants program for research. USDA established a Competitive Research Grants Office (CRGO) in 1978 to implement this section of the legislation. To award grants, CRGO adopted most of the same procedures used by the National Science Foundation. Grants are awarded on the basis of peer review and are open to applicants from the broadest possible spectrum of institutions. To ensure scientific stature and a regular infusion of new viewpoints, program manager positions are occupied by active research scientists on intermittent leave from their institutions. Panel members are also active scientists, selected according to the nature of their research to evaluate proposals.

*Current Program Emphasis in SAES*

In cooperation with USDA agencies, SAES develops projections of research programs every two years. These projections are done within the framework of the Current Research Information System (CRIS). Results are reported in four different categories of which one is program goals (Figure 8.1).

## Characteristics of the State Agricultural Experiment Station System

The performers of public-supported agricultural research and education are located in state and federal institutions with varying administrative and programmatic structures. Each institution/agency has specific roles. However, interaction among "performers" grows out of program linkages and coordination developed through cooperative planning and shared institutional processes. This informal set of linkages provides for articulation among scientists and promotes developments that have helped establish a system-wide approach in research, extension, and higher education. State-managed science and education programs must and do respond to needs expressed at state and local levels, but they also address those national and international issues that have implications for the agricultural and forestry sectors within that state's boundaries. The federally managed science and education programs are directed primarily at national and regional issues, but the findings often have implications at state and local levels, where producers and consumers make their individual decisions. What follows is a brief description of the significant differences between the USDA research system and the State Agricultural Experiment Station system (SAES).

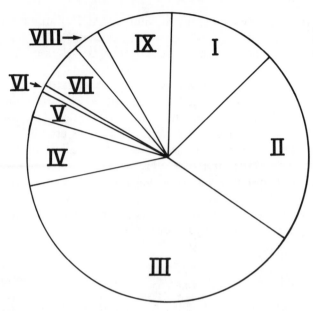

Figure 8.1   1985 Scientist Years of Effort by Goals (SAES)

| Program Goals | | Scientist Years | Percent |
|---|---|---|---|
| I. | Management of Natural Resources | 830 | 12.0 |
| II. | Protection from Pests and Other Hazards | 1559 | 22.6 |
| III. | Decrease Real Production Costs | 2558 | 37.1 |
| IV. | Expand Demand for Agricultural and Forest Products | 565 | 8.2 |
| V. | Improve Marketing Efficiency | 229 | 3.3 |
| VI. | Expand Export Markets: Assist Developing Nations | 49 | 0.7 |
| VII. | Protect Consumer Health and Improve Well Being | 357 | 5.2 |
| VIII. | Improve Rural Family Life | 230 | 3.3 |
| IX. | Community Improvement | 514 | 7.5 |
| | | 6891 | |

First, the SAES is decentralized in terms of administration and facilities. Each of the 50 states has an institutional complex consisting of a Land Grant University, a main experiment station and a network of branch stations. The substations are located in different production areas of each state with unique agro-climatic conditions. Each state's complex is autonomous and administered independently. Elaborate mechanisms have been established, however, for planning and coordinating research among states within regions, across regions and with the USDA research system. The in-house agencies of USDA—ARS, FS, and ERS—have networks of regional research facilities, but these are administered and managed as total units.

Second, the SAES complex within each state carries out three functions—research, teaching, and extension. Most of the time the scientist carries out a minimum of two functions, and sometimes three. The research function is concerned with the generation of new knowledge and technology while the extension function is concerned with its adoption and utilization by users. The educational function is usually closely integrated with the research function. Graduate students complete a research project under the direction of a scientist. The thesis or dissertation based on the research serves as a partial fulfillment for the degree requirements. Hence, the research function has dual outputs, a research product and an agricultural scientist or trained worker. The major supply of agricultural scientists in the U.S. and an increasing supply of agricultural scientists in developing countries are products of the SAES system. At the present time about 35 percent of the Ph.D. candidates are international students, mostly from developing countries. Needless to say, the impact of the SAES on agriculture and agricultural research programs in these countries have been enormous. In contrast, the USDA research agencies concentrate primarily on the research function and their scientists specialize in carrying out that function.

Third, the support of the SAES research programs comes from a number of sources. Part of the Federal support is administered by CSRS while other federal funds supporting those research programs comes from the research agencies of the USDA (ARS, ERS, FS, etc.), and from other federal agencies—the National Science Foundation (NFS), the National Institute of Health (NIH), the Department of Energy (DOE), the Department of Transportation (DOT), etc. The bulk of the support of SAES research programs, however, comes from non-federal sources—primarily state appropriations. The scientist working in the SAES system carrying out research, teaching and the extension functions is supported from multiple sources. However, in comparison, the USDA research agencies are supported almost entirely with federal funds. The individual scientists can therefore pursue research that contributes primarily to the agencies' mission.

The final major difference is in the area of organization. The SAES are organized primarily along the lines of disciplinary departments. This structure was established under the Morrill Act and firmly entrenched before the passage of the Hatch Act twenty-five years later. Moreover, the transfer of knowledge to students is on a disciplinary basis and therefore carried out in disciplinary departments. The three integrated functions—research, teaching, and extension are also carried out and generally managed at the department level within the institution. The research agencies of USDA are organized along problem area lines or other major categories of work that relate to the agencies' mission.

### Accomplishments of Agricultural Sciences

Scientific and technological progress in American Agriculture can be separated into three major periods—hand power to horse power; horse power to mechanical power; and the start of science power. The effect of these changes on labor and land productivity are illustrated in Figure 8.2.

From the Civil War to World War I, the change from human power to horse power and continuous inventions and improvements in farm implements heralded the first phase of productivity increases. These innovations resulted in an almost twofold increase in productivity. During this period, the United States made a commitment to scientifically based agriculture—institutionalized in the land-grant college system and the U.S. Department of Agriculture. The period between World Wars I and II saw the second phase of productivity increases in agriculture, based primarily on internal combustion tractors powered by cheap fuel. Along with the increased use of fertilizer, massive water projects, and a cooperative extension service to transfer this new knowledge, productivity doubled again. In the post–World War II period, both labor and land productivity increased from 70 to 120 (based on a 1967 index of 100). The key factors in this initial phase of scientific agriculture were the use of hybrid crop

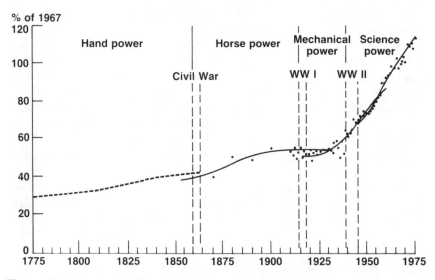

Figure 8.2 U.S. Agricultural Productivity Growth During the Past 200 Years

strains, widespread use of pesticides and herbicides, improved nutritional and medical practices in animal husbandry, and the increased use of energy and fertilizers.

Another way to demonstrate the contribution of Agricultural science to the economic and social well-being of U.S. citizens is through the use of a few examples.

## Hybrid Corn

For thousands of years Indians of the Western Hemisphere grew corn.* Their varieties were pollinated by the wind and bred largely by chance. Despite their lack of scientific insight, they transformed a wild grass from Mexico into one of the world's most productive plants. Sixteenth- and 17th-century farmers continued the practice of corn improvement. Distinct varieties were developed by selecting the best ears at the time of harvest and using seeds from those ears to produce the next year's crop. This kind of selection continued until about 1900 and resulted in scores of high-yielding, randomly pollinated varieties. Then, in the course of just a few years, scientists applied genetics to corn breeding—and brought about a major tranformation of agriculture.

The development of hybrid corn resulted from the exploitation of a phenomenon known as heterosis or hybrid vigor. It was geneticist George Harrison Shull who developed the heterosis concept as it is applied today. He and E. M. East, a contemporary whose experiments at the Connecticut Agricultural Experiment Station in New Haven closely paralleled Shull's, were the first to isolate pure strains of corn. These were then crossed to produce the vigor of hybrid corn.

The results of Shull's experiments were reported in two publications in 1908 and 1909. In a brief span of five years, Shull established a sound biological basis for hybrid corn—completely changing the course of corn breeding and establishing a model for the improvement of many crops. The adoption of hybrid corn was steady and dramatic. From 1930 through 1979 the average yields of corn increased from 22 to over a 100 bushels per acre, adding several billion dollars a year to the U.S. economy.

These genetic improvements in corn plants permitted intensive planting practices (high plant population, better drainage and moisture control, and higher levels of fertilizer and pesticide use) and the reduction of harvest losses through improved harvest and drying technology.

---

*This entire section is taken primarily from an article by William V. Brown appearing in *Science 84,* November.

The success of hybrid corn has also stimulated the breeding of other crops, such as sorghum hybrids, a major feed grain crop in arid parts of the world. Sorghum yields have increased 300 percent since 1930. Approximately 20 percent of the land devoted to rice production in China is planted with hybrid seed, which is reported to yield 20 percent more than the best varieties. And many superior varieties of tomatoes, cucumbers, spinach, and other vegetables are hybrids. Today virtually all corn produced in the developed countries is from hybrid seed. From those blue bloods of the plant kingdom has come a model for feeding the world.

## Broiler Industry

Changes in the broiler chicken industry have been phenomenal over the past 30 years. Broiler production in the U.S. has quadrupled and annual consumption of chicken meat increased to over 50 pounds per person in 1980. The farm price of broilers fell from $0.36 per liveweight pound in 1948 to $0.27 in 1982. After adjustment for inflation the real price of broilers has fallen dramatically.

Improvement in the efficiency of broiler production owes much to SAES and USDA research and to the use of university-trained geneticists by breeders. In addition to genetic improvement in feed conversion efficiency and quality of meat, there were accompanying changes in housing, feed and waste handling systems, and disease control methods. Over the past 30 years there has been significant changes in the structure of the industry. The size of broiler farms has increased while the total number has dramatically declined. These larger units employ forwarding contracts and have obtained large scale infusions of credit from feed suppliers (Teigen, 1984).

## Farm Management

Prices, weather, technology, institutions, and the needs, moods, attitudes, goals, and values of people change to influence profits and losses in farming. In this dynamic setting wrong decisions can easily result, wrong not only in terms of the needs of the decision-making units, but also in terms of social needs. Private and public costs of wrong decisions can be very high. Thus, it is argued that research and education are needed in farm management to reduce errors and the costs of errors in allocating and using farm resources.

Farm management specialists devote the great bulk of their farm-oriented research effort toward developing information and guides for farmers to use in choosing enterprises and methods of production. The largest single group of studies deals with enterprise costs and returns, with enterprise combinations, or with enterprise adjustments to changing technology or prices. Numerous studies deal with the economics of a single enterprise (beef, dairy, cotton, or fruit) and many, through budgeting or programming, determine optimal enterprise combinations within varying resource situations and constraints. Production studies are devoted to providing cost information on alternative ways of producing crops and livestock involving alternative irrigation systems, fertilizer combinations, fertilizer and seed, labor-machinery-equipment combinations, alternative rations, and dryland versus irrigation farming. Given our economy, rich in alternative farm technologies and highly dynamic in developing new technologies, it is not surprising that a great deal of effort is devoted to providing guidance in the choice of production methods. Nor is it surprising that the choice of enterprise is regarded as the most important decision problem, because comparative advantages shift as technologies, prices, and institutions change (Jensen, 1977).

The impact of farm management research cannot be measured as easily as the results of biological sciences, but anyone having knowledge of the farm enterprise realizes its importance.


**Future Challenges**

The urgency of short-term needs in the agricultural sector, e.g., for credit, should not obscure the continuing need of producers and the agricultural support infrastructure for scientific knowledge. Continued vigor of the food and fiber industry calls for improved productivity and higher quality goods and services—including more value-added products for the export market. The combination of traditional research methods and new biotechnology techniques offers tremendous potential for improving the competitive position of U.S. agriculture.

New and improved animal technologies point to faster growth rates, less feed per unit of output, increased disease resistance, and more offspring per animal. Animal diets can consist of more forages and crop by-products, and be supplemented with minerals, vitamins, amino acids, and other nutrients. Using biotechnology techniques and conventional plant breeding, crops will have increased resistance to disease, insects and nematodes. Variation in temperature, water availability, and competition from weeds will have less effect on new, more resistant varieties of tree crops, potatoes, corn, soybeans, and grain sorghum. Genetic engineering can alter plant structures and shapes to improve harvesting and maturing processes with a potential reduction in production costs and improvement in quality.

The public is increasingly aware of the relationship between personal well-being and diet. Statistical and scientific evidence suggests a relationship between what we eat and certain chronic diseases, such as hypertension, diabetes, and cancer. These developments create a conflict situation—with the results of human nutrition studies on one side and the affected farmers on the other—causing both confused consumers and an excess supply of some commodities.

Plant and animal scientists need to have a better understanding of the results of nutrition studies, and nutritionists should become more aware of the realities of agricultural production. Producers need help in adjusting to changing markets. They have made large investments and will resist changes until they can see reasonable options. Scientists and educators are in a good position to provide this help. Nutritious food cannot be provided without the cooperation of the farmer, the processor and others in the food system.

Other forces creating a need for improved technologies include the following:

- There are increasing concerns about the continued availability of the natural resource base. Improved resource-saving technologies need to be incorporated into current production practices. What resource use patterns are consistent with sustained agricultural uses over time?
- During the past century, converging scientific, economic, and technological developments have led to growing public concern over the effects of these developments on human health and quality of life. Such changes have prompted vigorous debate over the enforcement and adequacy of our laws and regulations. How do we effectively monitor unwanted contaminants in our food supply? How do we evaluate the safety of genetically engineered microbes which may be used in food processing or production? And how do we evaluate low-level carcinogenic risks from multiple sources? These are but a few of the scientific questions facing us today.
- The United States has extensive acreages of forest and range resources (71 percent of total land area). These resources provide jobs, wood, wildlife, water, forage, and energy—and a varied array of recreation opportunities. As with annual crops and domestic farm animals, improved forest and range technologies can increase yields, better protect the resource, reduce input costs, and enhance quality of outputs—all to meet changing demands of domestic and foreign customers.
- Scientific and technical exchanges with other countries make it possible to obtain and share agricultural data, collect exotic germplasm

and biological materials, and share information that can improve the efficiency of forestry, crop, and livestock production.

## Concluding Remarks

The State Agricultural Experiment Station System provides for the American people an enduring example of positive benefits for the tax paying public. As indicated by Thurow (1983) "the tremendous success of American agriculture depended on more than good soil, good climate, and hard working farmers, important as they were"—but also on the "significant contribution made by government cooperation and funds that have been provided to the industry, especially for research and education."

The station administrators in each generation have successfully maintained the separate identity and the localized control of the station establishment. Moreover, they have repeatedly illustrated the soundness of the principle, first formulated in the Hatch Act of 1887, that local responsibility for research, financed in part by Federal authority but never dominated by that authority, economically and efficiently produces scientific dividends in a democratic society.

A new generation of agricultural science will connect the expanded potential of science with the problems of agriculture. Innovative technologies will come from understanding both the basic biology of the plants and animals upon which we depend and the total systems of which they are a part. To keep the production system going, we will have to find ways to make it much more efficient; renewing our soils, conserving our water supplies, minimizing pesticide use, maximizing biological nitrogen fixation, and recycling byproducts.

On the one hand, this means new emphasis on biochemistry, microbiology, and genetics in order to understand the biological processes at the molecular level. On the other, it means new emphasis on the total ecological system, on the interactions among economic species and their pests, and on natural processes requiring minimal capital input.

The full potential of improved productivity will not be derived from technological advances alone. Unless there are complementary improvements in the human agents managing agricultural resources and adaptive modifications of agricultural institutions, then the full social return to the investment in science will not be realized.

## References

Brown, William L. 1984. "Hybrid Vim and Vigor." *Science 84* (November):77–78.
Jensen, H.R. 1977. "Farm Management and Production Economics, 1946–70." In *A Survey of Agricultural Economics Literature*, ed. L.R. Martin, Vol. 1. Minneapolis: University of Minnesota, 1977.

Knoblauch, H.C.; E.M. Law; and W.P. Meyer. 1962. *State Agricultural Experiment Stations. A History of Research Policy and Procedure.* USDA, Misc. Pub. No. 904. Washington, D.C.: U.S. Dept. of Agriculture.

Lu, Yao Chi, and Leroy Quance. 1979. "Agricultural Productivity: Expanding the Limits." USDA, ERS. Agriculture Information Bulletin 431. Washington, D.C.: U.S. Dept. of Agriculture.

Mayberry, B.D., ed. 1976. *Development of Research at Historically Black Land-Grant Institutions.* Tuskegee, Alabama: Association of Research Coordinators, Land Grant 1890 Colleges and Universities, Tuskegee Institute.

O'Connell, Paul F. 1984. "Research: Background for 1985 Farm Legislation." USDA, Science and Education. Washington, D.C.: U.S. Dept. of Agriculture.

Rasmussen, Wayne D., and R.J. Hildreth. 1983. *The USDA-Land Grant University System in Transition.* Report FS-16. East Lansing: Michigan State Cooperative Extension Service.

Teigen, L.D.; F. Spinelli; D. Harrington; R. Barry; and R. Farnsworth. 1984. "Emerging Technologies: Implications for Farm Programs," USDA, ERS. Unpublished staff paper. Washington, D.C.: U.S. Dept. of Agriculture.

Thurow, Lester C. 1983. "Farms: A Policy Success." *Newsweek,* May 16.

# Part IV

# Assessing Neglected Dimensions: Evaluative Concepts in Agricultural Research

# 9

# The Health Effects of Agricultural Production

## Molly Joel Coye

### Introduction

Agriculture is the only industry in which humans apply large quantities of synthetic chemicals directly and purposely to the environment. Pesticides are injected into the land, mixed with water for irrigation and sprayed into the air and onto plants; all of these compounds are specifically utilized for their properties as biocides.

Only belatedly in the history of chemical agriculture have we begun to evaluate the potential costs of these practices for human health. In fact, we have only recently begun to contemplate the health effects of other aspects of agricultural production. Over the past half century, the economic objectives of agricultural producers shaped the reorganization and industrialization of agriculture, the evolution of new cultivation practices replacing hand labor with machines or chemicals, the design of machinery, the development of pesticides and other chemicals, and the adequacy of housing, potable water and basic hygiene facilities for agricultural workers. Neither the producers nor the agricultural scientists in research and development questioned the potential impact of these practices on the health of agricultural workers or on the larger community and physical environment.

Populist and other small farmer movements have periodically called into question the ethics and values implicit in the dominant mode of agriculture, in some cases protesting practices which they experienced as damaging to their health: exhausting physical labor for fourteen and sixteen hour days, low pay, ramshackle housing, nonexistent sanitation facilities and polluted drinking water, and crippling tools like the short handled hoe. As elsewhere in the book, agricultural research and development activities within the land grant institutions and field research stations failed to address the problems identified by these movements.

In the 1960s, a new wave of farmworker organizing coincided with the emergence of the environmental movement and public concern about pesticide residues as contaminants in the environment and in humans. The need for improved environmental protection led to the creation of the Environmental Protection Agency (EPA), charged with the registration of agricultural chemicals for use, and enforcement of use restrictions. The EPA, the Food and Drug Administration (FDA), which samples food products for pesticide and other contaminants, and the Occupational Safety and Health Administration (OSHA), which has very limited responsibility for the enforcement of health and safety regulations in agriculture, are the agencies which have direct responsibility for the health impact of agricultural practices on agricultural workers and on the general public.

This chapter addresses the potential health impact of current agricultural practices, the regulatory approaches to pre-market and subsequent use evaluation of agricultural materials and equipment, and the need for integration of public health concerns into agricultural research and development. In studying the health externalities created by agricultural systems, there are two human "target" populations to consider: the community at large, exposed to pesticide contamination in drinking water, residues in food, and occasionally to drift from aerial application; and farmers and other agricultural workers, who face more intensive chemical exposures as well as health and safety problems related to the machinery used, the physical environment and strenuous labor, and to biologic agents such as plants and infectious organisms.

The first section reviews available information on the health of agricultural workers, data and criteria used to evaluate agricultural production materials, such as pesticides, for their potential health and safety effects before registration for use, and current public health monitoring of the health status of agricultural workers. The second section describes the impact of current production practices on the health of the general population: exposure to agricultural chemicals in the air as drift from treated fields, in drinking water, and as food residues; the resulting population body burdens; and associated health effects.

In both of these sections, I have tried to outline the values implicit in present methods of estimating and preventing adverse health externalities, and to describe some of the indicators and criteria that could be used in an alternative approach. In the final section, some of the issues fundamental to these problems are discussed—why health concerns have been "left out" of agricultural research and development, the rising incidence of environmental crises, the barriers to improvement in public health, and the alternative approaches which will be required to incorporate health concerns into agricultural research.

## Agricultural Production and the Health of Agricultural Workers

### The Industrialization of Agriculture

The enormity of the change represented by the industrialization of agriculture in the United States during the past two centuries is difficult to encompass within any academic field. Public health developed in the 1800s as a primarily urban phenomenon, as a response of the industrial manufacturers to infectious disease transmission in the dense populations of new industrial cities. Simultaneously, the non-urban population declined precipitously from 90 percent of the U.S. in 1840 to 25 percent in 1970, and the farm population declined from 42 percent to less than 5 percent over the same period.

As a result, public health and the field of occupational health have been slow to develop an analysis of agricultural health hazards, and have barely noted the impact of industrialization on the nature of agricultural work itself. Family farms have been consolidated into agribusiness with hired employees, frequently seasonal or migrant, and differing in class, racial and ethnic characteristics from the original farming community. Elements of industrialization in agriculture such as the sub-division and specialization of tasks, mechanization and the centralization of decision-making change the economic value of farm labor, change the traditional relationship of the farmer to the land, and alter the organization of the workforce. The health effects of such changes have been studied in urban industrial populations but rarely in agriculture, despite a wealth of anecdotal evidence that the impact has been profound. Finally, the lack of public health studies of these effects has crippled attempts to regulate agricultural practices.

### Changes in Agricultural Production Processes

THE INCREASING ROLE OF HIRED, SEASONAL AND MIGRANT LABOR. Although estimates of the total labor force vary in agriculture more than any other sector, four to five million persons probably work in agriculture as their primary means of earning a living. Hired, non-family farmworkers constitute between one-third and one-half of those primarily employed in agriculture. As the total farm population has declined in the United States, the proportion of hired farmworkers has risen rapidly; approximately half of all farmworkers are seasonal. Seasonal workers face the greatest occupational hazards in agriculture, because their work is concentrated in high risk crops and activities.

Of the one billion pounds of pesticides used annually in agriculture in the U.S., 800 million pounds are applied to approximately 20 percent of the total crop acreage (Pimentel, 1980); most of these crops involve seasonal field labor. More than 50 percent of seasonal workers are hired for harvesting operations, which involve contact with foliage during high pesticide application periods; of the 27 percent who work in the cultivation of crops, more than one-third work in cotton, a crop which uses a very high rate of pesticide applications (Task Group, 1975). There is also a geographic concentration of the workforce at highest risk: more than 50 percent of hired farmworkers on farms employing more than ten workers are found in just two states, California and Florida, and 65 percent are employed in production of vegetables, fruits, nuts, tobacco or sugar. Two-thirds of all vegetables are produced in California, Idaho, Michigan, Texas and Washington; California produces almost one-half of all fruit in the U.S., Florida another 20 percent. This pattern of seasonal and geographic concentration is paralleled to a lesser extent by agricultural services (applicators, machinery operators and other non-field production workers).

MECHANIZATION. The mechanization of agriculture has resulted in significant decreases in occupational injuries (both in absolute terms, by replacing workers, and as a rate, because many hazardous hand labor processes have been mechanized). Mechanization has also resulted in unemployment for large numbers of farmworkers, however, and has been eccompanied by other changes in agricultural production, some with more adverse effects on agricultural worker health. For example, the development of reduced tillage and no-till cultivation required herbicides to kill existing vegetation prior to planting. The reduced amount of cultivation also encourages increased insect populations and disease, resulting in increased use of chemicals to control the pests. As research for each new stage in agricultural technology research is done, the potential effects of such inter-relationships on worker or general community health are rarely contemplated. However, as some technologies prove themselves economically counterproductive, the adoption of alternative approaches may incidentally serve to benefit the health of workers—as has been the case with the lower rates of pesticide use involved in integrated pest management.

AGRICULTURAL CHEMICAL USAGE. The pattern of chemical use within agriculture has changed markedly since World War II. The organochlorine pesticides first used as anti-malarials in the war were widely and intensively used in the 1950s. In the 1960s, they were largely replaced by the organo-phosphate and carbamate compounds, and by a growing number of synthetic chemicals such as the pyrethroids. The use rate of herbicides doubled in the years 1966–1980, as farmers replaced mechanical cultivation with chemical weed control, and herbicides now account for two-thirds of the total poundage by active ingredient of all pesticides used in the U.S. In the same time period, the insecticide use rate has been halved and fungicide use has decreased substantially. Total pesticide usage in the United States has reached a plateau, and significant growth is expected only in exports to developing nations (Maddy, 1983).

In 1980, more than 45,000 individual products containing more than 1500 active ingredients were registered for use as pesticides by the EPA (Eichers, 1981). Approximately 2.5 billion pounds of active ingredients are used annually in the United States, but more than half of this consists of chlorinated compounds used for water treatment (anhydrous chlorine, chlorine dioxide, sodium hypochlorite). Approximately 1 billion pounds, containing slightly over 600 active ingredients, account for most chemicals used in agriculture. The general category "pesticide" includes chemicals used as insecticides, herbicides, fungicides, rodenticides, acaricides and other biocides; an even greater number of "inert" ingredients (called inert because they are not active against the target species, although they may have adverse health effects on humans) are also used in agricultural chemical formulations. Of the 45,000 individual products registered federally, not all are currently or widely used and the number registered for use in most states is much lower (Maddy, 1983).

*Evaluation of Implements and Materials Prior to Use*

In the USDA *Agricultural Research Service Program Plan*, the objectives of this major federal program are outlined in some detail, including the development of equipment, pest control methods and materials, improved nutrition, animal husbandry, and more efficient work processes. Considerations of farmworker health and safety or of consumer health effects are not substantially addressed in the objectives, nor in the elements by which they are to be approached (USDA, 1983). This is indicative of the lack of coordination between researchers developing agricultural production technology and those studying the health of workers or communities. There is, for example, no systematic or regulated review of agricultural tools and machinery for their impact on occupational health and safety before their introduction into use. The most significant exception to this pattern is the pre-registration evaluation of pesticides chemicals for toxicologic effects.

EVALUATION AND REGISTRATION OF AGRICULTURAL CHEMICALS. The Federal Insecticide, Fungicide and Rodenticide Act (also known as FIFRA, or the Federal Environmental Pesticide Control Act, PL 92–516) designates the Environmental Protection Agency as the federal body responsible for registering and regulating the use of pesticides in the United States. The EPA is also charged with enforcement of these regulations, and with conducting research on the toxicologic, environmental, and public health impacts of pesticides.

When the federal registration of pesticides was initiated in 1954, the only data required of manufacturers was that for acute toxicity (the $LD_{50}$, or lethal dose for 50 percent of animals exposed) and subacute toxicity (adverse effects of chronic exposure over a short time period, usually 90 days). Chronic feeding studies for oncogenicity (tumor induction) were first required in 1963, and studies on reproductive (fertility), teratogenic (birth defect) and mutagenic (genetic change) effects were not required until 1970. The test protocols required for carcinogenicity, reproductive, teratogenic and mutagenic effects were strengthened in the 1978 FIFRA amendments and again in Proposed Data Requirements published by the EPA in 1982 and currently under review.

## Data Gaps

When the responsibility for registration and tolerance-setting was transferred to the EPA in 1972, all pesticides currently in registration and all tolerances set for these pesticides were based on limited acute and subacute toxicity data. The need for adequate data on the potential reproductive, mutagenic and teratogenic effects of these compounds was considered a priority. Congress directed the EPA to put all such pesticides through a re-registration process requiring registrants to submit studies addressing these concerns. Approximately 600 of the 1200 pesticide active ingredients now in use were registered prior to the 1970–1972 amended study requirements, and 'data gaps' for these pesticides have been a subject of concern. In 1982, the House Agriculture Subcommittee on Department Operations, Research and Foreign Agriculture released a Staff Report on EPA's Pesticide Program, comparing information held by EPA on each active ingredient with the data required under FIFRA law (DORFA, 1982):

- 79 to 84 percent of active ingredients currently registered and used commercially lacked adequate oncogenicity studies,
- 90 to 93 percent of active ingredients currently registered lacked adequate mutagenicity studies,
- 60 to 70 percent of active ingredients currently registered lacked adequate teratogenicity studies, and

- 29 to 47 percent of active ingredients currently registered lacked adequate studies (other than on teratogenicity) to determine reproductive effects, such as on fertility.

The National Research Council, in a major review of available toxicologic data on commercial chemicals published this year, found that no toxicity data was available for 38 percent of 3,350 pesticides and inert ingredients of pesticide formulations listed. Available toxicity data was judged below the minimum required for assessment of toxicity in 26 percent of cases, adequate for a minimal assessment in 2 percent of cases, for partial assessment in 24 percent, and complete assessment in only 10 percent of cases (NRC, 1984). Moreover, because new chemicals are put into production each year, we are losing ground on the total proportion of pesticides for which adequate testing has been done.

### Quality of Data Submitted.

A further problem in the evaluation of pesticides has been the quality of data submitted for the registration of new products. Public attention was first drawn to this issue when a commercial toxicologic laboratory, Industrial Bio-Test Laboratories, was discovered to have provided inadequate or falsified data to the EPA. The laboratory was the largest private commercial toxicologic unit involved in pre-registration testing, and the registration of more than 200 pesticides was found to be based in part on IBT data, including 90 pesticides intended for use on food crops (EPA, 1983). Of 801 chronic health effects studies submitted to EPA, only 3 percent were found to be valid and sufficient to support registration (NRDC, 1984). Although the IBT studies are now being repeated for resubmission, this episode identified marked deficiencies in EPA'S Laboratory Audit Program. At the time of the IBT scandal, the Program employed only one full-time professional; with a current staff of four and responsibility for auditing all laboratories submitting data on all toxic chemicals, including pesticides, the staff is still unequal to this oversight role.

### EPA Review

The same staffing shortages which hamper the EPA Laboratory Audit Program also affect the internal review process for evaluation of toxicologic data submitted for product registration. When attention was drawn to several cases in which EPA scientific reviewers were directly incorporating information submitted by manufacturers in "cut and paste" operations, the Batelle Memorial Institute was asked to conduct a study of this problem at the EPA (*Pesticide and Toxic Chemical News,* 1984). Thirty-three percent of the 578 EPA reviews audited by Batelle were drawn directly from registrant-submitted data without independent analysis. This is a particularly critical issue because there is no public access for independent peer review of studies submitted to the EPA for product registration. The FIFRA amendments in 1978 in fact addressed this problem, and mandated public access; this was not implemented until the spring of 1984 because of a court challenge by Monsanto on the basis of trade secrets protection.

Once a pesticide is registered for use, subsequent findings of toxicologic effects meeting one of the risk criteria in federal regulations may trigger an RPAR (Rebuttable Presumption Against Registration) review. EPA has moved slowly both in placing pesticides in review (Kelthane, for example, was found to be carcinogenic in mice and rats by NCI in 1978, meeting one of the criteria for review, but was not placed in RPAR until spring of 1984), and in bringing RPAR reviews to completion.

## Assessment of the Health and Safety of Agricultural Workers

Farmworkers are specifically excluded from key labor laws, from almost all federal and state occupational safety and health laws and regulations, and in half the states in the U.S., from the workers' compensation system as well. Because of this, most of the information sources on working conditions, exposures, and health effects which are available for industrial, service, professional and other workers are not available for agricultural workers. In states where agricultural workers are not covered by workers' compensation, physicians lack incentives to report work-related injuries or illnesses, and are particularly unlikely to report occupational illness among field workers. Even in California, the only state to require that physicians report all possible pesticide-related illnesses to a County Health Officer within 24 hours (with a $250 fine for non-compliance), the state Department of Health Services estimates that only 1 percent of all pesticide-related illness among farmworkers is reported (Kahn, 1976).

EXPOSURE DATA. The 1970 Williams-Stieger Act, which created OSHA, and subsequent inter-agency agreements with the EPA specifically excluded farmworker exposure to pesticides from OSHA surveillance and enforcement programs. The EPA nationally does not conduct field monitoring of agricultural worker exposure except for research purposes. Enforcement of EPA regulations and investigation of exposure incidents has been delegated to state departments of agriculture.

The National Institute for Occupational Safety and Health (NIOSH) conducted a survey of worksites in the U.S. from 1972–74. This survey, the National Occupational Hazards Survey (NOHS), did not include farmworkers but did include agricultural services workers in the Standard

Industrial Classification two-digit code '07'; approximately half way through the survey, the scope was further restricted to Standard Metropolitan Statistical Areas (SMSAs) only.

In 1982–83, a second NIOSH survey entitled the National Occupational Environmental Survey (NOES) was conducted, also including agricultural services (SIC code '07'), but not production workers. Of twenty two worksites visited, two were in crop preparation services, ten were veterinarians, eight were lawn and garden treatment services, and two ornamental plant nurseries. Rural areas were included. This data is still being analyzed, but preliminary findings, when NOHS/NOES observations of exposures are cross-indexed with information in the Registry of Toxic Effects (RTECS), indicate that agricultural services workers are potentially exposed to a total of 175 chemicals which are potentially carcinogenic, mutagenic, teratogenic, or acutely toxic. Forty five of these are carcinogenic, mutagenic, teratogenic, or some combination thereof.[1] SIC 07 is within the upper one-third of all industries for relative health risk considering only these four health risks, according to the NIOSH model for identification of high risk occupational groups described here (NIOSH, 1983a).

The State of California Department of Food and Agriculture monitors worker exposure when suspect or high-toxicity pesticides are first placed in registration. When chlordimeform, which is a potent carcinogen in animals and has caused severe cystitis (bladder inflammation) in humans, was re-registered for use in California, the CDFA required extensive urine sampling. In addition, CDFA routinely does a random sampling of pesticide residues on foliage and potential worker exposure (air and dermal patch sampling, among other methods) in order to determine the adequacy of Departmental regulations and enforcement. This has provided a large body of specific data on worker exposure in California; comprehensive testing programs of this nature do not exist in other agricultural states.

All of these systems are concerned with estimating exposures to chemicals. Information on exposure to hazardous machinery (tractor hours, days of work with the short handled hoe, etc.), to biologic agents, to noise and to other occupational hazards is not systematically collected by public health or agricultural health and safety agencies.

THE GENERAL HEALTH STATUS OF AGRICULTURAL WORKERS. The general health status of many agricultural workers—not solely seasonal and migrant workers—is already significantly compromised by factors which are indirectly job-related but nevertheless derivable from occupation. In particular, low income and relative geographic and social isolation contribute to deficiencies in nutrition, housing, sanitation, education, and in access to preventive and medical care services.

Most of these factors exacerbate occupational health risks. Housing in or near fields exposes workers and their families to pesticide spray drift. Lack of adequate sanitation is associated with an increased prevalence of parasitic and infectious disease, something public health studies and migrant clinic reports have documented among migrant farmworkers. Lack of potable water in the fields and in some housing forces workers to drink irrigation water which is frequently contaminated with pesticide run-off and is increasingly used as a direct method of pesticide application. Lack of education makes it difficult or impossible for workers to read pesticide labels and posted signs, a problem which is even more serious for the increasing number of non-English speaking ethnic groups now working in U.S. agriculture.

Nutritional deficiencies increase the toxicity of many pesticides (Shakman, 1974, Mahaffey, 1979). Mild water deprivation and food restriction, similar to that experienced by many farmworkers, has been found to significantly increase the acute toxicity of the widely used organophosphate parathion (Baetjer, 1983). Finally, the same economic and geographic factors which limit access to medical care for farmworkers may also delay or prevent appropriate treatment for job-related injuries and illnesses.

Since 1971, OSHA standard §1910.141 has required basic sanitation facilities in all permanent workplaces in the U.S.; also, facilities for sanitation have been required in the construction industry, and in temporary labor camps. There is no evidence that field laborers differ in physiological and hygienic needs from other workers. Studies conducted during the development of rural water supply systems demonstrated that the availability of water for personal hygiene may significantly reduce disease transmission, and strategies promoted by the Centers for Disease Control for the control of acute enteric diseases emphasize the importance of hand washing. On these bases, farmworker organizations petitioned OSHA to regulate the provision of sanitation and hygiene facilities at agricultural worksites in 1974. However, it was not until 1984 that OSHA issued a proposed Field Sanitation Standard in response to a Supreme Court ruling ordering the agency to propose a standard or show cause for failure to comply. In 1985, OSHA determined that "adequate" cause for the promulgation of a standard had not been found.

A 1983 survey of Hispanic migrant farmworkers used the HANES instrument to investigate the health status of tomato harvesters in Indiana, Ohio and Michigan. Upper respiratory, dental, and back and neck problems were the most frequently reported complaints. Farmworkers reported having been sprayed by or otherwise exposed to pesticides an average of 6.6 times during the preceding year; 21 percent reported having been sprayed or otherwise exposed ten times or more. 97 percent of the sample were estimated to be in need of medical attention. Perceived problems of farmworkers in comparison with other Midwesterners include poorer housing and sanitation facilities (92 percent), more diseases and other health problems (84 percent), more child labor (76 percent), and greater exposure to pesticides and hazardous chemicals (79 percent) (Barger, 1983).

INJURY DATA. Injury and death rates rank agriculture consistently among the three most hazardous industries in the United States. The death rate for agricultural workers is 54 per 100,000 workers, in comparison with 57 and 63 for construction and mining, and the rate of disabling injuries is 54 per 1,000 workers, versus 53 and 50 for construction and mining, respectively. In considering the comparison between agricultural work and mining and construction, it is important to note that the latter two sectors are highly organized, and are uniformly covered by workers' compensation, enhancing the likelihood that work-related death and injury will be reported. Furthermore, since almost half of all farmworkers in labor surveys have worked less than 75 days per year, the death and injury rate per work hour in agriculture is presumably even higher in comparison with industrial occupations (Strigini, 1982).

The relative position of agricultural worker safety described above still holds, despite a steady decline in occupational injury rates for many sectors of agriculture. The fall in injury rates is due to mechanization of harvesting, changes in cultivation practices which reduce stoop labor and other crippling physical labor, and redesign of tools and implements. In a review of occupational injuries in California agriculture, Whiting showed a close correlation between the rate of decline in sprain-and-strain type injuries, including back strain, and changes in the physical demands of work in various crops. Field vegetable crops traditionally utilized stoop labor, but as the short-handled hoe was finally replaced in California in the late 1960s, these injuries fell by 34 percent. Workers on fruit and nut tree farms, where there is less stoop labor but much lifting, experienced an intermediate decrease of 19 percent. Workers on dairy, livestock and poultry farms, and in nursery and greenhouse work, showed almost no decline in such injuries for the same period because mechanization of these farms had taken place much earlier (Whiting, 1975).

Machines themselves remain the primary cause of reported work-related injuries in agriculture, however. Tractors alone are responsible for an estimated 40 to 60 percent of farm accidents and fatalities. Factors contributing to accidents include the complexity of many new machines, heat stress, and the effects of pesticide residues. Mechanization may actually represent potentially increased health risks for equipment operators, because harvesters and other equipment shake large amounts of foliage rapidly, dislodging pesticide residues and creating a substantial risk of inhalation exposure. Aerial application pilots are at particularly high risk, because equipment failure when flying may be compounded by chronic neurologic effects of low-level pesticide exposure, resulting in decreased ability to compensate for mechanical problems.

ILLNESS DATA. Like injury rates for agricultural workers, occupational disease rates rank among the most hazardous. In California, they are the highest of all sectors in the state labor force: occupational illnesses per 100 full-time workers in 1979 were: 0.3 for workers in all sectors combined, 0.5 for manufacturing, 0.3 for mining, 0.3 for construction, and 0.6 for agriculture (0.7 for agricultural production, and 0.5 for agricultural services) (Division of Labor Statistics, 1981). While injury rates have been declining, disease rates have not, and represent a rising proportion of all morbidity among agricultural workers. In public health terms, this resembles the broader shift in developed industrial societies to predominant patterns of chronic disease.

## Mortality.

Information about mortality rates among agricultural workers is obtained through two basic epidemiologic approaches. The first proceeds from occupation, and compares mortality rates between agricultural workers and other occupational groups or national rates. Early studies of this type identified excess death rates among farmers and farm laborers for such potentially work-related causes of death as leukemia, skin cancer, motor vehicle accidents, machinery accidents, cancer of the skin and asthma (DHEW Vital Statistics, 1963; Milham, 1971, 1976; Peterson, 1980). More recently, NIOSH published a further study by Milham in which a correlation between specific types of cancer and agricultural sub-groups (e.g., nurserymen, dairy farmers, poultry farmers) was noted. More studies of this type have been conducted for pesticide applicators than for farmworkers, because it is easier to establish and follow cohorts (groups) of registered applicators; excess lung cancer death rates have been found consistently in these studies (Blair, 1983).

The second approach is to compare the incidence of agricultural occupations among persons dying of one (possibly occupational) disease with that among persons dying of a second (presumably non-occupational) disease. For example, Stemhagen recently published a study in which persons dying of liver cancer were twice as likely to have worked as farm laborers as a matched control population (Stemhagen, 1983). A series of similar studies has repeatedly confirmed an excess risk of leukemia among farmworkers in several midwestern states; in each case, the risk has been associated with particular crops or livestock and with high insecticide or herbicide usage, although the specific patterns have not always been consistent (Blair, 1979; Burmeister, 1981, 1982, 1983).

The mortality from all causes is lower among farmers than the general population, probably as a result of two factors: the 'healthy worker effect', i.e., the self-selection of healthy workers into physically strenuous occupations such as farming and of unhealthy workers out of such occupations; and the lifestyle of farmers, which includes vigorous exercise and markedly low tobacco use. The excess mortality rates most consistently encountered in studies of agricultural workers have included cancers of the lymphatic and hematopoietic system (particularly leukemia), and of the prostate, skin and stomach, and motor vehicle accidents (farm machinery) (Blair, 1982).

In some studies, there is a significant difference in death rates between farm owners/managers and farm laborers. Stemhagen found that the risk of liver cancer was associated exclusively with the job title identified as 'farm laborer', and Carlson found that farm laborers had a three times greater rate of death from respiratory diseases than farm owners and managers (Carlson, 1978).

There is no standard death certificate across all states, nor a standard approach to obtaining or coding information on usual occupation. Partly because of this, and partly because it is even more difficult to identify cohorts (groups to follow over several decades) in agriculture than in other sectors, there are no reliable estimates of the mortality experience of farm laborers.

## Heat Stress.

Substantial medical evidence of the adverse health effects of work without adequate water intake under hot environmental conditions exists, although studies of the rate and limit of acclimatization among farmworkers in varying climates and occupational activities within the United States have not been done. Heat stress may lead to heat exhaustion, cramps, and stroke, and in its earlier stages, is frequently treated symptomatically by the worker and therefore is not reported (NIOSH, 1980, 1981). Rest periods and drinking increased quantities of water are the primary means of preventing heat stress, yet potable water is frequently unavailable to field workers; one study found that fewer than half of the agricultural employees interviewed were provided with drinking water (or handwashing or toilet facilities) in the field (Department of Labor, 1984).

## Musculoskeletal Disease.

The National Health Interview Survey data file contains information on self-reported conditions and injuries from a sample of U.S. households. Analysis of this data reveals that farmworkers have a higher prevalence of arthritis than white collar, blue collar, service, or all workers combined.

Seventeen percent of all conditions reported among farmers and farm managers during the period 1969–1977 were musculoskeletal and connective tissue diseases, versus 12 percent for all occupations combined. Musculoskeletal conditions were the most frequently reported ailments among both male and female farmers and farm managers; farmers reported over 50 percent more musculoskeletal disease than farm managers. Arthritis represented 68 percent of musculoskeletal disease reported by male farmers, and 74 percent of that reported by female farmers.[2]

Social Security Administration data show that 17 percent of disability awards granted to male farmers and 23 percent of those made to females were attributable to musculoskeletal and connective tissue disease, making it the second leading cause of disability among farmers of both sexes. The rigorous physical work of farming is presumed to be responsible for this excess in musculoskeletal disease, although no studies have been done to identify the equipment, tools, or work practices which are specifically associated with these adverse outcomes (NIOSH, 1983b).

## Dermatitis.

The most frequently reported occupational disease, for agriculture as for all industries, is dermatitis. The rate of occupational skin disease for all California industries combined was 2.1 per 1,000 workers in 1977. The rate for agriculture was 8.6; for manufacturing 4.1; for construction 2.5; and for mining 2.0. While agriculture represented only 3 percent of state employment, it accounted for more than 13 percent of all occupational dermatoses. The majority of cases are due to plant exposures, primarily poison ivy; however, 16 percent were attributed to agricultural chemical exposure (Division of Labor Statistics, 1982). Because 26 percent of these pesticide-related dermatoses required disability leave, the economic as well as the health significance of pesticide-related dermatitis for farmworker families is obvious.

## Pesticide-Related Illnesses.

Systemic pesticide illness is markedly under-reported, for reasons which include the non-specific nature of early and mild symptoms of pesticide exposure, the sociology and political economy of agriculture and its field labor force, and the lack of physician knowledge regarding occupational disease in general and pesticide-related disease in particular. Of reported illnesses in California, ground applicators, mixers, loaders and field workers represent the greatest proportion, approximately one-third. Greenhouse and nursery workers have relatively high rates, presumably because their workplaces are largely enclosed and pesticide applications are concentrated. Truck drivers, who handle highly concentrated pesticide formulations, and firemen, who are exposed in uncontrolled emergency situations, have rates only slightly lower than the greenhouse and nursery workers.

The pattern of systemic poisonings has also changed over the past two decades, perhaps most remarkably in California, where strengthened regulations on field re-entry were introduced in the early 1970s as part of a vigorous pesticide monitoring and enforcement program. Until that time, a large proportion of reported cases involved entire crews of field workers, frequently harvest crews in citrus orchards, who entered the orchard or field while high concentrations of pesticide residues were still present on the foliage. Cases of systemic illness reported in the last five to seven years have more frequently been individual or small groups of workers encountering re-entry violations or accidental exposures; almost all illnesses reported except dermatitis, however, are still acute illnesses (symptoms developing immediately after and directly referable to moderate or high exposures to pesticides).

Evidence has accumulated to suggest that the vast majority of pesticide-induced illnesses among agricultural workers in all job categories are in fact moderate and chronic rather than severe or acute—that is, continuous or intermittent symptoms in response to continuous or intermittent low-level exposures. A series of studies in California, New Jersey, Canada, Nebraska and other agricultural regions have examined the blood cholinesterase levels of farmworkers in comparison with either their own pre-season baselines or with groups of non-agricultural workers (cholinesterase enzyme activity is inhibited [decreases] upon exposure to organophosphate and carbamate pesticides). In each case, seasonal shifts correlated with pesticide application periods or significant differences from non-exposed population norms have been reported (Brown, 1976; Quinones, 1976; Spigiel, 1981).

Low-level exposure to organophosphate pesticides may produce a variety of non-specific central nervous system symptoms, that is, symptoms which also occur with influenza and many other common non-occupational diseases. These symptoms include headache, fatigue, drowsiness, insomnia and sleep disturbances, mental confusion, disturbances of concentration and memory, anxiety and emotional lability. Studies of farmworkers, and in some cases applicators and farmworkers separately, have found many of these symptoms to be prevalent at a higher rate than among comparable non-agricultural groups (Levin, 1976; Quinones, 1976).

The most detailed study of the prevalence of potentially pesticide-related morbidity among farmworkers was conducted by the California State Department of Health Services in 1974. Farmworkers reported physicians visits for potentially pesticide-related symptoms 15 times more frequently than a control population of the same ethnic background and socioeconomic status (Kahn, 1976). Based on a further investigation of the physician reporting for these cases, and on a similar study in another California county, the director of pesticide programs for the Department of Health Services estimated that as little as 1 percent of all pesticide-related illness in farmworkers reported in California—despite the fact that state regulation requires physicians to report such cases to their County Health Officer within 24 hours of diagnosis (Kahn, 1976). In 1982, 235 cases of pesticide-related illness among farmworkers were reported; if this represents 1 percent of actual illness, the "true" prevalence would be 23,500 cases among the estimated 300,000 farmworkers in the state. If this rate is applied to a conservative estimate of the national farmworker labor force, or 4 million workers, the prevalence may be 313,300 cases; if we apply the rate only to hired seasonal farmworkers who are at greatest risk for field residue exposures, the case prevalence would be 156,600.

These studies indicate that cholinesterase inhibition, taken as an index of exposure, is widely prevalent among a variety of agricultural work groups, and that certain non-specific but potentially pesticide-related symptoms are also more prevalent among farmworkers than the general population. While the extent of cholinesterase inhibition reflects organophosphate and carbamate exposure only, we must assume that low level chronic exposure to other pesticide residues also occurs.

Partly as a result of increased publicity about the potential toxicity of chronic pesticide exposure, many farmers and farm laborers have become more concerned about agricultural chemical usage. Of 1,959 Missouri farmers polled in a 1983 survey, 30 percent reported that "high use of chemicals" was "very important" as an issue. Out of a list of eight selected government programs, including agricultural research, soil conservation, and cooperative extension programs, farmers reported that they perceived less benefit from farm safety programs than most other programs (only price support programs and farm credit programs ranked lower) (Farm and Rural Life Poll, 1983).

There is no regular biologic monitoring of agricultural worker exposures to pesticides, except for periodic cholinesterase tests required of certified pest control operators handling organophosphates and carbamate compounds on a regular basis in the state of California. There are no regular examinations or surveys to identify the adverse health effects of pesticide or pesticide residue exposures.

## Other Agricultural Diseases.

A wide range of other diseases are associated with agricultural work, although the total numbers of persons affected are significantly less than for the three categories discussed above. Biologic agents cause such diseases as "valley fever" (coccidioidomycosis), anthrax, brucellosis, tetanus, tularemia, leptospirosis, Rocky Mountain spotted fever, Q fever, rabies, psitticosis and ornithosis, orf, histroplasmosis, sporotrichosis, and ringworm. Hypersensitivity pneumonitis, a form of allergic sensitization, is known as farmer's lung, and is also found among mushroom workers. Toxic gases accumulate in stored fodder and cause silo filler's lung. Vibration may cause circulatory and musculoskeletal system changes, and ultraviolet radiation causes skin cancer at excessive rates among farmers. Hearing impairment has also been found at high rates among agricultural workers, the result of operating machinery without ear protection.

### Psycho-Social Effects of Agricultural Work.

Several studies of mental illness in rural communities have found prevalence rates to be significantly higher than in urban communities; this prevalence rate has consistently been in the range of 10 percent of the rural population, defined as those cases probably in need of psychiatric care (NIMH, 1979). In Mazer's detailed study of a Massachusetts rural community, general physicians reported that 51.5/1,000 patient visits—or one out of twenty visits—were for psychiatric care (Mazer, 1976). An NIMH review of mental health and rural America concluded that these studies identify a marked "slippage" between the existence of mental illness in rural areas and the treatment of such disease (NIMH, 1979).

Many sociological descriptors of rural farm populations are consistent with these findings. Rural residents are poorer than urban residents, and rural farm families are poorer than non-farm families residing in rural areas. There is a higher ratio of dependent persons—those under age 18, or age 65 or greater—to productive age group persons in rural areas. While the general health status as well as the mental health status of rural residents is below that for urban residents, the quality of health facilities and services, the availability of transportation to reach health care centers, and the smaller number of practitioners working in rural areas results in less access to care for rural communities as well (NIMH, 1979).

More recently, sociologists and economists investigating rural communities have identified patterns which are known to contribute to mental illness in other settings. Changes in the structure and control of agriculture have concentrated not only on ownership, but also managerial control over production practices. In the Missouri Farm and Rural Life Poll (1983), 47 percent of the respondents felt that agricultural decisions are made predominantly by persons other than farmers. These structural changes are not only occurring in the family farm sector of agriculture, of course; the contracting of hired labor through marketing corporations rather than by individual growers has substantially changed job stability and work relations for many seasonal workers. Unemployment is an increasingly critical problem for both groups as well; for family farmers who fail financially and cannot find employment in their communities, and for seasonal workers displaced by mechanization. Despite these many indicators of distress among rural farmers, there are almost no studies of the potential relationship between agricultural production systems and mental stress and disease.

## The Impact of Agricultural Production on the Health of the Community

*The Quality of Food Products*

NUTRITIONAL QUALITY/ADEQUACY. There appears to be little question that the United States is capable of producing enough food with sufficient calories, protein, vitamins and minerals to afford a healthy diet for every citizen. Discrepancies between this capacity and the diet consumed by Americans may be therefore ascribed, in the view of many nutritionists, to problems of distribution and of processing and marketing approaches which affect the quality of foods as they reach the consumer (Gussow, 1984). The health externalities of these food processing, marketing and distribution policies are beyond the scope of this paper. It should be emphasized, however, that some food additives and a good many agricultural chemical residues commonly detected in marketed produce may affect the nutritional value of the produce itself, either because of interactions between the product and the contaminant or because one affects the body's metabolism response to the other. In the U.S. Senate Select Committee on Nutrition and Human Needs report on world food and nutrition (Select Committee, 1977) food additives and pesticide residues are not discussed; yet the presence of and health effects of these artificial contaminants may be the most significant remaining aspect of the inherent nutritional quality of foods produced in the U.S.

BIOLOGICAL CONTAMINANTS. Farmworkers frequently must urinate and defecate in open fields without benefit of latrines and handwashing facilities, a fact which should assault our sensibilities. As mentioned before, every other sector of the workforce has protection in this regard under OSHA regulations, including work sites sharing many characteristics with agricultural fields such as forestry and construction. The potential health effects of contaminated produce have increased in recent years because growers now prefer to have many crops picked, wrapped and crated right in the fields. Although no studies have been conducted to demonstrate the nature and prevalence of food contamination resulting from these practices, a NIOSH report submitted to OSHA on the need for a Field Sanitation Standard stated that the relationship between poor sanitation and disease is well known, and concluded that such a standard could be supported on the basis of good public health practice (Department of Labor, 1984).

PESTICIDE RESIDUES.

### Determination of Tolerances.

The EPA, as noted in the previous section, is responsible for registering and regulating pesticides and enforcing these laws and regulations. In addition, the EPA establishes "tolerances" for each crop or animal feed. The tolerance is the maximum amount of pesticide residue in either parts per million (ppm) or milligrams per kilogram (mg/kg) which may be legally present on foods or feed at the time of sale.

Tolerances are determined as follows: A "no observable effect level" (NOEL), which does not produce the adverse effects observed at higher dose levels, is derived from data supplied by the registrant. The NOEL is reduced by a safety factor (typically 100) because the extrapolation of tox-icologic doses from animals to humans is only approximate. This results in the "acceptable daily intake" (ADI), in milligrams of pesticide/body weight/day. Multiplied by the weight of an average adult, this becomes the "maximum permissible intake" (MPI) in milligrams/day. Differential toxicity among infants, pregnant women, the elderly or other sub-populations is not considered in deriving the MPI or provided for by the use of additional safety factors.

At this point, the potential dietary intake must be derived from studies of consumer dietary patterns. A "food factor" is the indicator of how much of each product is consumed, on average, per day. The "theoretical maximum residue contribution" (TMRC) is the proposed tolerance multi-plied by the food factor. If tolerances exist for a pesticide on more than one commodity, the TMRC is the total of all proposed and established tolerances times the food factors. The TMRC must be less than the max-imum permissible intake (MPI) for that pesticide.

There are several problems with the tolerance-setting process as it currently functions:

- Significant gaps exist in the registration data submitted by manufac-turers to EPA for many pesticides currently in use, as noted in the previous section.
- The food factors used to estimate potential daily intake may significantly under-estimate consumption by some subgroups within the U.S. population.
- A number of suspect carcinogens have been granted tolerances, despite the lack of evidence identifying 'safe' thresholds for any car-cinogen.
- The safety factor on which some tolerances are based has been an order of magnitude less than 100.

- Metabolic transformations of the pesticide residue during food processing are not part of the registration process; thus, they have not been included or evaluated.
- Additive and synergistic effects of separate pesticides are generally not considered in the determination of tolerances.

### Consumption Estimates (Food Factors).

The food factors for each commodity are derived from Department of Agriculture survey data either on agricultural production or on household consumption. In using the agricultural production data, total 1975 production of each commodity is divided by the total U.S. population. Household consumption data are currently based on a 1965/66 USDA survey. This has resulted in estimates of consumption which may be considerably lower than actual figures for many large subgroups of consumers. For example, average U.S. consumption of commodities such as mushrooms, nectarines, radishes, summer squash, cantaloupes, eggplant, kale, molasses, swiss chard, tangerines, and watercress is assumed to be less than 7.5 ounces, or approximately one-half pound per year. The EPA is currently revising the dietary estimates for subgroups such as children, the elderly, and ethnic groups, although how these revised estimates will be integrated into the tolerance setting process has not yet been decided.

### Tolerances for Suspect Carcinogens.

Federal law prohibits the use of carcinogens as food additives, and both international and national regulatory agencies have repeatedly found that there is no threshold for any carcinogen (a threshold is the level of exposure below which there is not increased risk of cancer among the exposed population). The EPA has stated that its policy in regulating carcinogens is based on a "no-threshold approach". Despite this, tolerances have been granted for a number of agricultural chemicals which are "suspect carcinogens" according to criteria established by these agencies. There is no scientific basis for the assumption that pesticide residues in food products are less biologically active than carcinogenic contaminants derived from other sources, such as diethylstilbestrol (DES).

The use of carcinogens in animal feed is exempted from the requirements of the Delaney Clause only if it leaves no residue in "any edible portion of such animal after slaughter or in any food yielded by or derived from the living animal." In 1979, the FDA policy was revised to allow some residues, provided that the residues would not pose more than an "insignificant" risk of cancer (i.e., a one-in-a-million chance).

A related issue arose in 1983 when melamine, a by-product of the feed-through pesticide Larvadex, was found to induce cancer in mice.

Larvadex is fed to chickens to prevent flies from hatching in the birds' manure, and leaves melamine in poultry flesh and eggs. Larvadex has never been registered by the EPA, but was in wide use in more than two dozen states under emergency permits until it was pulled off the market in August of 1983. Reduction of the estimated cancer risk for consumers to the usual criterion of one in a million would require restricting melamine residues to .06 ppm in eggs; however, at effective use levels of Larvadex, melamine levels may be as high as .25 ppm. In proposing to allow Larvadex use again, the EPA has challenged the FDA dietary estimates for eggs, and provided alternative estimates which would bring down the calculated risk to consumers.

### Detection of Cancelled Pesticides in Food Products.

A number of private market basket surveys, in addition to FDA monitoring, confirm that residues of cancelled pesticides such as DDT, endrin and dieldrin may be found in food products long after cancellation and termination of use. The contribution of this continuing exposure to human fat tissue levels is difficult to ascertain, because many of the cancelled compounds accumulate in these tissues and have been detected in population sampling over several decades.

### FDA Monitoring of Food Residues.

The Food and Drug Administration is responsible for monitoring food in order to determine that EPA's tolerances or maximum safe residue limits are not exceeded, and for taking enforcement action where necessary to prevent the sale of food with residues above these tolerances. Three hundred and eight pesticides are currently registered for use on food commodities. The multiresidue analytic method most commonly employed by the FDA can identify and quantify only 93 of these pesticides; other methods allow identification of an additional 57 pesticides. The multiresidue analytic method most commonly employed detects no more than 33 percent of the pesticides for which tolerances exist and which are suspect carcinogens; the additional methods increase this proportion to 50 percent (FDA, 1979). No currently available screening battery is capable of detecting all pesticides for which tolerances have been established.

The FDA regulates only interstate shipments of food. Approximately 10,000 samples, including 7,000 samples of domestically grown produce, are collected each year. (In addition, a Total Diet Study or market basket survey is conducted annually to estimate the total intake of pesticide residues for U.S. consumers. This is not used for enforcement purposes.) Since 1979, FDA has been issuing a Surveillance Index for each pesticide, including information on production volume, major uses, toxicity, significant impurities and metabolites and the potential for dietary exposure; these indices enable the agency and states to focus sample collection on pesticides representing the greatest potential health risk.

Intrastate commerce is regulated by the individual states, which vary widely in the quality and frequency of monitoring and in their enforcement programs. A problem common to both the state and federal enforcement programs is the time lag between sampling of commodities and enforcement actions: in many cases, the commodity has been distributed and marketed, and often consumed, before enforcement action is initiated. Approximately 3 percent of FDA's surveillance samples, and 7 to 10 percent of follow-up samples, violate established tolerances.

### Residues in Food Products.

Standard commercial techniques of food processing can significantly reduce the level of pesticide residues present in foodstuffs. The trimming or peeling of both vegetables and fruits and animal products such as meat, fish and poultry can mechanically remove a portion of the residues (trimmings from commercial food processing are utilized as animal feeds, however, thus reintroducing them into the food chain). It is estimated that as much as 50 percent of dietary residues are derived from dairy products, meat, fish and poultry, although these constitute less than 30 percent of the total U.S. diet (Tannenbaum, 1979).

OTHER RESIDUES AND CONTAMINANTS IN FOODSTUFFS. A wide range of other additives have been used in agriculture, particularly in animal feed, and may be found in meat, poultry and dairy products as they reach the consumer. Growth stimulants include the antibiotics (chloramphenicol, bacitracin, penicillins, tetracyclines), hormone analogues (hexoestrol, zernol, DES), arsanilic acid, and thiouracil. Antibiotics, corticosteroids and other compounds are used prophylactically and therapeutically as well. Almost one-half of the antibiotics used in the U.S. are fed to farm animals (Homberg, 1984).

This use of antibiotics presents a public health problem both in the high doses used to treat diseases such as mastitis in cows, and in the lower doses in which they are sold as premixes in animal feed. Products (meat and dairy) from treated animals must be discarded for specified time periods after the antibiotics have been discontinued, in order to prevent direct human consumption of antibiotics and the resulting development of resistant strains of microorganisms. Although the USDA conducts training for farmers on the correct use of antibiotics, there is no comprehensive monitoring and enforcement of the regulations regarding meat products and farmers frequently treat their animals with much higher doses than required, in the belief that "more is better."

Feeds containing penicillin and tetracyclines are also currently on the market, although Britain and other European countries have largely banned these premixes and the FDA attempted to ban their use in the United States as early as 1977. Congress placed a moratorium on the proposed ban, and requested more studies; each of the studies have confirmed the hazards associated with this practice. Antibiotic resistance has been shown to travel from animals to humans, where the antibiotic-resistant bacteria may then cause disease. Most recently, the Centers for Disease Control reported salmonellosis in eighteen persons in four Midwestern states who were infected by an antibiotic-resistant strain after eating hamburger originating from a herd of beef cattle fed subtherapeutic chlortetracycline for growth promotion; eleven persons were hospitalized for an average of eight days, and one person died (Holmberg, 1984).

*Contamination of Drinking Water with Agricultural Chemicals*

Contamination of the lower Mississippi River with many synthetic organic chemicals provided the impetus for the passage of the Safe Drinking Water Act (PL 93–523) in 1974, designed to monitor and protect groundwater sources of potable water. Unlike biological pathogens, chemical contaminants are not easily removed or treated from water supplies. In 1976, the EPA established National Interim Primary Drinking Water Regulations, setting Maximum Contaminant Levels (MCL) for six organic chemicals. All of these were pesticides: Endrin, Lindane, Methoxycholor, Toxaphene, 2, 4-D, and 2,4,5-T/Silvex. The gas chromatograph mass spectrophotometers required for determination of these synthetic organics are extremely costly and as a consequence only a few water supply laboratories are equipped to monitor this type of contaminant.

The past decade has witnessed an increasing number of regional problems with pesticide contamination of groundwater, including rising levels of nitrates in some communities due to heavy use of fertilizers. Extensive well-water contamination with DBCP was discovered in the late 1970s throughout many parts of the state of California; about 35 percent of wells in the San Joaquin Valley, a major agricultural area, are contaminated (Maddy, 1983). An initial study by the State Department of Health Services found an increased mortality rate for stomach cancer in this region, which has caused concern because the primary site for tumor induction in animals experimentally exposed to DBCP is the stomach.

Other chemicals which were not expected to persist in groundwater have contaminated drinking water sources in many states. Temik (aldicarb) is a highly toxic carbamate which has been heavily used on many crops, including potatoes in Wisconsin and Long Island. Although laboratory and field studies had indicated that aldicarb could not reach groundwater, aldicarb levels above the state recommended guideline of 7 ppb were found in 13.5 percent of 6500 drinking water wells sampled in

Suffolk County, New York in 1979. Residents were advised not to use the water from these wells for drinking or cooking. Levels greater than ten times the recommended guideline were found in 16 percent of these wells (Zaki, 1982). Aldicarb is now under a Rebuttable Presumption Against Registration (RPAR) review at EPA.

Groundwater is the primary source of drinking water for almost half of the U.S. population, and for 75 percent of the major cities in the U.S. The Senate Committee on Environment and Public Works commissioned a report reviewing 128 cases of groundwater contamination which resulted in well closings. The contaminants (most wells were multiply contaminated) responsible for the closings were: organic chemicals 242, insecticides 201, chlorides 26, nitrates 23, and metals 619. There are no standards for many of the chemicals now commonly found in groundwater, although the EPA estimates suggest that as much as 1 percent of the nation's usable ground water has already been contaminated (Pye, 1983). Because the health effects of low-level exposures across very broad populations are difficult to capture without the collection of standardized morbidity and mortality data, it will be difficult to evaluate these potential problems epidemiologically. In 1984 the EPA issued "data call-ins," requiring that studies be provided to address outstanding data gaps, for over 80 pesticides with the potential to contaminate ground water.

*Agricultural Community Exposure*

Public health and agricultural officials in rural and agricultural areas frequently receive complaints about aerial pesticide applicators directly spraying buildings and living areas, or about drift from aerial applications. Although almost no studies have been done of the health effects of community exposure to spray and drift, there is good reason to suspect that specific locations in close proximity to fields may be at high risk; drift from treated fields often accounts for as much as half or more of the pesticide applied. Complaints have increased with the rising public consciousness of the potentially adverse effects of pesticide exposure, and with the out-migration of urban and suburban populations into rural areas. In many regions, housing tracts have been developed in the midst of cultivated fields, and even ground spray applications have been a source of conflict in these communities.

Communities also encounter unregulated dumpsites with many years' accumulation of agricultural chemicals. In poor communities, or where safety education has been inadequate, pesticide cans and barrels are used for washing clothes, carrying water and cooking. Children walk through or·play in recently treated fields, and even use pesticide containers as toys. Surveys or inspections which would provide information about the prevalence of related illnesses or about the effectiveness of public health education and intervention to enforce pesticide regulations is lacking.

### Residues of Agricultural Chemicals in Humans

Some pesticides and their metabolites remain in human tissues and fluids for prolonged periods of time after initial exposure. These residue levels depend not only upon the amount of initial exposure and absorption into the body, but also upon the patterns and rates of metabolism, storage, and elimination. Most organophosphorus and carbamate pesticides are rapidly metabolized and excreted, and some organochlorines and chlorophenoxy herbicides are rapidly excreted without any metabolic alteration. Many of the organochlorine compounds, however, are lipophilic and are assimilated and stored in the lipid portion of adipose (fat) tissues. Certain organophosphorus compounds which are also lipophilic may remain temporarily sequestered in adiposed tissues for as long as several weeks. Measurement of these residues and their metabolites, therefore, can serve as a useful indicator of general population exposures, and in combination with toxicologic data may identify potential public health hazards and areas for further research.

Most multiresidue analytic techniques used in these surveys can detect only a limited number of all the pesticide residues which may exist in body tissues, as indicated in the discussion of food and water contamination. In the EPA project discussed below, the method used permitted characterization of approximately 38 pesticides and toxic compounds.

IN THE GENERAL POPULATION. The EPA National Human Monitoring Program, a probability sampling of human adipose tissue initiated in 1970, is a continuing program to assess general population exposures to pesticides. The National Center for Health Statistics later joined with the EPA program in order to correlate blood serum and urine specimen residues with health information collected during the Second Health and Nutrition Examination Survey (NHANES II).

In blood samples, 99 percent of all subjects tested had detectable DDT and its analogs. Approximately 80 percent of the urine samples had detectable levels of pentachlorophenol. Residues of carbamate pesticide metabolites occurred in 2 to 4 percent of urine samples, and dialkyl phosphate residues ranged from 6 to 12 percent of those tested. Adipose tissue residue levels also indicate that there is in fact widespread exposure of the general population to these compounds (Murphy, 1983).

IN RURAL RESIDENTS. Rural residents in agricultural areas often have more pesticide exposure than does the general population, through ingestion of freshly harvested foodstuffs recently sprayed, through contamination of local drinking water supplies, and through drift or overspray during aerial pesticide applications in addition to occupational exposures for those directly employed in farm work. A study of chlorinated hydrocarbon residues in the serum of nonoccupationally exposed pregnant women in Mississippi was reported in 1976. The major crops in the area were cotton, soybeans and rice, on which large quantities of chlorinated hydrocarbons were used as insecticides during the early 1970s. Serum samples from mothers and from the umbilical cord at delivery were obtained and analyzed over a one-year period for 350 pairs of mothers and newborns. All of the subjects had at least one, and usually two DDT metabolites in their serum. The mean levels of residues were higher among rural subjects and black subjects, and were comparable to the mean levels reported in occupationally exposed chemical company employees, and two to five times higher for both mothers and newborns that the average levels for the total U.S. population (D'Ercole, 1976).

SOCIOECONOMIC DIFFERENCES. The difference in serum residues between the white and black populations has been found in other studies, as has a prevalence of higher serum level in individuals with lower socioeconomic status. In Davies' 1972 report, subjects stratified by Hollingshead socioeconomic classification showed an inverse correlation between class level and residue levels within racial groups as well, indicating that the determining factor is class rather than race (Davies, 1972). In terms of causes, both the socioeconomic and racial differences in serum residues are probably due to poorer housing, quality of sanitation, availability of running water, to greater proximity of housing to cultivated areas, and to less education in use practices.

IN HUMAN MILK. In an analysis of human milk samples from 1436 women residing in the U.S. testing for residues and metabolites of four specific chlorinated hydrocarbon insecticides, dieldrin was found above the detection limit (1.0 ppb) in over 80 percent of the samples collected. Although chlordane was not recovered from any of the samples, and heptachlor from only 2 percent of the samples, their principal metabolites were found in 74 percent and 63 percent of all samples, respectively. Mirex, the fourth insecticide, was not positively identified in any of the samples. There was significant geographic variation in the proportion of samples with values above detection limits, with the southeastern U.S. having the highest mean residue level for dieldrin, chlordane and heptachlor. Mean fat adjusted residue levels for samples above the detection limit were in the 100 ppb range for all three residues (Savage, 1981).

**Public Health and Agriculture: The Need for Integrated Research and Development**

As we have seen in the material presented here, the relationship between agricultural production and health is a special case, unlike that existing in other sectors of economic production. A much higher rate of injury and illness appears to exist among farmworkers than most other sectors of the workforce. Workers' compensation does not cover farmworkers in half the states in the country. Farm workers are also excluded from general benefits such as social security. Regulations which entitle workers to basic worksite sanitation, the right to know the name of chemicals used in a workplace, and other occupational health and safety programs routinely exclude agricultural workers.

The criteria used to evaluate and regulate agricultural chemical residues in air, water, and food are also different from those used for industrial pollutants, particularly in regulating potentially carcinogenic pesticide residues in foods. The reporting and monitoring of health effects associated with agricultural practices are much weaker than for industrial, service, and other sectors of the workforce. All of these issues are health externalities—costs not incorporated into the economy of the individual agricultural producer, costs borne instead by the agricultural laborer and by the larger society.

There is no single explanation for this phenomenon. Listed below are three questions, each representing a component of the relationship between agricultural production and health and a facet of the central issue of inequity just outlined. In discussing these questions, alternative approaches which incorporate these concerns into agricultural research and development and into public health programs are suggested.

*Why have health concerns been excluded from the research, development, and implementation of agricultural production?*

I have already noted the urban roots of public health, and the delayed response of public health professionals and agencies to the occupational health problems of agricultural workers. Given the evidence reviewed in this chapter showing very high rates of occupational injury and disease among workers in agriculture, however, we may ask why these problems were not identified and addressed by agricultural researchers, as they have been in other high-risk industrial sectors.

Part of the larger problem involved in recognizing externalities, or here the public health costs of agricultural production, lies in a narrow definition of agriculture as a technological intervention in nature, rather than as a social process of production. The cost/benefit analysis is therefore encapsulated within the triad of land, labor, and implements as units of production cost. Because structural constraints, such as workers compensation and unionization of the workforce have been kept minimal in the agricultural sector, agricultural managers encounter neither economic nor social pressures to incorporate health externalities into their evaluation of costs and benefits. This situation has begun to change over the past decade as environmental groups, farmworker unions, and advocate organizations have pressed regulatory agencies for improved standards and stricter enforcement.

Increased research on the health effects of agricultural production and improved reporting systems for injury and illnesses would markedly improve the quantity and quality of information available for assessment of costs which have been externalized from agriculture. Strengthened pre-market evaluation of agricultural production materials and technologies for their potential health impacts would encourage the incorporation of health concerns into earlier stages of research and development. Extension of workers' compensation coverage and increased utilization of economic policies, such as the millage tax on pesticide sales which finances health and safety research and regulation in California, may result in the internalization of some of the health costs of past and present practices. Finally, there has been increasing interest in agricultural technologies which utilize lesser amounts of pesticides, loosely referred to as integrated pest management programs, a development which may substantially reduce the potential for both worker and community exposures.

In this context, questions of whether pesticide use on surplus crops or in situations where continued cultivation may be counter-productive for the larger agricultural eco-system have also received increasing attention. In California, these issues were raised during regulatory consideration of Bolero and Ordram use on rice; there was already a one year supply of the crop in storage and large payment-in-kind allotments had been made. They were also debated when use of the suspect carcinogen chlordimeform on cotton in the Imperial Valley was considered (and finally approved), because of the large cotton surplus and the fact that the Imperial Valley crop serves as a land bridge for pest movement between Arizona and the more productive, valuable, and uninfested crops in the Central (San Joaquin) Valley.

*What structural changes would improve the pre- and post-market evaluation of agricultural processes and materials?*

The public has frequently assumed that chemicals are fully and adequately tested before marketing, and that public agencies possess enough information to definitively evaluate the substances. Material presented in this chapter questions both of these assumptions. Adverse public reaction to discoveries of contaminated drinking water, residential areas, and foodstuffs has escalated through a series of 'environmental crises' over DBCP, dioxin, aldicarb, EDB and other chemicals. Concerns about the long-term effects of chemical exposures have also begun to surface among family farmers and field laborers.

This pressure, compounded by the escalating costs of clean-up operations where land and water systems are contaminated, has stimulated the interest of state and federal legislative bodies in new forms of regulation and oversight in agricultural research and in agricultural practices. Among the structural changes proposed, the strengthening of pre-market evaluation and the establishment of environmental and health monitoring systems are critical to the intelligent design of public health and agricultural evaluation policy. While adequate models for environmental and health surveillance already exist, approaches to pre-market evaluation and regulation may require some fundamental revisions.

Because of the historical evolution of the legal and regulatory system in the United States, chemicals—like corporations—have individual standing and are "innocent until proven guilty". That is, the necessity and advisability of regulating each chemical has been considered individually, an unwieldy process given the rapid evolution of agricultural chemical technology and the limitations of agency review staff. It may be that only generic standards will be able to adequately address the urgent need for improvements in the regulatory assessment of chronic health effects of pesticide exposure. Generic standards classify and regulate groups of chemicals by pre-determined criteria; the EPA classification of pesticides in Categories I, II and III on the basis of acute toxicity is an example of this approach.

The NIOSH Criteria for a Recommended Standard for Occupational Exposure During the Manufacture and Formulation of Pesticides and the standard for Identification, Classification and Regulation of Toxic Substances Posing a Potential Occupational Carcinogenic Risk proposed by OSHA in 1977 are examples of generic standards which address chronic effects (primarily carcinogenicity). In the proposed OSHA standard, all chemicals shown to cause cancer in human beings, or in two mammalian species, or in a single mammalian species if the tests have been replicated in another experiment, or in a single mammalian species if the results are supported by short-term tests, would be classified as Category I; worker protection (labeling, training, protective equipment, engineering controls) is regulated according to the Category in which a chemical is classified (OSHA, 1977).

The strengthening of pre-market evaluation and the establishment of environmental and health monitoring systems will not justify public confidence, however, if independent scientific review is not ensured as well. Public access to toxicologic information submitted by manufacturers for the registration of pesticides was mandated in the 1978 FIFRA revisions, but was subsequently blocked by court rulings until 1984, preventing independent scientific review of EPA regulatory decisions. Peer review is a basic principle in all of the sciences concerned with agricultural health—medicine, toxicology, industrial hygiene, epidemiology—and it is certainly the most effective insurance against problems such as those which have plagued the regulatory process in recent years.

*How could public health programs contribute to the integration of health concerns into agricultural research and development?*

There is no routine surveillance of occupational disease among any sector of the workforce, so agricultural workers are not at a disadvantage in comparison with other workers in this respect. Because the reporting of work-related injury and illness among agricultural workers is weak, however, increased efforts in surveillance and research are needed simply to accurately determine the extent of actual morbidity and mortality among this population.

Even in the absence of symptoms, such monitoring should address biological "contamination" (body burden of residues in tissues) and physiologic change (e.g., cholinesterase inhibition, electroencephalographic abnormalities and other changes) as well as the presence of disease and disability. Public health agencies such as NIOSH or the Migrant Health Office of the Public Health Service and county and state health departments have important resources to offer to agricultural researchers, and would gain much by a more frequent interchange with researchers and with technical personnel such as field advisors in agriculture as well.

Unfortunately, even increased efforts in medical surveillance cannot promise to substantially mitigate the controversy which surrounds the interpretation of occupational and environmental health studies. Cholinesterase blood test results are a good example of a clinical test which is frequently interpreted in widely differing ways, with major implications for the health and economic well-being of the affected worker. While the public sees such tests as objective and neutral, health scientists should know better, and agricultural scientists would benefit from education regarding the complexities of these issues.

There is a tremendous need for research on the health effects of agricultural production. The skills required for this research exist within the public health community, but are unlikely to be brought to bear on the environmental and occupational health risks of agriculture unless researchers in agriculture view this area as a genuine priority. As agricultural technologies change and the public grows increasingly agitated about the suspected effects of chemical exposures, we have every reason to expect new and more vigorous regulatory interventions in agricultural practice. The wisdom and success of these interventions will depend in large part on our ability to bring the two worlds of public health and agriculture together, and on our willingness as scientists to address the most pressing and troubling questions at this interface.

## Notes

1. Information extracted for this paper courtesy of David H. Pederson, Industrial Hygenist, Division of Surveillance, Hazard Evaluations and Field Studies, NIOSH.
2. Information extracted for this paper courtesy of Shiro Tanaka, M.D., Industry Wide Studies Branch, Division of Surveillance, Hazards Evaluations and Field Studies, NIOSH.

## References

Baetjer, Anna M. 1983. "Water Deprivation and Food Restriction on Toxicity of Parathion and Paraoxon." *Archives of Environmental Health* 38:3:168–171.

Barger, Ken, and Elizabeth Reza. 1984. "Survey of Midwestern Farmworkers." Unpublished project summary, March 7, 1984. Bloomington: Department of Anthropology, Indiana University.

Barthel, E. 1981. "Increased Risk of Lung Cancer in Pesticide-exposed Male Agricultural Workers." *Journal of Toxicology and Environmental Health* 8:1027–1040.

Blair, Aaron, and Terry L. Thomas. 1979. "Leukemia among Nebraska Farmers: A Death Certificate Study." *American Journal of Epidemiology* 110:264–273.

Blair, Aaron. 1982. "Cancer Risks Associated with Agriculture: Epidemiologic Evidence." *Basic Life Sciences* 21:93–111.

Blair, Aaron, and D.J. Grauman; J.H. Lubin; and Jerold F. Fraumeni. 1983. "Lung Cancer and Other Causes of Death among Licensed Pesticide Applicators." *Journal of the National Cancer Institute* 71:1:31–37.

Brown, J.R.; F.C. Chai; L.Y. Chow; *et al.* 1978. "Human Blood Cholinesterase Activity— Holland Marsh, Ontario, 1976." *Bulletin of Environmental Contamination and Toxicology* 19:617–623.

Burmeister, Leon F.; S.F. Van Lier; and P. Isacson. 1982. "Leukemia and Farm Practices in Iowa." *American Journal of Epidemiology* 115:5:720–728.

Burmeister, Leon F.; G.D. Everett; S.F. Van Lier; and P. Isacson. 1983. "Selected Cancer Mortality and Farm Practices in Iowa." *American Journal of Epidemiology* 118:1:72–77.

California Department of Food and Agriculture. 1983a. *Report of Pesticides Sold in California for 1982 by Pounds of Active Ingredients.* Prepared by the Enforcement Unit, Division of Pest Management; HS-1159 May 1, 1983.

_____. 1983b. "1982 Summary of Priority Pesticide Exposure Investigations Conducted by Counties Pursuant to EPA/State/County Cooperative Agreement." Prepared by the Enforcement Unit, Division of Pest Management; HS-1158 December 20, 1983.

Carlson, Mark L., and Gerald Petersen. 1978. "Mortality of California Agricultural Workers." *Journal of Occupational Medicine* 20:1:30–32

Davies, John E.; W.F. Edmundson; A. Raffonelli; J.C. Cassady; and C. Morgade. 1972. "The Role of Social Class in Human Pesticide Pollution." *American Journal of Epidemiology* 96:5:334–341.

Department of Labor, Occupational Safety and Health Administration. 1984. "Field Sanitation: Proposed Rule; Request for Comments." 29 CFR Part 1928. (Docket No. H-308). *Federal Register* 49:42:7589–7604, March 1, 1984.

D'Ercole, A. Joseph; R.D. Arthur; J.D. Cain; and B.F. Barrentine. 1976. "Insecticide Exposure of Mothers and Newborns in a Rural Agricultural Area." *Pediatrics* 57:6:869–874.

Division of Labor Statistics and Research. 1981. *Occupational Injuries and Illnesses Survey: California, 1979.* San Francisco: California Department of Industrial Relations, May, 1981.

_____. 1982. *Occupational Skin Disease in California.* San Francisco: California Department of Industrial Relations, January, 1982.

_____. 1983. *California Work Injuries and Illnesses, 1981.* San Francisco: California Department of Industrial Relations, December, 1983.

DORFA (Subcommittee on Department Operations, Research, and Foreign Agriculture). 1982. *EPA Pesticide Regulatory Program Study.* House Committee on Agriculture, 97th Congress, 2d. Sess., 1982.

Eichers, T.R. 1981. *Agricultural Economic Report Number 464.* U.S. Department of Agriculture, Farm Pesticide Economic Evaluation, 1981.

Environmental Protection Agency (EPA). 1983. *Summary of the IBT Review Program.* Washington, D.C.: EPA, Office of Pesticide Programs, July 11, 1983.

Farm and Rural Life Poll. 1983. "Summary Tables for 1983 Missouri Farm and Rural Life Poll." Colombia: University of Missouri, Department of Rural Sociology.

Food and Drug Administration (FDA). 1979. *FDA Monitoring Programs for Pesticide and Industrial Chemical Residues in Food.* Washington, D.C.: Study Group on FDA Residue Programs, June, 1979.

Gussow, Joan A. 1983. "Food Security in the United States: A Nutritionist's Viewpoint." In *Food Security in the United States,* ed. Lawrence Busch and William Lacy, pp. 207–230. Boulder, Colo.: Westview Press, 1983.

Holmberg, Scott D.; Michael Osterholm; Kenneth A. Senger; and Mitchell Cohen. 1984. "Drug-resistant Salmonella from Animals Fed Antimicrobials." *New England Journal of Medicine* 311:617–622.

House Committee on Interstate and Foreign Commerce, Subcommittee on Oversight and Investigations. 1978. *Cancer-Causing Chemicals in Food.* 95th Congress, 2d. Sess.

Joint Council on Food and Agricultural Sciences. 1984. *Summary: Needs Assessment for the Food and Agricultural Sciences. A Report to the Congress from the Secretary of Agriculture.* Washington, D.C.: U.S. Department of Agriculture.

Kahn, Ephraim. 1976. "Pesticide Related Illness in California Farm Workers." *Journal of Occupational Medicine* 18:10:693–696.

Kutz, F.W.; F.C. Strassman; and A.R. Yobs. 1977. "Survey of Pesticide Residues and their Metabolites in Humans." In *Pesticide Management and Insecticide Resistance,* ed. D.L. Watson and A.W. Brown. New York: Academic Press.

Levin, Harvey S., and R.L. Rodnitsky. 1976. "Behavioral Effects of Organophosphate Pesticides in Man." *Clinical Toxicology* 9:391–405.

Levin, Harvey S.; R.L. Rodnitsky; and D.L. Mick. 1976. "Anxiety Associated with Exposure to Organophosphate Compounds." *Archives of General Psychiatry* 33:225–228.

Maddy, Keith T. 1983. "Pesticide Usage in California and the United States." *Agriculture, Ecosystems and Environment* 9:159–172.

Mahaffey, Kathryn R., and John E. Vanderveen. 1979. "Nutrient-toxicant Interactions: Susceptible Populations." *Environmental Health Perspectives* 29:81–87.

Mazer, Milton. 1976. *People and Predicaments.* Cambridge, Mass.: Harvard University Press.

Milham, Samuel. 1976. "Occupational Mortality in Washington State, 1959–1971." Washington, D.C.: Dept. of Health, Education, and Welfare, PHS/CDC/NIOSH Pub. No. 76–175–C.

Milham, Samuel. 1983. "Occupational Mortality in Washington State, 1950–1979." Washington, D.C.: U.S. Dept. of Health and Human Services, PHS/CDC/NIOSH Pub. No. 83–116, October, 1983

Mott, Laurie, and M. Broad. 1984. "Pesticides in Food: What the Public Needs to Know." San Francisco: Natural Resources Defense Council, March 16, 1984.

Murphy, Robert S.; F.W. Kutz; and S.C. Strassman. 1983. "Selected Pesticide Residues or Metabolites in Blood and Urine Specimens from a General Population Survey." *Environmental Health Perspectives* 48:81–86.

National Research Council. 1984. *Toxicity Testing: Strategies to Determine Needs and Priorities.* Washington, D.C.: National Academy Press.

National Institute of Mental Health (NIMH). 1979. *Mental Health and Rural America: An Overview and Annotated Bibliography.* Ed., J.W. Flax, M.O. Wagenfeld, R.E. Ivens, and R.J. Weiss. Washington, D.C.: U.S. Dept. of Health, Education and Welfare, PHS/ADAMHA Pub. No. 78–753

National Institute of Occupational Safety and Health (NIOSH). 1980. *Hot Environments.* Washington, D.C.: U.S. Dept. of Health and Human Services, PHS/CDC/NIOSH Pub. No. 80–132

————. 1981. *Proceedings of a NIOSH Workshop on Recommended Heat Stress Standards.* Washington, D.C.: U.S. Dept. of Health and Human Services, PHS/CDC/NIOSH Pub. No. 81–108

————. 1983a. "A Model for the Identification of High Risk Occupational Groups using RETCS and NOHS Data." Washington D.C.: U.S. Dept. of Health and Human Services, PHS/CDC/NIOSH Pub. No. 83–117

————. 1983b. "Musculoskeletal Disease in Agricultural Workers." Internal Document.

Occupational Safety and Health Administration (OSHA). 1977. "Identification, Classification and Regulation of Toxic Substances Posing a Potential Occupational Carcinogenic Risk." Department of Labor, Proposed Ruling, in: *Federal Register* 42:192:54148, Tuesday, October 4, 1977.

*Pesticide and Toxic Chemical News.* 1984. "Audit of Scientific Review Process of Chronic Toxicology Studies Submitted to EPA in Support of Pesticide Registration." Report on Batelle Columbus Laboratories. January 11, 1984:26–29.

Peterson, Gerald R., and Samuel Milham. 1980. "Occupational Mortality in the State of California 1959–61." Washington, D.C.: Dept. of Health, Education, and Welfare, PHS/CDC/NIOSH Pub. No. 80–104.

Pimentel, David; D. Andow; R. Dyson-Hudson; D. Gallahan, *et al.* 1980. "Environmental and Social Costs of Pesticides: A Preliminary Assessment." *Oikos* 34:126–140.

Pye, Veronica, and Ruth Patrick. 1983. "Ground Water Contamination in the United States." *Science* 221:713–718.

Quinones, Michael A.; J.D. Bodgden; D.B. Louria; and A.E. Nakah. 1976. "Depressed Cholinesterase Activities among Farm Workers in New Jersey." *Science of the Total Environment* 6:155–159.

Savage, E.P.; T.J. Keefe; J.D. Tessarie; H.W. Wheeler; F.M. Applehans; E.A. Goes; and S.A. Ford. 1981. "National Study of Chlorinated Hydrocarbon Insectaice Residues in Human Milk, USA." *American Journal of Epidemioloby* 113:413–422.

Select Committee on Nutrition and Human Needs. 1977. *Report of Study Team 9 (Nutrition): World Food and Nutrition Study.* U.S. Senate, U.S. Government Printing Office.

Shakeman, R.A. 1974. "Nutritional Influences on the Toxicity of Environmental Pollutants." *Archives Of Environmental Health* 28:105–113.

Spigiel, Robert W.; D.R. Gourley; and T.L. Holcslaw. 1981. "Organophosphate Pesticide Exposure in Farmers and Commercial Applicators." *Clinical Toxicology Consultants* 3:41–45, 45–50.

Stemhagen, Annette; John Slade; Ronald Altman; and Joanne Bill. 1983. "Occupational Risk Factors and Liver Cancer: a Retrospective Case-control Study of Primary Liver Cancer in New Jersey." *American Journal of Epidemiology* 117:4:443–54.

Strigini, Paulo. 1982. "On the Political Economy of Risk: Farmworkers, Pesticides, and Dollars." *International Journal of Health Services* 12:2:263–292.

Tannenbaum, Steve R. 1979. *Nutritional and Safety Aspects of Food Processing.* New York: Marcel Dekker.

Task Group on Occupational Exposure to Pesticides. 1975. *Occupational Exposure to Pesticides (Report to the Federal Working Group on Pest Management).* Washington, D.C.: U.S. Government Printing Office Publication No. 0–551–026.

USDA. 1983. *Agricultural Research Service Program Plan.* Washington, D.C.: U.S. Dept. of Agriculture, Miscellaneous Publication No. 1429.

Wang, H.H., and B. MacMahon. 1979a. "Mortality among Pesticide Applicators." *Journal of Occupational Medicine* 21:741–744.

_____. 1979b. "Mortality of Workers Employed in the Manufacture of Chlordane and Heptachlor." *Journal of Occupational Medicine* 21:745–748.

Waters, M.D.; V.F. Simmon; A.D. Mitchell; T.A. Jorgenson; and R. Valencia. 1980. "An Overview of Short-term Tests for the Mutagenic and Carcinogenic Potential of Pesticides." *Journal of Environmental Science and Health* B15:6:867–906.

Whiting, William B. 1975. "Occupational Illnesses and Injuries of California Agricultural Workers." *Journal of Occupational Medicine* 17:3:177–180.

Zaki, Mahooz H.; Dennis Moran; and David Harris. 1982. "Pesticides in Groundwater: the Aldicarb Story in Suffolk County, NY." *American Journal of Public Health* 72:1391–1395.

# 10

# *Review and Evaluation of Social Externalities*

## William D. Heffernan

### Introduction

Providing food for its people is one of the most basic responsibilities of a society. However imperfectly, the United States has fulfilled this social responsibility, but one can question whether the abundance of food has led to a higher quality of life for all Americans. It has made more food available to all, even to the economically less fortunate families who spend 30 to 40 percent of their incomes for food. Most of our farm programs over the past 50 years have addressed what is assumed to be "excessive," not "inadequate," production of food for our population.

Many factors have converged to make this abundance possible. Among these are ecological factors such as quality soil and favorable climate as well as those societal factors which have created the infrastructure which supports the productive sector. Given the interdependency of these factors and numerous others which contribute to production, it is somewhat misleading to focus on any single factor and discuss its consequences in isolation from others. By itself, agricultural research does not inevitably lead to particular social outcomes. Unlocking new knowledge and information may make possible certain outcomes, but many other factors, such as governmental farm programs and taxation policies, interact to produce particular social outcomes.

Many researchers, especially those more oriented toward basic research, have little concern or control over how the knowledge they create will be used. Their perceived role is to create knowledge. Yet, the researcher and the research process are influenced by the social and political contexts within which they operate (Hightower, 1973; Busch and Lacy, 1983).

Often the social consequences stem more from the applications of the research than from the basic knowledge which was discovered. Still, there exists a close link between the basic and the applied in agricultural research. So-called "basic research" is often encouraged by the agribusiness sector because it has use in their applied research. This may occur even without the researcher's awareness.

My purpose is to explore some of the negative social consequences made possible by agricultural research. This is important because these social consequences are ignored in most analyses of the social benefits of agriculture research. I shall then examine and challenge the efficiency model typically utilized in evaluating agricultural research. Given the close social and economic ties between public and private agricultural researchers (Hightower, 1973), it is not always possible to clearly differentiate the social consequences of public versus private research. Even so, there are certain types of research done at publicly supported institutions which can be examined for their social consequences even though one recognizes that private research may also contribute to negative social consequences (Ruttan, 1982).

When raising questions regarding the human dimensions of agricultural research, we must recognize that all research does not have the same impact. Each new research discovery in agriculture is unique and carries with it a unique set of possible social consequences. Thus, it is with considerable trepidation that I group all agricultural research discoveries together and develop generalizations about them. Some comments apply more to certain research efforts than to others.

## The Neglect of Social Consequences

Typically, researchers as well as the public are surprised that agricultural research has had unanticipated consequences and has generated unintended social costs. Much of the reason for this is that public researchers often simply do not ask what the social consequences of their work might be. It is also quite probable that those in the private sector also do not fully understand the social impact of the changes made possible by research.

In the 1930s, there had been an attempt by social scientists in the Bureau of Agricultural Economics of USDA to ask questions about social aspects of agriculture (Kirkendall, 1966). The negative social consequences highlighted by these researchers were not appreciated by some influential politicians, and the Bureau was soon eliminated (Goldschmidt, 1978). The elimination of the Bureau of Agricultural Economics not only brought a halt to the asking of more general questions at the USDA, but it served as a notice to all researchers who were part of the land grant system that such research would not be evaluated favorably (Busch and Lacy, 1983).

Since some of the forefathers of rural sociology were a part of the Bureau of Agricultural Economics, it is not surprising that the interest of rural sociologists in examining some of the larger social issues related to agriculture was extinguished. Even as late as the 1950s and '60s, sociological research focused on agriculture limited itself to asking how a system could be established which would cause farmers to rapidly adopt new practices researchers had discovered. Although an occasional critic raised the question of whether farmers should adopt a particular innovation (Campbell, 1968), for the most part, these questions and questions concerning the social consequences of adopting these practices were never asked. With the rise of external critics in the 1970s, this "adoption/diffusion" research thrust began to fade, and a set of broader questions was again raised. Today, the literature on the broader social causes and consequences of changes in agriculture is developing rapidly. (Rodefeld, *et al.*, 1978; Newby and Buttel, 1980; Berardi and Geisler, 1984; and Schwartzweller, 1984).

**Categories of Agricultural Research**

Recognizing that agricultural research can be categorized in many different ways, I will divide it into two broad categories. The first category is research which has as a major goal that of reducing the need for labor. Specifically, this includes research oriented toward producing larger equipment, as well as research designed to facilitate increased mechanization and automation. Included here is research that develops strains of plants and animals that will facilitate mechanization.

The second broad category of research is that which is designed to increase the output per unit of non-human input. This category includes increasing the yield per acre or increasing the useable energy from a given quantity of fuel. Even these categories are not discrete. For example, a researcher might have as his goal that of increasing the productivity of a dairy cow through improved nutrition or genetic selection. Such an innovation indirectly reduces the need for labor because the added milk output is obtained with very little added labor.

*Research to Reduce Labor*

Historically one major and on-going research thrust has been to reduce the labor needed in agricultural production. The assumption has been that less labor will lead to lower labor costs in food production and thus to lower priced food for the consumer. (Farm families hoped that by producing more, usually by increasing the size of their operation, they could increase their income.) The results of this process have been called—in cold economic terms—the "transferring of labor resources out of agriculture." In human terms it has involved costly social adjustments. Consumers may have benefited from lower prices, but, as citizens of this country, they have paid a price in other ways.

During this century, there have been periods of relative prosperity for farmers which were followed by periods of economic crisis in the farming community, such as we are now experiencing. During these times, not only young people, but established farm families have been forced to quit farming (and often to leave their house and community) (*Newsweek,* 1984). Most farm families did not voluntarily leave their farms. They were forced to leave when they could not survive on their farm because research designed to increase labor efficiency led to "over production" and lower prices. They left only after their creditors refused to loan them more funds or after their economic misery became so great that they were forced to leave behind their relatives, friends, recreational opportunities and the community of their birth and forefathers. They moved to urban areas hoping to find jobs that could provide them with basic economic necessities (Heffernan, 1967).

The social costs stemming from these changes can be grouped under three headings: costs to individuals and farm families, costs to rural communities, and costs to urban communities.

COSTS TO INDIVIDUALS AND FAMILIES. In contrast to the quiet, peaceful existence depicted by writers and artists, a recent study done by the National Institute for Occupational Safety and Health reports that farming ranks in the upper ten percent of 130 high stress occupations. Stress occurs when one is unable to control events which have a serious consequence for one's life. Although this is a general characteristic of all farmers, family stress is greatly increased when a farm family faces foreclosure. Because the family's life is so closely tied to the farming operation, an occupational change usually leads to a change in the family's way of life. It also usually means a severing of social ties as the family is forced to move to other communities in search of employment. The personal cost to family members can not be calculated in economic terms. For those unable to cope with the stress accompanying such events, the social costs may be high.

Stress leads to illness. Medical experts estimate that from one-half to three-fourths of all illness is psychosomatic or stress-related (Pelletier, 1977). In a recent study we conducted of farm families, illness was identified as the major source of stress. Thus, stress leads to illness, and illness leads to stress.

Those unable to cope with stress may ultimately commit suicide.  In Missouri we have experienced almost a fourfold increase in suicide among farmers less than 65 years of age, from six suicides in 1982 to 23 in 1983. As the economic crisis facing Missouri farmers intensifies, health authorities anticipate even greater increases.

The social costs of stress are also seen in family and community life. Often persons experiencing great stress show changes in their behavior, such as aggressiveness or withdrawal.  Family relations are often strained at such times.  These personal costs have not received much attention, and while the economic cost to society of the increased cost of health care and problems stemming from fragmented families might be estimated, the personal costs defy an economic assessment.  One need only attend a farm foreclosure sale to feel the personal cost to a young farm family and their neighbors and friends.

COSTS TO THE RURAL COMMUNITIES.  As farm families have been forced from their farms, they have seldom found job opportunities in rural communities because the social and economic well-being of many rural communities has been dependent upon the farm segment.  Rural trade centers, which draw a major portion of their economic support from farming, have shared the farmers' economic conditions.  Fewer farm families has meant the need for fewer goods and services in rural communities.  The uprooting of farm families has carried over to include the families of small business persons, as small towns across the country have seen their economic base decline.  It has not been just the farmers who have been forced into the cities, but all of those who have been dependent on farm families for economic support.

In the 1970s, many states began making a major effort to attract industry into their rural areas.  This, along with tourism and a growing rural population which depends on social security and pensions, has altered the economic base for many rural communities.  For some rural communities, such an effort stemmed the tide of outmigration.  In many rural communities, a reverse migration occurred.  Even by the late '70s, however, many rural communities continued to decline.  As the population was lost, schools, churches and business organizations had to be reduced and consolidated.  Many facilities were abandoned and friendship and kinship ties were strained or broken.  Most families were not eager to give up the rural life and the non-economic benefits they received from farming (Kliebenstein, *et. al.,* 1982), but they had no alternative.

COSTS TO URBAN AREAS.  As families from farms and rural communities have moved into the cities, their problems have gone with them.  In rural areas, a belief exists that rural youth learn to work hard and to take responsibility. The belief further suggests these virtues will serve the youth well in the urban labor market. However, a vast research literature developed in the '50s and '60s indicated that rural youth did not fare well in the urban labor market (Burchinal, 1962). Farm-reared youth were disproportionately represented in the lower segments of the occupational hierarchy. If rural youth did poorly, older persons forced to leave the farm did even worse. They were not prepared educationally, occupationally or socially for urban jobs or urban living. Most of the older displaced farmers were forced into unskilled occupations and thus were the first to be fired during recession and the last to be hired during an economic upswing.

Many of the urban industrial centers were not prepared for the mass influx of migrants from rural areas. The schools and housing conditions were inadequate. The social and economic conditions into which these families were forced provided few opportunities for the children. Most of the children were unable to improve their life chances. Today we hear about third generation welfare recipients. Many of these are the descendents of rural families forced into urban areas.

Classical economic theory suggests that after a period of adjustment the labor resources released from one sector will be utilized by other sectors to improve the economic well-being of the society. This theory may eventually be supported by the agricultural experience, but the so-called "adjustment period" has been marked by human misery for one, two and three generations. Even during this time some scholars were asking whether, in a post industrial society, there would be enough work for all persons during their productive years (Galbraith, 1969). Will these descendants ever be integrated as productive workers into the industrial or service sector of this country? Or will they continue as largely unemployed workers often surviving on government welfare?

The flight to the suburbs of those who were economically better off and the deterioration of the central city as the poor and jobless remained is well-documented. As labor was forced out of agriculture, the human problems became urban problems which erupted into major urban crises in the late '60s. I do not mean to suggest that agricultural research was the cause of the urban problems. Many of the families that ended up in the most dire straits in urban areas were experiencing poor living conditions in rural areas as well. But perhaps some of these problems could have been solved more easily if agricultural research had been less concerned with reducing the labor in agriculture. It is ironic that at a time when unemployment in the city was an obvious problem, some agricultural research was oriented toward forcing more persons from the agricultural sector.

One could spend much time discussing in detail the social consequences for rural and urban communities of the mass exodus from rural communities. The point is that as consumers we may purchase food more cheaply because of agricultural research, but as taxpayers responsible for providing certain social services for all members of society, we have paid a price for the change. Some of these costs could be estimated in economic terms, but many of the human costs can not be calculated in dollars.

However, with less than two and one-half percent of the population listed as farmers and with over half of the farm family's income now coming from non-farm sources (Census of Agriculture, 1982), the social consequences stemming from the reduced labor in agriculture may be of more historical than current or future interest in this country. More important to the society today are some of the consequences which flow from research which attempts to increase efficiency in ways other than reducing the labor input.

*Research Designed to Increase the Productivity of Non-Labor Inputs*

The major effort of agricultural researchers has been to increase the productivity of non-labor factors of production such as an acre of land, either through increased efficiency or increased inputs. The question frequently asked is "Can two blades of grass be grown where there is now one?" Agricultural research has been very successful in increasing yields per acre and improving other measures such as rate of gain or feed efficiency in livestock. The assumption behind this research is that increased food production from a given resource, such as a land or animal unit, will reduce the cost of food because increased efficiency reduces the cost of production. As in the case of research designed to reduce labor, there are social consequences which have not been anticipated and questions to be asked concerning the present and future cost as well as regarding impacts on the availability of food.

The major increases in production per acre have come from additional inputs to that acre of land. In the case of corn, the increases in yield from 35 to 150 bushels per acre (and in some cases much higher) have resulted from the use of hybrid seed, commercial fertilizers and chemicals. After World War II, the horse was also put aside as researchers opted for tractors and elaborate machines and the fuel necessary to build and to run them (Telleen, 1978). All of these inputs had to be purchased and thus required capital.

Today, commercial farmers have thousands of dollars invested in equipment. They must have access to even more capital to purchase other inputs. Recent data from the Missouri Mail-In-Record Association members suggest almost $150 of operating capital is required to produce an acre of corn. This is in addition to land costs (rented or purchased). It represents a sharp contrast to farms prior to World War II and some farms using organic or other alternative agricultural techniques today. The major social consequences of this research stem not from the research directly, but from the need for additional capital.

SOCIAL CONSEQUENCES OF THE CHANGING IMPORTANCE OF CAPITAL. In many ways, the research designed to reduce labor and the research designed to increase production, which requires more capital, have worked together to move selected farm families out of agriculture.

As farm prices dropped or failed to keep pace with the rising price of purchased inputs, net farm family income dropped. Thus, it became impossible for farm families to generate necessary capital from retained farm earnings (Tootell, 1966). Farming, an occupation once available to all persons willing to put forth the necessary labor, now became one of the most restrictive of all occupations. Only those individuals from families with considerable wealth were able to farm.

Agricultural research has benefited those that have access to capital both because capital was usually required to purchase the products associated with new innovations and because capital facilitates access to education and information. The adoption-diffusion studies clearly revealed that operators of large farms, with high family incomes, high education and access to a wide range of information were the early adopters of new practices (Rogers and Shoemaker, 1971). Many of those innovations proved to be very profitable to the innovators and early adopters. As a consequence, the innovations contributed to increasing the capital of those individuals. As more and more farmers adopted the new innovation, as in the classic case of hybrid seed corn, overall production of corn increased, and the price declined. Eventually the price of corn was reduced to the point that a farmer could not profitably produce with open-pollinated corn (Ruttan, 1982). If one could not generate the funds to purchase hybrid seed corn, he/she was forced out of corn production. (For a discussion on the organizational changes stemming from the introduction of hybrid corn, see Kloppenburg, 1984.) Thus, while labor-saving technologies reduced the need for labor, they increased the need for capital.

In current conditions, when the economic crisis is especially severe and a disproportionate number of farm families are facing bankruptcy, it is access to capital which determines who survives. Those farm families unable to generate sufficient capital from family resources are forced into the commercial money market to secure capital. But, the low rate of return to capital in agriculture makes the repaying of commercial loans with interest of twelve to twenty percent difficult or impossible. Over the decade of the '70s, when farm prices were generally strong, return to capital invested averaged only 7.3 percent for members of Missouri's Mail-In-

Record Association (Hein, 1983). When land prices were inflating rapidly during the 1970s, the consequence of this low rate of return relative to interest rates was masked. But as land prices have leveled off (or declined) the impact of borrowing capital for agricultural production has become more obvious. As more farmers entered the commercial loan market for large amounts of capital, control of production agriculture began to shift away from farm families.

Since most of the wealth in this country is located in urban centers, the trend for the past several decades has been for capital to move from urban areas into farm production. As urban capital moved to agricultural production, control of that production moved to urban areas. Usually the capital from urban areas is concentrated and channeled through financial and agribusiness organizations, but tax policies encourage more direct ownership patterns such as limited partnerships. These organizations have gained increasing control over agricultural production. Those organizations with major control have also been successful in extracting most of the profits from farm operations. Keeping the rate of return low prevents farmers from ever developing sufficient capital to regain control of agricultural production. It is becoming increasingly clear that in many sectors of the farm economy, it is no longer the farmers who are benefiting from public research.

The final consequence of research which emphasizes capital-intensive approaches has been the growing concentration and control of the food industry. Again, it may not have been the intended consequence of many agricultural researchers, but the concentration of control was greatly facilitated by research which required capital inputs.

THE BROILER INDUSTRY AS AN EXAMPLE. To demonstrate the consequences—both for the farmer and the consumer—of the relationship between the increased need for capital and the organization of the food system, I will focus on the broiler industry (Heffernan, 1984). The organization and structure of the broiler industry has probably undergone greater changes during the past 30 years than the organization of any other agricultural commodity.

In the 1940–50s, one part of poultry science research was focused on health problems. The concern was to eliminate such communicable diseases as coccidiosis so that larger numbers of poultry could be raised in a given area. As the disease problems were overcome, research on facility design increased rapidly. Newly designed buildings were constructed and new "labor saving" equipment was developed.

At the same time, nutritionists began to develop rations which would improve feed efficiency. This meant a movement away from home grown poultry feed to a more highly processed feed which included various feed additives.  Geneticists were at work attempting to develop strains of chickens that would perform best under confined conditions.  As a result, farmers became more dependent on hatcheries for genetic stock, on feed companies for feed, on pharmaceutical companies for feed additives and on purchased buildings and equipment.

As the capital required for producing poultry increased, farmers were unable to generate it.  This presented an opportunity to those hatcheries, feed companies, and processing companies which had available capital and which were looking for predictable markets for their products and reliable sources of poultry for processing.  By providing some capital, they saw they could obtain control of that segment of the industry.

The integrating companies did not have to provide all the capital to control the industry.  They began to make short-term capital available to the poultry producers.  Basically, these firms provided the capital for the feed, birds and health care.  In exchange, they required that a formal contract be signed by the farmer giving the integrating firm the right to decide the breed of the chickens, the ration to be fed, the health care practices to be followed, the date at which birds would be delivered and the time at which the birds would be picked up.  The farmer gave up all of the major management decisions.  In exchange, the farm family was paid on the basis of the pounds of chicken produced, which in an industrial setting would be called "paid on a piece rate."

The farm family still had to provide the labor and the long-term capital for the buildings and equipment by borrowing and using their land as collateral.  Of the 95 broiler producers that we interviewed in Union Parish, Louisiana, in 1981, only three were debt free (Heffernan, 1984).  Most growers obtain a 20 or 30 year loan on their buildings, but the contract with the integrating firm extends only for the time period from when a batch of chicks is received until they are marketed.  This is usually less than two months.  The growers gave up all management responsibility, and total control of production was shifted to the integrating firm (Heffernan, 1974).

As the poultry industry was becoming vertically integrated, it also was becoming horizontally integrated.  The long-term profitability of the industry was apparent to several agribusiness firms.  There followed within the industry a very competitive fight for dominance of the broiler industry in this country.  The large firms had more capital, and for the most part, these are the firms which are operating today.  But large did not necessarily mean the largest broiler integrating firms.  Large in this case meant large multinational conglomerates.

Today, there are fewer than 130 integrating firms in the United States.  The largest four companies produce about a third of all the poultry in this country, and the top 20 firms produce over two thirds of all the broilers.

Companies among the largest fifteen include Con-Agra and Imperial Foods of England (which is one of the three largest food corporations in England), Cargill, Tyson, Federal Milling Company, Continental Grain Company, Archer Daniels Midland, and Central Soya. Today, ninety-five percent of all broilers which are produced and sold in this country are produced and sold under this system.

No markets are available to farmers who are not willing to accept the contract of the integrating firms. Furthermore, these firms have a total of 243 processing plants, and they will not go beyond 30 miles from their plants for growers. This means that if one wants to produce poultry commercially in this country, he/she must live within 30 miles of one of the processing companies. In addition, growers must be willing to build a building to company specifications at a cost of approximately $80,000 and sign a formal contract with one of the integrating firms.

Within three decades, a commodity which was produced, processed and distributed in one of the most competitive market systems, which could be produced by large and small farmers alike, and which could be produced almost anywhere in this country has become one of the most organizationally and geographically concentrated segments of the food industry.

There is no doubt that poultry is produced more cheaply and is made available to consumers at a lower cost than at any other time in our history. But, the low price of poultry during the past couple of decades is at least partially the result of extreme control-seeking competition within the poultry industry. Information we received suggests that some conglomerates were for many years operating their poultry divisions at a loss. Those conglomerates with profits from other sectors could survive, but single product firms were forced out. As we move toward a more oligopolistic type of market, it is safe to assume that integrating firms will not continue to produce poultry at a loss. In the past year, profits have returned to the industry.

Agricultural research did not "cause" this radical change in the poultry industry, but it made the change possible. More importantly, few questions were asked by researchers about the social or organizational implications of their work.

Who benefits from poultry science research today? Clearly not the growers. The companies determine the rate at which growers will be paid. In many ways, agricultural research in poultry science today is done for the benefit of a few integrating firms. These integrating firms basically have a monopoly on the poultry supply in this country. They are now in a position to determine how much of this publicly-funded research benefit they will pass on to the consumer.

Although the poultry industry may be farther along the route of concentration than other segments of the food industry, it is not entirely unique. For example, Iowa Beef Producers (a subsidiary of Occidental Petroleum) and Cargill (under the name of Excel), slaughter 45 percent of all beef cattle in this country. (*The Record Stockman,* 1983; *The Drovers Journal,* 1984). Two hundred and one feedlots feed 45 percent of all the beef cattle. The largest feed lots are operated by Cargill. During the past year, Cargill tried to buy three beef slaughtering facilities from Land-O-Lakes. An antitrust suit brought by Mumfort of Colorado has prevented that merger.

A few giant conglomerates control the vast majority of the grain shipped in the world today (Hamilton, 1972), process most of the soybeans and grain (Martinson, 1978), and control the production of both red and white meat. With this type of control, farmers and consumers are no longer interacting in a competitive market (Martinson and Campbell, 1980). They must interact with a few specific companies, and these companies determine the quality and the price of the product. They also determine how much profit producers make. By and large, the profit margin has been so low that, in areas such as poultry and beef feeding, farmers have not been able to generate sufficient capital to produce independently.

The decentralized production system of the past served the consumer quite well. Many questions need to be asked of this new centralized system. For example, how will the benefits of poultry research be shared with the consumer in the future? What has happened to the quality of the product? Some consumers are concerned with the consequences of feed additives and would prefer to purchase poultry not fed such products, but they have no choice. What will be the future consequences of a few firms having virtual control over the genetic stock used in poultry production? As "unneeded strains" of poultry are allowed to become extinct, could we lose our diverse genetic base? The recent Avian flu scare in the northeast reminds one of the southern corn blight where reliance on genetically similar monocultures greatly increased losses. Are there unforeseen environmental factors which might suggest the need for other types of production systems in the future?

INCREASED SPECIALIZATION. Agricultural research has lead to increased specialization in agricultural production. As research developed more sophisticated equipment, the cost of the equipment increased dramatically. Farmers can no longer afford to own the expensive equipment that is required for the production of a large variety of commodities. Also, the information required to produce a particular commodity has and is continuing to increase rapidly. Farmers have difficulty in acquiring the necessary information for a variety of commodities. The consequence has been to limit the number of commodities produced on a farm.

In some areas of the midwest, many farms produce only corn and soy-beans. Current farming practices require that these crops be planted during two months in the spring and harvested during a two month period in the fall. Chemicals have virtually eliminated any labor requirements the remaining eight months of the year. Thus, the farm family is usually over-employed during four months of the year, but underemployed the remaining two-thirds of the year.

The work schedule varies, of course, depending on the commodity produced. The schedule is much shorter for broiler producers. Broiler growers are over-employed the first week or ten days following the receiving of the young chicks. But for the next month, they are underemployed. The production of some commodities, especially livestock such as dairy, is much more uniform in the labor requirement.

The problem with the work schedule resulting from increased specialization is that it is difficult for farmers to find non-farm jobs for the slack periods. This becomes another case of labor being released from agricultural production and not being absorbed and utilized by other segments of the society.

ECONOMIC IMPACT ON RURAL COMMUNITIES. Research which has led to a capital-intensive agriculture and relies heavily on purchased inputs has had an impact on rural areas in ways other than just the migration of farmers. The commercial farm of today has become an assembly plant. The farmer assembles land, seed, fertilizer and chemicals and distributes them in a particular geographic pattern so that he/she can utilize the sun's energy in the production process. After what is a relatively long production time period, the farmer collects the finished product and sells it.

From the community standpoint, this process contributes little to the economic well-being of the local area. In a sense, most of the production is not done in the rural area. The production is done in the oil refineries, farm equipment plants and chemical plants in urban areas. These products are then moved to their rural assembly plants. The farmer assembles all the inputs, but adds little value. Most of the value obtained from the "farm product" goes to those firms that produce the fertilizer, seed, chemicals and equipment. If capital is borrowed, some of the income has to go to make the interest payments. Much of the value of the agricultural product is simply passed through the rural community. The rural community receives no economic benefit.

Only a small portion of that which the farmer receives is circulated in the rural community. For example, if the fertilizer or equipment is sold through a local dealer, that dealer retains a small portion of the farmer's cost in exchange for his retail services. Many of the large farm operators, however, bypass the local retailers completely and buy directly from a company or distributor. In this case, none of the cost for the inputs contributes to the economic viability of the rural community. Since large farmers bypass local markets no economic contributions are made to the local community from the sale of the commodity.

This leaves only the return on labor to be circulated in the local community, and today the labor cost is frequently less than 10 percent of the total input costs. Although we can speak of the value of agricultural products in a community, often less than 10 percent of that value ever makes any contribution to the economic base of the community. As more farm purchased inputs are produced in urban centers, farm production contributes less and less to the economic base of rural communities.

On this basis the farm family is no more important to the economic base of the rural community than is the family which receives its income from some other work organization in the community, such as the post office. Fifty years ago (or today on organic farms), the farm added a higher percentage of value to the agricultural products and thus had the potential to provide a stronger economic base for the rural community. Today, the value of the agricultural products produced in an area tells us little about the contribution agriculture makes to the economic vitality of that community.

SOCIAL IMPACTS ON RURAL COMMUNITIES. The poultry industry is one example of a system in which the farm family and corporation jointly provide the capital. This opportunity is not available to producers of most commodities. For most persons in agricultural production, the choice is to provide the capital and be a family farmer or, if one does not have capital, to become a wage laborer working for a larger-than-family farm. An increasing proportion of agricultural goods are produced on large, industrial-type farms. In these structures, capital is provided by stockholders who are often far removed from the production process. Both labor and management are hired.

As land, labor, and capital, the three elements provided by the farm family, begin to be provided (as well as subdivided) by different individuals or groups, the social relationships that govern the way people interact begin to change. No longer are all of those involved in production agriculture farmers. In corporate farms, there are owners, managers, and workers. Although farmers with large operations have more status, economic power, and more political influence in the community than small farmers, they do not have control over small farmers. In corporations, however, managers have a major control over the well-being of workers. As the organizational structure of the production unit begins to be altered, the social implications are felt in the farm community.

Several studies conducted by researchers in the past few decades suggest that changes in the structure of agriculture are related to social changes in the community. A study by Goldschmidt (1978) in the 1940s compared two communities in California. Arvin was a rural community surrounded by large farms that employed a hired labor force. Duniba was a rural community surrounded predominately by family farms. The two communities were compared using numerous measures of quality of life including family income, level of living, social and religious institutions, and the degree of local control over the political process. Duniba, the community surrounded by family farms, ranked higher on more than fifteen different measures of quality of life.

These communities were examined by other researchers in 1970 (La Rose, 1973) and in 1977 (Community Services Task Force of the Small Farm Viability Project, 1977). Although neither of these two studies were as comprehensive as the original Goldschmidt study, the results of both indicated that the differences in the level of services provided by the communities were as great or greater than they were in the 1940s.

Another study in the Goldschmidt tradition was conducted in the San Joaquin Valley of California. This study avoided some criticisms of the Goldschmidt study by comparing 130 towns (Community Services Task Force of the Small Viability Project, 1977). The researchers concluded again that the communities surrounded by small-scale farming tended to offer more to local residents than those surrounded by large farms operated with hired labor.

In 1969, I interviewed contract poultry producers and family farmers, as well as owners (or managers) and workers on larger-than-family farms in Louisiana (Heffernan, 1972). Few differences were found between contract producers and family farmers with regard to involvement in formal and informal community activities. Small differences were found between these two categories of producers and owner-managers of larger-than-family farms, but major differences were found when compared to workers. Workers felt more alienated, were less involved in formal voluntary associations, and less active in political activities.

Numerous other studies have been conducted at different times in different geographic regions and using different methodologies (Rodefeld, 1974; Martinson, *et al.*, 1976; Flora and Conley, 1977; Heffernan and Lasley, 1978; and Harris and Gilbert, 1979). The results of all these studies affirm a relationship between the type of agricultural structure and the social consequences for rural communities.

The list of social consequences related directly or indirectly to agricultural research could be continued. Specific packages of research discoveries, such as those that led to the development of the mechanical tomato harvester, could be selected and traced and additional consequences could be identified (Friedland, 1973; Friedland, *et al.*, 1981). However, my major purpose is not to present an exhaustive list of social consequences but to suggest that there are a host of social consequences that have been ignored as agricultural research has focused almost exclusively on increased efficiency. To underscore the importance of these social factors, one needs only to suggest that a serious consideration of them throughout the research process might well have caused a redistribution in the use of public research funds.

## Reasons for Ignoring Social Consequences

Why did agricultural research go in the direction of energy- and capital-intensiveness? The easy answer is to blame leaders of agricultural research stations and the agricultural researchers. This suggests that the only solution needed is to enlighten those responsible for research. The real answer is much more basic. The problem originates in the social system of which the researchers are a part. The roots of the problem lie both in the failure of the society (or government) to develop a food policy for this country and in an economic system which focuses on a narrow view of efficiency.

### The Lack of a National Food Policy

This country has never attempted to develop a national plan for the food system. Because of abundant agricultural production (in part due to agricultural research), this country has never had to worry about national food shortages. Thus, the food system has never become the center of public attention and deliberate planning. As a consequence, the accepted goal for the food system is the same as for the rest of the economy: to produce as much as possible in the short run. This is most obvious when examining farm policy over the past half century.

Because there is no plan or policy for the food system, there is no plan or goal to orient agricultural research. Researchers are left on their own to determine what they pursue. They learn through their socialization experience what is considered good research. The research tends to emphasize discovery and is oriented toward a narrow view of efficiency (Busch and Lacy, 1983). Few persons inside the agricultural research establishment have ever challenged this narrow view of efficiency, nor have they asked what the longer-term environmental, health, and social ramifications of this research are.

### The Dominance of the Efficiency Paradigm

One of the major reasons that agricultural research has taken the direction of replacing labor with capital, energy, and chemicals is an over-reliance on the efficiency paradigm which serves as the basis for economic theory. It is not surprising that I, a sociologist, should raise this issue since this is a frequent topic of debate between economists and sociologists (Gardner, 1984). Perhaps it is not as much a problem with the paradigm per se as it is a problem with the way that it is operationalized, at least in the agricultural sector. In the process of operationalizing the efficiency model, those variables which are not easily measured empirically are omitted. Some of the basic values in this society, such as freedom, independence, and human dignity, do not lend themselves well to empirical measurement and are omitted from empirical models. Sometimes they are recognized in the abstract development of a utility function, but they are omitted in the empirical models. Future-oriented factors such as concern for public health, for the environment, for the substainability of agriculture are also difficult to operationalize and are not accounted for in the "market place." Thus, the very paradigm which has directed agriculture and agriculture research has simply not been effective in reflecting basic societal values nor in assessing real, but difficult to measure health, environment, and social costs.

Even staying within the rather narrow confines of the efficiency model, one can raise some questions regarding its application to agriculture. More specifically, why have labor, and to a lesser extend land, been the major input variables considered to be in scarce supply, when neither appear to be a constraint to adequate food production in this country? Unemployment is increasingly a problem facing this society, but research continues to focus on releasing more labor. Much agricultural research is designed to produce more per acre. But last year the government paid billions of dollars to reduce agricultural production by taking land out of production.

On the other hand, the crux of the current farm crisis is the huge debt farmers have incurred. Several government policy alternatives designed to reduce the principle or interest are being suggested. Yet, agricultural research continues to focus on new technologies and practices which require huge sums of capital. "Efficient" agricultural production in this country continues to be understood as a large agricultural output per unit of input of labor and, to a lesser extend, land. If attention was focused on other input variables such as energy, chemicals or capital, the results would be quite different. Our agriculture is very inefficient relative to capital invested, energy utilized, or chemicals utilized. Only a couple of the numerous inputs required have been selected for emphasis. Other resources utilized in food production such as quality water and topsoil are usually overlooked entirely. In short, agricultural research has been guided by an efficiency model which emphasizes only two input resources. Even if we stay with the efficiency model, a much larger number of variables needs to be considered.

EFFICIENCY AND SURVIVAL OF THE FITTEST. In addition to questions of resource efficiency, one has to raise questions concerning whether or not our system, which selects farmers on the basis of who can provide the necessary capital, really selects the best managers. When comparing those farm families who are in financial trouble and being forced out of agriculture today with those who continue to operate their farms, there is evidence to suggest that it is not necessarily the poor managers who are being forced out of agriculture.

A family farm has a life cycle that coincides with the farm family's life cycle. Four phases—establishment, development, maintenance, and retirement—have been identified (Bennett, 1982). If the farm family is in the later part of their development phase (between 35 and 45 years of age) when economic conditions for the commodities they produce turn sour, they are doomed to failure (Campbell, *et al.*, 1984). This is because they have acquired large debts in the early part of their development phase in order to obtain the necessary capital to set up a commercial farming operation. If they get through the development phase during good economic conditions, they have already begun to start paying off much of their farm debt and are likely to survive during the maintenance phase, even if conditions turn sour. Most of the farm foreclosures at this time are on those operations farmed by families in their late 30s and early 40s (*Newsweek,* 1984). They were in the development phase at the wrong time.

Recent data from the Missouri Mail-In-Record Association provide additional explanation. Using 1981 data, researchers divided all members of the Mail-In-Record Association into three categories based on their percent equity in the operation (Hein and Kirtley, 1982). One-third had 85 percent equity in their operation. A second third had between 65 and 85 percent equity. The remaining third had less than 65 percent equity in their operation.

Those in the first category had a net family income in 1982 of $16,000. Those in the second category broke even, but those in the last category had large negative family incomes. The explanation is quite simple. It goes back to the 7 percent return on their investment mentioned earlier. Of course, during the 1970s, land ownership, not farming, was very profitable because of the rapidly rising value of farmland. But the downturn in land prices in the 1980s has erased much of that benefit. Farmers receiving 7 percent or less return on their investments cannot pay 12 to 20 percent interest on a very large proportion of their total assets and still make a profit. The interesting point was that farmers in the third category, those with less than 65 percent equity, were the most efficient farmers when using measures such as pigs weaned per litter, pounds of milk per cow and bushels of grain per acre. Many of the farmers who are currently being forced out of agriculture because they do not have sufficient capital are some of the best farm managers we have ever had.

HISTORICAL FOUNDATIONS OF THE BELIEF IN EFFICIENCY. The belief system supporting the need for increasing the efficiency of farm workers appears to come from two major sources. From early on in our history scholars, entrepreneurs and politicians alike realized that cities could not be built and industries could not be developed unless a large proportion of the society's workers could be released from food production. The development of industries and cities required that agricultural technology be developed which would release huge numbers of workers from food production. Secondly, classical economic theory supported this exodus of farm labor by arguing that labor which is released in one productive sector of society will be transferred to another productive sector. After a period of adjustment, the whole society will be moved to a higher level of well-being. Today, these beliefs continue to be supported by farmers and others who defend agriculture and agricultural research by stressing the small number of farmers required to produce food.

The agricultural establishment points with pride to the fact that one farmer can produce enough to feed 10, 20, 30, 40, 50 and now, up to at least 70 to 80 other persons. This type of statement is misleading because, as I noted earlier, farmers today add little value in the food production process. Prior to World War II, when it was said that one farmer produced enough to feed 20 other people, it meant that most of the inputs in the food production process were provided by the farm family. Over half of the input costs for food production were in the form of labor, horsepower, and energy.

The saying that one farmer produces enough food for 70 or 80 other persons is erroneous. It is not just one farmer. It is a farm family and the host of workers and managers providing farm supplies and processing and distributing the produce. We continue to reduce the number of farmers required, but the number of persons in the food system continues to be between one-quarter to one-third of the labor force. We have changed people's occupations and possibly their place of residence, but the number of persons in the food system has changed little. We have not increased the efficiency of workers in the food system.

## Conclusion

Although most farmers and agricultural researchers subscribe to the belief that reducing labor in agriculture is good, they did not develop the belief, and they are not alone in supporting it. The belief is as prevalent in the industrial sector as it is in the agricultural sector. Agriculture is not unique. And it is more integrated into the larger society both economically and culturally than it has ever been.

One can be rather critical of some of the social consequences of agricultural research, but we should remember that agricultural research is not unique here either. The concerns I have expressed regarding the need for capital and its relationship to the concentration and control of agriculture are similar to those which have been raised regarding the many other industrial organizations which have already traveled along this path.

A critical examination of agricultural research forces us to review the whole value system of the society and the compatibility of that system with the social structure. Any attempt to develop an effective food policy would require us to order our priorities. This process would highlight some of the contradictions that exist between our values and what is. For example, the concentration of ownership and control is challenging one of our society's basic values which emphasizes individual opportunity and equality.

Agricultural research is not unique in the way it operates. It simply reflects our larger social, political and economic system. If there is any uniqueness to agriculture and agricultural research, it is that it contributes to the most basic need of mankind. The assurance of food now, and in the future, is one of society's major functions. Perhaps then it is fitting that we start with an evaluation of the food system as we attempt to understand the relationship between the social system in which we exist and the values we espouse.

The agricultural research organization in this country has proven to be very effective in achieving the goal of efficient use of labor and land in the short term. We have an abundance of food in this country. Thus, in the United States, we have the "luxury" of being able to focus some attention on other important social consequences.

## References

Bennett, John. W. 1982. *Of Time and the Enterprise.* Minneapolis: University of Minnesota Press.

Berardi, Gigi M., and Charles C. Geisler. 1984. *The Social Consequences and Challenges of New Agricultural Technologies.* Boulder, Colo.: Westview Press.

Burchinal, Lee G. 1962. "Career Choices of Rural Youth in a Changing Society." North Central Publication No. 142. Agricultural Experiment Station Bulletin 458. Minneapolis: University of Minnesota.

Busch, Lawrence, and William B. Lacy. 1983. *Science, Agriculture, and the Politics of Research.* Boulder, Colo.: Westview Press.

Campbell, Rex R. 1966. "A Suggested Paradigm for the Individual Adoption Process." *Rural Sociology* 31:458–466.

Campbell, Rex R.; William D. Heffernan; and Jere L. Gilles. 1984. "Farm Operator Cycles and Farm Debts: An Accident of Timing." *The Rural Sociologist.* Forthcoming.

Flora, Jan L., and Judith Lee Conby. 1977. "Impact of Type of Agriculture on Class Structure, Social Well-being, and Inequalities." Paper presented at the annual meetings of the Rural Sociological Society, Madison, Wisconsin.

Friedland, William H. 1973. "Social Sleepwalkers: Scientific and Technological Research in California Agriculture." Research Monograph No. 13. Santa Cruz: University of California.

Friedland, William H.; A. Barton; and R.J. Thomas. 1981. *Manufacturing Green Gold: Capital, Labor and Technology in the Lettuce Industry.* New York: Cambridge.

Galbraith, John Kenneth. 1969. *The Affluent Society,* 2nd ed., rev. Boston: Houghton Mifflin.

Gardner, Delworth B., and Carole Frank Nuckton. 1984. "Two Agricultural Economists Look at Rural Sociology." *The Rural Sociologist,* pp. 100–109, March.

Goldschmidt, Walter. 1978. *As You Sow: Three Studies in the Social Consequences of Agribusiness.* Montclair, N.J.: Allanheld, Osmun.

Hamilton, Martha M. 1972. "The Great American Grain Robbery and Other Stories." Washington, D.C.: Agribusiness Accountability Project.

Harris, Craig K., and Jess C. Gilbert. 1979. "Large-scale Farming, Rural Social Welfare, and the Agrarian Thesis: A Re-Examination." Paper presented at the Annual Meetings of the Rural Sociological Society, Burlington, Vermont.

Heffernan, Judith B. 1967. "A Comparative Study of Selected Characteristics of Nonmigrants and Migrants in Price County, Wisconsin." Unpublished Masters Thesis. Madison: University of Wisconsin.

Heffernan, William D. 1972. "Sociological Dimensions of Agricultural Structures in the United States." *Sociologia Ruralis* 12:481–499.

_____. 1974. "Social Consequences of Vertical Integrations: A Case Study." Unpublished Manuscript. *Proceedings of the Rural Sociology Section of the Society of Southern Agricultural Scientists.* Memphis, Tenn.

_____. 1984. "Constraints in the U.S. Poultry Industry." In *Research in Rural Sociology and Development,* ed. Harry K. Schwartzweller, Vol. I, pp. 237–260. Greenwich, Conn.: JAI Press.

Heffernan, William D., and Paul Lasley. 1978. "Agricultural Structure and Interaction in the Local Community: A Case Study." *Rural Sociology* 43:348–361.

Hein, Norlin A. 1983. "Missouri Farm Business Summary." University of Missouri Extension Division.

Hein, Norlin A.; Carroll L. Kirtley; and Donald Osburn. 1982. "Interest Costs: A Heavy Burden on Leveraged Operations." University of Missouri Farm Management Newsletter. September 10.

Hightower, Jim. 1973. *Hard Tomatoes, Hard Times.* Cambridge, Mass.: Schenkman.

Kirkendall, Richard Stewart. 1966. *Social Scientists and Farm Politics in the Age of Roosevelt.* Columbia: University of Missouri Press.

Kliebenstein, James B.; William D. Heffernan; Donald A. Barrett; and Carroll L. Kirtley. 1981. "Economic and Sociologic Motivational Factors in Farming." *Journal of the American Society of Farm Managers and Rural Appraisers,* pp. 10–14.

Kloppenburg, Jack, Jr. 1984. "The Social Impacts of Biogenetic Technology in Agriculture: Past and Future." In *The Social Consequences and Challenges of New Agricultural Technologies,* ed. Gigi M. Berardi and Charles C. Geisler, pp. 291–321. Boulder, Colo.: Westview Press.

LaRose, Bruce L. 1973. "Arvin and Dinuba Revisited." Hearing before Subcommittee on Monopoly, Select Committee on Small Business, U.S. Senate. Washington, D.C.: U.S. Government Printing Office.

Mann, Susan A., and James M. Dickinson. 1978. "Obstacles to Development of a Capitalist Agriculture." *Journal of Peasant Studies* 5:466–481.

Martinson, Oscar B. 1978. "The American Grain Marketing System: An Organizational Analysis." Unpublished Ph.D dissertation. Madison: University of Wisconsin.

Martinson, Oscar B., and Gerald R. Campbell. 1980. "Betwixt and Between: Farmers and the Marketing of Agricultural Inputs and Outputs." *The Rural Sociology of the Advanced Societies: Critical Perspectives,* ed. Frederick H. Buttel and Howard Newby, pp. 215–253. Montclair, N.J.: Allanheld, Osmun.

Martinson, O.B.; E.A. Wilkening; and R.D. Rodefeld. 1976. "Validity and Reliability of Indicators of Alienation and Integration Applied to a Selected Rural Sample." Unpublished manuscript. Madison: Department of Rural Sociology, University of Wisconsin.

Newby, Howard, and Frederick H. Buttel. 1980. "Toward a Critical Rural Sociology." *The Rural Sociology of the Advanced Societies: Critical Perspectives,* ed. Frederick H. Buttel and Howard Newby, pp. 1–35. Montclair, N.J.: Allanheld, Osmun.

*Newsweek,* April 2, 1984, pp. 60–62.

Pelletier, Kenneth R., 1977. *Mind as Healer, Mind as Slayer.* New York: Dell.

Rodefeld, Richard D.; Jan Flora; Donald Voth; Isao Fujimoto; and Jim Converse. 1978. *Change in Rural America: Causes, Consequences, and Alternatives.* St. Louis: C.V. Mosby.

Rogers, Everett M., and F. Floyd Shoemaker. 1971. *Communication of Innovations.* New York: Free Press.

Ruttan, Vernon W. 1982. "Changing Role of Public and Private Sectors in Agricultural Research." *Science* 216:23–28.

_____. 1982. *Agricultural Research Policy,* Minneapolis: University of Minnesota Press.

Small Farm Viability Project (editors). 1977. *The Family Farm in California.* Sacramento, California: Small Farm Viability Project.

Schwarzweller, Harry K., ed. 1984. *Research in Rural Sociology and Development,* Vol. 1. Greenwich, Conn: JAI Press.

*The Drovers Journal.* 1984. "Big Packers Getting Bigger." June 28.

*The Record Stockman.* 1983. "Beef Packing May be Nation's Most Concentrated Industry." August 4.

Tootell, Robert B. 1966. "Credit for the Farm Family." *What's Ahead for the Family Farm,* pp. 23–30.

# 11

# Beyond Conventional Economics— An Examination of the Values Implicit in the Neoclassical Economic Paradigm as Applied to the Evaluation of Agricultural Research

## Patrick Madden

## Introduction

### Initial Definitions

If we follow Jacob Viner's axiom that "economics is what economists do," then we find that economics is a multifaceted profession embracing a wide range of philosophical, theoretical, and methodological perspectives. The orthodox or neoclassical approach perhaps comes closest to the popular view that economics is a science of business transactions—although Von Mises contends the science is more accurately described as dealing with "all market phenomena and with all their aspects" (1962:77). However, this definition is far too restrictive, for it excludes much of the work in important areas and schools of thought, such as public finance (Musgrave, 1959), natural resource economics (Butlin, 1981; Castle, *et al.,* 1981; Ran-

Helpful suggestions in preparing this chapter were offered by Ken Dahlberg, Glenn Johnson, Jim Shortle, Spiro Stefanou, Ted Alter, and Emery Castle. Opinions expressed herein are those of the author.

dall, 1981), institutional economics (Gordon, 1980; Samuels, 1980; Schmid, 1980) and behavioral economics (Weaver and Stefanou, 1984).

*Neoclassical economics* is the theoretical framework and the backbone of the academic training of most economists educated in this country. Neoclassical economics focuses primarily on *microeconomics,*

> . . . those parts of economic analysis whose concern is the behavior of individual units, in particular, consumers and firms, rather than with aggregates such as unemployment, the price level, national income, etc. which are the subject of *macroeconomics.* [Neoclassical economics is] a theory of allocation of scarce resources in a static economy . . . a subjective value theory of price determination, based on demand and supply, a marginal productivity theory of distribution . . . and the vision of a harmonious economic system [Pearce, 1983:278,308].

Kuttner (1985:74) defines neoclassical economics as follows:

> Neoclassical economics, the reigning school, marries the assumptions of the classical invisible hand—the principle of self-regulating economy—to the keynesian insight that macroeconomic stabilization by government is necessary to keep the clockwork operating smoothly. In method, standard economics is highly abstract, mathematical, and deductive, rather than curious about institutions. Neoclassical economic theory posits an economic system of "perfect competition." All transactions in the economy are likened to those that occur in simple marketplaces, like fish markets, in which prices rise or fall exactly enough to move the merchandise. As economists say, adjustment of price based on supply and demand serves to "clear the market." That is, if there is an oversupply of herring on a given day, the shrewd fishmonger will lower his price; otherwise the market will fail to clear and the fish will rot. If there is high demand for lobster but short supply, the fishmonger will raise his price; otherwise there will be too many willing buyers. From this stylized picture of a small market, standard economics projects a "general equilibrium" that is said to characterize the entire economy. . . .
> The model also assumes that markets are composed of many sellers and many buyers, who individually have too little market power to dictate prices or to manipulate choices, and can only offer or accept bids. . . .
> Perfect competition requires "perfect information." Consumers must know enough to compare products astutely; workers must be aware of alternative jobs, and capitalists of competing investment opportunities. Otherwise, sellers could charge more than a competitive price and get away with it, and workers could demand more than their services were worth. Moreover, perfect competition requires "perfect mobility of factors." Workers must be free to seek the highest available wage, and capitalists to shift their capital to get the highest available return; otherwise, identical factors of production would command different prices, and the result would be a deviation from the model.

Despite the apparent naïvete of the strict assumptions of the neoclassical model, the concensus among economists is that the model is rather robust; that is, while deviations from these assumptions are commonly recognized, the predictive value of the model in many contexts nonetheless remains quite strong.

Economists who study *public finance* are typically trained in neoclassical economics, but they relax some of the key assumptions. Musgrave (1959:3) defines public finance as "the complex of problems that center around the revenue-expenditure process of government." The concerns of public finance include resource allocation, the distribution of income, full employment, price-level stability and economic growth—those factors that determine the material well-being of individuals, groups, and society as a whole; public finance inquires how these phenomena are affected by taxation and government spending. Musgrave (1959:4) identifies two categories of public finance: *predictive* inquiry which seeks to explain why existing policies are pursued and to predict which policies may be adopted; and *normative* analysis which addresses the political and social values of society that interact with the market sector of the economy.

Economists specializing in *resource economics* are also steeped in neoclassical theory, but here again, they lay aside key assumptions. Also, training in natural resource economics typically develops an acute awareness of the value assumptions underlying the neoclassical paradigm. Perhaps the most definitive essay on the nature and scope of natural resource economics is the review article by Castle *et al.* (1981). This essay traces the intellectual geneology of natural resource economics, the methodologies widely used, and the major research accomplishments of that field since World War II, in applied areas such as water, resource scarcity, environmental economics, and others. Resource economists are eclectic—drawing upon both neoclassical and institutional economics in their works.

*Institutional economics* is a school of thought founded by Thorstein Veblen, Wesley C. Mitchell, and John R. Commons. Prominent exponents of this school include Clarence Ayres (1952), Gunnar Myrdal (1978), and Philip Klein (1978). Myrdal (1978:773–774) for example, characterizes institutional economics as follows:

> The most fundamental thought that holds institutional economists together is our recognition that even if we focus attention on specific problems, our study must take into account the entire social system, including everything else of importance for what comes to happen in the economic field. Foremost, among other things, is the distribution of power in society and, more generally, economic, social, and political stratification; indeed, all institutions and attitudes. To this must be added, as an exogenous set of factors, induced policy measures, applied with the purpose of changing one or several of these exogenous factors.

Klein (1978:264) observes that "Institutionalists give a very different meaning to the word *value* than do standard economists, who more often than not merely equate value with price." Neoclassical economics takes political and market institutions as fixed and given; institutionalists take a different view: "Growth and progress, conflict and its resolution through change, these are the processes that interest institutionalists, not mechanistic equilibrium" (Klein, 1978:265).

Whereas "conventional" or neoclassical economics is inherently reductionist in assuming away troublesome realities, institutional economics is more holistic, seeking to formulate logically integrated systems. And whereas most conventional economists do not regularly account for the value assumptions underlying their theories and methods, institutional economists are schooled to be acutely aware of, and to acknowledge clearly, their key assumptions. Reaching beyond the range of concepts of conventional economics, institutionalists seek to form a bridge with sociology, political science, ethics, and history.

To be commended for their breadth of perspective, institutionalists are nonetheless in frequent peril of holistic paralysis. Impatient policymakers often embrace the relatively quick and seemingly more precise solutions offered by neoclassical analysts, rather than wallow through the necessarily more complicated, but more realistic analysis offered by institutionalists.

Created in part as a reaction against the reductionist perspective of neoclassical economics (Samuels, 1980:8–16), institutional economics was initially predicated on the assumption that technology (including both "hardware" and "software") determines the opportunities and ultimately the welfare of individuals and societies. Institutional economics has gradually developed several intellectual positions (Klein, 1978; Gordon, 1980:8–16). One—evolutionary or developmental theory—focuses on the processes by which institutions affecting property rights and other rules change. Another, illustrated by the works of Schmid (1978), is concerned with assessing the impact of changes in institutions, as a guide to better public and private decision making.

An emerging school, *behavioral economics* (Weaver and Stefanou, 1984), questions the predictive efficacy of neoclassical economics. This school orientation recognizes, for example, that individual preferences are ambiguous, that individuals rarely make decisions based upon complete or accurate information, and that uncertainty clouds a firm's prediction of production processes—particularly in agriculture. Behavioral economists postulate that instead of limiting their models to those predicated on "fixed decision environments in which information is instantaneously available and rationally processed," economists should construct models consistent with observed behavior of the decision makers (Weaver and Stefanou, 1984:174). Based largely upon cognitive psychology, this school of thought seeks to explain deviations between the optimizing behavior predicted by neoclassical analysis and the actual behavior of firms and consumers. Simon's (1978) concepts of bounded rationality and satisficing illustrate the conceptual innovations proposed by the behavioralists.

Beyond the question of the neoclassical model's predictive power, however, and more germane to the present discussion, is the impression given by many economists that they have adopted the model as their norm or ideal: "Perfect competition, in a sleight of epistomological hand, is said to describe the best possible as well as the actual world. . . . Neoclassical economics, with its reliance on the efficiency of markets, is a lavishly embroidered brief for laissez-faire" (Kuttner, 1985:74,83).

A vast array of work is performed by economists in various employment contexts. One important task has been the evaluation of publicly funded programs. Particularly in the past decade, agricultural economists have performed studies to evaluate agricultural research. Most of this research has been done by rather orthodox neoclassical researchers who rarely ask how the value assumptions underlying their analysis influence the findings and their interpretation. Indeed, to ask them this question is close to heresy because of their belief that economics is a value-free science.

Myrdal (1972:33) draws an important distinction between "values" and "valuations." He observes that the term "values" connotes something "solid, homogeneous, and fairly stable, while in reality valuations are regularly contradictory, even in the mind of a single individual, and also unstable, particularly in modern society." Through a process of valuation, a person reaches a value position.

For purposes of this chapter, it is convenient to distinguish between two ways in which value positions enter into the world of economists: value judgments and value assumptions. The former are explicit; the latter are implicit and often unrecognized by the economist. The distinction, then, between value judgments and value assumptions is taken to be strictly cognitive. If the economist realizes and admits to embracing a particular value assumption, it thereby becomes a value judgment for purposes of this analysis. At one end of the cognitive continuum is the economist who realizes fully the nature and implications of the value assumptions within which he operates, and candidly acknowledges these value positions. At the other extreme is the "positive economist," who believes his profession is free of value positions.

## Scope of Inquiry

The first part of this chapter examines the general value judgments and assumptions upon which conventional or neoclassical economics is based. The specific value assumptions underlying current economic evaluations

of agricultural research are then scrutinized. Finally, the value characteristics of a more socially and ecologically responsible approach to agricultural science and technology are delineated.

## Value Assumptions in Economics

It is universally acknowledged that economists make both value judgments and assumptions—as citizens, as consumers, or as adherents or
non-adherents to a particular religious faith. Those espousing positive
economics, however, contend that economists, in their role as economists,
are ethically neutral. A rather extensive (and in my judgment, convincing) literature argues that the economist *qua* economist conducts his or
her professional work in a context replete with both value judgments and
assumptions—those of colleagues, of peer review committees, of contract-
funding clients, of the editorial boards of professional disciplinary journals, of governmental bodies that determine budgets for research, and of
the body politic which establishes the laws and institutions that shape
market structures and determine the distributions of income and wealth
(Machlup, 1969:113–115). All of these contextual values set the stage
upon which the economist performs. They exert great leverage upon the
economist's choice to research problem and method, the resources at his/
her disposal, decisions as to which phenomena or categories of subjects
are relevant to be researched, the emphasis and interpretation given to
specific findings—even the decision whether to be an economist.

In addition to operating within this larger value context, the economist
takes either explicit (value judgment) or implicit (value assumption) positions on several strategic matters, including his or her philosophical orientation toward science, reductionism and mathematization, harmlessness,
monetization of value, consumer sovereignty, efficiency, productivity, and
intertemporal equity.

### Philosophic Orientation Toward Science

Important aspects of the economist's philosophic orientation toward science typically include a series of value positions favoring veracity, curios-
ity, measurement or quantification, and objectivity (Boulding, 1970:119;
McCloskey, 1983:484–485). While most economists make a preeminent
value judgment in favor of what is often termed "positive" as opposed to
"normative" economic analysis, the definitions underlying this choice are
often fuzzy, if not untenable (Machlup, 1969; Katouzian, 1980:135–153).
The feature of positive economics most attractive to economists is
(presumed) objectivity or value neutrality. "Objective" decisions are more
easily defended than "subjective" ones—hence objectivity is a source of

security to the economist. Furthermore, the economist's clients typically expect objectivity—an analysis of the effects that given means will have upon given ends.

Friedman (1953:4) states that "positive economics is in principle independent of any particular ethical position or normative judgments. . . . In short, positive economics is, or can be, an 'objective' science, in precisely the same sense as any of the physical sciences." Normative economics is thought to deal with value judgments as to "what ought to be," while positive economics presumably deals with "what is." When economists decide that positive economics is superior to normative economics, they are making a preeminent value judgment which determines in large part what kinds of work they will do, how they will do it, and how they will interpret the results.

The philosophical progenitor of positive economics is generally considered to be logical positivism (McCloskey, 1983:485). It turns out, however, that positive economics is at best an illegitimate offspring estranged from its alleged parent. While logical positivism is predicated strictly upon systematic reasoning based on observable phenomena and testable propositions, many of the theoretical constructs upon which the work of positive economics is erected are not directly testable nor observable (Machlup, 1969:112–113; Katouzian, 1980:56–71). For example, constant returns to scale, which implies equiproportional changes in *all* resource inputs, is not strictly testable; firms in the real world do not hold the ratios of all resources constant as they expand or contract (Madden, 1984b). Katouzian also contends that neoclassical consumer theory is not strictly testable due to logical circularity—for example, consumer choices are strongly affected by prior knowledge of relative prices—and because the available data are imperfect reflections of their referent concepts.

Adherents of positive economics frequently contend that positive means measurable, while normative (considered by them the polar opposite of positive) economics involves non-measurable phenomena (Machlup, 1969:102). Neither component of this argument is entirely valid. Much of the data used in positive economic analysis is critically flawed—a reality conveniently ignored by economists rushing toward completion of statistical estimation of parameters and a longer list of refereed journal articles. Secondly, the realm of values is far from non-measurable. Witness, for example, the many scientifically designed opinion polls and the landmark study by Busch and Lacy (1983) reporting the reasons given by agricultural economists (among other disciplines) for their choice of research topics.

Seemingly more defensible than the measurability criterion for distinguishing positive from normative economics is the instrumentalist nature of much positive economic analysis, wherein findings are stated as conditional propositions. If the decisionmaker prefers goal A, then option X will attain A at lower cost then will option Y. But if goal B is preferred, then Y is the more efficient option. As far as it goes, this type of instrumental statement appears to be value free. Looking deeper, however, it becomes clear that value assumptions are imbedded in the findings. The criterion of choice between options X and Y was cost—which is based upon market prices and institutions that are a reflection of consumer and societal values. Exclusion of other criteria (ecological impact, equity considerations, etc.) is a *de facto* value assumption that these non-market criteria are irrelevant. Other important value assumptions are the decisions to ignore options Z and W and to inquire only about goal preferences A and B and not C and D.

Many economists who profess to practice "positive economics" routinely engage in normative activity when they attack the wisdom of various public policies. Such analysis is ordinarily presented in an "objective" manner—if our nation wants to continue to prosper, then the massive structural deficits in the federal budget must be greatly reduced, for example.

Coats (1964:11) observes that in economics there is "a continual interplay between logic and observation, and considerable scope for individual judgment in the selection of 'potentially' influential from 'actually' influential variables, . . . strictly formal procedures cannot eliminate all individual judgments."

Ulmer (1980:175–176) states that:

> It is not the presence of value judgments in standard economics that is reprehensible, but the fact that they are unacknowledged, hidden, the fifty-third card in the casino deck, the medium's helper behind the arras, the sacred unmentionable that never can be exposed in the forum of public opinion. Such value judgments have a capacity only for harm, for distortion, for retarding or obscuring knowledge rather than advancing it.

He goes on to say that it is inevitable that economics deal in value judgments, and that if the science became truly value free it would thereby also become substance free, useless. He argues that value judgments can and should be tested in research based on actual experience (1980:178). Glenn Johnson (1982:72–73), substantially in agreement with Ulmer on this point, proposes an "iterative-interaction" form of research to test simultaneously both positive and normative hypotheses: "Problem solving is an *iterative* process with many feedbacks as a decisionmaker or researcher proceeds through the steps of problem definition, observation, analysis, decisionmaking, execution, and responsibility bearing." In this way, the researcher learns what the decisionmaker considers "good or bad," in an iterative process whereby progressively better informed choices are offered.

In his critique of standard (read neoclassical) economics, Daly (1980, ix-x) contends that:

> We absolutely must revise our economic thinking so that it will be more in conformity with the finite energy and resource limits of the earth, and with the finite limits of man's stomach. Standard economics confines its attention to the study of how best to allocate given means among given ends. It does not inquire very deeply into the nature of means or the nature of ends. . . . Our narrow economics is likely to commit the error of wishful thinking (assuming that just because something is desirable it must also be possible). Likewise, unless we inquire into the nature of ends and face the questions of ultimate value, ethics, and the ranking of our ends, we are likely to commit the opposite error, that of technical determinism (assuming that just because something is possible it must also be desirable).

Castle (personal communication, 1985) contends that Daly's argument is flawed by an apparent assumption of a constant knowledge base. History has demonstrated repeatedly that what is desirable often (though not universally) becomes possible through advances in science and technology. And while it may be foolhardy to take the extreme position of assuming that all present and future problems will be somehow solved by new knowledge, the opposite position is equally untenable. One's position between these polar extremes is a matter of subjective judgment. Studies of the agricultural science and technology enterprise (such as Ruttan, 1982, and Feller *et al.* 1984) demonstrate that a wide range of problems can be solved and opportunities realized through the commitment of adequate scientific and educational resources, within a congenial organizational and institutional setting. However, it is important to recognize explicitly the value assumptions built into much conventional (neoclassical) economic analysis that ignores externalities and treats the use of non-renewable resources as ordinary expenses, valued at current market prices, a common analytical procedure assailed by critics such as Daly (1980) and Schumacher (1973). Certain schools of thought (notably the institutionalists) and subject matter areas (natural resource economics and environmental economics for example) have demonstrated an awareness of the "side effects" often assumed away in conventional economic analysis (Castle, 1965). Castle *et al.* (1981:427–428) in summarizing an extensive literature in which economists have given explicit attention to "externalities" and other "market failures," have noted,

> Failure to appreciate the implications of the basic externality literature significantly handicapped any economist in the analysis of the social problems of the 1960s and 1970s. . . . At least some of our economic progress has been the result of decisions that were not based on full accounting of the social costs. To the extent that economists have supplied decision makers with information that has not reflected these costs, they must bear part of the responsibility.

In summary, the positive-normative dichotomy is misleading as a descriptor of the philosophy of science actually embraced by economists. Value positions are universally taken by economists, whether they know it or not. The most doctrinaire neoclassical economists deny it but the institutionalists, natural resource economists, and members of other schools and subject matter areas make a concerted effort to give explicit attention to value assumptions, externalities and social costs often ignored in conventional economic analysis. As Castle has stated, (personal communication, 1985) "We need to work harder at getting those imbedded values into the open so that their effects can be judged." The integrity and usefulness of economics is enhanced when explicit attention is given to value positions (Leontief, 1971).

## Reductionism and Mathematization

Increasingly economists are turning their attention to mathematical representations of the economy or various logically reduced subsets thereof. This trend has lent an air of sophistication and precision to economics, and has led to rigorous treatment of concepts. However, some economists have expressed alarm over this trend. One comment often made is that increased use of mathematics has led to a false sense of security on the part of economists (Kamarck, 1983:3–6). McCloskey (1983:512) contends that "economists are stumbling towards conventions of prose that are bad for clarity and honesty." Robert Solo, (1969:24–27) posits that the current generation of economists tends to confuse mathematical proficiency for increased economic knowledge. Solo summarizes this trend, which started in the 1930s and accelerated after the second World War, as being driven by the value judgment that economics must become a "true science," after the model of physics. He recognizes two powerful value sets—the "Hicks Effect" and the "Samuelson Effect"—which shaped this trend and work together to the detriment of economics.

The Hicks Effect (named after the Oxford economist Sir John Hicks) centers on the demand that economics become: "free of values and entirely neutral with respect to the comparative needs and wants, pains and pleasures, frustrations and opportunities of the different persons or groups or classes that compose the social universe." Solo then critically assails the Hicks Effect as follows: "Consuming vast energies and lots of paper, the endeavor to establish a value-free economics of welfare yielded nothing. Yet, that the enterprise so long withstood the assault of common sense can be explained only by the fact that it was insulated from any queries concerning its relevance or meaning by a dense wall of esoteric symbolism—the Samuelson Effect."

Whereupon, Solo defines and critiques the Samuelson Effect:

When Paul Samuelson wrote *Foundations of Economic Analysis,* his declared intention was to recast economic theory into a set of mathematical propositions *in order that those propositions could be tentatively verified or definitely refuted through experimental test,* thus giving to economics the same empirical base that physics had. In one sense, Samuelson was enormously successful. He set the tone and direction for his generation. He became a man of great influence and affluence, a Nobel Prize winner and a millionaire. In another sense, he failed completely. He and those who followed him succeeded certainly in recasting the whole of economics in complex and esoteric mathematical symbolism, *but not a single one of the propositions of theory has, as a consequence, been exposed to refutation through experimental test.* The basis for the acceptance or rejection of the propositions of economics remains as much a matter for intuitive judgment as ever before [emphasis in the original].

As economists have sought to be respected and rewarded in academic and other professional circles as "true scientists" they have honed their quantitative skills to a fine edge, with increasingly sophisticated and mathematical techniques. Criticizing the propensity of economists to substitute compactness and obscurity for simplicity and clarity, Leontief (1971:1–2) has stated: "Uncritical enthusiasm for mathematical formulation tends often to conceal the ephemeral substantive content of the argument behind a formidable front of algebraic signs. . . . it is the empirical validity of the assumptions on which the usefulness of the exercise depends." Leontief (1971:3) also contended that the tendency to increasingly mathematize economics has distorted the values of the academic community: "Continued preoccupation with imaginary hypothetical, rather than with observable reality has gradually led to a distortion of the informal valuation scale used in our academic community to assess and to rank the scientific performance of its members. Empirical analysis, according to this scale, gets a lower rating than formal mathematical reasoning." He goes on to observe that an economist is likely to earn a higher professional status by devising a new statistical procedure for estimating an unknown parameter (often from data whose exact meaning and validity remain unclear to the analyst and to readers), than by performing a successful quest for more and better data "that would permit us to measure the magnitude of the same parameter in a less ingenious, but more reliable way" (1971:35).

Leontief (1971:5) cites Agricultural Economics as an "exceptional example of a healthy balance between theoretical and empirical analysis and of the readiness of professional economists to cooperate with experts in the neighboring disciplines." While Agricultural Economics may be more "healthy" than its parent discipline in this regard, it is tending inexorably in the direction of more disciplinary isolation and mathematical sophistication. The editorial policies of the "most prestigious" refereed journals, in combination with the "publish or perish" syndrome in the awarding of academic tenure and in promotions and merit pay increases, constitute a valuation system that strongly modifies the behavior of agricultural economists. This behavior modification scheme encourages more theoretical and mathematical research as opposed to projects requiring the creation of new or improved data bases; it rewards sole- or senior-authored articles, thus discouraging interdisciplinary team efforts relative to "one-man shows;" it encourages research in which value judgments are implicit and shared by the reviewers, but it rejects research dealing explicitly with controversial values and conflicting goals; it prefers form over content, technique over problem-solving, mathematics over economics; it glorifies the analysis of hypothetical puzzles as opposed to substantive problems; it rewards elitism and chauvinism while disparaging practicality (Katouzian, 1980:204–206; Busch and Lacy, 1983:229–234; Johnson, 1984:5–9).

Like most scientists, economists frequently select research topics on the basis of the requirements of the method they wish to employ. As the methods have become more highly mathematical and abstract, the scope of inquiry has often been reduced accordingly. Decrying this reductionist trend, Boulding (1970:157) states: "If the formal study of economics boxes itself in so much that real economics problems will have to be studied outside it, this will be worse for economists than it is for mankind."

*Harmlessness*

Another widely embraced value assumption postulates that it is desirable to avoid inflicting pain upon one individual or class at the expense of another. This value assumption is manifested in a huge body of economic research based on Pareto and Hicks-Kaldor criteria. The Pareto-safety approach assumes that any innovation is desirable if it makes at least one person "better off" without making others "worse off." A closely related concept, "Pareto-efficiency," is defined as "a situation in which everyone is so well-off that it is impossible to make anybody better-off without simultaneously making at least one person worse-off" (Randall, 1983:41,113). The economist starts by asking how each property owner or consumer can maximize his/her "welfare" without infringing upon the rights of others—the Pareto-better criterion. Less restrictive than the Pareto-better criterion is the Hicks-Kaldor criterion, which permits changes that would make someone worse off if the benefits to the gainers are large enough to more than compensate the losers. Such payments are not assumed to actually occur (Page, 1977: 145–146).

The Pareto and Hicks-Kaldor concepts lie at the center of the so-called "new welfare economics" (Arrow and Scitovsky, 1969:387–433). While most orthodox practitioners of neoclassical economics seem to take for granted that only those innovations should be permitted that pass the Pareto or Hicks-Kaldor criteria, this value presumption gives preference to the existing institutions, distribution of property rights, and income. As Schmid (1978:202), a prominent institutionalist, observes:

> Initial income distribution is exogeneously determined in most economic models. The determination of factor ownership is somehow made prior to economic analysis. There is some assumed political process that allocates ownership. The economist proceeds to ask how each property owner can maximize welfare without infringing on the property of others. The conventional answer uses the doctrine of Pareto-better efficiency as a guide to institutional choice. That institution is better that makes it possible, when starting from some given factor (or goods) ownership for some person to be made better off without anyone else being made worse off.

Pareto optimality requires, in effect, a unanimous voting rule which is clearly unworkable in most public and private decisionmaking contexts. The Hicks-Kaldor condition is less restrictive, but is also impractical in many situations. Both criteria rest on questionable value assumptions as Boulding (1970:126) has pointed out:

> Many, if not most, economists regard the Paretian optimum as almost self-evident. Nevertheless, it rests on an extremely shaky foundation of ethical propositions. The more one examines it, for instance, the more clear it becomes that economists must be extraordinarily nice people even to have thought of such a thing, for it implies that there is no malevolence anywhere in the system. It implies, likewise, that there is no benevolence, the niceness of economists not quite extending as far as goodwill. It assumes selfishness, that is, the independence of individual preference function, such that it makes no difference to me whether I perceive you as better off or worse off. Anything less descriptive of the human condition could hardly be imagined. The plain fact is that our lives are dominated by the very interdependence of utility functions which the Paretian optimum denies. Selfishness, or indifference to the welfare of others, is a knife-edge between benevolence on the one side and malevolence on the other. It is something that is very rare. We may feel indifferent toward those whom we do not know and with whom we have no relationships of any kind, but toward those with whom we have a relationship, even the frigid relationship of exchange, we are apt to be either benevolent or malevolent. We either rejoice when they rejoice, or we rejoice when they mourn.

## The Monetization of Value

Oscar Wilde has been quoted as saying, "a cynic is a man who knows the price of everything and the value of nothing." While neoclassical economists widely deny that their analysis includes normative components, the market prices they use so widely in economic analysis are, in fact, normative data. As Johnson (1982:68) states, ". . . prices are values in exchange that reflect the underlying values of the parties involved." Market prices are a reflection of preferences for goods and services expressed by present-day consumers who have the income and the will to spend it—which in turn reflect the existing distributions of income and wealth. Prices are also a reflection of marketing and other institutions, which are another reflection of the values of some components of society—those most influential in shaping the rules of property ownership (Schmid, 1978:4).

Institutional and resource economists (Georgescu-Roegen, 1971; Randall, 1981; Karmack, 1983) have been among the most vocal critics of the use of market prices as weights in deriving value aggregates. For example, in reviewing a series of essays on the national income accounts in general, and gross national product (GNP) in particular, Jaszi (1971) expresses regret that market prices must be used in determining indicators of economic performance. For all the deficiencies of GNP and its related measures, however, a more acceptable method than the national income accounts has yet to be developed for reflecting the economic tempo of the nation—the rate at which the nation generates goods and services (as well as some "bads" and "dis-services").

While the market mechanism is widely recognized by economists as a highly efficient system for meeting the private wants of individual consumers, this mechanism fails to reveal consumer preferences for public wants. One category of public wants is "social wants," those satisfied by services consumed equally by all residents regardless of their monetary contribution—such as defense. The second category is "merit wants," things like free education and innoculations that are considered so meritorious that they are supported through the public budget in a priority manner over-riding consumer preferences (Musgrave, 1959:9–13).

Some humanist critics of neoclassical economics are rather strident in their characterization of economics in general and its monetization of value in particular (Schumacher, 1973:9). Intimately related to the monetization of values is the value assumption of consumer sovereignty.

## Consumer Sovereignty and the Enthronement of Greed

The key value assumption here is that the individual consumer is the best judge of what goods and services will satisfy him. Neoclassical demand theory assumes "consistent maximization of a well-ordered function, such as a utility or profit function" (Becker, 1976:153). Varien's (1984:112) representation of the neoclassical theory of consumer preference includes (among several assumptions required for mathematical manipulation) the assumption of "strong monotonicity," which, translated, means that "more is better." Or, as Kamarck (1983:80) has described it: "it is assumed that consumers are rational and selfish: they know which commodities will satisfy them best and they spend their money accordingly."

Several economists have taken issue with this assumption. Simon (1979) claims, for example, that instead of making a set of optimum choices among all possible combinations of commodities and services available to them, they exhibit what he calls "bounded rationality." Lacking omniscience, consumers are unaware of both available choices and their prices. Operating with prior opinions and limited information, the consumer searches only until he finds an alternative that meets his level of aspiration, stops the search, and settles on that alternative. This decision process is called "satisficing," rather than optimizing (Kamarck, 1983:84; Weaver and Stefanou, 1984:6–9).

Another value assumption central to much of neoclassical economic theory is that the greatest good for the greatest number of people will result naturally from an economic system governed by consumer sovereignty. This is coupled with faith in Adam Smith's "invisible hand" of greed among producers striving to increase their profits by satisfying consumer wants (Boulding, 1970:126).

Schumacher and the various proponents of humanistic economics (see for example Lutz and Lux, 1979) point out the importance of distinguishing between human needs and wants. The poorest of the poor, for example, have unmet food and housing needs which may threaten their very existence, but because they lack purchasing power, these needs are not translated into demand in the market place. However, even if one ignores needs and focuses on wants, there are other difficulties. For example, Ulmer (1980) argues that the fundamental assumption of demand theory—which postulates that consumer tastes are given and constant, as well as exogenous to the economic system—is flatly false. He points out that tastes are flexible and are shaped by economic events, such as changes in income, advertising, the appearance of new products, keeping up with the Joneses, etc. Another problem is that consumer demand and market prices are not strictly based on the "wants" of *all* persons. Rather, demand is principally driven by the preferences of contemporary (as opposed to future) consumers who have ample money and the will to spend it on certain categories of goods and services. The wants (much less the needs) of the very poor and of future generations are imperfectly registered in the market place.

Modern economics, it seems, has become largely a science of greed. As Schmid (1978:24), a prominent institutional economist, has pointed out: "Modern Western economics has tried hard to make love superfluous for the working of the economy. The competitive market is thought to be a system where welfare is maximized without anyone caring for anyone else. Selfishness is guided by Adam Smith's unseen hand and produces Pangloss's best of all possible worlds." The engine driving a capitalistic economy is greed. The engine is sparked by sales promotional activity (such as advertising) which creates greater and greater wants, inducing a sense of dissatisfaction with things of the past. In the process "Economics is reduced to 'the mechanics of utility and self-interest,'" as Georgescu-Roegen (1971:318) has observed. It seeks to predict quantitatively the behavior of entrepreneurs and consumers under the assumption that they are acting "rationally," that is, seeking to maximize their own short-term material gain. Just as physics is useful in predicting the velocity of a falling object, neoclassical economics is intended to be useful in predicting the behavior of firms, consumers, prices, and production.

While the value assumption of "economic rationality" underlies the logical structure of most neoclassical economic models of behavior, many economists slip into yet another value judgment, the habit of equating such rationality (read selfishness) with intelligence, the virtue most highly esteemed by academics. Anyone who refrains from acting in ways that maximize his own material "well-being" is considered irrational and *ipso facto* defective and inferior. Thus, the more doctrinaire neoclassical economists have enthroned the vice of greed as a cardinal virtue.

## Efficiency and Productivity

Closely akin to the value assumption of consumer sovereignty are the widely held value assumptions *efficiency* and *productivity*. Efficiency is assumed to be good. Efficiency in turn is broken down into technical or "X" efficiency and allocative efficiency. If a process is technically efficient, the firm cannot obtain a greater level of output while using smaller quantities of any of the required inputs or resources. Allocative efficiency, on the other hand, depends on the market prices of the various ingredients; cheaper resources are substituted for more expensive ones, relative to their incremental contribution to the firm's revenue through production of the various products for which they are ulitized.

During a time of high unemployment, many observers question the social validity of a valuation criterion which implies it is universally "good" to eliminate the jobs of people thereby destined to become redundant, unemployed, and impoverished of self-esteem as well as of money. Lester Thurow addresses this and other trade-offs in his book *The Zero*

*Sum Society*. Many economists brush aside the suggestion that displaced workers are made worse off through the market mechanism of allocative efficiency, by embracing two more assumptions: (a) that (labor) resources are perfectly mobile, both able and willing to relocate to places and occupations where their services are most valuable; and (b) the"*trickle-down*" value assumption that allocative efficiency adjustments will make the economy stronger, thus enhancing the employment and income opportunities of all workers.

Closely related to the assumed preeminence of consumer sovereignty and efficiency is that of *productivity*, which posits that—other things being equal—more goods and services are better than less. One manifestation of this value assumption is the fact that economists consider the best measure of a nation's well-being to be its per capita real income after taxes—the volume of goods and services consumers can afford, on the average. Productivity can be enhanced through relocation or improvement of resources (e.g., irrigation of the deserts, education of workers) or through various forms of technological change. As productivity increases, fewer resources are required to produce a given amount of output, or a greater level of output can be produced with given inputs. Thus, either greater production or lower costs and output prices can be expected as a result of increases in productivity—assuming that other things are equal and that the industry is competitive rather than monopolistic.

Thus, the economist embraces the value assumption that increases in productivity are good, "other things being equal." In some instances, however, serious detrimental side effects accompany the increases in productivity—faster soil erosion, chronic unemployment, environmental pollution by farm chemicals, culturing of resistant strains of germs through routine feeding of antibiotics to livestock, etc. Such "side effects" are often ignored by those doctrinaire neoclassical economists who are unaware of the social and physical environment in which the economy operates. Other economists have made serious efforts to deal with *externalities (Castle et al.,* 1981: 426–429).

### Intertemporal Equity

The value assumptions underlying consumer sovereignty, efficiency, and productivity may be extended to a multiple-year context, in which future generations of producers and consumers compete with the present and past generations for limited resources. Likewise, in this context, future generations benefit from permanent investments made and institutions created by present and past generations. Economists have sought rigorous ways of equating past, present, and future economic values through mathematical compounding and discounting formulas (Page, 1977; Lind, *et al.,* 1982).

In private transactions, both the compounding rate and the discount rate are ordinarily keyed to some appropriate market rate of interest. In evaluating the future benefits and costs of public projects and investments, however, such as construction of bridges and dams, the choice of appropriate discount rate is obscured by political, methodological, and ethical controversy (Page, 1977:155; Castle *et al.,* 1981:423–434; Lind *et al.,* 1982:55–77). Page has observed, for example, that "Raising the Army Corps' [of Engineers] discount rate from the 2.625 percent it used in 1962 to 8 percent would have killed off 80 percent of the dam projects approved that year." Precisely because of this the discount rate has been a political football between conservationists and Congressional "pork barrelers."

Lind (1982:57) argues that the market rate of interest is probably methodologically irrelevant to discounting as applied to public investments and public policies, primarily because that procedure results in the systematic undervaluation of future events and service flows. He states, "... the government, in making public investments and public policy decisions, is the guardian of future generations as well as the servant of the present ones." He goes on to defend, however, the exercise of estimating the current value of future net benefits of public projects. Such analysis provides a rough approximation to guide policymakers away from the grossly non-economic choices, while acknowledging that political considerations will continue to hold sway in choices among projects exhibiting benefit-cost ratios in some wide acceptable range.

Boulding (1970:129) observes that the "real" dollars of constant purchasing power so widely computed in benefit-cost analysis of social alternatives is a "dangerously imperfect measure of the quality of human life and human values." Furthermore, benefit-cost analysis is highly vulnerable to manipulation to suit the prejudices of the persons hoping to influence the policy decisions. Nonetheless, Boulding contends that these studies provide an "extremely valuable first approximation" for guiding choices among competing alternative public policies and investments.

In his discussion of the socially optimum rate of depletion of exhaustible resources, Grout (1981:88–109) contrasts the depletion paths resulting logically from alternative value presumptions: Pareto efficiency, compensation tests, utilitarianism, maximin, and fairness. After discarding the Pareto-efficient approach as ambiguous and impractical, he concludes that the choice among the other four depends upon societal values regarding present and future generations. He observes that it is highly unlikely that the present generation would act so selfishly as to use their position of power to maximize their lifetime consumption by depleting all of the resources in their lifetime. He suggests that such actions would be precluded by their presumed affection for their children, grandchildren, and perhaps great-grandchildren.

However, if today's resource depletion plans are extended to encompass only four generations, then the second through fourth generations will be deprived of the "joy of giving" enjoyed by the first generation in providing for its visible descendents. Specifically, barring some major technological breakthroughs rendering the exhaustible resources unnecessary, the great-grandchildren would be faced with the awful prospect of being utterly incapable of providing them for the future of their children, grandchildren and subsequent generations. Even if all four generations were able to consume equal amounts of the resources, or to attain equal incomes or consumption of goods and services—one could not logically conclude that they would be equal in satisfaction unless one assumed the spark of human compassion for one's descendents became extinguished: a grim and unlikely event. Thus, the value assumptions underlying efforts to determine a socially optimum rate of depletion of resources are diametrically opposite the ethic of conservationism, which is based on a concern for distant as well as presently visible generations, plus the prudential judgment that an uncertain future technology should not be relied upon to bail mankind out of future shortages caused by excessive current consumption.

## Counterpoint

Just as good health is taken for granted until one becomes ill or encounters a very sick person, the value assumptions underlying conventional economic analysis are best understood when contrasted with other views. For example, Schumacher (1973) has perceptively criticized a number of value assumptions underlying the economic analysis of productivity and efficiency. He points out, for example, that in the process of analyzing how a firm could maximize its profits or minimize costs, the economist typically ignores the distinction between renewable and non-renewable resources: the current market value of each resource is simply entered into the calculus with no regard for the permanence of the production processes and consumption patterns. Recommendations made on the basis of such analysis have the effect of encouraging and rewarding greed, ecological irresponsibility, and indifference to future generations. Schumacher (1973:24) quotes John Meynard Keynes, the great 1930s advocate of federal deficit spending, as saying: "For at least another hundred years we must pretend to ourselves and to everyone that fair is foul and foul is fair; for foul is useful and fair is not. Avarice and usury and precaution must be our gods for a little longer still. For only they can lead us out of the tunnel of economic necessity into daylight."

Rejecting totally this philosophy, Schumacher (1973:33) claims the assertion that "foul is useful and fair is not" is the antithesis of wisdom.

> The hope that the pursuit of goodness and virtue can be postponed until we have attained universal prosperity and that by the single-minded pursuit of wealth, without bothering our heads about spiritual and moral questions, we could establish peace on earth, is an unrealistic, unscientific and irrational hope. The exclusion of wisdom from economics, science, and technology was something that we could perhaps get away with for a little while, as long as we were relatively unsuccessful; but now that we have become very successful, the problem of spiritual and moral truth moves into the central position.
>
> From an economic point of view, the central concept of wisdom is permanence. We must study the economics of permanence. Nothing makes economic sense unless its continuance for a long time can be projected without running into absurdities.

Quoting Gandhi as saying, "Earth provides enough to satisfy every man's need, but not for every man's greed," Schumacher contends that permanence is incompatible with value assumptions that encourage conspicuous consumption at the expense of irreplaceable resources and the environment. At the same time, he contends the economic-political system is destroying opportunities for man to live a meaningful and satisfying existence, something that combines a satisfying work experience with spiritually enriching leisure activity. He advocates a norm called "Buddhist economics," whose principal goal is a "Right Livelihood." Buddhist economics attempts to maximize human satisfaction by the optimal pattern of productive effort, including where possible, the substitution of cheaper for more expensive resources. And where irreplaceable natural resources and unspoiled environment are not priced dearly, they tend to be depleted and damaged. Thus, Schumacher contrasts the value assumptions of conventional economic analysis with those of a philosophy emphasizing permanence rather than immediate enjoyment, inner satisfaction rather than outer materialism.

Economists are not alone in making value judgements as an integral part of their professional endeavors. Rudner (1953) has argued that scientists *qua* scientists routinely make value judgements that intimately affect their conclusions, the most notable being their choice of conceptual framework within which to interpret empirical reality. Far from castigating scientists for making value judgements, however, Rudner argues that if true objectivity is to be attained, the best place to start is for scientists to recognize explicitly the value judgements they are making. Beyond this initial step, he calls for establishment of a "science of ethics," which would accommodate an orderly and objective inclusion of value judgements intrinsic to the scientific enterprise.

Up to this point, it has been demonstrated that conventional economic analysis, far from being value-free, is loaded and surrounded with value assumptions that strongly affect its choice of topics, methods, outcomes and interpretations. It is not the purpose or message of this chapter to argue that economists should somehow expunge all value assumptions from their work as economists. On the contrary, it is hoped that as economists become aware of the value assumptions implicit in their standard *modus operandi,* they may choose to alter some and admit explicitly to others.

We turn now to an examination of the role played by economists' value assumptions in their evaluations of agricultural research.

## Value Assumptions in the Economic Evaluation of Agricultural Research

It is beyond the scope of the present chapter to review the findings of the many economic evaluations of agricultural research. This has been done in previous works (for example, Evanson *et al.,* 1979; Norton, *et al.,* 1981; and Ruttan, 1982). Rather, the purpose here is to unpack the major value assumptions underlying the methodologies chosen by economists in conducting such studies.

In their review of methods used to evaluate returns to agricultural research, Norton and Davis (1981) found a large number of *ex post facto* evaluations of agricultural research that could be classified into three major groups: (a) those that explicitly or implicitly used a concept of consumers and producers surplus and which, in general, estimated an average rate of return to research, and (b) regression-type studies that include research as a variable in a production function used to estimate a marginal rate of return to research, and (c) an important category, not ordinarily considered in the "evaluation" literature, comprised of a large body of mathematical programming studies—specifically those studies that evaluate the results of agricultural research indirectly by including their findings as alternative technologies (that is, in the form of different yields or resource requirements) in economic analyses. These studies are done at various levels of aggregation—some at the level of the individual firm, others at the regional or national level. One feature distinguishing the third approach from the first two is that it can focus on rather specific categories of research, rather than aggregate expenditures for research at the state or national level.

In evaluating the three types of studies, the value assumptions and value judgments that influence the direction, form, and content of their inquiries can be categorized only in a very general way. Those studies most nearly reflecting logical positivism are those employing methods keyed most closely to neoclassical economic theory—particularly the first category of studies based on consumer surplus or producer surplus. The second major category of studies, those employing some form of statistical inference method involving regression, seem less closely tied to economic theory and more pragmatically based. The third general category, mathematical programming studies incorporating comparative analysis of agricultural technologies, are intermediate between the first and second types in regard to their dependence upon neoclassical theory. In this approach, however, important value positions are taken in the selection of optimizing criterion, technologies analyzed, and constraints imposed on the models, as discussed below.

All three types of study rely upon some form of data for estimating the productivity of research, rather than simply constructing hypothetical theoretical arguments. However, the quality of the data in relation to the real-world phenomena they are intended to represent is often seriously flawed, and resources are rarely available to develop improved data sets (Leontief, 1971). Rather than refraining from making estimates on the basis of inadequate data, the practical-minded economist usually proceeds to analyze the best of imperfect data sets, under the value assumption that "halitosis is better than no breath at all." Specific value assumptions underlying each of the three major categories of evaluation study are now examined.

### Consumer and Producer Surplus

The consumer and producer surplus approach (Hicks, 1941) has been very widely used in economic analysis of agricultural research productivity (Norton and Davis, 1981). Consumer surplus represents the total satisfaction consumers as a whole receive from buying a product at a given price when some of them would have been willing to pay a higher price rather than do without the product. Geometrically it is defined in relation to a specific quantity (Q) of a product that is sold at a given price (P), shown by the intersection of supply and demand curves in the PQ plane. The area below the demand curve and above the horizontal price line represents consumer surplus. The corresponding area lying above the supply curve and below the price line represents producer surplus—conceptually defined as the summation of "satisfactions" gained by all producers who would have been willing to produce their share of Q at a price lower than P (Pearce, 1983:99,354).

As applied to analysis of changes in agricultural productivity associated with technological change, the consumer and producer surplus approach entails estimation of two quantities: the market value of purchased input saved because of the more efficient production technology, and the lower market price consumers pay for their current level of consumption as a result of the improved technology. The discounted present value of the future streams of changes in consumer and producer surplus are combined into a monetary benefit, which is then compared with some estimate of the cost of research and development.

Practitioners of this approach have employed a variety of assumptions regarding the unknown demand and supply functions for agricultural products. Study results are strongly influenced by these assumptions. Ruttan (1982:252–254) reports that many of the early studies of the payoff to agricultural research were strongly biased, over-estimating the rate of return. Major defects were the failure to include the costs of essential complementary inputs (most notably extension), and the use of rather naive forms of supply and demand function. He says many of these deficiencies have been corrected in the more recent studies. However, the data on both the benefits and the inputs remain problematic and thus limit the confidence one can place in the results.

An important assumption inherent in consumer and producer surplus approach is that discounted future streams of costs and benefits accurately represent the actual social costs and benefits. As discussed earlier, there are several important problems with this assumption; in addition, there are the value questions of how the preferences of future generations are to be taken into account.

Most of the studies in the literature have ignored the actual distribution of benefits and the costs. Only recently have studies attempted to estimate the differential impacts of technology adoption on various classes or groups (for example, Schmitz and Seckler, 1970; de Janvry, *et al.*, 1980; Brandt and French, 1983).

In his discussion of the distribution of benefits from agricultural technology, Sundquist (1983) notes that it is primarily the early adopters of the new technologies that tend to reap major gains in income, but later on as total output is increased enough to suppress prices, consumers become the beneficiaries.

Another benefit not mentioned is the impact on the national economic well-being, especially increases in the balance of trade which are stimulated by increased productivity and lower prices. National economic growth, employment, and the incomes of the vast majority of Americans have increased significantly as a result of increases in agricultural production and productivity.

Only in recent decades have agricultural economists taken note of such negative impacts of agricultural technologies as employment losses due to mechanization, environmental degradation due to excessive soil erosion and misuse of chemicals, and taxpayer burdens due to the high cost of dealing with massive surpluses. Sundquist suggests two ways of coping with such adverse effects: regulatory constraints on the use of technology, and compensation paid to persons harmed by adoption of the technology, such as the mechanical tomato harvester. These two approaches are essentially reactive, taking as inevitable and exogenous the nature and pace of technology generation and adoption. Economists typically have taken a "value-neutral" position with regard to the quality and velocity of technological change emanating from agricultural research. However, as Katouzian has argued, indifference is also a value judgment.

In their examination of the adoption of the tomato harvester, Schmitz and Seckler (1970) extended their analysis beyond the usual consumer and producer surplus by unpacking the "value of inputs saved." By including the financial losses experienced by displaced farm laborers, this study offered a useful departure from a rash of rather narrowly conceived consumer and producer surplus studies of earlier vintage. However, it was criticized as being flawed by de Janvry et al. (1980). First, while Schmitz and Seckler found that social returns to tomato harvester research were in excess of 1000 percent of public investment costs, de Janvry et al. contends that important components of the public research costs were ignored: the cost of breeding new varieties of tomatoes amenable to mechanical harvesting, the cost of educating farmers as to the practical ways of employing the new machines, and other related costs.

Another flaw pointed out by de Janvry et al., was that the analysis had assumed that all cost-savings were passed along to the consumer in terms of lower food costs, with none of the savings being captured by producers, processors, wholesalers, or retailers in the form of monopoly profits. They contend this assumption is inconsistent with the obvious oligopoly power within the tomato processing and distribution industry.

A key value assumption of all studies examined, including that of Schmitz and Seckler, was that the accounting of "social benefits and costs" was to be restricted to the American scene. Ignored were the indirect effects on other nations. For example, Mexico could have realized a major economic benefit if, instead of mechanizing, the U.S. tomato industry had simply moved to Mexico as it was starting to do when the tomato harvester was developed in the early 1960s. The role of publicly and privately supported research and development in the case of the tomato harvester has been documented by Madden (in Feller et al., 1984, vol. 4).

Friedland and Barton (1975) go far beyond the conventional consumer and producer surplus approach in their examination of the social consequences of agricultural research. In analyzing the mechanization of the harvest of tomatoes, lettuce, and other crops, they considered the well-being óf farmworkers, both in terms of their incomes and the quality of life inherent in the nature of work they do. They note, for example, the transition from a self-directed pace of the stoop laborer hand picking tomatoes to the machine-directed pace of workers standing in a restricted space on a mechanical harvesting machine. These costs are also noted by de Janvry, *et al.* (1980) in their dialectical analysis of the contradictions inherent in a system which promotes invention and adoption of labor-saving mechanical technology in the face of high unemployment, low income and displaced workers, and increasing dependence upon fossil fuel energy. It remains unclear how these "non-monetary" considerations are to be weighed or otherwise combined with monetary values in evaluating research. Decisions on this matter, of course, involve important value judgments. In most economic evaluations, these considerations are ignored, based on a value assumption that they are unimportant or not measurable.

*Regression Studies*

The second general approach to economic evaluation of agricultural research mentioned by Norton and Davis is the estimation of production functions featuring research as a variable, permitting an estimate of the "marginal rate of return to research." Many examples of such research are found in the literature (Norton *et al.*, 1981). The dependent variable in these studies is usually some measure of agricultural productivity; independent or explanatory variables include, among others, various measures of research activity. Problems of discounting future streams of benefits and costs are avoided with this approach, because an array of annual data are used, typically at the state level rather than the national level of aggregation.

Let us first consider the dependent variable. In his seminal study of the impact of research on agriculture, Ruttan (1982) notes the distinction between increases in production versus increases in productivity. An increase in production is simply an expansion of output, which can result from planting more acres or milking a larger herd, or it can be caused by an increase in productivity—such as a higher yield per acre or milk pro-duction per cow. Productivity is a ratio whose numerator is production and whose denominator is input. When a single input is used in the denominator, the resulting "partial productivity" ratio can be misleading. For example, an increase in crop yield per acre can be the combined result of increased levels of fertilization, a more effective herbicide, and an improved seed variety. An increase in one partial productivity ratio may be accompanied by a decrease in another, as when higher milk production per cow is accomplished by increasing the number of times each cow is milked per day, thereby reducing the milk output per labor-hour.

In an attempt to overcome this confusion, economists have constructed a measure of "total productivity," where the numerator is an estimate of the current market value of production, and the denominator is some measure of total inputs. Ordinarily, the various classes of inputs, such as fertilizer, labor, seed, and so forth, are aggregated into an index using market prices of the inputs as weights—in other words, the total cost of the inputs valued at market prices. Valuation of land and of operator and management inputs is always a sticky problem, and no universally satisfactory method has been found to deal with it. In the case of estimating the productivity of research, the denominator is an estimate of the total costs of the research, or in the more detailed studies, the total cost of researching, developing, and transfering the new technology.

A widely accepted but nonetheless questionable procedure used in the measurement of productivity is the inclusion of government payments as part of the numerator, value of output. Conceptually, if the effect of research on agricultural productivity is to be measured, then only those components of increased value of production attributed directly to it (or, if indirectly, at least by some tangible linkage) should be permitted in the accounting. Government payments to farmers, either directly or through overt supply control programs, are a result of political rather than scientific activity, and should be accounted for accordingly.

Other conceptual difficulties are inherent in the way agricultural productivity is measured for purposes of evaluating agricultural research in regression studies. One of these difficulties has to do with the accounting of costs. Only out-of-pocket cash costs are taken into account; the market prices used in making these calculations fail to reflect externalities associated with environmental degradation or the health impacts resulting from adoption of the new technologies, as well as the preferences of future generations.

Paramount among the list of independent or explanatory variables is some measure of research activity. The measure most often utilized is the annual research budget of the state agricultural experiment station, corrected for changes in an index of faculty salaries and subtracting the costs of capital construction. This approach, of course, ignores the massive research presence of the USDA's Agricultural Research Service, the growing volume of non-land-grant university research, and agricultural research done by the private sector—which has reached a level nearly double the budget of publicly funded agricultural research (Feller et al., 1984). Another conceptual difficulty with the use of experiment station budget data to represent research activity (specifically it should be termed "land-grant university research") is the matter of homogeneity of the data set. In particular, the use of such data glosses over the differences among states (and changes over time) in the mixture of various disciplines, as well as the mix of kinds of research being done. Consequently, the parameter estimates may be biased and are difficult to interpret precisely.

For example, Ruttan draws the distinction between science-oriented and technology-oriented research. Science-oriented research seeks to enhance the technology-generating capability of disciplinary fields such as biochemistry, botany, plant pathology, soil science, etc. Technology-oriented research is directed toward the creation of a new technology as the primary objective, rather than the advancement of science (Ruttan, 1982:246–247). Johnson and Wittwer (1984) refer to the former as "disciplinary" research and the latter as "problem-solving" research. They also identify a third kind, "subject matter" research, which has as its purposes the enhancement of the ability of a department or other administrative unit to deal with a wide range of problems. This would include research done to strengthen the capacity of interdisciplinary departments such as agronomy, for example, often composed of plant geneticists, soil scientists, forage specialists, and other disciplines.

Bonnen (1983:959) points out that some observers of agricultural research contend that the necessary and sufficient condition for enhancing agricultural productivity is basic or disciplinary research. Taking issue with this belief, Bonnen argues that basic research is necessary but not sufficient, requiring linkages to applied or problem-solving research, extension, and farmer education.

It is perhaps in recognition of this principle that Dean Hess of the University of California at Davis strongly advocates what he calls "targeted basic research," wherein some of the scientists with a bent for basic research are housed with those deeply emersed in subject matter, problem-solving, or technology-generating research in the various departments of the University (Feller *et al.*, 1984, vol. 2).

Evanson *et al.* (1979) conclude that, while the annual rate of monetary return to agricultural research is often found to be in the neighborhood of 50 percent and sometimes higher, it matters very much how the research is organized. Based on regression analysis, they conclude that the returns to agricultural research are increased as research becomes better articulated (linked) with extension and farmers, and as it is decentralized, even to substations within states (see also Feller *et al.*, 1984, vol. 4).

The purpose of the regression approach is ordinarily to estimate the separate impact of research, while holding other factors constant. However, given what is known about the strength and significance of interactions between research and extension, as documented by Evanson *et al.* (1979), it is a logical fallacy to attempt to estimate a statistical "main effect" for research alone. Where clear statistical interaction patterns are found, conditional impact statements are required, stipulating the productivity response to research under specific kinds of linkages with extension, the private sector, and other key actors in the system. Even within the domain of research, Ruttan (1983:247) notes that interaction is important: "Science-oriented research does not have a significant independent effect. The high payoff to science-oriented research is achieved only when it is directed toward increasing the productivity of technology-oriented research."

Regardless of what it is called, the results of the regression studies clearly indicate that science-oriented (often called basic) research has a low payoff in terms of the direct effect on agricultural productivity; its effect is felt only in interaction with technology-oriented or problem-solving research and extension. Likewise, interactions between publicly and privately funded research, uniformly ignored in existing studies, should not be overlooked in analyzing the impact of agricultural research; to ignore these realities is to make naive assumptions regarding the causes of agricultural productivity.

## Mathematical Programming Approaches

Another important way in which economists "evaluate" agricultural research is to include the results of that research in their mathematical programming models in ways that permit comparisons of new and previous technologies. The scope of individual studies varies from the individual farm to the national level. For several decades, farm management researchers and extension experts have incorporated the financial implications of emerging new technology into their analysis of farm plans, to determine what effects various technologies may have on farm income and production of various commodities. The results of agricultural research are implicitly introduced into the analysis in the form of coefficients reflecting changes in yields, resource requirements, and costs.

When the analysis is done at the farm level, it is ordinarily reasonable to assume that the prices of the farm commodities and purchased inputs remain constant. That is, the decisions made by an individual farmer or small number of farmers are assumed to have an insignificant effect on total market supplies or the demand for farm inputs. This assumption historically has been valid, since farms have been very numerous and "atomistic," meaning that each farm accounts for a minute fraction of the total market. As the trend toward fewer or larger farms continues, however, this assumption will eventually become erroneous; it already may be naive in the case of highly concentrated industries such as poultry and eggs.

While earlier research estimated how farm income would be affected by alternative production technologies, some current research studies are taking a broader view. For example, a study in Illinois by Eleveld and Halcrow (1982) evaluates the effects of the various tillage systems (up-and-down-hill cultivation, contouring, contouring plus terracing), soil erosion, as well as farm income. Trade-offs between income and soil erosion vary from one tillage system to another; different locations have different results due to variations in soil type, slope, rainfall, and other factors. Agricultural research illumines these trade-offs and, in many cases, improves the options available to farmers and policymakers. Various forms of conservation tillage, for example, are found to be both more profitable and less vulnerable to soil erosion (a win-win situation) as compared with conventional plow-oriented tillage (Feller *et al.*, 1984, vol. 4, ch. 6). The results of previous research on tillage systems, in terms of potential effects on farm income, are essential in predicting the potential adoption of the technologies by farmers.

In a recent study, Crowder (1984:24), analyzed the effects of farming methods not only on soil erosion but also on pesticide and nutrient pollution of streams and underground water. Soil erosion was limited to three tons per acre, since this was considered the "tolerable" limit for most Pennsylvania farms. Annual losses of nitrogen and phosphorus in surface runoff were constrained to 14 pounds and 6.5 pounds per acre, respectively. Crowder admits these limits may be too high, possibly posing ecological problems, but he felt these levels were "practical." Simulated soil losses of plant nutrients (nitrogen and phosphorus) and pesticides as well as tonage of soil erosion, were fed into a linear programming model to select among alternative cropping systems. The study found that:

> Reduced tillage and no-till reduced pollutant levels with little impact on farm income [as compared with conventional tillage]. . . . Fewer pollution problems were associated with CCAAA [a rotation of 2 years corn and 3 years alfalfa] compared to other rotations because of the relatively large amount of land devoted to alfalfa, a relatively less erosive and chemical-polluting activity. . . . Significant problems were associated with [continuous corn], including not only surface runoff losses but also high levels of nitrate in deep percolate.

The scope of this study could have been extended to consider other alternative cropping systems (such as organic or regenerative methods, for example). And the levels of all pollutants could have been limited to ecologically harmless levels (established or presumed). Nonetheless, studies such as this illustrate the potential contribution of ecology-oriented economic analysis to informed decision making by farmers considering alternative rotations or tillage systems, and by policymakers concerned about limiting non-point source pollution in ways that do not destroy the profitability of farming. This trend is hopeful in view of T. W. Schultz's axiom, "An economist who is only an economist is likely to be a nuisance if not a positive danger" (Hoch, 1984:7). An economist who is aware of ecological relationships can incorporate them into his/her analysis in ways that yield useful results.

Economists recognize that adoption of new technologies by vast numbers of farms (or even by a small number of gigantic ones) can change total output of farm commodities by amounts large enough to affect prices. In a similar vein, the prices of inputs can be changed. This realization has led to development of analysis beyond the farm level, featuring regional or even national aggregates of production and demand. These studies are termed "spatial equilibrium" or "inter-regional competition" studies. Historically, most of these studies have looked exclusively at the financial implications of various production technologies and public policies (via changes in prices and permissible levels of acreage or other restrictions or inducements).

In recent years, spatial equilibrium studies have undergone a metamorphosis reflecting changes in public policy concerns. Starting with the petroleum price escalation of the 1970s, studies began to examine the impacts of technology changes and policy options, not only with regard to farm income and prices, but also considering energy requirements. And very recently, these studies have considered soil erosion (Heady, 1982). These trends reflect the value assumption by economists that their research should be useful in addressing emerging policy concerns. This is consistent with the findings of Busch and Lacy (1983:111), that agricultural economists report "importance to society" is the leading criterion for selection of research topics (5.6 on a 7 point scale).

## Values, Economics, and Agricultural Research

While most publicly supported research and extension personnel like to assume a posture of value neutrality, saying they are not biased for or against any philosophical orientation, the fact remains that neither extension nor research personnel can be value free (Laue, 1979). Value positions are taken explicitly or assumed at many essential junctures—one's choice of research or extension topic, conceptual model, and analytical methods, as well as the order of presentation, the presenter's enthusiasm, emphasis on key points, and other subtleties are based on (usually unknown and unstated) value assumptions and judgments. The intrusion of value positions is inescapable as long as human beings are doing the research and educational activities. Therefore, it makes little sense to argue that persons in the publicly funded sector of the technology delivery system remain value-free. Instead, scientists should be called upon to make their value positions explicit. In this way, the effects of their value positions cen be examined. Also, the various publics can more effectively have a voice in achieving "better" value judgements, and consequently more socially desireable technologies.

Public debate regarding the optimum mix of scientific autonomy and social responsibility in publicly funded research organizations has intensified in recent years. For example, public interest organization, California Rural Legal Assistance, has brought suit against the University of California and that State's Cooperative Extension program, with charges that funds are being misappropriated and the fundamental mission of the land grant system betrayed in the choice of research objectives and extension methods. CRLA is demanding as relief that UC be required to delay initiation of publicly supported agricultural research until the potential social impacts have been studied and a committee of non-involved persons has approved the proposed research. Kendrick (1984:1) has responded as follows:

> This allegation fails to recognize the nature of the benefit [of agricultural research] and its distribution among producer, supplier, and consumer.
>
> The social impact analysis of contemplated research called for by the plaintiffs would have a destructive impact on creativity and innovation in research. All research, whether in agriculture, engineering, physical science, medicine, the arts, humanities, or social sciences, has potential positive and negative impacts on societal values and structural configurations.
>
> The challenge to us as a people is not to stifle inquiry into the unknown, but to be wise enough to incorporate new knowledge into the fabric of living a better life within an organized society. Programs conducted by the Land-Grant Agricultural Experiment Stations and Cooperative Extension are undertaken on the assumption that an enlightened society will accept or reject findings and practices based on what it sees as being in its best interests.
>
> The broadest participation in the benefits from a technologically based agriculture in the United States accrues to the consuming public. The national interests of the United States are served by supporting, through research, extension, and other actions, the efficient production, processing, and marketing of the products of agriculture.

In this statement, Kendrick is clearly emphasizing the impact of agricultural research on consumer surplus—lower prices for food.

The contention that society will serve its own best interest by abundantly supporting agricultural research, with no "social accounting" strings attached seems to be based on three implicit value assumptions:

1. The "greatest good for the greatest numbers of people" is assumed to be promoted by an ever increasing abundance of agricultural commodities. Agricultural research that enables producers to

increase production, productivity, and efficiency are assumed inevitably to enhance the welfare of consumers through greater availability at lower prices.

2. It is assumed that if emerging technologies carry detrimental side effects (pollution, social dislocation, unemployment, carcinogenic residues, etc.), then society will omnisciently anticipate these side effects.

3. It is further assumed that, in view of the anticipated impacts, entrepreneurs and other decision makers will automatically reach a rational decision as to whether these disadvantages outweigh the advantages; that is, if the social disadvantages are expected to outweigh the anticipated advantages of adopting a technology, that technology will not be adopted.

These assumptions have been subject to extensive criticism both from within and outside the agricultural research establishment. For example, the axiom that more is better than less can be questioned in view of agricultural surpluses costing billions in federal funds. It is reasonable also to question whether the human condition is improved indefinitely with successively higher levels of wealth and income, at a time when one of the leading causes of death, even among affluent teenagers, is suicide. Similar incongruities have been observed between so-called economic measures of well-being, such as per capita income and wealth, and various social indicators (Strumple, 1976). Even the wealthy suffer from anomie, alienation, depression, disease, drug addiction, etc. This incongruity does not imply, however, that efforts to further improve the income (equitably distributed) and employment of this and other nations should be suspended or even slowed. Rather, it raises the challenge of finding ways to enrich the meaning of life, its ethical and spiritual content, in addition to overcoming material deprivation.

The second and third assumptions have also been severely questioned. Predictions of the long term effects of chemicals and other technology have frequently been found to be incorrect. And the adoption of technology by private decision makers is known to be affected more strongly by the promise of greater profits than by anticipated social and environmental impacts whose costs are not borne by the firm adopting the technology. Thus, the assumptions underlying the argument for a *laissez-faire* approach to agricultural research are doubtful.

Among the most eloquent critics of the agricultural research system are some enlightened economists within the land-grant university system. For example, *Bonnen* (1983:964) has written that:

Organizations, foundations, legal advocacy groups, and others . . . now constitute a Greek chorus of criticism of the performance of U.S. agricultural institutions. Most cluster around the growing *externalities* of agricultural technology and public policy. These issues include *environmental degradation*; concerns for *animal welfare*, impacts on *health* and *safety of farmers*, agricultural workers, and consumers; adverse *nutritional effects* of production and processing technologies; the extrusion of *smaller family farmers* from agriculture, erosion of rural communities, and the concentration of agricultural production and economic welfare; adequate conservation and commercial exploitation of *fragile lands* that should not be in cultivation.

Focusing R&D investment on productivity and ever increasing growth is not enough today. Equity, but also safety, quality of life, stability, and preservation of the environment for future generations, to name a few, must become major goals of agricultural R&D, as well as productivity and growth. In an urban society, soured on paying for malfunctioning farm programs to support farmers who are far wealthier than the typical taxpayer, these concerns must be dealt with or agricultural scientists can expect to lose public support of agricultural R&D. . . . *Greed* is not a sufficient condition upon which to base public policy.

Changes in society's values and social agenda, in part the consequence of externalities to agricultural policy and production, will remain an important source of disequilbria. This will require not only social science, physical and biological science, but also humanities research on the ethical and *value conflicts* in the choices that must be made.

Various public interest organizations, highlighting possible links between agricultural research and the well-being of society, have called for conscious *social planning*. For example, Marty Strange (1984:20) of the Nebraska-based Center for Rural Affairs has taken issue with the *laissez-faire* philosophy espoused by proponents of unbridled agricultural research:

There is a sort of feeling throughout the land that the unwanted is necessary. I simply can't accept that. I don't believe American agriculture has to unfold in any pre-determined way—we can have the kind of agriculture we want. That is, we can have the kind of agriculture we want within the limitations of nature, within the constraints established by the laws of nature—which constraints we've pretty well ignored in the last 100 years.

It should not be beyond the wits of man to articulate a set of fundamental social goals related to agriculture, and then to devise strategies for shaping the agricultural technology delivery system to better attain these goals. The fact that the vast majority of agricultural R&D is done outside public organizations (*Feller et al.*, 1984, volumes 1 and 5) simply intensifies the social responsibility and the challenge facing publicly supported organizations, such as *land-grant institutions* and USDA, to take a *pro-active* rather than exclusively a reactive mode of thinking about agricultural technology.

Key assumptions underlying the conventional (neoclassical) economic analysis have been scrutinized; some were found to be naïve. Nonetheless, the neoclassical model "works" in the pragmatic sense that the predictions stemming from neoclassical economic analysis are found to be accurate in many contexts. The task of the behavioralist school of economics is to identify those contexts where the neoclassical model does or does not predict well, and to formulate new models where needed to better predict economic reality. Many enlightened economists, notably natural resource economists and institutionalists, were found to be exemplary in avoiding the restrictive assumptions of their more doctrinaire neoclassical brethren, by recognizing explicitly the importance of value assumptions, externalities, and a more complete accounting of social costs in both public and private decision making. The value assumptions inherent in alternative approaches to economic analysis of agricultural research have been explicated. The consumer and producer surplus approach was found to carry the strongest value assumptions; findings of such studies are subject to considerable doubt as to their proper interpretation. Measurement problems plague all economic analysis, not least the analysis of agricultural research. Difficulties have been noted in attempts made by economists to make regression estimates of the impact of agricultural research. Mathematical programming (economic simulation or optimization model) constrained by reasonable ecological considerations such as soil erosion and run-off of agricultural chemicals, while not without deficiencies, was found to be a promising approach to the estimation of the potential impacts of alternative technologies and, *ipso facto*, of research and development work and technology transfer efforts required for the widespread adoption of that technology.

In the usual conduct of public and private decision making regarding agricultural research, economic analysis inevitably is and should be taken into account. As the economist becomes more acutely aware of the value assumptions underlying his/her analysis, and as alternative assumptions are incorporated into their studies, decision makers will be given a richer and more useful basis for choice. The task of envisioning society as it can and should be must not be left to economists or academics alone to decide. All who have a stake in the outcome should have the opportunity to become informed as to the choices and their implications.

The challenge before the agricultural research establishment is to organize itself and conduct its work in ways calculated to create science and technology that will lead to a "better" society, better according to ethics and values far beyond those embodied in current market prices. With sensitivity to that broader set of ethics and values, as well as to the integrity of natural and living systems, economic analysis can illumine many decisions by predicting the outcome of alternative courses of action.

# References

Arrow, Kenneth J., and Tibor Scitovsky. 1969. *Readings in Welfare Economics.* Homewood, Ill.: Richard D. Irwin.

Ayres, Clarence E. 1952. *The Industrial Economy.* Boston: Houghton Mifflin.

Becker, Gary S. 1976. *The Economic Approach to Human Behavior.* Chicago: University of Chicago Press.

Bonnen, James T. 1981. "Agriculture's System of Developmental Institutions: Reflections of the U.S. Experience." Paper presented at Symposium on Rural Economics, Quebec, Canada: University of Laval.

_____. 1983. "Historical Sources of U.S. Agricultural Productivity: Implications for R&D Policy and Social Science Research." *American Journal of Agricultural Economics* 65:958–966.

Boulding, Kenneth E. 1970. *Economics as a Science.* New York: McGraw-Hill.

Brandt, Jon A., and Ben C. French. 1983. "Mechanical Harvesting and the California Tomato Industry: A Simulation Analysis." *American Journal of Agricultural Economics* 65:265–272.

Breimyer, Harold F. 1983. "Food for People and Profit: Ethics and Capitalism—An Alternative Interpretation." *The Farm and Food System in Transition.* Report FS5. East Lansing: Michigan State Cooperative Extension Service.

Brown, Lester R.; William Chandler; Christopher Falvin; Sandra Postell; Linda Stark; and Edward Wolfe. 1984. *State of the World, 1984.* New York: W. W. Norton.

Busch, Lawrence, and William B. Lacy. 1983. *Science, Agriculture, and the Politics of Research.* Boulder, Colorado: Westview Press.

Butlin, J. A. (ed.). 1981. *Economics of Environmental and Natural Resources Policy.* Boulder, Colorado: Westview Press.

Castle, Emery N. 1965. "The Market Mechanism, Externalities, and Land Economics." In *Journal of Farm Economics* 47:542–556.

Castle, Emery N.; Maurice M. Kelso; Joe B. Stevens; and Herbert H. Stoevener. 1981. "Natural Resource Economics, 1946–75." In *A Survey of Agricultural Economics Literature,* ed. Lee R. Martin, Vol. 3, pp. 393–500. Minneapolis: University of Minnesota Press.

Coats, A. W. 1964. *The Role of Value Judgments in Economics.* The Thomas Jefferson Center for Studies in Political Economy. Charlottesville: University of Virginia.

Crowder, Bradley M.; Donald J. Epp; Harry B. Pionke; C. Edwin Young; James G. Beierlein; and Earl J. Partenheimer. 1984. "The Effects on Farm Income on Constraining Soil and Plant Nutrient Losses." University Park, PA: Agricultural Experiment Station Bulletin 850, May 1984.

Daly, Herman E. 1980. *Economics, Ecology, Ethics—Essays Toward a Steady-State Economy.* San Francisco: W. H. Freeman.

Davis, Jeffery S., and Willis Peterson. 1981. "The Declining Productivity of Agricultural Research." In *Evaluation of Agricultural Research,* ed. G. W. Norton *et al.,* pp. 97–104. Minneapolis: University of Minnesota Agricultural Experiment Station.

Day, Richard H. 1977. "Economic Optimization in Agricultural and Resource Economics." In *A Survey of Agricultural Economics Literature,* ed. Lee R. Martin, Vol. 2, pp. 57–156. Minneapolis: University of Minnesota Press.

_____, ed. 1982. *Economic Analysis and Agricultural Policy.* Ames: Iowa State University Press.

de Janvry, Alain; Philip LeVeen; and David Runsten. 1980. *Mechanization in California Agriculture: The Case of Canning Tomatoes.* San Jose, Costa Rica: Inter-American Institute of Agricultural Sciences, Misc. Pub. 223.

Eleveld, Bartelt, and Harold G. Halcrow. 1982. "How Much Soil Conservation is Optimum for Society?" In *Soil Conservation Policies, Institutions, and Incentives,* eds. H. G. Halcrow, E. O. Heady, and M. L. Cottner, pp. 233–250. Ankeny, Iowa: Soil Conservation Society of America.

Evanson, Robert E.; Paul E. Waggoner; and Vernon Ruttan. 1979. "Economic Benefits from Research: An Example from Agriculture." *Science* 205:1101–1107.

Feller, Irwin; Lynne Kaltrieder; J. Patrick Madden; and Dan E. Moore. 1984. *Agricultural Technology Delivery System: A Study of the Transfer of Agricultural and Food-Related*

*Technologies.* Final report to USDA; five volumes. University Park: Institute for Policy Research and Evaluation, The Pennsylvania State University.

Ferguson, C. E. 1969. *The Neoclassical Theory of Production and Distribution.* New York: Cambridge University Press.

Fishel, Walter L. 1981. "Changes in the Need for Research and Extension Evaluation Information." In *Evaluation of Agricultural Research,* ed. G. W. Norton *et al.,* pp. 9–17. Minneapolis: University of Minnesota Agricultural Experiment Station.

French, Ben C. 1976. "The Analysis of Productive Efficiency in Agricultural Marketing: Models, Methods, and Progress." In *A Survey of Agricultural Economics Literature,* ed. Lee R. Martin, Vol. 1, pp. 94–208. Minneapolis: University of Minnesota Press.

Friedman, Milton H. 1953. *Essays in Positive Economics.* Chicago: University of Chicago Press.

Georgescu-Roegen, Nicholas. 1971. *The Entropy Law and the Economic Process.* Cambridge: Harvard Univeristy Press.

Gordon, Wendall. 1980. *Institutional Economics: The Changing Systems.* Austin: University of Texas Press.

Grout, Paul. 1981. "Social Welfare and Exhaustible Resources." In *The Economics of Environmental and Natural Resources Policy,* ed. J. A. Butlin, pp. 88–109. Boulder, Colorado: Westview Press.

Halcrow, Harold G.; Earl O. Heady; and Melvin L. Cottner, ed. 1982. *Soil Conservation Policies, Institutions, and Incentives.* Ankeny, Iowa: Soil Conservation Society of America.

Harwood, Richard R. 1983. "International Overview of Regenerative Agriculture." Proceedings of Workshop on Resource-Efficient Farming Methods for Tanzania, May 16–20, 1983. Emmaus, Penn.: Rodale Press.

Haynes, Richard, and Ray Lanier, ed. 1982. *Agriculture, Change and Human Values.* Gainesville: University of Florida, Humanities and Agriculture Program.

Heady, Earl O. 1982. "Trade-offs Among Soil Conservation, Energy Use, Exports and Environmental Quality." In *Soil Conservation Policies, Institutions, and Incentives,* ed. H. G. Halcrow, E. O. Heady, and M.L. Cottner, pp. 254–273. Ankeny, Iowa: Soil Conservation Society of America.

Heilbroner, Robert L. 1969. *Economics Means and Social Ends—Essays in Political Economics.* Englewood Cliffs, New Jersey: Prentice Hall.

Heilbroner, Robert L., and Arthur M. Ford. 1976. *Economic Relevance—A Second Look.* Pacific Palisades, California: Goodyear.

Hicks, John R. 1941. "The Rehabilitation of Consumers' Surplus." *The Review of Economic Studies* 9:108–116.

Hock, Irving. 1984. "Retooling the Mainstream: Discussion." *American Journal of Agricultural Economics* 66(5):793–797.

Hurwicz, Leonid. 1969. "Optimality and Infrastructional Efficiency in Resource Allocation Processes." In *Readings in Welfare Economics,* ed. K. J. Arrow and T. Scitovsky, pp. 61–80. Homewood, Ill.: Richard D. Irwin.

Jaszi, George. 1971. "An Economic Accountant's Ledger." *Survey of Current Business* 51 (7, Part 2):183–227. (Fiftieth Anniversary Issue, "The Economic Accounts of the United States: Retrospect and Prospect").

Jeske, Walter E., ed. 1981. *Economics, Ethics, Ecology: Roots of Productive Conservation.* Ankeny, Iowa: Soil Conservation Society of America.

Johnson, Glenn L. 1982. "An Extension to 'What Can a Research Man Say about Values?'" In *Economic Analysis and Agricultural Policy,* ed. R. H. Day, pp. 66–74. Ames: Iowa State University Press.

————. 1984. "Academia Needs a New Covenant for Serving Agriculture." Mississippi State: Mississippi Agriculture and Forestry Experiment Station, Special Publication.

Johnson, Glenn L. 1982. "An Extension to 'What Can a Research Man Say about Values?'" In *Economic Analysis and Agricultural Policy,* ed. R. H. Day, pp. 66–74. Ames: Iowa State University Press.

Judge, George G. 1982. "On the Theory and Practice of Econometrics." In *Economic Analysis and Agricultural Policy,* ed. R. H. Day, pp. 91–103. Ames: Iowa State University Press.

Kamarck, Andrew M. 1983. *Economics and the Real World.* Philadelphia: The University of Pennsylvania Press.

Katouzian, Homa. 1980. *Ideology and Method in Economics.* New York: New York University Press.

Kendrick, J. B. 1984. "Agricultural Research is on Trial." *California Agriculture* 38 (5 and 6).

Klein, Philip A. 1978. "American Institutionalism: Premature Death, Permanent Resurrection." *Journal of Economic Issues* 12:251–276.

Kuttner, Robert. 1985. "The Poverty of Economics." *The Atlantic Monthly* 255 (2):74–84.

Laue, James H. 1979. "Value-Free, Objective Educators." In *Coping with Conflict: Strategies for Extension Community Development and Public Policy Professionals,* pp. 1–6. Ames, Iowa: North Central Regional Center for Rural Development.

Leontief, Wassily. 1971. "Theoretical Assumptions and Nonobserved Facts." *American Economic Review* 61:1–7.

Lind, Robert C.; Kenneth J. Arrow; Gordon R. Corey; Partha Dasgupta; Amartya K. Sen; Thomas Stauffer; Joseph E. Stiglitz; J. A. Stockfisch; and Robert Wilson. 1982. *Discounting for Time and Risk in Energy Policy.* Baltimore: John Hopkins University Press.

Lutz, Mark A., and Kenneth Lux. 1971. *The Challenge of Humanistic Economics.* Menlo Park, California: Benjamin/Cummings.

Machlup, Fritz. 1969. "Positive and Normative Economics." In *Economic Means and Social Ends,* ed. Robert L. Heilbroner, pp. 99–129. Englewood Cliffs, New Jersey: Prentice-Hall.

Madden, J. Patrick. 1970. "Social Change and Public Policy in Rural America: Data and Research Needs for the 1970's." *American Journal of Agricultural Economics* 52:308–14.

_____. 1984a. "What to do with those Empty Boxes—Fill or Decorate Them?" In *Economies of Size Studies,* pp. 104–108. Ames: Iowa State University Center for Agricultural and Rural Development.

_____. 1984b. "Regenerative Agriculture: Beyond Organic and Sustainable Food Production." *The Farm and Food System in Transition.* Report FS33. East Lansing: Michigan State Cooperative Extension Service.

Madden, J. Patrick, and Irene Johnston. 1984. "A Case Study of the Mechanical Tomato Harvester." In *Agricultural Technology Delivery System: A Study of the Transfer of Agricultural and Food-Related Technologies,* ed. I. Feller, *et al.,* Vol. 4, pp. 4.1–4.69. University Park: Institute for Policy Research and Evaluation, The Pennsylvania State University.

Mansfield, Edwin. 1975. *Microeconomics: Theory and Applications.* New York: W. W. Norton.

McCloskey, Donald N. 1983. "The Rhetoric of Economics." *Journal of Economic Literature,* 21(2):481–517.

Musgrave, Richard A. 1959. *The Theory of Public Finance.* New York: McGraw-Hill.

Myrdal, Gunnar. 1973. *Against the Stream—Critical Essays on Economics.* New York: Pantheon Books.

_____. 1978. "Institutional Economics." *Journal of Economic Issues* 12:771–783.

Norton, George W.; W. L. Fishel; A. A. Paulsen; and W. B. Sundquist. 1981. *Evaluation of Agricultural Research.* Proceedings of NC–148 Workshop. Minneapolis: University of Minnesota, Agricultural Experiment Station, Misc. Pub. 8.

Norton, George W., and Jeffrey S. Davis. 1981. "Review of Methods Used to Evaluate Returns to Agricultural Research." In *Evaluation of Agricultural Research,* ed. G. W. Norton *et al.,* pp. 26–47. Minneapolis: University of Minnesota Agricultural Experiment Station.

Okun, Arthur M. 1971. "Social Welfare Has No Price Tag." *Survey of Current Business* 51 (7, Part 2):129–133. (Fiftieth Anniversary Issue, "The Economic Accounts of the United States: Retrospect and Prospect").

Pearce, David W. 1981. *The Dictionary of Modern Economics.* Cambridge: MIT Press.

Perleman, Michael. 1977. *Farming for Profit in a Hungry World—Capitalism and the Crisis in Agriculture.* Montclair, New Jersey: Allanheld Osmun.

Peterson, Willis, and Yujiro Hayami. 1976. "Technical Change in Agriculture." In *A Survey of Agricultural Economics Literature,* ed. L. R. Martin, Vol. 1, pp. 497–540. Minneapolis: University of Minnesota Press.

Randall, Alan. 1981. *Resource Economics.* New York: Wiley.

Rodale, Robert. 1983. "Breaking New Ground: The Search for a Sustainable Agriculture." *The Futurist* 17:15–20.

Rudner, Richard. 1953. "The Scientist *Qua* Scientist Makes Value Judgements." *Philosophy of Science* 20(1):1–6.

Ruttan, Vernon W. 1982. *Agricultural Research Policy.* Minneapolis: University of Minnesota Press.

Samuels, Warren J., ed. 1980. *The Methodology of Economic Thought.* New Brunswick, New Jersey: Transactions Books.

Schmid, A. Allan. 1978. *Property, Power, and Public Choice: An Inquiry into Law and Economics.* New York: Praeger.

Schmitz, A., and D. Seckler. 1970. "Mechanical Agriculture and Social Welfare: The Case of the Tomato Harvester." *American Journal of Agricultural Economics* 52:569–78.

Schumacher, E. F. 1973. *Small is Beautiful—Economics As If People Mattered.* New York: Harper and Row.

Shepard, Geoffrey S. 1982. "What Can a Research Man Say about Values?" *Journal of Farm Economics* 38:8–16.

Simon, Herbert A. 1979. "Rational Decision Making in Business Organizations." *American Economic Review* 69:493–513.

Solo, Robert. 1976. "New Maths and Old Sterilities." In *Economic Relevance—A Second Look,* ed. R. L. Heilbroner and A. M. Ford, pp. 24–27. Pacific Palisades, California: Goodyear.

Strange, Marty. 1984. "Down on the Farm," NOVA TV program, interview. First broadcast on March 20.

Strumpel, Berkhard, ed. 1976. *Economic Means for Human Needs: Social Indicators of Well-Being and Discontent.* Ann Arbor: Survey Research Center, The University of Michigan.

Sundquist, W. Burt. 1983. "Technology and Productivity Policies of the Future." *The Farm and Food System in Transition.* Report FS4. East Lansing: Michigan State Cooperative Extension Service.

Swanson, Earl R. 1984. "The Mainstream in Agricultural Economics Research." *American Journal of Agricultural Economics* 66(5):782–792.

Thurow, Lester C. 1980. *The Zero-Sum Society.* New York: Basic Books.

Tweeten, Luther. 1983. "Food for People and Profit: Ethics and Capitalism." *The Farm and Food System in Transition.* Report FS5. East Lansing: Michigan State Cooperative Extension Service.

Ulmer, Melville, J. 1980. "Human Values and Economic Science." In *The Methodology of Economic Thought,* ed. W. J. Samuels, pp. 171–181. New Brunswick, New Jersey: Transaction Books.

Varien, Hal R. 1984. *Microeconomic Analysis.* Second edition. New York: W. W. Norton & Co.

Von Mises, Ludwig. 1962. *The Ultimate Foundation of Economic Science.* Kansas City: Sheed Andrews and McMeel.

Weaver, R. D., and S. E. Stefanou. 1984. "Toward a Behavioral Approach to Modelling Dynamic Production Choice Structures." *Northeastern Journal of Agricultural and Resource Economics* 13(2):163–176.

# 12

# Energy and Other Natural Resources Used by Agriculture and Society

## David Pimentel and Susan Pimentel

**Introduction**

In recent decades, the fertile cropland of the United States and technical innovations in agriculture have made this country the major food producing nation in the world. We have become so at great cost. The high production level has caused a gradual degradation of cropland and led to the rapid depletion of water and energy resources.

At a time when supplies of arable land, ground water, and fossil fuel are diminishing, the need for a dependable food supply, ample in quantity and nutritive quality, is expected to increase. Already the U.S. population numbers about 240 million, more than a ten-fold increase since 1850 (Figure 12.1). The fact that the per capita consumption of resources, many of them nonrenewable, has grown several fold as well, is cause for even greater concern.

Conservative projections are that the world population will increase from more than 4 billion to over 6 billion in the next 20 years. To feed this population, food production will have to be increased two-fold over present levels. Dwindling resources make this task difficult. We will not succeed unless agricultural policy is based on sound ecological principles.

In this chapter, we will explore the energy flow in agriculture, discuss resource interdependence, and identify alternative strategies that could be adopted to improve the management of land and water resources and reduce the dependency on fossil fuel (Figure 12.2).

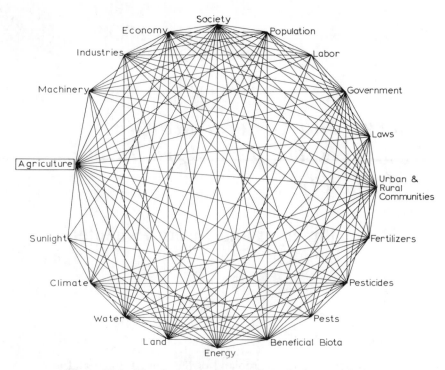

Figure 12.1   The Interdependency of Agriculture and the
Ecological System

## Historical Perspective:  Energy Flow in Agricultural Production

For centuries humans had little control over their environment and existed in what can be characterized as a hostile world.  Slowly we progressed and found ways to manage the natural environment to our advantage.  Each advance, from hunting and gathering of food to producing food by modern, fossil-driven agricultural systems, has increased our control and allowed us to produce a more dependable food supply.  These advances, however, have pushed us ever closer to overstepping the earth's carrying capacity.

The revolution in agricultural technologies that has occurred during the past two centuries is illustrated by examining the changes in U.S. corn production from 1700 to present day.

### Swidden Agriculture

Before agricultural systems were developed, humans obtained most of their food by gathering seeds, nuts, and berries, and hunting mammals,

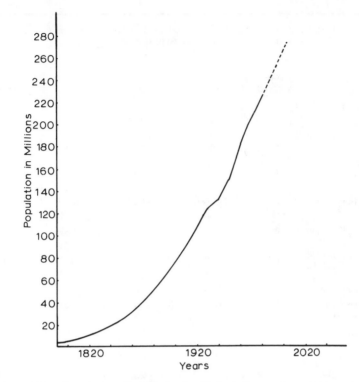

Figure 12.2   Population Growth in the United States, Actual (_____) and
Projected (_ _ _ _)

birds, and fish.  When human numbers increased, many regions could no
longer support a hunting-gathering economy and a shift had to be made
to a more permanent type agriculture (Boserup, 1965).

Swidden agriculture was the first technology employed.  Vegetation was
cut and burned on site to kill weeds and release nutrients to the soil for
crop production.  Slash and burn crop technology required few tools but
much manpower.  To raise corn by hand required about 1,200 hours of
labor per hectare (Table 12.1).  A big handicap of this system was that
land could be tilled and planted to crops for only a couple of years before
soil nutrients were depleted.  Then the land had to lay fallow for some 20
years to enable the vegetation to regrow and the soil nutrients to be
replenished.

### Draft Powered Agriculture

Early Native Americans and the first European settlers also raised corn by
hand, but beginning with United States independence, most corn culture

**Table 12.1  Quantities of Various Inputs to Produce Corn Using Only Labor, Draft Animals, and Mechanization from 1910 to 1983**

| | Hand-produced | 1910 | 1920 | 1945 | 1950 |
|---|---|---|---|---|---|
| Labor (hrs) | 1,200[a] | 120[b] | 120[b] | 57[f] | 44[f] |
| Machinery (kg) | 1[c] | 15[b] | 15[b] | 22[g] | 30[g] |
| Draft animals (hrs) | 0 | 120[b] | 120[b] | * | * |
| Fuel (liters) | | | | | |
| Gasoline | * | * | * | 120[i] | 135[i] |
| Diesel | * | * | * | 20[i] | 25[i] |
| Manure (kg) | * | 4,000[n] | 4,000[n] | 3,000[n] | 2,000[n] |
| N (kg) | 0 | 0 | 0 | 8[g] | 17[g] |
| P (kg) | 0 | 0 | 0 | 8[g] | 11[g] |
| K (kg) | 0 | 0 | 0 | 6[g] | 11[g] |
| Lime (kg) | 0 | 10[d] | 10[d] | 145[e] | 195[e] |
| Seeds (kg) | 11[d] | 11[d] | 11[d] | 11[g] | 13[g] |
| Insecticides (kg) | 0 | 0 | 0 | 0[g] | 0.1[g] |
| Herbicides (kg) | 0 | 0 | 0 | 0[g] | 0.05[g] |
| Irrigation (%) | 0 | * | * | 1[l] | 1[l] |
| Drying (kg) | 0 | 0 | 0 | 43[d] | 48[d] |
| Electricity (10³ kcal) | 0 | * | 1[d] | 8[d] | 16[d] |
| Transport (kg) | * | 25[m] | 25[m] | 170[m] | 210[m] |
| Yield (kg) | 1,880[e] | 1,880[e] | 1,880[e] | 2,132[g] | 2,383[g] |

involved draft animal power. Pressures from a growing population made this shift necessary.

During this period, U.S. agriculture was organic-based. That is, nutrients for crop production were provided by livestock and green manures. This farming system required the cultivation of 2 hectares of land to produce one hectare of a crop: one hectare would be planted to a legume such as clover and the following year this legume would be plowed under and planted to corn. Although this two-year rotation system provided an adequate amount of nitrogen for the corn crop each year, the soils were slowly depleted of phosphorus, potassium, and calcium. Still, this system enabled substantially more land acreage to be productive than under the earlier swidden technology.

In addition, the use of 200 hours of oxen power per hectare of corn reduced the manpower input from 1,200 to about 400 hours (Pimentel and Pimentel, 1979). Thus, each hour of oxen input replaced 4 hours of manpower input. When horsepower came into prominence during the early 1900s, the labor input was further reduced. Each hour of horsepower replaced about 10 hours of manpower (Pimentel, 1984) (Tables 12.1 and 12.2).

**Table 12.1 Continued**

| 1954 | 1959 | 1964 | 1970 | 1975 | 1980 | 1983 |
|---|---|---|---|---|---|---|
| 42[f] | 35[g] | 27[g] | 22[g] | 17[h] | 12[h] | 10[d] |
| 35[g] | 42[g] | 49[g] | 49[g] | 50[h] | 55[h] | 55[d] |
| * | * | * | * | * | * | * |
| 150[i] | 155[i] | 125[i] | 120[i] | 60[h] | 50[b] | 40[d] |
| 30[i] | 35[i] | 65[i] | 80[i] | 70[h] | 75[b] | 75[d] |
| 1,000[n] | 1,000[n] | 1,000[n] | 1,000[n] | 1,000[n] | 1,000[n] | 1,000[n] |
| 30[g] | 46[g] | 65[g] | 125[g] | 118[j] | 146[j] | 152[j] |
| 13[g] | 18[g] | 20[g] | 35[g] | 65[j] | 74[j] | 75[j] |
| 20[g] | 34[g] | 32[g] | 67[g] | 75[j] | 96[j] | 96[j] |
| 124[e] | 158[e] | 203[e] | 220[e] | 220[h] | 426[k] | 426[d] |
| 17[g] | 19[g] | 21[g] | 21[g] | 21[h] | 21[h] | 21[d] |
| 0.3[g] | 0.8[g] | 1.1[g] | 1.1[g] | 2[h] | 3[b] | 3[d] |
| 0.1[g] | 0.3[g] | 0.4[g] | 1[g] | 4[h] | 7[b] | 8[d] |
| 2[o] | 3[o] | 5[p] | 9[q] | 16[r] | 17[s] | 18[s] |
| 77[d] | 271[d] | 725[d] | 1.880[e] | 2,290[d] | 3,200[d] | 3,300[d] |
| 24[d] | 36[d] | 60[d] | 80[d] | 90[d] | 100[d] | 100[d] |
| 262[m] | 287[m] | 325[m] | 305[m] | 298[m] | 326[m] | 322[m] |
| 2,572[g] | 3,387[g] | 4,265[g] | 5,080[g] | 5,143[t] | 6,500[t] | 6,500[u] |

[a] Estimated from Lewis, 1951.
[b] Estimated from Pimentel, 1984.
[c] Pimentel and Pimentel, 1979.
[d] Estimated.
[e] USDA, 1970.
[f] USDA, 1954.
[g] Pimentel *et al.*, 1973.
[h] Pimentel and Burgess, 1980.
[i] Quantities from Pimentel *et al.* (1973) and proportions estimated.
[j] USDA, 1979; USDA, 1982b.
[k] USDA, 1981.
[l] Percentage of corn acreage irrigated (USBC, 1952).
[m] Transport of machinery, fuel, and nitrogen fertilizer.
[n] Estimated amount of livestock manure containing 80% moisture.
[o] Percentage of corn acreage irrigated (USBC, 1962).
[p] Percentage of corn acreage irrigated (USBC, 1967).
[q] Percentage of corn acreage irrigated (USBC, 1973).
[r] Percentage of corn acreage irrigated (FEA, 1976).
[s] Estimated percentage of corn acreage irrigated.
[t] Three-year running average yield (USDA, 1976; USDA, 1982a).
[u] Estimated.

*Asterisk means greater than 0.

*Note:* All units per hectare.

**Table 12.2 Enery Input for Various Items Used in Corn Production from 1700 to 1983 (1,000 kcal per hectare)**

|  | 1700 | 1910 | 1920 | 1945 | 1950 |
|---|---|---|---|---|---|
| Labor[a] | 653 | 65 | 65 | 31 | 24 |
| Machinery[b] | 19 | 278 | 278 | 407 | 555 |
| Draft animal[c] | 0 | 886 | 886 | 0 | 0 |
| Fuel (liters)[d] |  |  |  |  |  |
| Gasoline | 0 | 0 | 0 | 1,200 | 1,350 |
| Diesel | 0 | 0 | 0 | 228 | 275 |
| Manure[e] | 0 | 0 | 0 |  |  |
| N[f] |  |  |  | 168 | 357 |
| P[g] | 0 | 0 | 0 | 50 | 69 |
| K[h] | 0 | 0 | 0 | 15 | 28 |
| Lime[i] | 0 | 3 | 3 | 46 | 61 |
| Seeds[j] | 44 | 44 | 44 | 161 | 322 |
| Insecticides[k] | 0 | 0 | 0 | 0 | 7 |
| Herbicides[l] | 0 | 0 | 0 | 0 | 3 |
| Irrigation[m] | 0 | * | * | 125 | 125 |
| Drying[n] | 0 | 0 | 0 | 9 | 10 |
| Electricity[o] | 0 | * | 1 | 8 | 16 |
| Transport[p] | * | 25 | 25 | 44 | 58 |
| Total | 716 | 1,301 | 1,302 | 2,492 | 3,260 |
| Ratio[q] | 10.5 | 5.8 | 5.8 | 3.4 | 2.9 |
| Yield[r] | 7,520 | 7,520 | 7,520 | 8,528 | 9,532 |

[a]Food energy consumed per laborer per day was assumed to be 3,110 kcal from 1700 to 1970, 3,300 kcal for 1975, and 3,500 kcal for 1980–1983.

[b]The energy input per kilogram of steel in tools and other machinery was 18,500 kcal (Doering, 1980).

[c]The food energy per hour of draft animal use was calculated to be 7,380 kcal (Pimentel, 1984).

[d]A liter of gasoline and diesel fuel was calculated to contain 10,000 and 11,400 kcal (Cervinka, 1980). These values include the energy input for mining and refining.

[e]No charge was made for the manure input. This input was assumed to be included in either the draft animal input or the machinery and fuel inputs.

[f] Nitrogen = 21,000 kcal/kg (Dovring and McDowell, 1980).

[g]Phosphorus = 6,300 kcal/kg (Dovring and McDowell, 1980).

[h]Potassium = 2,500 kcal/kg (Dovring and McDowell, 1980).

[i] Limestone = 315 kcal/kg (Terhune, 1980).

[j] From 1700 to 1920, it was assumed that each kilogram of corn equaled 4,000 kcal, whereas when hybrid seed was used from 1945 to 1983 the cost was 24,750 kcal/kg (Heichel, 1980).

[k]Chlorinated insecticides dominated use from 1945 to 1964, and the energy input was calculated to be 67,000 kcal; whereas from 1970 to 1983 carbamate and phosphate

## U.S. Farm Population

When the U.S. population numbered only 5 million, most people were farmers in a rural setting in the northeastern region of the nation. By 1850 the pressure on the forests to provide fuel and agricultural land to

**Table 12.2 Continued**

| 1954 | 1959 | 1964 | 1970 | 1975 | 1980 | 1983 |
|---|---|---|---|---|---|---|
| 23 | 19 | 15 | 12 | 10 | 7 | 6 |
| 648 | 777 | 907 | 907 | 925 | 1,018 | 1,018 |
| 0 | 0 | 0 | 0 | 0 | 0 | 0 |
| 1,500 | 1,550 | 1,250 | 1,200 | 600 | 500 | 400 |
| 342 | 399 | 741 | 912 | 912 | 878 | 855 |
| 630 | 966 | 1,365 | 2,625 | 2,478 | 3,066 | 3,192 |
| 82 | 113 | 126 | 221 | 410 | 466 | 473 |
| 50 | 85 | 80 | 168 | 188 | 240 | 240 |
| 39 | 50 | 64 | 69 | 69 | 134 | 134 |
| 421 | 470 | 520 | 520 | 520 | 520 | 520 |
| 20 | 54 | 74 | 110 | 200 | 300 | 300 |
| 7 | 20 | 40 | 100 | 400 | 700 | 800 |
| 250 | 375 | 625 | 1,125 | 2,000 | 2,125 | 2,250 |
| 15 | 54 | 145 | 376 | 458 | 640 | 660 |
| 24 | 36 | 60 | 80 | 90 | 100 | 100 |
| 67 | 79 | 89 | 84 | 82 | 90 | 89 |
| 4,118 | 5,047 | 6,101 | 8,509 | 9,342 | 10,784 | 11,037 |
| 2.5 | 2.7 | 2.8 | 2.4 | 2.2 | 2.4 | 2.4 |
| 10,288 | 13,548 | 17,060 | 20,320 | 20,575 | 26,000 | 26,000 |

dominated use, and the energy input for these was calculated to be 100,000 kcal/kg (Pimentel, 1980).

l Phenoxy herbicides dominated use from 1945 to 1959, and the energy input was calculated to be 67,000 kcal/kg; whereas from 1964 to 1983 other types of herbicides dominated use, and the energy input for these are calculated to be 100,000 kcal/kg (Pimentel, 1980).

mWater used per irrigated hectare was assumed to be 37.5 cm from 1945 to 1970 and 45 cm from 1974 to 1983. The percentage of corn acreage receiving irrigation are shown in Table 12.1. The energy required per kilogram of irrigation water pumped from a depth of 100 meters was calculated to be 300,000 kcal/cm.

nThe quantity of corn per hectare that required drying is shown on Table 12.1. The energy required per kilogram dried was 200 kcal (Peart *et al.*, 1980).

oIncludes energy input required to produce the electricity.

pFor the goods transported to the farm, an input of 275 kcal/kg was included (Pimentel, 1980).

qRatio is output/input.

r An input of 4,000 kcal/kg of corn.

*Asterisk means greater than 0.

supply food reached a critical stage due to the four-fold increase in population.

Shortages of food resources forced many farmers to move to the Midwest and use the rich agricultural soils of that region for food production. The rail and barge transportation systems that developed moved grains and other foods to the eastern urban areas and moved manufactured goods back to the West.

Centralization, specialization, and large farms typify U.S. agriculture today. Only about 3 percent of the U.S. population is now directly involved in on-farm production.

### Energy Use in U.S. Crop Production

Beginning in the twentieth century, energy from fossil fuels flowed into the new agricultural crop production systems to run farm machinery and also as the raw material needed to produce fertilizers and pesticides. With the advent of heavy mechanization of agriculture, the labor input in corn production was reduced to about 10 hours per hectare, about 1/20th of the input required to produce corn by hand (Tables 12.1 and 12.2). Meanwhile, the fossil energy input increased dramatically.

Since 1945, however, the total amount of fuel consumed by farm machinery has declined from about 140 liters/ha to about 115 liters/ha today because of improved engines, larger farm machinery, and a change from gasoline to diesel fuel.

Initially, the primary fuel burned in tractors was gasoline. Only 15% used diesel fuel (Table 12.1). There has been a gradual shift away from gasoline to today's situation with 65% of U.S. tractors using diesel fuel (Table 12.1). Diesel has the advantage over gasoline of providing 20–25 percent more power or greater efficiency per unit of fossil energy (Council for Agricultural Science and Technology, 1975).

Another reason for this reduction is the use of larger farm equipment that performs more operations in substantially less time than the smaller machines. The result is less fuel expended per hectare in corn production. But while liquid fuel inputs have declined, the fossil energy inputs for construction of the machinery have risen dramatically.

### Commercial Fertilizers

U.S. corn yields remained relatively static at about 1,880 kg/ha from 1909 to 1940 (Figure 12.3). Then they started to increase rapidly about 1945 when hybrid corn varieties were planted and commercial fertilizers and pesticides were applied (Pimentel *et al.*, 1973). From 1945 to date, corn yields have increased three-fold (Figure 12.3), but at the cost of a four-fold increase in total energy inputs.

In 1945, an average of 8 kg of nitrogen and phosphorus and 6 kg of potassium were applied per hectare of corn (Figure 12.4). By 1983, nitrogen application rates reached a high of 152 kg/ha, nearly a twenty-fold increase. Note that the energy inputs of nitrogen alone in 1983 about

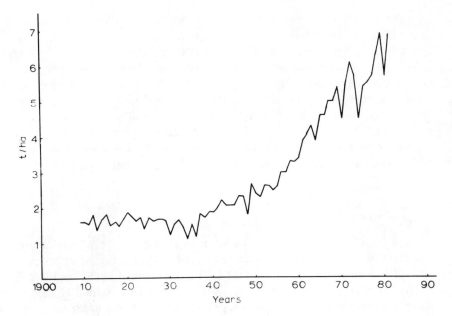

Figure 12.3   U.S. Corn Yields from 1909 to Present

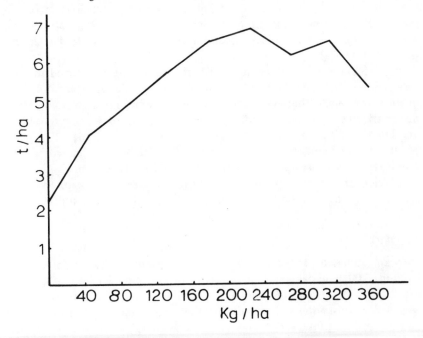

Figure 12.4   Corn Yields (t/ha) with Varying Amounts of Nitrogen with the Phosphorous Application held Constant at 38 kg/ha (Source: Munson and Doll, 1959)

equalled the total energy inputs for all inputs used in 1945 corn production (Table 12.2). Thus a clear picture emerges of how much U.S. agricultural technologies have changed in just four decades.

Although the amounts of phosphorus and potassium applied per hectare rose significantly from 1945 to 1983, clearly they did not grow as rapidly as nitrogen inputs did. The ten to fifteen-fold increase in the use of these minerals is less significant because both require significantly less energy per kilogram to produce (Table 12.2) than nitrogen.

Lime is the least energy costly of the fertilizers used in corn production (Table 12.2) and quantities of lime applied rose about three-fold from 1945 to 1983.

*Pesticide Use*

As with fertilizers, little or no pesticide was used in corn production before 1950 (Table 12.1), but once employed, the quantity of insecticide applied to corn rose quickly, from 0.1 kg/ha in 1950 to 3 kg/ha by 1983.

The insecticides used in the early '50s and '60s were primarily chlorinated insecticides. Then there was a gradual shift to carbamate and phosphate insecticides when selected chlorinated insecticides were banned in the 1970s. The change in the chemical makeup of insecticides increased the energy inputs per kilogram of pesticide produced by about 50 percent. The total inputs for chemical insect control rose forty-five-fold over this period (Table 12.2).

In this same time span, changes in herbicide use also occurred in corn production. The first herbicide used in corn production was 2,4-D, a phenoxy herbicide that was relatively energy efficient to produce. The newer triazines and other herbicides that were added during the 1960s and later are 50 percent more energy costly to produce (Table 12.2). As a result, the total energy input for chemical weed control increased two hundred and sixty-seven-fold from 1950 to date. Hence, not only were there changes in the quantities of pesticide applied but there were significant changes in the kinds of insecticides and herbicides utilized.

*Summary*

Only an estimated 716,000 kcal were used to produce a hectare of corn by hand in 1700, whereas today in U.S. corn production 11.1 million kcal are expended. This translates into a fifteen-fold increase in energy inputs. Matched against inputs, yields during this period have grown only three and a half-fold (Tables 12.1 and 12.2). The energy crisis that struck the United States in 1973 did not slow the growth of energy use in corn production, although there is evidence to suggest that there has been some improvement since then. Grain yields have increased 26 percent, whereas energy use has increased only 18 percent.

Overall, however, it is important to keep in mind that the fossil fuels used in agriculture simply facilitate the harvest of solar energy. The solar energy reaching a hectare during the year in the United States is about 14 billion kcal. During a 4-month summer growing season in this region nearly 7 billion kcal or about 1/2 of the total reach an agricultural hectare. When we harvest 7,000 kg of corn per hectare, we harvest only 0.2 percent of the total solar energy input. The solar energy input represents about 93 percent of the total energy input to produce a hectare of corn. The fossil energy input of 9.6 million kcal represents only 7 percent (Table 12.2). Our concern is not about the solar energy but about the 7 percent which is a non-renewable resource being rapidly depleted.

## Interdependence of Resources

In industrialized nations like the United States, fossil energy has become as vital a resource for crop production as land and water resources. In fact, energy inputs are being pumped into agricultural crop production systems to compensate for shortages of arable land and rainfall.

### Land and Soil Losses

Croplands have been shifted out of production predominantly in the eastern section of the United States and in parts of the Great Plains and Great Lakes States. Since 1945, the total cropland lost to highways, urbanization, and other related uses has been about 45 million acres—an area nearly that of the state of Nebraska. The development of highways accounts for 50 percent of the total loss. Increasing human populations, growing urban- and sub-urban populations, and industrialization account for the remainder.

Several million more acres have been lost from production because of soil erosion damage. Erosion has severely reduced the productivity potential on the cropland remaining in use, having removed at least one-third of the land's topsoil. Soil loss adversely affects crop productivity by reducing organic matter (including basic plant nutrients) and fine clays. The latter affect the water holding capacities of soil. In addition, as soil thins, rooting depth is restricted and soil tilth is reduced.

In some regions of the southern United States, soil losses during the past 200 years have resulted in yield reductions that range from 25 percent to 50 percent for crops such as corn, soybeans, cotton, oats, and wheat (Pimentel *et al.*, 1983). Nonetheless, crop yields in most U.S. regions have been rising despite the effects of soil erosion because of increased energy inputs in the form of fertilizers and pesticides and the use of such advanced technologies as high-yielding crop varieties.

For example, in corn production the yield of corn from 2 hectares of land, with energy inputs of about 2.2 million kcal per hectare, is about 2,500 kg per hectare, or a total of about 5,000 kg (Pimentel and Pimentel, 1979). If less land is available and there is a need to produce 5,000 kg of corn on only one hectare of land, then the energy inputs have to be increased to about 6.5 million kcal (Pimentel, 1980). Thus, to reduce the land area by half and maintain corn yields, about 3 times more fossil energy must be expended. With energy resources now at a premium, the U.S. cannot afford to lose valuable cropland and continue to make up the deficit with fossil fuel.

In general, for each 1 kg of reduction in yield due to soil erosion and degradation, an estimated 1,000 kcal of fossil energy is required to offset the loss (Pimentel et al., 1981). For example, if corn yields were reduced in a region by 25 percent from 7,000 kg/ha to 5,250 kg/ha, an estimated 1.8 million kcal/ha (60 gal of oil/ha) in energy would be required to maintain the corn yield. A reduction in soil organic matter and soil tilth increases the energy required to till the soil.

## Water Shortages

In recent decades the agricultural system of the U.S. has become increasingly water intensive and in some areas high crop yields are directly dependent on irrigation practices. Presently, agriculture consumes 83 percent of the fresh water that is withdrawn (Figure 12.5) and this demand is expected to increase 17 percent from now until 2000 (USWRC, 1979).

Pumping underground water to the surface is energy intensive. To irrigate a hectare of corn in an arid region for one growing season requires more than three times the total energy input needed to grow the same crop under normal rainfall conditions (Pimentel et al., 1982a).

Water shortages are fast becoming a major resource problem in this country (Pimentel et al., 1982a). The amount of ground water being removed greatly exceeds replenishment throughout most of the nation, but this is especially true in the West (Pimentel et al., 1982a). Water overdraft in regions over the Ogallala Aquifer in the Great Plains, water deficits along the Colorado River, and water shortages in the San Joaquin Valley are symptomatic of the pressure for irrigation water. A study of 32 counties in the Texas Panhandle, where the Ogallala Aquifer is unusually shallow, estimated that by 1995 the combination of fuel increases and water depletion will eliminate irrigation and force a return to dryland farming (Brown, 1981). Indeed, the use of ground water in parts of the West now exceeds the limits of natural water recharge and recycling. In

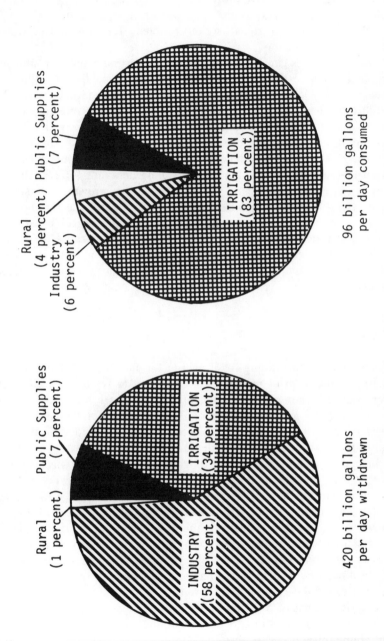

WATER
WITHDRAWN

Rural
(1 percent)  Public Supplies
(7 percent)

IRRIGATION
(34 percent)

INDUSTRY
(58 percent)

420 billion gallons
per day withdrawn

FRESHWATER
CONSUMED

Rural
(4 percent)  Public Supplies
(7 percent)
Industry
(6 percent)

IRRIGATION
(83 percent)

96 billion gallons
per day consumed

Figure 12.5   Off-channel Water Withdrawals in the United States and the Proportion of Freshwater Consumed in 1975

adjoining states, water overdraft exceeded replenishment by about 25 percent, while in the Texas-Gulf area overdraft is as high as 77 percent (USWRC, 1979). This signals serious problems for all who need water for agricultural production.

Water shortages can be hedged by increasing the acreage of unirrigated cropland. Where there is limited rainfall, land can be left fallow every other year to accumulate sufficient moisture to grow another crop. But to do this two hectares of land are needed to grow the same crop of wheat per year that under better rainfall conditions could be harvested from one hectare of land. However, the amount of such unirrigated cropland that is not marginal, fragile, or subject to serious soil erosion problems is limited. What this means, then, is that the conflicting demands for available water among irrigated agriculture, urban population growth, industry, and fossil-energy mining portend major changes in water use throughout the world. Among the four competing groups, evidence suggests that the proportion of water allotted to agriculture will decline because the economic yields from agriculture are far less than yields from industry and mining. If so, the potential shift in water use could seriously curtail agricultural productivity.

## Labor Substitutes

In addition to substituting fossil energy for shortages of water and land, energy in the form of machinery is also used to replace the labor input. For example, when corn is produced by hand, nearly 1,200 hours of manpower effort are needed per hectare (Table 12.1). As noted earlier, when a mechanized system is substituted, corn can be produced with an input of only 10 hours of manpower (Table 12.1).

Indeed, a gallon (3.79 liters) of gasoline, which contains 31,000 kcal energy, has tremendous power and the potential to do work. When one gallon of gasoline is used to operate a mechanical engine, which is about 20 percent efficient in converting heat energy, an equivalent of 6,200 kcal of work is produced, equal to about 9.7 hp-h of work or the work equivalent of one horse working at capacity for nearly a 10-hour day. Since man produces only 1/10th of a hp-h working at capacity, the gallon of gasoline is equivalent to 97 manhours of work or one man working 8 hours a day, 5 days a week for 2.5 weeks.

Clearly, the use of fossil fuel drastically reduces the input of manpower or horsepower needed in agricultural production. As long as fuel supplies are abundant and cheap, this will continue to be an acceptable tradeoff. Note, however, that mechanization itself has not increased the crop yield per hectare except where growing seasons are short and mechanization facilitates timing and increases the speed of planting and harvesting.

### Effective Resource Management Policy

Beyond the basics of food, water and shelter humans also need more than just crop and livestock species. Maintenance of a quality environment both for agriculture and the natural ecosystem depends upon an estimated 200,000 species of plants and animals (Pimentel *et al.,* 1980a). Many of these species help renew atmospheric oxygen. Some prevent us from being buried by human and agricultural wastes, while others help purify our water.

The relative impact that various natural species groups have in the environment can be judged in part by their biomass per unit area. The average biomass of humans, for example, in the nation is about 18 kg/ha (16 lb/A). Figure 12.6 illustrates the great abundance (compared with that of man) of living protoplasm in the other species groups such as insects, earthworms, protozoa, bacteria, fungi, and algae. Insects and earthworms average about 1,000 kg/ha (Wolcott, 1937; Edwards and Lofty, 1977); protozoa and algae about 150 kg/ha (Alexander, 1977); bacteria about 1,700 kg/ha (Alexander, 1977); and fungi, 2,700 kg/ha (Alexander, 1977).

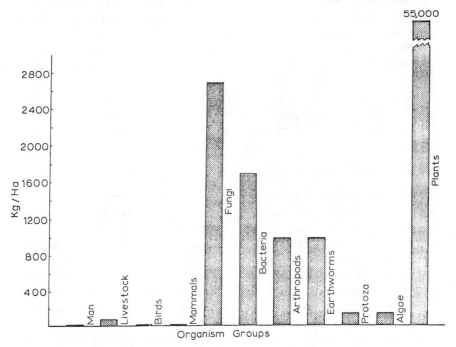

Figure 12.6   The Average Biomass Weight of Man and His Livestock per acre in the United States (Pimentel, et al., 1975) and the Estimated Biomass of Natural Biota Species Groups of Birds, Mammals, Arthropods (Lauer, et al., 1976), Earthworms (Edwards and Lofty, 1977), Protozoa, Bacteria, Algae, and Fungi (Alexander, 1977) in the Environment.

These species total about 6,700 kg/ha in biomass—approximately 350 times the average human biomass in the United States.

In addition to playing a major role in waste degradation in agriculture, the many small organisms are essential in the release of nitrogen into the soil. When one considers that it costs approximately $2.5 billion to apply 10 million tons of nitrogen fertilizer annually, the estimated 14 million tons of nitrogen that are biologically fixed in the United States every year have a calculated value of about $3.5 billion (Delwiche, 1970). The great economic advantage of protecting these nitrogen-fixing bacteria and other natural biota so they may contribute to crop production is obvious.

Pollinating forage, fruit, and vegetable crops is a vital activity carried out by insects. A total of 90 U.S. crops, valued at nearly $4 billion, are dependent upon insect pollination, and 9 additional crops, valued at $4.5 billion, are significantly benefited by insect pollination (USDA *et al.*, 1969). In addition to the cultured plants, large numbers of wild plants require cross-pollination for their propagation.

Despite our many technological advances, substitutes for insect pollination of plants, both cultivated and wild, do not exist. On a bright sunny day in July, for example, honeybees and wild bees pollinate about 8 trillion blossoms in New York State alone (Pimentel and Pimentel, 1979).

There are many viable, alternate practices presently known to man that are more in harmony with the natural ecosystem and could, if employed, lessen the manipulation of the ecosystem. These alternatives would help decrease the use of fossil-based fertilizers, pesticides and large machinery and improve the management of soil and water resources. Some of the most promising alternatives are discussed in the following section.

## Soil Nutrients and Alternative Fertilizers

Whenever crops are harvested, significant quantities of nutrients that once were in the soil are removed because they have been incorporated into the growing plant material. In recycling these nutrients, livestock manure offers a traditional substitute for some or all commercial fertilizer presently being used. Manure not only is a source of nutrients that crops need, but it helps to reduce soil erosion and improves soil structure (Neal, 1939; Zwerman *et al.*, 1970). In the United States, current manure production is estimated to be 1.1 billion tons per year, with about 420 million tons produced in feedlots and other confined rearing situations (Miller and McCormac, 1978; Van Dyne and Gilbertson, 1978). Although more than 70 percent of this collected manure is applied to land, it provides agriculture with only about 8 percent of the needed nitrogen, 20 percent of phosphorus, and 20 percent of potassium.

The amount of nitrogen from manure applied to U.S lands could be doubled if proper management practices were employed in handling livestock manure (Muck, 1982). When manure is left standing in the barn and/or placed on the surface of agricultural land, most of the ammonium nitrogen is lost. To prevent this loss, manure should be collected promptly and stored in large tanks or immediately turned under the soil when application is made to the land (Muck, 1982).

Although livestock manure can be effectively applied to land to reduce use of commercial fertilizers, its enormous volume and weight relative to amounts of nutrients contained makes the handling of manure labor intensive compared with commercial fertilizers. This energy investment is calculated to be about 30,000 kcal of fuel per ton of manure, collected and spread by tractor when the manure is located about 1.5 km from the cropland (Linton, 1968; Pimentel *et al.*, 1983).

Thus, 25 tons of manure applied to the land would require a fuel input of 750,000 kcal. But if the same amount of nutrients contained in 25 tons of manure were obtained from commercial fertilizer, the fuel input would be 2.3 million kcal. Thus, using manure provides more than a three-fold energy saving over commercial fertilizer. Obviously, as distance between field and manure source increases, so does the energy expenditure. Indeed, this is the major problem associated with making efficient use of manure from feedlots, which are usually far from agricultural land.

Before commercial fertilizers were so universally used in corn production, corn was planted in rotation with a legume crop such as sweet clover (Pimentel, 1981). Although legume rotations are not always feasible, legumes could be planted between corn rows in August. Then these plants, considered "green manure," would be plowed under in early spring when the field is being prepared for reseeding. Winter vetch and other legumes, for example, planted in this manner yield about 15 kg/ha of nitrogen (Mitchell and Teel, 1977). Also the use of a cover crop such as this protects the soil from wind and water erosion during the winter and has the additional advantage of adding organic matter to the soil. One disadvantage is that the green manure must be plowed under during the spring when the farmer is pressed for time to plant the major crop.

*Alternate Pest Controls*

Pesticides, because of their widespread use, have taken their toll on the natural environment. The effects, varied and complex, are often ignored when total assessments of benefits and costs are calculated. Pesticides have influenced the structure and function of ecosystems, altered the stability of natural communities, and reduced species population numbers. They have changed the normal behavior patterns in animals, stimulated or suppressed growth in animals and plants, and modified the reproductive capacity in some animals. In addition, their use has altered the susceptibility of certain plants and animals to diseases and predators and has affected the natural evolution of species populations (Pimentel and Edwards, 1982).

A wide variety of alternative pest controls can be used as substitutes for pesticides (Pimentel et al., 1982b). One of these is biological control, or the use of parasites and predators to control insects and weeds. Under this approach, pesticides are applied only when the pest population threatens to exceed the natural enemy controls and when economic damage will take place in the crop. Not only is care used as to when a pesticide is applied but also only those pesticides are used that have a major impact on the pest and minor impact on natural enemies. The use of natural enemies and other biological controls is ideal from an energy standpoint. Because parasites and predators obtain their food-fuel directly from the pests, they are solar powered.

Yet another successful way to control pests without pesticides is breeding food and fiber crops with resistance to plant pathogens, pest insects, and weed damage (Pimentel et al., 1973; Pimentel et al., 1982b). Most crops now planted in the United States have had some resistance to plant pathogens bred into them. This is documented by the fact that only about 2 percent of U.S. agricultural acreage is treated with fungicides for plant pathogen control (Eichers, 1981).

In addition to the alternatives mentioned, various agronomic or cultural practices may be modified to enhance pest control (Pimentel et al., 1982b). For instance, when corn is planted after a legume or small grain, the injurious corn rootworm complex is controlled (Pimentel et al., 1982b). Crop rotations have proven successful for control of many other insects, plant pathogens, and weeds.

Other cultural practices for pest control include altering planting times to elude pests, tilling the soil to destroy weed and insect pests, applying irrigation water to control growth sequences of crop and pests, plus the judicious use of organic and plastic mulches (Pimentel et al., 1982b). All of these techniques have some energy and environmental costs, but for certain pests of a particular crop and region they may be highly beneficial both in terms of total energy conservation and the maintenance of a quality environment.

## Substitute Crop–Cultural Practices

To reverse further land productivity losses caused by soil erosion, alternate cultural practices already known to man could easily be employed. The most common methods are contour planting, crop rotation, application of livestock manure, no-tillage crop production technology, cover-crop planting during the winter months when the crop is not on the field, interseeding a legume with a crop in later summer, and building structures to trap sediment and stabilize stream channels. All these strategies are known to decrease soil erosion.

Why, if these practices have proven so successful, are they not regularly employed by a majority of the farmers? Several studies attempting to answer this question reveal a variety of reasons: the failure of farmers to appreciate the need for recommended practices because of custom and inertia; the reluctance of many farmers to change the layout of their farm; the large number of corporate and rented farms whose operators have little incentive to maintain long-term soil quality; and the need of farmers for immediate income.

Economic considerations discourage many farmers from employing soil conservation techniques. Often the benefits that accrue from their use are diminished by added production costs. For example, contour planting increases both farm labor and fuel use from 5 to 7 percent. No-till corn has the advantage of requiring less labor and conserving soil moisture, but it increases pest problems and thus, ultimately, pesticide usage. Then too, high fixed costs are often associated with the incorporation of soil conservation techniques into a farm operation because new management skills, improved varieties of plants, new machinery, and different chemicals may be needed. Nevertheless, most investigators report that soil conservation eventually results in a net revenue increase that is realized through increased crop yields.

No-till or minimum-till crop culture has several advantages over conventional tillage but there are also some disadvantages. Reliance on a no-till or minimum-till system does reduce the tractor fuel inputs normally required to plow and disc soil by conventional tillage. About 60 liters of diesel fuel are used per season to till one hectare with a 50-hp tractor, compared with about 15 liters for no-till planting. Thus, in a season, the saving could amount to about 45 liters or 513,630 kcal of fossil fuel per hectare if a no-till system were adopted.

On the other hand, with a no-till system, herbicide and insecticide use must be increased over conventional tillage to control weeds and deal with the increased insect and slug problems that often occur (USDA, 1975). Sometimes with no-till, pesticide use is doubled, thereby making the total energy inputs greater than with conventional tillage. Another energy input associated with no-till is the cost of the larger amount of corn seed (about 13 percent more than conventional tillage) that is required to offset poorer germination in the no-till environment (Phillips *et al.*, 1980).

*Conservation of Water*

Numerous techniques are available for conserving water and, not surprisingly, most of these are the same as those that prevent soil erosion. The use of organic mulches, no-till crop culture, the terracing of crops, the planting of strip crops, and planting crops on the contour—all of these slow runoff and help retain the water on the growing crops where it is needed.

If water must be used for agricultural irrigation, the quantities of water required for crop production can be conserved by employing efficient technologies. For example, surface irrigation uses a much larger quantity of water than drip irrigation (Batty and Keller, 1980). Drip irrigation delivers the needed amount of water directly to individual crop plants, but of course piping the water to each plant is energy costly in terms of the capital equipment required. Drip irrigation, however, saves energy where high lifts are involved because pumping energies are much greater than energy costs of installing a drip piping system (Batty and Keller, 1980). Future shifts in both irrigation technology and the use of crops best adapted to irrigation farming will probably reduce both water and energy use per irrigated hectare.

For the future, consideration should be given to shifting vegetable and fruit production back to the Northeast and Sun Belt because western agriculture is both water and energy inefficient and transporting food to distant areas where a great percentage of the U.S. population resides, is energy costly.

## Modifying American Diets

Because food production uses energy, the food system and ultimately food consumption patterns in the United States may need to be changed—especially when fossil energy supplies become scarce. To feed each American, about 1,500 liters (400 gallons) of oil equivalents are expended per year. Furthermore, a total of 17 percent of U.S. energy is expended to supply the population with food (Pimentel and Hall, 1984). Of this, agricultural production uses about 6 percent, food processing and packaging use another 6 percent, while distribution and home preparation account for the remaining 5 percent.

Interestingly, different food crops require different levels of energy inputs. Fruit and vegetables provide 1 kcal of food energy for 1 to 5 kcal of energy input. Production of grains is more energy efficient than vegetables, providing from 2 to 4 kcal of food energy per kcal of input (Table 12.3).

**Table 12.3  Energy Inputs and Returns for Various Food and Feed Crops Produced per Hectare in the United States**

| Crop | Crop yield (kg) | Yield in protein (kg) | Crop yield in food energy ($10^6$ kcal) | Fossil energy input for production ($10^6$ kcal) | Kcal food/feed output per Kcal fossil energy input | Labor input (manhours) |
|---|---|---|---|---|---|---|
| Corn (U.S.) | 7,000 | 630 | 24.5 | 6.9 | 3.5 | 12 |
| Wheat (North Dakota) | 2,022 | 283 | 6.7 | 2.5 | 2.7 | 6 |
| Oats (Minnesota) | 2,869 | 423 | 10.9 | 2.1 | 5.1 | 3 |
| Rice (Arkansas) | 4,742 | 272 | 14.0 | 12.5 | 1.1 | 30 |
| Sorghum (Kansas) | 1,840 | 202 | 6.0 | 1.5 | 4.0 | 5 |
| Soybean (Illinois) | 2,600 | 885 | 10.5 | 2.3 | 4.5 | 8 |
| Beans, dry (Michigan) | 1,176 | 285 | 4.1 | 3.1 | 1.3 | 19 |
| Peanuts (Georgia) | 3,720 | 320 | 15.3 | 10.9 | 1.4 | 19 |
| Apples (East) | 41,546 | 83 | 23.3 | 26.2 | 0.9 | 176 |
| Oranges (Florida) | 40,370 | 404 | 19.8 | 11.8 | 1.7 | 210 |
| Potato (New York) | 34,468 | 539 | 21.1 | 15.5 | 1.4 | 35 |
| Lettuce (California) | 31,595 | 284 | 4.1 | 19.7 | 0.2 | 171 |
| Tomato (California) | 49,620 | 496 | 9.9 | 16.6 | 0.6 | 165 |
| Cabbage (New York) | 53,000 | 1,060 | 12.7 | 16.8 | 0.8 | 289 |
| Alfalfa (Minnesota) | 11,800 (dry) | 1,845 | 47.2 | 3.6 | 13.1 | 12 |
| Tame hay (New York) | 2,539 (dry) | 160 | 5.5 | 0.6 | 8.6 | 7 |
| Corn silage (n.e. U.S.) | 9,400 (dry) | 753 | 29.1 | 5.2 | 5.6 | 15 |

*Source:*  From Pimentel and Pimentel, 1979, and Pimentel, 1980.

Although fruits and vegetables require larger energy inputs per food calorie than grain, no food crops are as energy expensive as the U.S. approach to producing animal protein. Ten to 90 kcal of fossil energy must be expended to produce 1 kcal of animal protein (Table 12.4). The major reason that animal protein products are significantly more energy expensive than plant protein foods is that initially energy has to be expended to produce the forage and grain crops to sustain the herd. Then too, the forage and feed used to maintain the breeding herd are auxiliary energy costs. About 1.3 head of breeding cattle must be maintained to produce one calf per year (Pimentel et al., 1975). In the United States, over 90 percent of all grains produced are fed to livestock (a high percentage in confinement operations) to yield the meat, milk, and eggs preferred by the American consumer. Overall, cycling plant protein through animals to produce meat protein is costly in both land and energy. However, rangeland-based livestock production has the major advantage of making marginal agricultural land productive. This is because forages grown on pasture and rangeland unsuitable for production of food crops, can be fed to animals effectively to produce valuable livestock protein (Pimentel et al., 1980b). The practice of grazing cattle on marginal land deserves more attention in the future.

Some argue in favor of changing U.S. dietary practices and using more grains directly for human consumption. The grain presently consumed by cattle each year could feed about 400 million humans or nearly twice the U.S. population.

Energy expenditure, however, is not the only factor to be considered when dietary changes are suggested. Food choices are based on social and cultural attitudes as well as taste, texture, color, and other palatability characteristics of the foods.

Of major consideration are the nutritional differences between the pure vegetarian diets and those that include animal products. Because vitamin B-12 (an essential nutrient) is lacking in pure vegetarian diets, it must be taken as a dietary supplement. Then, too, the quality of protein consumed may not be adequate in the vegetarian diet unless the essential amino acids of different plant foods are matched or "complemented." The large volume and bulk of vegetarian diets often make it difficult for young children and women to consume the quantities necessary to meet all nutritional needs. Further, infants, rapidly growing adolescents, pregnant and lactating women, and other nutritionally vulnerable groups consuming pure vegetarian diets may need nutritional supplements of vitamins A and D and iodine.

Modifying human diets is a complex issue because it involves personal habits and choices. Nutritionists working in community settings will be able to help people at least include more plant proteins in their daily menus, while ensuring the nutritional adequacies of these changes.

**Table 12.4 Energy Inputs and Returns per Hectare for Various Livestock Production Systems in the United States**

| Livestock | Animal product yield (kg) | Yield in protein (kg) | Protein as Kcal (10³) | Fossil energy input for production (10⁶ kcal) | Kcal fossil energy input/ Kcal protein output | Labor input (manhours) |
|---|---|---|---|---|---|---|
| Broilers | 2000 | 186 | 744 | 7.3 | 9.8 | 7 |
| Eggs | 910 | 104 | 416 | 7.4 | 17.8 | 19 |
| Pork | 490 | 35 | 140 | 6.0 | 42.9 | 11 |
| Sheep (grass-fed) | 7 | 0.2 | 0.8 | 0.07 | 87.5 | 0.2 |
| Dairy | 3270 | 114 | 457 | 5.4 | 11.8 | 51 |
| Beef | 60 | 6 | 24 | 0.6 | 25.0 | 2 |
| Dairy (grass-fed) | 3260 | 114 | 457 | 3.3 | 7.2 | 50 |
| Beef (grass-fed) | 54 | 5 | 20 | 0.5 | 25.0 | 2 |
| Catfish | 2783 | 384 | 1536 | 52.5 | 34.2 | 55 |

*Source:* Pimentel *et al.,* 1980b.

## Land and Soil Preservation by Legislation

Although loss of agricultural land is widely recognized as a serious problem, little legislative action has been taken to preserve the existing U.S. farmland. The problem is complex. Each state faces a different set of physical and political factors that are important not only to the feasibility of enactment but also to the ultimate success of a land use policy designed to protect cropland.

One of the primary considerations in formulating a land use policy is the degree of urban pressure present in the area. As one moves from rural to semi-suburban areas, farmland sells for many times more than its farm value. Land prices in semi-suburban areas have reached what some describe as "trigger levels"—prices at which farmers can sell their land, use the profit to buy an equivalent amount of equal or better farmland in another location, and cover all costs of selling and relocating as well.

### Assessment Policies

Land preservation policies now in effect vary widely across the nation. The most prevalent farmland preservation tool in use today is differential tax assessment, which has been adopted in varying forms by over 40 states (Davies and Belden, 1979). Basically, the method involves assessing land according to its farm use value. Since a farmer's property holdings are generally large in comparison to his income, his property taxes are likely to embrace a significant percentage of his income. The aim here is to maintain farm property taxes at levels that farmers can afford.

Yet the efficiency of differential assessment as a tool to preserve agricultural land remains in question. Differential assessment provides no assurances that a critical mass of farmland will be preserved. Experience has shown that when a farmer is offered a high price for his land, a mere reduction in real estate taxes seldom prevents the land sale.

### Exclusive Zoning

A second land preservation tool used to protect private agricultural lands has been the imposition of zoning. This mandates that certain lands may be used only for agriculture and may not be sold for urban development. The experience so far with this approach has been unsatisfactory, perhaps because states have delegated zoning power and enforcement to local governments.

Political considerations tend to become important in the process of enacting local zoning measures. Landowners who have high expectations of selling farmland for nonfarm uses at tremendous profits often oppose attempts by local governments to prevent them from realizing these economic gains. Local zoning is only a short-term solution, for there is no guarantee that future political pressures will not lead to an abdication of agricultural zoning as the monetary stakes grow higher.

## Developmental Rights Purchased

Of all the land use policies surveyed, the developmental rights purchase technique appears to offer the most promise. Under this policy the government purchases only the development rights of the land, leaving all other property rights with the farmer. The farmer continues to farm while receiving payment for the nonfarm increment in the value of his land. An obvious disadvantage of the plan is its high monetary cost to taxpayers in the district.

## Land Use Policies

Closely related to the problem of "land use" policies that may actually promote the loss or degradation of agricultural land are those policies that encourage the inefficient use of such land. Since the Agricultural Adjustment Acts of 1933, there have been nationwide efforts to control the production levels of our basic crops. The goal underlying such legislative efforts is to stabilize commodity prices in order to assure favorable financial conditions for farmers. Land retirement is one such device chosen to achieve the price-support objective.

Studies comparing United States agriculture under the land retirement program with a free land market situation reveal that to produce equal quantities of agricultural commodities, the total acreage needed under the land retirement program is considerably more than under the free land market situation. For example, 5.2 million acres are required to produce about 10 million bales of cotton under government controls, whereas only 4.4 million acres would be required to produce the same quantity of cotton without such controls (Pimentel and Shoemaker, 1974). In part, this discrepancy occurs because the land retirement program restricts production on a portion of the most highly productive land, forcing crop production onto less productive land in other areas. Consider the situation with respect to cotton production in the rich delta cropland of the southcentral United States. Soil moisture and insect conditions make this some of the most productive cotton land in the region. However, under land retirement roughly 50 percent of the land that once grew cotton in the delta is now idle from production. Individual growers obviously retire their poorer land, but the "poorer" land in the delta region is still significantly more productive on the average than the land outside the delta. As a result, yields in the nation as a whole are lower and more land must be used to guarantee an adequate cotton supply. Cotton production is marginally profitable on the poorer land because the price support program artificially raises the price of cotton on the market.

Government land controls also result in higher production costs and higher fossil fuel consumption. Extra equipment and additional fertilizer and insecticide applications are necessary to compensate for poorer soil and pest conditions. Without even including the cost of the government price support system, production costs are roughly 50 percent higher for cotton under the government land retirement program.

Economic efficiency and land conservation would result if acreage controls were abandoned. For example, in cotton production without acreage controls, production would shift away from the southeast and concentrate more in the western, southcentral, and southwestern regions. In addition, the treatment for the boll weevil often destroys the natural enemies of two other cotton pests, the bollworm and budworm, thus magnifying the pest problem. In order to recoup pest losses both the amount of insecticide used and the number of acres of land planted must be increased. All this adds to land degradation and increases in fossil fuel consumption.

## Conclusion

Clearly agricultural production depends on humans, land, water, energy, and natural biota and is influenced by the standard of living of society. There is a need for a holistic approach in resource management in agriculture and society. In simple terms we should "know what we are doing" and where we are headed in the future for resource policy and planning. This would help us focus agricultural research and develop sound policies for resource management.

From 1950 to 1960, a large portion of vegetable and fruit production shifted from the Northeast to the western region. With a good transport system and cheap energy, this was an economically sound policy. But in the future, we expect that some vegetable and fruit production will shift back to the Northeast. There are several reasons for this shift: (a) western agriculture is irrigated (energy costly); (b) transport to the East is energy costly; and (c) a heavy distribution of the U.S. population exists in the East. Food production employing irrigation is often about three times more energy intensive than rain-fed crop production. In addition, shipping foods across the country may add three to four times more energy to production costs.

A careful analysis of the various resource factors that influence agricultural production is needed to determine potential strategies for agricultural production recognizing the distribution of land and water resources and the location of the human population. In addition, the availability and price value of fossil energy must be included in the assessment.

# References

Alexander, Martin. 1977. *An Introduction to Soil Microbiology.* New York: John Wiley and Sons.

Batty, J. Clair, and Jack Keller. 1980. "Energy Requirements for Irrigation." In *Handbook of Energy Utilization in Agriculture,* ed. David Pimentel, pp. 35–44. Boca Raton, Florida: CRC Press.

Boserup, Ester. 1965. *Conditions of Agricultural Growth.* Chicago: Aldine-Atherton.

Brown, Lester R. 1981. *Building a Sustainable Society.* New York: Norton.

Cervinka, Vashek. 1980. "Fuel and Energy Efficiency." In *Handbook of Energy Utilization in Agriculture,* ed. David Pimentel, pp. 15–21. Boca Raton, Florida: CRC Press.

Council for Agricultural Science and Technology (CAST). 1975. *Potential for Energy Conservation in Agricultural Production.* CAST Rep. No. 40. Ames, Iowa: Council for Agricultural Science and Technology.

Davies, R., and J. Belden. 1979. "A Survey of State Programs to Preserve Farmland." Paper presented at the National Conference of State Legislators, Washington, D.C.

Delwiche, Constant C. 1970. "The Nitrogen Cycle." *Scientific American* 223(3):137–158.

Doering, Otto C. III. 1980. "Accounting for Energy in Farm Machinery and Buildings." In *Handbook of Energy Utilization in Agriculture,* ed. David Pimentel, pp. 9–14. Boca Raton, Florida: CRC Press

Dovring, Folke, and Donald R. McDowell. 1980. "Energy Used for Fertilizers." Department of Agricultural Economics Staff Paper 80 E-102. Urbana-Champaign: University of Illinois.

Edwards, Clive A., and J.R. Lofty. 1977. *Biology of Earthworms.* London: Chapman and Hall.

Eichers, Theodore R. 1981. "Use of Pesticides by Farmers." In *Handbook of Pest Management in Agriculture,* Vol. II, ed. David Pimentel, pp. 3–25. Boca Raton, Florida. CRC Press.

Federal Energy Administration (FEA) and the U.S. Department of Agriculture (USDA). 1976. *Energy and U.S. Agriculture: 1974 Data Base.* Vol. 2. Washington, D.C.: U.S. Government Printing Office.

Heichel, Gary. 1980. "Energy Attributable to Seed." In *Handbook of Energy Utilization in Agriculture,* ed. David Pimentel, pp. 27–33. Boca Raton, Florida: CRC Press.

Lauer, Gerald J.; David Pimentel; Angus MacBeth; Bert Salwen; and John Seddon. 1976. "Report of the Biological Communities Task Group Report No. 8." Hudson Basin Project. New York: Rockefeller Foundation.

Lewis, Oscar. 1951. *Life in a Mexican Village: Tepoztlan Restudied.* Urbana: University of Illinois Press.

Linton, Robert E. 1968. "The Economics of Poultry Manure Disposal." Cornell Extension Bulletin 1195. Ithaca, New York: Cornell University.

Miller, Robert H., and Donald E. McCormack. 1978. "Improving Soils with Organic Wastes." USDA Task Force. Washington, D.C.: U.S. Department of Agriculture.

Mitchell, William H., and M.R. Teel. 1977. "Winter Annual Cover Crops for No-tillage Corn Production." *Agronomic Journal* 69:569–573.

Muck, Richard E. 1982. Personal communication. Dept. of Agricultural Engineering. Ithaca, New York: Cornell University.

Munson, Robert D., and John P. Doll. 1959. "The Economics of Fertilizer Use in Crop Production." In *Advances in Agronomy,* XI, ed. A.G. Norman, pp. 133–169.

Neal, O.R. 1939. "Some Concurrent and Residual Effects of Organic Matter Additions on Surface Runoff." *Soil Science Society of America Proceedings* 4:420–425.

Peart, Robert M.; Roger Brook; and Martin R. Okos. 1980. "Energy Requirements for Various Methods of Crop Drying." In *Handbook of Energy Utilization in Agriculture,* ed. David Pimentel, pp. 49–54. Boca Raton, Florida: CRC Press.

Phillips, Ronald E.; Robert L. Blevins; Grant W. Thomas; Wilber W. Frye; and Shirley H. Phillips. 1980. "No-tillage Agriculture." *Science* 208:1108–1113.

Pimentel, David, ed. 1980. *Handbook of Energy Utilization in Agriculture.* Boca Raton, Florida: CRC Press.

_____. 1981. "The Food-Land-Fuel Squeeze." *ChemTech.* 11:214–215.

_____. 1984. "Energy flow in Agroecosystems." In *Agricultural Ecosystems: Unifying Concepts,* ed. R. Lowrance; B.R. Stinner; and G.J. House, pp. 121–132. New York: John Wiley & Sons.

Pimentel, David, and Marcia Pimentel. 1979. *Food, Energy and Society.* London: Edward Arnold.

Pimentel, David, and Michael Burgess. 1980. "Energy Inputs in Corn Production." In *Handbook of Energy Utilization in Agriculture,* ed. David Pimentel, pp. 67–84. Boca Raton, Florida: CRC Press.

Pimentel, David, and Clive A. Edwards. 1982. "Pesticides and Ecosystems." *BioScience* 32:595–600.

Pimentel, David, and Carl W. Hall, eds. 1984. *Food and Energy Resources.* New York: Academic Press.

Pimentel, David, and C. Shoemaker. 1974. "An Economic and Land Use Model for Reducing Insecticides on Cotton and Corn." *Environmental Entomology* 3:10–20.

Pimentel, David; Larry E. Hurd; Anthony C. Bellotti; Michael J. Forster; Ida N. Oka; Owen D. Sholes; and Richard J. Whitman. 1973. "Food Production and the Energy Crisis." *Science* 182:443–449.

Pimentel, David; William Dritschilo; John Krummel; and John Kutzman. 1975. "Energy and Land Constraints in Food-protein Production." *Science* 190:754–761.

Pimentel, David; Eric Garnick; Alan Berkowitz; Stuart Jacobson; Sam Napolitano; Patrick Black; Sally Valdes-Cogliano; Bill Vinzant; Ellen Hudes; and Sue Littman. 1980a. "Environmental Quality and Natural Biota." *BioScience* 30:750–755.

Pimentel, David; Pascal A. Oltenacu; Malden C. Nesheim; John Krummel; Michael S. Allen; and Sterling Chick. 1980b. "Grass-fed Livestock Potential: Energy and Land Constraints." *Science* 207:843–848.

Pimentel, David; Mary Ann Moran; Sarah Fast; George Weber; Robert Bukantis; Lisa Balliett; Peter Boveng; Cutler Cleveland; Sally Hindman; and Martin Young. 1981. "Biomass Energy from Crop and Forest Residues." *Science* 212:1110–1115.

Pimentel, David; Sarah Fast; Wei L. Chao; Ellen Stuart; Joanne Dintzis; Gail Einbender; William Schlappi; David Andow; and Kathryn Broderick. 1982a. "Water Resources in Food and Energy Production." *BioScience* 32:861–867.

Pimentel, David; Carol Glenister; Sarah Fast; and David Gallahan. 1982b. *Environmental Risks Associated With the Use of Biological and Cultural Pest Controls.* Final Report. NSF Grant PRA 80–00803. 165 pp.

Pimentel, David; Gigi Berardi; and Sarah Fast. 1983. "Energy Efficiency of Farming Systems: Organic and Conventional Agriculture." *Agriculture, Ecosystems, and Environment* 9:359–372.

Terhune, Elinor C. 1980. "Energy Used in the United States for Agricultural Liming Materials." In *Handbook of Energy Utilization in Agriculture,* ed. David Pimentel, pp. 25–26. Boca Raton, Florida: CRC Press.

United States Bureau of the Census (USBC). 1952. *Census of Agriculture 1950.* Vol. III. Washington, D.C.: U.S. Government Printing Office.

_____. 1962. *Census of Agriculture 1959.* Vol. III. Washington, D.C.: U.S. Government Printing Office.

_____. 1967. *Census of Agriculture 1964.* Vol. II. Washington, D.C.: U.S. Government Printing Office.

_____. 1973. *Census of Agriculture 1969.* Vol. IV. Washington, D.C.: U.S. Government Printing Office.

U.S. Department of Agriculture (USDA). 1954. *Changes in Farm Production and Efficiency.* Agricultural Research Service. Washington, D.C.: U.S. Department of Agriculture.

U.S. Department of Agriculture and the State Universities and Land-Grant Colleges. 1969. *A National Program of Research for Bees and Other Pollinating Insects Affecting Man.* Washington, D.C.: U.S. Government Printing Office.

U.S. Department of Agriculture (USDA). 1970. *Agricultural Statistics 1970.* Washington, D.C.: U.S. Government Printing Office.

_____. 1975. "Minimum Tillage: A Preliminary Technology Assessment." Office of Planning and Evaluation. Washington, D.C.: U.S. Department of Agriculture.

_____. 1976. *Agricultural Statistics 1976.* Washington, D.C.: U.S. Government Printing Office.

_____. 1979. *1980 Fertilizer Situation.* Economic Statistics Cooperative Service FS-10. Washington, D.C.: U.S. Department of Agriculture.

_____. 1981. *Agricultural Statistics 1981.* Washington, D.C.: U.S. Government Printing Office.

_____. 1982a. *Agricultural Statistics 1982.* Washington, D.C.: U.S. Government Printing Office.

_____. 1982b. *Fertilizer: Outlook and Situation.* Economic Research Service FS-13. Washington, D.C.: U.S. Department of Agriculture.

U.S. Water Resources Council (USWRC). 1979. *The Nation's Water Resources. 1975–2000.* Vols. 1–4. Second National Water Assessment. Washington, D.C.: U.S. Government Printing Office.

Van Dyne, Donald L., and Conrad B. Gilbertson. 1978. "Estimating U.S. Livestock and Poultry Manure and Nutrient Production." USDA-ESCS Publ. No. ESCS-12, March. Washington, D.C.: U.S. Department of Agriculture.

Wolcott, George N. 1937. "An Animal Census of Two Pastures and a Meadow in Northern New York." *Ecological Monographs* 7:1–90.

Zwerman, Paul J.; Alfred B. Drielsma; George D. Jones; Stuart D. Klausner; and Donald Ellis. 1970. "Rates of Water Infiltration Resulting from Applications of Dairy Manure." In *Relationship of Agriculture to Soil and Water Pollution,* Proceedings of the 1970 Cornell Agricultural Waste Management Conference, pp. 263–270. Washington, D.C.: Graphics Management Corp.

# Part V

# Emerging Alternatives and Their Implications

# 13

# *Alternative Agriculture*

## William Lockeretz

### Overview

The term "alternative agriculture" has come into quite general use in the past decade. However, as is often the case with terms that describe new trends or movements, it has no precise nor universally accepted definition. Strictly speaking, any agricultural system could be called "alternative" if it differs substantially from the prevalent system, even one resulting from accelerated movement in the direction in which the prevalent system is already moving. However, in practice the term is reserved for certain kinds of alternatives; people calling themselves "alternative agriculturalists" would not include in their number advocates of greater use of synthetic pesticides or a switch to fewer but larger farms.

Rather, "alternative agriculture" can be taken to refer to agricultural systems that share certain broad goals, at least in some loose way. These include reduced dependence on the larger industrial economy, greater decentralization and self-sufficiency for farms and regions, better protection of environmental values, long-term sustainability through conservation of finite resources and maintenance of soil productivity, and production of more healthful foodstuffs. In addition, a less tangible theme that runs through much of the alternative agriculture literature concerns the place of agriculture in American society. This view—in some ways a modern form of agricultural fundamentalism—seeks to enhance the understanding, awareness, and appreciation of farming among non-farmers and to revitalize many traditional agrarian values that have substantially been supplanted by the values of a modern industrial economy.

Not all alternative agriculturalists agree on the relative importance of these various goals, and certainly not on the desirability of one or another specific way to achieve them. Still, alternative agriculturalists more or less know who they are. Thus the term is a useful one for many purposes, and it would be quibbling to worry too much about its vagueness.

The idea of alternative agriculture is strongly associated with that of organic farming. In fact, the former term is sometimes taken as virtually the equivalent of the latter (Youngberg, 1978). The definition of organic farming has been the subject of considerable disagreement among supporters and critics alike, but two concepts are important in any definition. The first is fertilization through leguminous crops, livestock manures and organic wastes, or minerals that are not readily soluble, as opposed to fertilizers whose nutrients are in highly available form. The other is the control of insect pests, weeds and diseases through biological control and integrated management, with resistant crop varieties and cultural practices such as crop rotations and residue management favored over synthetic pesticides (USDA, 1980).

Alternative agriculture also gives high priority to reducing the use of energy. Beyond that, farmers might replace fossil fuels by renewable sources, such as solar energy, alcohol from grain, diesel fuel substitutes from oilseeds, or solid fuel from crop residues.

Alternative agriculture also involves important changes in animal husbandry, including the elimination of antibiotics (at least their routine use) and growth hormones, and greater use of open pens and low-density housing rather than confinement in environmentally controlled facilities. The feeding regime makes greater use of forages, roughages and grazing, and less use of grains and concentrates. All these changes mean settling for—or actually preferring—a slower daily weight gain to raise the animal in what is regarded as a more natural manner.

Some alternative agriculturalists look beyond specific production techniques to consider the structure of the agricultural sector as a whole and its relation to the larger economy. This group usually favors small to moderate sized farms, especially independent, family farms worked by resident owner-operators. They also seek to reduce the ties to the industrial economy and instead to increase the self-sufficiency of farms. Thus reducing fossil fuel use is seen as desirable not only because fossil fuel is a finite resource, but also because farmers must buy it from a powerful economic entity over which they exert no control. This also explains a small but persistent interest in traditional open pollinated varieties of corn; irrespective of agronomic differences compared to hybrids, open pollinated seed can be saved from the previous crop instead of having to be purchased each year from a seed company.

On the output side they favor more direct sales to consumers, with less reliance on intermediates such as transporters, processors, distributors, and packers. This change implies that more of the consumer's food supply will come from sources that are close both geographically and in the sense of having passed through fewer hands. Typically, a greater portion of the diet is expected to be in the form of unprocessed or "minimally processed" foodstuffs.

The goals of alternative agriculture are quite broad, and sometimes are stated rather vaguely. Moreover, many systems have been proposed to achieve them, in part because alternative agriculturalists typically prefer to select systems specifically keyed to the physical and socioeconomic conditions of a particular region, rather than thinking entirely in national terms.

This diversity of goals and outlook raises several questions. For example, the different goals are not necessarily compatible; at the least, a particular method for achieving one might inadvertently conflict with another. Nor can we automatically assume that a particular technique in fact will achieve its intended purpose. Finally, realistic techniques intended for practical application must be reconciled with idealized, abstract goals and values. Alternative agriculturalists vary considerably in how they balance pragmatism and commitment to an ideal. Put even more generally, this last question concerns whether alternative agriculture implies a fundamentally different set of values regarding agriculture as a whole and the entire economic system, or whether the alternative agriculturalist's task is to work towards the more tangible goals listed earlier, but within the prevailing value system.

Alternative agriculture has not yet been analyzed sufficiently to provide definitive answers to these questions. This is not intended to be a condemnation. The term "alternative agriculture," although unfortunately singular in form, does not refer to a single, monolithic movement. It has many components; its advocates have many different motivations. The absence of universally accepted definitions and principles could just as well be regarded as a sign of intellectual vigor as an intellectual gap. However, it would be a very serious mistake—but one that has been made all too often—to fail to acknowledge the heterogeneity of alternative agriculture and to assume, without critical examination, that it is possible simultaneously to achieve all the goals put forth by all the people calling themselves "alternative agriculturalists." Nor are alternative agriculturalists always conscientious about acknowledging the legitimacy of different values held by other people who can equally well claim that label.

The remainder of this paper will discuss the problems that can arise when these points are overlooked. But alternative agriculture is not alone in this regard; the same questions can be raised regarding the existing agricultural system as well. Indeed, given the far greater commitment of people and money to research on the prevailing system, it is striking that so many of its basic assumptions and values could remain immune to critical examination for so long.

For example, sentiment for supporting small and moderate farmers has been sufficiently strong among the non-farming majority to make commodity programs a fixture of the agricultural political agenda for the past half century. Yet it seems clear that the main beneficiaries of these programs are those who hold the land, not necessarily those who work it. Moreover, quite apart from secondary structural consequences that conflict sharply with the reason for non-farmers' willingness to pay for these programs, they have not even been particularly effective in achieving their primary purpose, as shown by the record level of price support payment in 1983, exactly 50 years after the creation of such "temporary" programs under the New Deal.

A related issue concerns the beneficiaries of public agricultural research, which has helped bring about an overwhelming transformation of production methods, especially since World War II. To be sure, consumers—who as taxpayers have borne the costs—have benefited substantially from the resulting efficiencies. But historically, public support of agricultural research also has roots in a broadly held wish to improve the well-being of farmers. Yet one can argue that besides consumers, the main beneficiaries have been the industries that provide commercial inputs— machinery, improved seeds, chemicals, fuel, etc.,—that have replaced farm-produced inputs, along with the largest, best capitalized farmers who could afford the newer technologies and for whose farms the new technologies were best suited. Farmers in general certainly produce more now, but they also spend more; in real dollars, they often do not end up keeping more. Moreover, many observers have noted the obvious conflict between government research to increase output (which is not necessarily the same as increasing income) and government payments to reduce output.

To be sure, in the past decade the dominance of a production orientation—"to make two blades grow where one grew before"—has been supplanted by a more mixed agenda that also asks "why," "whether" and "for whom" (also "against whom"), not just "how to" and "how much." But this questioning has been stimulated largely by outsiders, both officially through reviews of the nation's agricultural research program and unofficially through pressure from groups who previously were substantially excluded from shaping that program (Paarlberg, 1980). These outsiders—including many advocates of alternative agriculture—have reminded us that from time to time we need to reexamine the basic principles and goals behind specific agricultural research programs.

But this same point applies equally well to alternative agriculture, even if it has been little discussed. The following discussion therefore will seek to apply the questions raised above to three important and widely discussed areas of alternative agriculture:  organic farming, energy, and local food production.

## Organic Farming

*Goals*

Organic farming has many different kinds of supporters, and therefore several subtly different definitions.  Fertilization and pest control techniques, as discussed earlier, lie at the heart of all of these definitions.  A purely operational definition—what techniques and materials should or should not be used—avoids the difficulty of explaining precisely what one means concerning the more general principles of organic farming, such as sustainability, working with nature, healthy soil, ecosystem compatibility or a holistic approach.  Hodges (1982) nicely bridges these two important sides of the meaning of "organic," but understandably does not boil down such a complex matter to a one or two sentence definition.  Coleman (1985) favors developing some simple, precise, and easily followed steps that any farmer could take to convert to organic methods; he would like to avoid losing potential organic farmers because they think that they have to have an entirely new way of thinking about farming.  But a "least common denominator" technique-based definition, although appealingly concrete and pragmatic, does not address points that to some other advocates of organic farming represent its most important differences as compared to conventional methods.  Thus Friend (1983) criticizes a purely operational definition on the grounds that it "reduces a system of agriculture to a mere collection of techniques."  To him, "though conventional farmers and many biological farmers can be found doing many of the same things, such as spreading manure, the differences are profound."  Oelhaf (1978: 125–126) includes in organic farming one's attitudes towards the land, towards future generations, and towards nature and the universe.  Vail and Rozyne (1982) give interesting examples of farmers who are organic as far as not using prohibited materials, but whose system conflicts with the spirit, if not the letter, of the more commonly accepted understanding of the term.

How a particular organic farming system deals with these more intangible matters is important in terms of its compatibility with the broadest and most general goals of alternative agriculture.  For example, most definitions do not say whether power is to be supplied by animals, humans, or machinery, nor, for machinery, what size is preferred.  Some organic farmers have a decided preference for animal power or small machinery, while for others organic farming refers only to soil fertility and pest control. The latter group will not rule out large tractors or combines if they make sense for their particular farms, and in fact their equipment is typically similar to that of their conventional neighbors (Klepper, *et al.,* 1977).

Which attitude is more consistent with the goals of alternative agriculture described earlier? The immediate answer might be that large machinery is not an "alternative," and that a farmer with smaller machinery or animal power is less dependent on external inputs. On the other hand, under some conditions organic farming is commercially feasible only with fairly powerful tractors to cultivate mechanically for weed control. A frequent but superficial criticism is that organic farming is how everyone farmed fifty years ago (before herbicides were introduced), and that weed problems either cut yields severely or required an economically burdensome amount of labor. However, this criticism does not take account of the fact that farmers of that time could not perform mechanical weed control in nearly as timely a manner as they can with today's larger tractors. Thus, an organic farmer who rejects the use of large machinery because of a commitment to a more far-reaching concept of alternative agriculture may have to accept some sacrifices regarding the economic goals of organic agriculture, that is, to achieve an adequate yield and economic return without using toxic materials. The same point can be made about many other purchased inputs, such as hybrid seed. Let us take for granted that economically and agronomically the purchased version is clearly advantageous. One still must decide whether the fact that it is bought makes an input automatically unattractive compared to the farm-produced version. The minimalist organic farmer would answer very differently from the more thorough-going kind who chooses to reject certain technologies even though they are acceptable under the minimal definition of organic farming. Thus, a broad and deep commitment to alternative agriculture in general is different from a commitment to one particular (but certainly important) component of it, namely, non-use of certain toxic chemicals.

### Marketing

A similar question arises with marketing of organic products. Organic farmers generally believe that their products are more healthful, at the very least because of the absence of toxic residues, and perhaps also because of beneficial physiological effects of organic fertilizers (USDA, 1980). Some consumers also value these differences and are willing to pay more for organic foods. How to develop appropriate marketing mechanisms and pricing policies for organically grown food is a complicated matter that should receive careful consideration if organic production becomes more important in the future.

First, we cannot easily and simply state whether organic products in fact offer the claimed nutritional advantages, and we may never be able to do so, given the wide range of both organic and conventional methods and the complex effects of weather, soil, and production practices on the nutritional value of a crop. Second, even if we could assign an unquestioned advantage to organic methods, certifying that a particular product indeed was produced organically is difficult, and some fraud and deception may be inevitable. Third, even if this problem is resolved, not all consumers will agree on how much of a premium, if any, they would be willing to pay for the advantages of organic over conventionally produced foods.

Many organic farmers consider that they are justified in charging a premium, and sometimes would not be able to survive without it. Even if not, they take pride in their methods and would prefer to have their products identified as organic in the marketplace. On the other hand, the previous discussion suggests that organic producers should not expect any premium outside the circle of consumers who particularly value organic foods. Moreover, maintaining the identity of organic products from farm to marketplace imposes additional handling, packaging, and distribution costs. Therefore, the retail price of identifiable organic products can be expected to be higher even if the producer does not receive a premium.

What does this mean for future expansion of this alternative? Actually, some organic production is already marketed through conventional channels, with the producer receiving no premium and the product not identified as organic at the point of sale (Wernick and Lockeretz, 1977; USDA, 1980). This happens because the volume of production exceeds the demand for organic foods, or because no middleman has stepped in to connect the existing supply and demand in a particular area. In these cases, farmers have chosen to be organic because they prefer it as a production method, regardless of how the product gets sold. For them organic farming either is as profitable as conventional, or they are willing to accept an economic sacrifice. As long as additional farmers are willing to adopt organic methods on these terms, the issues raised above are irrelevant—no special prices or marketing channels are called for. But here the choice of marketing arrangement has been settled only by putting aside certain "alternative" aspects of organic farming, namely more direct marketing and explicit recognition of (presumed) nutritional superiority.

## Consumer and Governmental Support for Organic Methods

But what about those farmers who need a premium price? Barring significant future changes in consumer preferences, how can aggregate production expand beyond the volume that can be sold at the higher price?

If indeed additional economic support of organic farming is needed, a basis for it may lie in the production process itself, rather than in the supposed superiority of the product. That is, either the consuming public or the government may choose to subsidize organic production because it is a socially preferable system with regard to environmental protection and resource conservation. In traditional economic language, it internalizes certain costs that are external to the balance sheet of a conventional farm (Breimyer, 1980).

Although low cost food is repeatedly cited as a great achievement of the U.S. agricultural system, in fact consumers have sometimes let considerations other than price and value influence their purchasing decisions. Two well-publicized examples are the boycott of non-union lettuce and grapes in the 1970s in support of unionization of farm workers, and the more recent boycott of Nestlé products in reaction to that company's aggressive promotion of infant formula in the developing world. In neither case was quality or price the issue; rather, consumers wished not to support certain kinds of producers because of the practices they followed. Beyond the food sector, the slogan "Buy American" and the union label appear to have considerable influence with some classes of consumers. Similarly, judging by the large amount of "corporate image" advertising, consumers also are influenced—or so advertisers assume—by a company's record on environmental protection and other social issues. It seems plausible that concern over environmental contamination by pesticides is strong enough to generate a similar sentiment in support of organic farming. It would not depend on consumers being scared—rightly or wrongly—about toxic pesticide residues in their food, such as in the recent flare-up over EDB. It would be enough that the organic producer has not put such substances into the environment, regardless of whether they would have also ended up in the food. Organic farming's value in controlling soil erosion could also be a source of public support, at least in areas where this problem has been well publicized.

Similarly, in an attempt to improve the economic well-being of farmers, the Federal government permits the price of food to be higher than it need be through price supports, marketing orders, and production adjustments. Whether these programs are effective and equitable—a matter of considerable dispute—is immaterial. Nor does it matter that, as has been argued, in the long run these programs may in fact benefit the consumer as well. The point is that the general public, either as consumers or as taxpayers, are supporting producers in the interest of a presumed national goal—an economically healthy and stable agricultural sector—that could not be achieved through individual purchasing decisions in the marketplace. Moreover, depending on the particular program, the benefits may be targeted to a particular class of producers deemed to deserve special support, namely small and moderate sized operators. Again, the notorious ineffectiveness of ceilings on payments and the overriding importance of "unintended" advantages for larger farmers are beside the point—we are talking here about the principle of helping the family farmer, a principle that undoubtedly has a lot to do with the non-farming majority's willingness to pay for these benefits (Breimyer, 1977: Chap. 8; USDA, 1981: Chap. 7).

Moreover, these benefits traditionally have been tied—again, in principle, at least—to soil conservation. Unfortunately, there is considerable evidence to show that despite the substantial government payments, soil conservation has been poorly served (Cook, 1983). Price supports and payments are offered in exchange for a reduction in acreage of grains and other cultivated crops. But little attention has been given to what is done with the land taken out of cultivated crops. In theory it must be put into a "soil conserving" use, but a persistent theme in the debate over soil conservation and price support policies has been the need for a "cross-compliance" mechanism to insure that farmers pay adequate attention to the former to be eligible for the benefits of the latter (Dinehart and Libby, 1981). Moreover, farmers are free to undo any conservation measures when grain price increases stimulate an increase in acreage. In organic farming, the rotation of cultivated crops with meadow is an intrinsic part of the system, and not an expedient to be adopted or discarded according to a particular year's market conditions.

Consequently, there are linkages, both positive and negative, between organic methods and PIK-type programs. At present, there is no discernible support for organic farming in the administration, but there certainly is in Congress, as shown by House passage of the Agricultural Productivity Act of 1983, formerly the Organic Farming Act. It is not unreasonable to suppose that at some point, the combined problems of soil erosion, grain surpluses, and pesticide contamination might lead the federal government to modify existing commodity programs in ways that would have particular advantages for organic farmers, even if the term "organic farming" is not used explicitly.

Such a development could stimulate much wider adoption of organic farming, but would also raise difficult questions for alternative agriculturalists. Involvement in such programs would imply foregoing some other items on the alternative agenda, and in a symbolic way would signal acceptance of certain features of national agricultural policy that may be inimical to certain alternative values.

Organic products under government payment programs would have a difficult time maintaining their identity after leaving the farm, let alone receiving premium prices in the market. Also, the proposals discussed here emphasize the commercial aspects of agriculture, with subsistence or marginal farmers benefiting little, if at all. Those wishing start out farming at this level could actually be hurt to the extent that commodity programs tend to increase land prices. It is often said—although in such a complex matter conventional wisdom may be an oversimplification at best—that the commodity programs of the past half century have tended to help larger, more specialized farms at the expense of the family-sized, diversified farms that are more consistent with traditional agrarian models (USDA, 1980). (Of course, such an effect is independent of whether commodity producers use organic-type methods, so the point is of more symbolic than practical significance.) There already exist some large, highly capitalized organic farms that rival their conventional neighbors in terms of standard "top management" criteria and that sell into the nationally integrated marketing system that handles most U.S. farm products. If official support of organic-like methods ever comes about, serious thought will have to be given to balancing the clear benefits for one version of alternative agriculture focusing on non-use of toxics, for example, to the exclusion—and possibly even the detriment—of some fundamentally different visions of the most desirable alternatives (those emphasizing small-scale, diversified farming communities, for example).

## Energy

The deterioration in the energy situation that began about a decade ago has been regarded as an important incentive for adoption of alternative agricultural methods. Our current dependence on fossil fuel figures prominently in discussions of agriculture's sustainability or lack of it. Alternative methods may either reduce the quantity of fuel needed or replace fossil fuel with a renewable source. Some conservation measures are very straight-forward and do not raise any fundamental issues. Indeed, some have already been adopted by many farmers and could hardly be regarded as "alternative agriculture." Others, however, are considerably more subtle and complex, and it is not always clear that the effect of a particular alternative will actually be in the desired direction.

### Direct and Indirect Effects on Agricultural Sustainability from Changes in Energy Use

Clearly, dependence on a finite resource such as fossil fuel conflicts with sustainability. But a major change in fossil fuel use—either a decrease or an increase—necessarily entails other changes that could either enhance or detract from the system's sustainability. Indeed, these changes could be far more important than the direct effect of the changes in fuel use as such (Lockeretz, 1984).

For example, fossil fuel has permitted greatly expanded production of grain in the Great Plains with water pumped from the Ogallala formation, a deep, non-recharging aquifer. High energy prices in the late 1970s seriously disrupted this system. However, sustainability is threatened even more by the adverse ecological consequences of on-going irrigation on the one hand (Strange, 1983), and the expected abandonment of irrigation in some areas because of drawdown of the aquifer on the other (Frederick, 1980). Both these threats can certainly be called consequences of fossil fuel use—for without fossil fuels, pumping from deep wells would not have been possible. But they would remain as threats even if fossil fuel problems were eliminated once and for all, say by an efficient and economical solar pump.

On the other hand, fossil fuel use can reduce certain threats to sustainability. In dryland agriculture on the Great Plains, summer fallow with herbicidal weed control offers much greater protection against wind erosion than does the older system of clean-tilled fallow. Soil conservation stabilizes the region's agriculture more than the energy requirement of herbicide manufacture threatens it. In the days of the "Dust Bowl," emergency tillage was important for controlling soil loss once the soil started blowing. Farmers with tractors could perform more timely emergency tillage than those with animal power; dryland agriculture without power machinery was one of the most unstable agricultural systems in the country's history. But then again, if it weren't for tractors, cropping in the Great Plains would not have reached quite the same scale as it did in the 1920s, and it would not have been quite so critical to be able to perform emergency tillage with the timeliness that is possible only with tractors (Lockeretz, 1981a).

## Overall Energy Consumption of an Agricultural System

The entire production system must be examined to answer the more prosaic question of how much energy a given alternative would save. A change intended to save energy in one area may require other changes that actually increase the total energy consumption of the system. Hauling and spreading manure as fertilizer requires fuel. Therefore, depending on the distance involved, it does not automatically save energy in comparison to fertilizers manufactured from fossil fuel. Similarly, although herbicides are produced from petroleum, the main alternative to herbicides is mechanical weed control (cultivation), which also requires petroleum. Conversely, no-till is an alternative that reduces the fuel required for cultivation, but usually requires more herbicides. This means that typically, overall energy requirements are reduced by only a modest fraction (Lockeretz, 1983). (No-till is sometimes put forth as a "conventional" alternative that in some sense is supposed to be related to organic farming. Actually, the herbicide requirements of no-till in its most commonly advocated versions make it unattractive to organic farmers, although some have attempted to work out their own methods for doing it without herbicides, thereby capturing the best of both systems.)

Similar difficulties affect the analysis of production of fuels from agricultural materials, such as grain or crop residues. Some of the most widely publicized systems for producing alcohol apparently are net energy consumers. However, how to analyze the energy balance of alcohol production is debatable, and the matter may never be resolved to everyone's satisfaction (Chambers *et al.,* 1979). For example, it is hard to know how much energy credit to give to the by-product feeds from alcohol production, or how much to charge for the nutrients not returned to the soil if crop residues are used either as a feedstock or a boiler fuel. It is even more complicated to take account of the erosion that can result from residue removal for fuel production. It would be ironic if one goal of alternative agriculture, conservation of fossil fuel, were achieved by a strategy that directly violated another, namely soil conservation. Nevertheless, there are good reasons for being concerned that this will occur, at least in cases where the strategy is poorly thought out or applied under inappropriate conditions (Lockeretz, 1981b).

Despite these problems, cases in which an intended energy-saving alternative "backfires" should not be parlayed into a criticism of alternative methods in general—as is sometimes done by certain critics who prefer cheap shots to careful analysis. It merely may indicate that the alternatives selected for experimentation were not the most suitable.

*Appropriate Size for a Renewable Energy Facility*

The scale of the conversion facility is critical in the production of alcohol and other fuels from agricultural materials. The higher efficiency and profitability of larger alcohol fuel plants are well documented. Indeed, it is not clear that an on-farm plant can be a net producer of liquid fuels, except perhaps at a substantial economic loss or with a very high labor input that might be incompatible with the farm's other requirements (Lockeretz, 1982).

However, a large industrial type facility does not offer the farmer the particular benefits claimed on behalf of on-farm alcohol production, such as an assured fuel supply. The farmer becomes just as dependent on fuel alcohol plants as on the petroleum industry. Farmer-owned cooperatives have been proposed as a way around this. Such cooperatives would have to be quite large to be economically attractive, but farmer cooperatives that size typically end up looking a lot more like private companies. A cooperative alcohol fuel plant's behavior under fuel scarcity has not yet been tested, and we don't really know just how cooperative an individual farmer member will find it. Thus, one self-sufficiency aspect of alternative agriculture conflicts with the resource conservation aspect. If a biomass conversion approach is selected, one must choose a particular system for obtaining fuel from agricultural materials. Depending on the choice, either the nation saves fossil fuel or farmers become more self-sufficient, but not both. In fact, with some of the systems that have been put forth, we get neither.

## The Reliability of Renewable and Fossil Fuel Supplies

Even those fuel alcohol plants that use the very best technology and that are large enough to capture the full economies of scale are of questionable profitability, as shown by the substantial federal and state subsidies necessary to get even a modest fuel alcohol industry established and by the failure of the industry to grow nearly as fast as was predicted in the late 1970s. The justification for subsidies was that alcohol fuel is a more reliable energy source than petroleum, especially than imported petroleum. However, it is not clear that a fuel supply that depends on grain is more stable. True, international political forces do not enter, but the output of grain is extremely variable, as shown by the sharp drops caused by drought in 1974, 1980, and 1983. Moreover, the price is even more variable, since it is affected by the international economy as well as weather and domestic economic conditions. Once we have committed ourselves to obtaining a certain portion of our fuel supply from grain, we cannot turn that source off when grain is expensive or scarce. Thus an almost inelastic demand is imposed on a portion of our grain supply, which in turn means that the price of alcohol from this grain will be very volatile. Alternatively, if the demand for grain for food and feed can bid grain away from this use in short years, our fuel supply is reduced, just as if a portion of our oil imports were cut off.

## On-Farm Alcohol Production and Food Self-Sufficiency

With on-farm production, the farmer can assure that the feedstock is available, since it is produced on the farm itself. However, using one's own grain for alcohol production does not change the fact that when grain prices are high the alcohol produced from it is expensive; this point is sometimes obscured in some materials on farm alcohol, which do not put opportunity costs (the value foregone in not selling the grain) on the same footing as cash costs (the price of purchased grain). On the other hand, the alcohol produced on a farm cannot meet the farm's entire energy needs, and complete energy self-sufficiency can be achieved, if at all, only through several drastic and expensive changes. One therefore should ask how much value can be attached to partial fuel self-sufficiency.

A farm that has eliminated half of its fuel needs still is dependent on outside supplies, and is still vulnerable to disruption of those supplies. It has no guarantee that during a fuel shortage it will be any easier getting half its supply than getting the full amount. Thus an on-farm source offers only partial protection. But the same protection is offered by doubling the farm's fuel storage for liquid fuels or by a backup generator or dual-fuel system for electricity and natural gas respectively. Only complete self-sufficiency offers a higher degree of protection, namely, protection even against a fuel shortage of indefinite length that would exhaust any reasonable fuel reserve. But even if one wants to imagine such a situation, it seems pointless to discuss the continued normal operation of such a farm. We would be talking about an emergency so severe that the entire food system—not just the production, but the transportation and storage of farm products and deliveries of inputs—would be disrupted as well. On-farm fuel production would hardly be enough to cope.

It is simplistic to think that because dependence on fossil energy is a source of instability, switching to an alternative automatically enhances stability. The possible reasons for favoring such a switch are manifold—reduced pressure on the nation's fossil fuel resources, greater dependability of the energy supplies of the nation as a whole or of farmers in particular, reduced farm production costs, or greater autonomy of farmers with respect to the petrochemical industry. Before a particular alternative can be recommended, the goals it is intended to achieve must be made explicit, and possible conflicts must be reconciled, or at least acceptable tradeoffs must be determined.

## Localized Food Production

### Comparative Advantages of Local and National Food Systems

For several decades the United States food system has been a national rather than regional one. Food consumed in a particular region may come from any part of the country, not primarily from within the region itself. With a few exceptions, such as fluid milk, transportation even of perishables has reached the point where the economics of production rather than of transportation is the main determinant of where a particular region gets its food. Given the United States' heterogeneity in climate and soils, one clear advantage of this is that a much greater variety of food is available at a particular location. In the winter, when fresh produce is out of season in New England, it can be obtained from California, say. Moreover, New Englanders can enjoy foods that cannot be grown in their own region at any time of year.

On the other hand, a national food system is not entirely advantageous. Distant producing regions sometimes have displaced local production not only during seasons when local sources are unavailable, or for those products that can never be produced locally, but across the board. Of course, this would not have happened if it were not for substantial reasons. However, the conditions that once made it desirable (assuming that it was really desirable) could change. If so, the earlier loss of local production may prove irreversible. It is very difficult to bring back the people, cropland and support facilities necessary to revive agriculture.

The decline of local agriculture raises several concerns (Toner, 1979; Dunford, 1981). Dependence on distant sources makes the food supply vulnerable to transportation disruptions, such as those caused by an energy shortage. This concern has prompted a flurry of state and local plans for increasing food self-sufficiency, especially in severe deficit areas such as the Northeast (e.g., Burrill and Nolfi, 1976; Fellows and Cody, 1979; N.Y. State Assembly, 1980). On a national scale, loss of agricultural land decreases the nation's ability to meet future increases in demand, whether domestic or international, or to compensate for declines in production in certain regions because of depletion of energy, irrigation water, or other resources. Loss of agricultural land can mean a loss of environmental values, such as open space, wildlife habitat, and an interesting and diversified landscape. It also entails a loss of economic activity in handling and distributing farm products and in supplying farm inputs. Finally, loss of local agriculture forecloses a career option to the young people of the area; even if farm-raised youths appear to be leaving agriculture, a new development is the increasing interest in agriculture being shown by some young people with non-farm backgrounds. This phenomenon may be connected with the rising interest in alternative agriculture. New entrants may be more attracted by alternative values, and may be better able to afford smaller, less commercial farms.

*Regional Food Self-Sufficiency: Just What Does It Mean?*

GEOGRAPHIC EXTENT. The concept of regional food self-sufficiency needs to be refined before one can discuss its merits or evaluate particular programs to achieve it. First, for what geographic area is self-sufficiency being sought? The concept has been variously discussed for a several state region, a single state, a part of a state, or even a metropolitan area. Biological and physical factors might be one basis for delineating the relevant area, infrastructure such as transportation networks another, and political considerations a third. The ultimate idea is for each person to be assured of an adequate food supply, but personal food self-sufficiency is clearly out of the question for the population at large.

Thus, some level of aggregation is required. The larger the area of aggregation, the easier it is for the area to be self-sufficient. Any proposal for self-sufficiency on a very small scale must take into account the fact that the food supply of a very small area is highly vulnerable to disruption from pests or adverse weather. The United States is fortunate in that its heterogeneity buffers it against very sharp fluctuations in total output; if a particular area can draw from the total output, not just its own, its food supply is similarly buffered. Even the drought-related grain shortages of 1974, 1980, and 1983 mentioned earlier were minor compared to drops in production in a smaller area, say a county.

But at the same time, it is commonly assumed that forces of human rather than physical origin are more readily controlled over a smaller area. Thus it is more likely that a smaller area can distribute equitably and efficiently whatever it can produce. How small a region does one need to achieve this advantage? Suppose, for example, that New England as a whole were to become self-sufficient, but not the individual states. How confident can consumers in Connecticut be that they will always get their accustomed supply from Maine, say? Trucker strikes that can disrupt transportation from California to New England can also disrupt it within New England. Going one step further, let us even suppose that somehow Connecticut managed to achieve self-sufficiency. Can the residents of the populous southwest portion of the state depend on food from the agricultural Connecticut River Valley? The question is not frivolous. Granted, the shorter the distance, the easier is transportation in a purely energetic sense. But it is not simply a matter of energy—we also must consider the infrastructure and the human factors involved. The record of metropolitan areas in handling emergencies—and we are really talking only about emergencies, since self-sufficiency doesn't matter when everything is flowing smoothly—hardly inspires confidence. In fact, even with energy problems, nearness of food producer and consumer is only a partial solution. The gas lines of 1974 and 1979 primarily arose from local logistical problems and human nature (hoarding) rather than from aggregate supply problems. That local distribution of groceries consumes less energy than cross-country hauling is irrelevant if the local distribution is facing a tight local supply of fuel.

SEASONAL AVAILABILITY AND TYPES OF FOODS. The time dimension as well as the spatial dimension of self-sufficiency must also be specified. Are we seeking a year-round local source of food, or are we only concerned with the growing season? The former may require a prohibitively expensive investment in greenhouses and facilities for storing perishables. It could also entail considerably higher food prices, and doing without certain foods (as discussed below). In-season self-sufficiency is very much easier to achieve, but offers very much less in the way of food security.

A related question is whether we wish to produce locally the same foods as already consumed, or whether eating habits should adjust to whatever is easiest to produce locally. The easiest way to achieve food self-sufficiency is simply to give up what you can't produce. Most parts of this country have been food self-sufficient throughout most of our history. But most people, throughout most of our history, have had diets that at best could be called drab, at worst nutritionally deficient. It is easy to argue in favor of local production of tomatoes, where the appeal of the locally grown version is obvious compared to one picked green and shipped 3,000 miles. One might even point to the local product's nutritional superiority. But what about citrus? Which is more appealing and more healthful, an orange from California, 3,000 miles away, or an orange grown in Massachusetts?

STORAGE. One must also take account of within-region storage of foods produced outside the region. Once we consider stored products, food self-sufficiency is no longer a life-and-death issue, if indeed it ever is in a country like the United States. It is quite simple to stockpile an adequate supply of foods like grains, dried beans, and powdered milk to insure that even a very populated metropolitan area will have enough food to sustain itself—granted not in a very interesting way—for months or even years. In a populous area with limited land, should one even bother to think about self-sufficiency in a staple like wheat, say? Or is it sufficient for the area to keep an adequate reserve of wheat brought in from Kansas? If the latter choice is made, food self-sufficiency comes down to perishables. Insofar as perishables generally are luxuries—very nice to have, certainly, but not essential to sustain life—this changes what a region might be willing to spend in money or in foregone opportunities for the sake of this limited version of food self-sufficiency.

We can generalize from this discussion to the value of any kind of self-sufficiency that is only partial, whether in time, or total quantity, or type of food. How validly can one use the argument of food security to support a program that realistically will permit only a portion of the region's food supply to be produced within the region? The partly self-sufficient region will still be critically dependent on the rest of the country. For staples, producing only a part of one's food needs (without adequate reserves, that is) means risking famine. In fact, even if a region came up short by just a few percent, some people would suffer seriously, just as on a world scale even a very small discrepancy between total supply and a total demand is enough to cause severe hardships because of the way in which the available supply is distributed (or rather, not distributed). Thus even if a region were substantially, but not completely self-sufficient, stockpiling would be essential. But it is not qualitatively more difficult to stockpile against a cutoff when the entire supply comes from outside than when only part of it does. With luxury foods, as discussed earlier, a partial supply is better than nothing, but one can get by with nothing.

*Strengthening Local Agriculture Compared to Strengthening the
Local Food Supply*

The concept of regional food self-sufficiency clearly raises many difficult questions, and it is not at all clear that it is an appropriate goal for every region. But even if not, this does not mean that the region should ignore opportunities to strengthen its agriculture. Although food self-sufficiency, farmland preservation, and regional support of agriculture are commonly discussed as though they were all part of the same issue, there are good reasons for a region to try to strengthen its agricultural production, quite apart form the vulnerability of its current food supply. Indeed, of all the reasons given earlier for concern over agricultural decline, only the first relates to food security. One can regard producing more food within a region as something good without necessarily considering it bad to bring food in from outside.

Serious contradictions will arise from ignoring the distinction between food self-sufficiency and strong local agriculture. The main reason that agriculture declines in a region is that farming is unprofitable. Conversely, regional agriculture can revive only if it becomes economically attractive. But suppose that the most economically advantageous crop is one that is already in surplus within the region. (That a particular crop is in surplus suggests that indeed it is a good one for the region.) Producing more of it might help agriculture's economic well-being but would not enhance local food self-sufficiency. In fact, producing non-food crops is sometimes the economically soundest strategy for producers in a particular location. Should this be encouraged? No, if you care about food security; yes, if you care about keeping farms and farmers around.

Similarly, one must decide just why one wants to have farms and farmers around. If it is to keep the land in its current use for its open space value, it does not matter much who owns the land, or how large the farms are. Thus, if current farm size is too small to realize full economies of scale, then consolidation into fewer but larger farms would help insure the economic viability of the region's agriculture, and therefore help keep the land from going to other uses. But this would reduce opportunities for would-be entrants who would like to keep this career option open, certainly not a desirable result if one would like to see agriculture restored to a more established position in the American social and cultural value system. If inadequate capital for upgrading the region's farms is a limiting factor, one would welcome investment from outside the region. But this would conflict with the goal of keeping within the region the flow of income generated from agriculture. Indeed, there already is considerable resentment in many parts of the country against non-agricultural investors who have no commitment to the region's overall well-being, but rather look at farming simply as a convenient tax shelter. If one is interested in preserving farmland for the sake of future food production capability, then the increasingly popular strategy of purchasing development rights makes sense. But this strategy is expensive and can go just so far. It is interesting that it sometimes is undertaken in an area where other farmland is sitting idle—not because it is being developed, but simply because it is not profitable to farm it. In such a case, one clearly cannot justify purchase of development rights as necessary to permit the region to raise more of its food, at least not in the short run.

This discussion indicates that what might be thought of as a single item on the alternative agriculture agenda—regional food self-sufficiency/farmland preservation/regional agriculture—is in fact a complex of related but distinct components. Their ultimate aims are not the same, and in fact may conflict. In any case, an advocate of a particular strategy within this general area should articulate his or her goals explicitly rather than simply counting on a general feeling among alternative agriculturalists that food security and farmland preservation and strong regional agriculture are all good and all worthy of support.

One must be clear about what one hopes to achieve and why, not just how. Moreover, one must also analyze whether the achievement of other goals will be adversely affected, even to the point of outweighing the benefits. Perhaps when taken together, the full range of advantages sought by the proponents of various aspects of alternative agriculture will prove too broad. If so, judicious balancing and integration will be needed in going from these goals in their full generality—however admirable—to their realization in specific cases. This seems to be true not just for food self-sufficiency, but also for organic farming and energy. Perhaps we can generalize from these three examples to the need for careful and critical analysis of all alternative agriculture. But for that matter, why stop with alternative agriculture?

## References

Breimyer, Harold F. 1977. *Farm Policy: 13 Essays.* Ames: Iowa State University Press.
_____. 1980. "Economics of Organic Agriculture." Paper No. 1980–35. Columbia: University of Missouri, Dept. of Agricultural Economics.
Burrill, George C., and James R. Nolfi. 1976. *Land, Bread, and History: A Research Report on the Potential for Food Self-Sufficiency in Vermont.* Burlington Vt.: Center for Studies in Food Self-Sufficiency.
Chambers, R.S.; R.A. Herendeen; J.J. Joyce; and P.S. Penner. 1979. "Gasohol: Does It or Doesn't It Produce Positive Net Energy?" *Science* 206:789–795.
Coleman, Eliot. 1985. "Towards a New McDonald's Farm." In *Sustainable Agriculture and Integrated Farming Systems,* ed. Thomas C. Edens, Cynthia Fridgen, and Susan Battenfield, pp. 50–55. East Lansing: Michigan State University.
Cook, Ken. 1983. "Soil Conservation: PIK in a Poke." *Journal of Soil and Water Conservation* 38:475–476.
Dinehart, Stephen, and Lawrence Libby. 1981. "Cross-compliance: Will It Work? Who Pays?" In *Economics, Ethics, Ecology: Roots of Productive Conservation,* ed. Walter E. Jeske, pp. 407–415. Ankeny, Iowa: Soil Conservation Society of America.
Dunford, Richard W. 1981. "Farmland Retention: Efficiency vs. Equity." In *Economics, Ethics, Ecology: Roots of Productive Conservation,* ed. Walter E. Jeske, pp. 367–379. Ankeny, Iowa: Soil Conservation Society of America.
Fellows, Irving F., and Patrick H. Cody. 1979. "A Food Production Plan for Connecticut, 1980–2000: A Guide to the Purchase of Development Rights on Farmland." Bulletin 454. Storrs: University of Connecticut, Agricultural Experiment Station.
Frederick, Kenneth D. 1980. "Irrigation and the Future of American Agriculture." In *The Future of American Agriculture as a Strategic Resource,* ed. Sandra S. Batie and Robert G. Healy, pp. 157–190. Washington, D.C.: Conservation Foundation.
Friend, Gil. 1983. "The Potential for Sustainable Agriculture." In *Sustainable Food Systems,* ed. D. Knorr, pp. 28–47. Westport, Conn.: AVI Publishing Co.
Hodges, R.D. 1982. "Agriculture and Horticulture: The Need for a More Biological Approach." *Biological Agriculture and Horticulture* 1:1–13.
Klepper, Robert; William Lockeretz; Barry Commoner; Michael Gertler; Sarah Fast; Daniel O'Leary; and Roger Blobaum. 1977. "Economic Performance and Energy Intensiveness on Organic and Conventional Farms in the Corn Belt: A Preliminary Comparison." *American Journal of Agricultural Economics* 59:1–12.
Lockeretz, William. 1981a. "The Dust Bowl: Its Relevance to Contemporary Environmental Problems." In *The Great Plains: Perspectives and Prospects,* ed. M.P. Lawson and M.E. Baker, pp. 11–31. Lincoln: University of Nebraska Press.
_____. 1981b. "Crop Residues for Energy: Comparative Costs and Benefits for the Farmer, the Energy Facility, and the Public." *Energy in Agriculture* 1:71–89.
_____. 1982. "On-farm Fuel Alcohol Production: Economic Considerations and Implications for Farm Management." *Energy in Agriculture* 1:171–184.
_____. 1983. "Energy Implications of Conservation Tillage." *Journal of Soil and Water Conservation* 38:207–211.
_____. 1984. "Energy and the Sustainability of the American Agricultural System." In *Agricultural Sustainability in a Changing World Order,* ed. Gordon Douglass, pp. 77–88. Boulder, Colo.: Westview Press.
New York State Assembly. 1980. "Subcommittee on Food, Farm and Nutrition Policy, 1980 Report." Albany, N.Y.
Oelhaf, Robert C. 1978. *Organic Agriculture: Economic and Ecological Comparisons with Conventional Methods.* Montclair, N.J.: Allanheld, Osmun.
Paarlberg, Don. 1980. *Farm and Food Policy: Issues of the 1980s.* Lincoln: University of Nebraska Press.
Strange, Marty. 1983. "Of Whooping Cranes and Family Farms: Another Look at the High Plains Study." *Journal of Soil and Water Conservation* 38:28–32.
Toner, William. 1979. "Local Programs to Save Farms and Farmlands." In *Farmland, Food and the Future,* ed. Max Schnepf, pp. 189–202. Ankeny, Iowa: Soil Conservation Society of America.

U.S. Department of Agriculture (USDA). 1980. *Report and Recommendations on Organic Farming.* Washington, D.C.: U.S. Dept. of Agriculture.

U.S. Department of Agriculture (USDA). 1981. *A Time to Choose: Summary Report on the Structure of Agriculture.* Washington, D.C.: U.S. Dept. of Agriculture.

Vail, David, and Michael Rozyne. 1982. "Contradictions in Organic Soil Management Practices: Evidence from Thirty-one Farms in Maine." In *Basic Techniques in Ecological Farming,* ed. Stuart Hill, pp. 32–40. Basel/Boston/Stuttgart: Birkhäuser Verlag.

Youngberg, Garth. 1978. "The Alternative Agriculture Movement." *Policy Studies Journal* 6:524–530.

# 14

# Biotechnology and Agricultural Research Policy: Emergent Issues

## Frederick H. Buttel

### Introduction

It seems like just yesterday that the public agricultural research system was defending itself from "post-Hightower" critics in public interest organizations and adjusting to the social equity concerns that were sent forth sporadically from the Bergland-led USDA. But this era of the final Jimmy Carter years also seems far behind us. We now have a new Administration and new cluster of buzzwords—genetic engineering, biotechnology, recombinant DNA, the "new biology"—that have captured the fancy of the agricultural research policy community. Some will applaud and others regret the apparent passing of what were a short time ago called the "new agenda" items (e.g., the impacts of public agricultural research on farm structure, environmental quality, and rural communities). It is, however, my view that the issues raised by the descendents of Hightower and given brief consideration in the late 1970s will not disappear. Indeed, these issues will be redefined and reshaped by the very emergence and development of biotechnology.

The purpose of this chapter will be to suggest that the rise of biotechnology as a focus of agricultural research and development (R&D) has

The author acknowledges the collegial interchange with and assistance of present and former graduate students at Cornell University, especially Martin Kenney and Jack Kloppenburg, Jr., and the helpful comments of J. Patrick Madden and Kenneth A. Dahlberg on an earlier draft. This research was supported by the Rockefeller Foundation and the Cornell University Agricultural Experiment Station.

begun and will continue to generate a number of policy dilemmas, the resolution of which will have a major influence on the U.S. public agricultural research system in the decades to come. The reader who has a penchant for clarity of expression and a distaste for an overuse of superlatives to the point of triteness will no doubt take exception to how often I use the expressions "unprecedented," "profound," and "unparalleled" in the passages that follow. But I must request forgiveness in my perhaps excessive use of these superlatives; I feel that it is important to underscore the profound—there I go again—nature of the changes in the public agricultural research system that are being induced by biotechnology.[1]

Before proceeding, it is important to indicate in specific terms what is meant by "biotechnology." It has now become common to refer to conventional plant breeding, crop physiology, and other techniques of similar vintage as "old biotechnologies." The concern here is with the "new biotechnologies" of more recent vintage, such as recombinant DNA, cell and tissue culture, hybridomas and immobilized enzymes, and so forth. Some may note, however, that tissue culture has been practiced now for over 20 years and, as such, is not new. Even so, the use of tissue culture exploded in the late 1970s and early 1980s because of advances in molecular biology and genetics. Thus, whereas the "old biotechnologies" were ultimately rooted in the basic science exemplars of organismic-level biology and organic and inorganic chemistry, the "new biotechnologies" are based on the disciplines of molecular biology, cell biology, and biochemistry. Put somewhat differently, these new agricultural technologies involve far greater ability to manipulate genetic information directly than did their predecessors.

There are four major reasons, which are elaborated upon in some detail below, why biotechnology promises to become pivotal in agricultural research policymaking in the U.S. First, the emergence of biotechnological approaches to agricultural research comes at a time when the land-grant and larger public agricultural research system is both reeling from trenchant criticisms and lacks the financial and scholarly resources with which to play a clearly dominant role in the development of this new technology. Second, biotechnology will serve to increase greatly the number of groups and actors who wish to influence the course of public agricultural R&D. Third, biotechnology portends a substantial shift in the division of labor between public and private research in the U.S., which will create major challenges in the formulation of research priorities and in the management of the socioeconomic and ecological impacts of research. Finally, biotechnology will likely give rise to a fundamentally new institutional structure for agricultural technology development for, and transfer to, the Third World.

## The Context of the Emergence of Biotechnology in Agricultural Research

Crucial to an understanding of the socioeconomic and ethical aspects of biotechnology is a recognition of the fact that biotechnology is not emerging in a vacuum. Indeed, the rise of biotechnology has been superimposed on a number of important trends and controversies that have affected the U.S. agricultural research system for over a decade.

The most important benchmark year for our purposes is 1972. It was in 1972 that two very different but equally penetrating critiques of the U.S. agricultural research system were initially published. The first such critique, Jim Hightower's *Hard Tomatoes, Hard Times,* was published in preliminary form by the Agribusiness Accountability Project and was later to be reissued by a commercial publisher (Hightower, 1973). Hightower's book was a scathing, uncompromising indictment of the public agricultural research system on social equity or social justice grounds. Hightower argued that the land-grant system, though initially established to serve the mass of rural and agricultural people, had become a publicly subsidized research arm of agribusiness and large farmers. While Hightower's viotriolic style and questionable treatment of certain data led many people in the land-grant system to dismiss *Hard Tomatoes, Hard Times* as not being a serious or balanced analysis, Hightower's book was the catalyst for a large number of successor volumes (e.g., Hadwiger, 1982; Busch and Lacy, 1983) that were more dispassionate, persuasive, and influential. Moreover, Hightower's work has by now placed the issues of the social determinants of research choice and the socioeconomic consequences of technology more squarely on the agenda of particular disciplines (especially rural sociology) and of a number of public interest groups. Biotechnology in the future will no doubt be subjected to scrutiny on social equity or social justice grounds as it becomes clearer what will be the major thrust of agricultural biotechnologies and their likely impacts on agricultural structure.

A second line of criticism of public agricultural research initiated in 1972 was the publication of the so-called Pound Report (National Academy of Sciences, 1972). The Pound Committee, organized under the auspices of the National Academy of Sciences, prepared what was then perceived as a surprisingly critical analysis of the conduct and accomplishments of agricultural research. To borrow Mayer and Mayer's (1974) notion of "island empire," the Pound Committee argued that public agricultural research had become highly insular and largely divorced from the frontiers of knowledge in the basic biological sciences. The Committee was strongly critical of what it perceived to be the dominant thrust of United States agricultural research—highly applied research geared primarily toward specific agricultural commodities—and urged that land-grant university (LGU) and Agricultural Research Service (ARS) scientists orient their work more toward basic biology in two important ways. First, the agricultural science disciplines were encouraged to become more familiar with, and indeed contribute to our knowledge of, the frontiers of basic research in biology. Second, the Pound Committee argued that the public agricultural research system should embrace the more comprehensive peer review system of the basic biological science research community and, in so doing, eliminate much of the low-quality or routine research that it saw as characterizing the land-grant and ARS systems.[2]

Almost exactly ten years later a subsequent report was published, the so-called Winrock Report (Rockefeller Foundation, 1982), that reinforced many of the conclusions of the Pound Report. The Winrock Report, based on a small workshop co-sponsored by the Rockefeller Foundation and Office of Science and Technology Policy (OSTP) of the Executive Office of the President, repeated the Pound Committee's criticisms of the lack of basic research in the land-grant universities and ARS. Moreover, the Winrock Report advocated quite sweeping organizational and funding reforms—basically arguing for a levelling off of formula funding, for a vast expansion of competitive grants for basic research, and for unprecedented participation of nonland-grant and non-ARS scientists in agricultural research. The Winrock Report also differed in another respect from the Pound Report, one that has quite significant implications for the future conduct of biotechnological research in ARS and the land-grant universities. The Winrock conferees placed major stress on public agricultural researchers increasing their emphasis on basic biology for one specific purpose: to enable the rapid transfer of basic or fundamental biological knowledge to the private sector for commercial exploitation. At several junctures in the report the conferees called attention to the fact that there is emerging an unprecedented degree of international competition in technological innovation. Agricultural researchers and administrators were, in effect, encouraged by the Winrock conferees to enlist their efforts in the international struggle for technological superiority. The conferees were also quite clear in their view that aiding the U.S. cause in international technological competition would necessarily involve agricultural scientists working more closely with private sector firms in research and development; accordingly, there would need to be a shift in who are defined to be the objects or direct beneficiaries of agricultural research, moving more and more away from farmers and their needs.

Remembering that both the Pound and Winrock Reports were authored in large part by "insiders" to the public agricultural research system, why should they have been motivated to argue for major reforms of an R&D system that engendered widely acknowledged accomplishments? There are, in my view, four reasons for these prominent land-grant and ARS figures to try to "fix" the system when it was not entirely clear that anything was broken.

First, by the 1970s it had become clear that the center of gravity of U.S. agricultural research had shifted to the private sector (Ruttan, 1982). Over two-thirds of funds spent on agricultural R&D in the U.S. were accounted for by private firms by the mid-1970s (Ruttan, 1982). To be sure, much private R&D is quite routine and of a product differentiation or product testing character, but the fact remains that a number of agribusiness firms had begun to prefer to do more and more of their R&D "in-house." Second, it was recognized in the 1970s that public funding of agricultural research was stagnating. Federal funds remained a relatively small component of total public agricultural research funding in the land-grant institutions. In addition, state governments were no longer providing major increases in agricultural research funding and, indeed, the fiscal crisis of the late 1970s and early 1980s had led to significant declines in state funding of some state agricultural experiment stations (SAESs). Thus, it was becoming increasingly apparent that the role of the land-grant and ARS systems was in some doubt due to fiscal austerity in the federal and state governments and to the increased technical capacities of agribusiness firms.

Third, the 1970s witnessed unprecedented concern about possible stagnation in agricultural productivity growth (see, for example, Cochrane, 1979). Many came to argue that the post-World War II trajectory of U.S. agricultural development had reached genetic ceilings and diminishing returns to applications of purchased inputs. The significance of biotechnology to this concern about productivity stagnation was twofold. On one hand, biotechnology came to be viewed as a set of techniques and eventual products that would raise photosynthetic ceilings and cheapen the production of purchased inputs (especially petrochemically-related inputs). On the other hand, it became apparent that most land-grant universities and ARS stations did not have significant expertise in molecular and cell biology. Thus, there came to be considerable concern that to the degree that biotechnology would significantly reshape agricultural technology, public agricultural research institutions in the U.S. might not be able to play a fundamental role in this transformation.

Fourth, the late 1970s and early 1980s have been a period of sustained national and global recession. Intimately associated with the post-1974 slide into prolonged recession was the decline of mature (often called "sunset") industries, such as steel, rubber, glass, autos, and chemicals. These industries experienced saturated markets, and their managements became motivated to relocate their production facilities in low-wage areas (the U.S. "sunbelt" and the Third World) in order to lower production costs and maintain profitability. The result was widespread economic dislocation as the advanced industrial countries, particularly the U.S., experienced significant declines in industrial employment and income and the socioeconomic disintegration of older industrial regions.

While proponents of various "industrial policies" to address the economic problems of the U.S. often had major differences of opinion, virtually all tended to agree on one aspect of public policy: the need to encourage "high-technology" (or "sunrise") industries. This notion has been prominent in virtually all advanced industrial countries and has precipitated unprecedented technological competition among the countries of Western Europe, North America, and Japan. Biotechnology is, of course, one of the most prominent high-technology or "sunrise" industries and has been the object of significant public R&D subsidies in most industrial countries.[3] The U.S. government has not entered the international competition over biotechnology nearly as aggressively as have other countries. Indeed, U.S. science and technology policy before the 1970s recession was largely confined to lavish funding of basic research and military R&D, with agricultural research being essentially the only arena within which the U.S. federal government intervened to encourage and subsidize applied, civilian R&D.

It is with this background that we can begin to understand the significance of recent claims that the land-grant and ARS systems need to expand their basic biology programs, especially in molecular and cell biology, and to develop institutions for rapid transfer of this fundamental knowledge to the private sector. The Winrock Report represented one of the first steps by the OSTP of the White House to begin to address international technological competition and to ensure continued U.S. dominance in science and technology—including, but not limited to, biotechnology. The U.S. federal government has apparently begun to take unprecedented steps to block the transfer of biotechnologies to other nations (e.g., its decision, along with Japan's, to withhold support for an International Centre for Genetic Engineering and Bio-Technology [ICGEB], sponsored by the United Nations Industrial Development Organization [UNIDO] to facilitate the transfer of biotechnologies for Third World applications; see U.S. Government Interagency Working Group on Competitive Transfer Aspects of Biotechnology, 1983).[4]

Nevertheless, what is significant about this new federal intervention in agricultural R&D policy is the thinly veiled notion that agricultural research should become subject to considerations of U.S. competitiveness in global markets. *What is so striking about this proposed reorientation of agricultural research policy is the absence or infrequent mention of how U.S. farmers will fare in the coming biotechnological transformation of agriculture.* It should be kept in mind that the global recession also involved near-depression conditions for many U.S. farmers. While the farm recession was largely induced by sagging international agricultural export markets caused by income declines and the attentuation of international trade, relentless—albeit less rapid—increases in agricultural productivity have served to exacerbate the farm crisis. Thus, the biotechnological transition, insofar as it would allow researchers to break through existing productivity plateaus, would promise to reinforce longstanding overproduction (and consequent commodity policy) problems in U.S. agriculture. It is also striking that post-Hightower social equity considerations, which had acquired considerable prominence and legitimacy in the late 1970s, have been almost totally absent from discourse on the role that biotechnology should play in agricultural R&D. Proponents of a rapid shift of agricultural R&D resources into biotechnology have rarely given much thought as to what types of farmers will be advantaged or disadvantaged by the new biotechnologies. Moreover, given the embryonic nature and complexity of biotechnology, post-Hightower critics have been limited in their ability to raise important questions about the future course of biotechnology. More often than not, the posture of the critics has been to urge the discontinuation of recombinant DNA processes for ethical reasons or as biohazards. But given the massive private investments already made in agricultural biotechnology and the commitment by many land-grant universities (especially the University of California, Davis; Cornell; Wisconsin; Michigan State; Illinois, and others) to become leaders in biotechnology, it is unlikely that any anti-biotechnology movement will be able to halt this type of research.

It was noted earlier that private firms are currently playing a major role in biotechnology R&D in the U.S. It has often been pointed out that any one of the two or three largest firms undertaking agricultural biotechnology R&D in the U.S. (e.g., Monsanto, DuPont) spends more annually on plant molecular biology research than the total publicly funded plant molecular biology program in the land-grant universities. In one sense this is not surprising, given the trend toward the predominance of private sector agricultural research over the past few decades. But submerged within this longstanding trend has been a crucial biological fact, which has always limited the commercialization of biologically-based inputs: *The production process not only reproduces but also multiplies its fundamental biological input.* For example, farmers utilizing a new non-hybrid variety of seed will, in the course of the production process, produce 100-fold or more the quantity of the seed input that they purchased in the spring and from which they can save seed for the next season.[5] Thus, until 1970, private sector agricultural research in the United States placed relatively little emphasis on developing biological input products such as seeds and instead focused primarily on machinery, food processing, and inorganic soil amendments and plant protection substances.[6]

Two major legal innovations have, however, changed this state of affairs quite profoundly. The first, the Plant Variety Protection Act of 1970, extended patent-like protection to crop varieties of sexually reproduced cultivars. The second, the U.S. Supreme Court's 1980 decision in the *Diamond v. Chakrabarty* case, established the legality of obtaining patents for novel life forms. The effect of these two legal institutions, which privatize both biological knowledge and matter, has been to stimulate greatly the level of private investment in agricultural biotechnology. One of the most dramatic indicators of the commercial importance of the privatization of biotechnological knowledge has been the massive trend since 1970 toward the acquisition of small, independent seed companies by large chemical and pharmaceutical firms. This acquisition movement was clearly stimulated initially by the Plant Variety Protection Act (and, as well, by world food shortages and rising world market prices for food, which made agriculturally-related investments more attractive). However, it was given even further impetus by the development of commercial biotechnology and by the favorable Supreme Court decision on the patenting of novel life forms. The result has been an unprecedented legal milieu favoring the privatization of biological knowledge and for considering genetic information potentially to be "proprietary molecules" for private firms to "create," patent, and withhold from competitors.

The unquestioned dominance of the private sector in applied plant molecular biology represents a marked departure from the status of molecular biology at the beginning of the 1970s. Molecular biology in the U.S., which has long been acknowledged as the best in the world, had virtually no commercial significance at the beginning of the 1970s. Molecular biology research had been quite lavishly funded by the federal government (especially by NIH and NSF) since the 1950s, but by the early 1970s there had been virtually no funding by industry of molecular biology research in universities, nor was there much private in-house R&D activity involving molecular biology.

The meager role of the private sector in molecular biology research was radically altered by two events during the 1970s. The first was the discovery of the basic technology of DNA recombination by Stanley Cohen and Herbert Boyer in 1973. It should be emphasized, however, that despite the attention received by the Cohen-Boyer discovery, this scientific breakthrough did not itself lead to major private sector investments. What did, in fact, generate the vast flood of investments in the late 1970s and early 1980s was, somewhat ironically, the "recombinant DNA debate" (see Krimsky, 1982) over the safety of genetic manipulation of microorganisms and of the creation of novel life forms. Influential members of the molecular biology research committee generated the debate by cautioning their colleagues that recombinant DNA might involve unforeseeable and unprecedented "biohazards." But from the point of view of many in the scientific community, this act of self-regulation began to get out of hand as environmental, community, and other citizens groups began to clamor for public regulation of basic research in molecular biology. Molecular biologists, many of whom were among those who a few years earlier had expressed reservations about the safety of recombinant DNA, then began to launch a campaign to resist federal regulation of molecular biology research. Among their appeals was the argument that recombinant DNA would ultimately be of major commercial significance and would be able to provide solutions to many pressing economic and environmental problems; federal regulation, it was said, would unnecessarily delay the development of these pathbreaking new technologies. Wall Street and venture capital investment firms as well as members of Congress began to take notice of this new message from the basic research community.[7] It was thus during the late 1970s that investors with venture capital began to explore the commercial potential of biotechnology, attracted as they were by the enthusiastic pronouncements of molecular biology researchers.

One of the most contentious aspects of the rapid commercialization of biotechnology during the late 1970s focused around the fact that the basic science roots of the technology were publicly funded and that many molecular biologists were irresponsibly translating their publicly funded knowledge into private gain. Indeed, many of the molecular biologists who mobilized in the mid-1970s to resist federal regulation of recombinant DNA were later among those to receive lucrative offers to work part-time for biotechnology start-up companies and to receive an equity interest in these firms.

What is revealed in the pattern of institutional affiliations of these "scientist-entrepreneurs," and so crucial for the future role of the land-grant system in biotechnology, is that only a handful of these scientists were from land-grant universities. In part this is a reflection of the relative deemphasis of basic research in the land-grant system, as discussed previously. However, it should also be noted that the aggregate impact of NIH and NSF programs for the funding of basic biology research has been to concentrate grant funds (and hence talent and graduate training programs) among a relatively small number of universities, most of which are nonland-grant, if not private universities. Thus, while Harvard, MIT, Yale, Stanford, Chicago, and other such universities have experienced major expansion of their biology programs as a result of federal funding, the majority of land-grant universities have received very little federal funding of basic research in molecular biology. Only a small number of land-grant universities (California, Wisconsin, Minnesota, and Cornell) are generally regarded as being among the top two dozen universities in the United States in molecular biology.

The rise of commercial biotechnology has thus occurred in a critical transition period for the public agricultural research system in general and the land-grant system in particular. The agricultural research establishment, which had been accustomed to receiving nothing but unqualified praise before the 1970s, became the subject of heated criticisms, from two very different directions. There were new pressures to restructure the division of labor between public and private research. The land-grant universities were being asked to emphasize basic research that could be transferred to private industry to serve the "national interest" in international technological competition. However, the capability of most of the land-grant universities in molecular and cell biology generally proved to be inadequate for a major new thrust focusing around basic molecular biology. Given the historical patterns of NIH and NSF funding of basic biology and the stagnation of public funding of agricultural research, it became unclear as to whether more than just a handful of land-grant universities could continue to play their historic role in pioneering the development of new agricultural technologies. Moreover, the elaboration of legal institutions of privatizing biological knowledge increased the attractiveness of private sector agricultural research and led many companies to recruit the land-grant system's best scientists away from the university. The land-grant system is therefore in the midst of some profound challenges, the responses to which will fundamentally affect the system in the decades to come.

## Agricultural Biotechnology Research Policymaking: The Emergence of New Actors

The previous section suggests four reasons why new biotechnologically-induced structures of research decision making are likely to be more complex and involve far more actors than the traditional system. First, biotechnology tends to be a private-sector-dominated, proprietary technology. Second, given the proprietary stakes involved, the private sector has begun to push for a new division of labor between public and private research, which will be discussed at substantial length below. Third, biotechnology is developing in a milieu of international technological competition. Finally, the tendency toward—or, at a minimum, the fear of—"technological protectionism" (Barton, 1984) by the advanced industrial states is causing Third World-oriented research organizations to express increasing concern about whether new agricultural technologies will be available to these research institutions. The remainder of this section will briefly summarize the nature of the new actors in agricultural research policy and the major reasons for their keen interest in how policy is currently being made.

While the forces that shaped agricultural research decision making during the bulk of the post-World War II period were by no means lacking in complexity, I would argue that one of the most important aspects of the rise of biotechnology R&D for agriculture will be the insertion of a host of new actors, and hence greater complexity, in the decision making process. Heretofore the research decision making system in the land-grant universities has been highly decentralized, something that in substantial measure reflected the predominant role of state governments (rather than the federal government) in research funding. Individual researchers occupied the central position in the decision making process. Responding primarily to the dictates of the reward system within professional associations and the land-grant university and to various communications about the immediate problems being experienced by farmers, individual investigators would propose and, more often than not, receive state agricultural experiment station (SAES) funding for their research ideas. In many universities and departments, commodity groups would play a major role in shaping the research choices of land-grant scientists, but with considerable variation across the SAESs. Agribusiness firms and their research interests have also been a significant factor in research decision making in many contexts, again with substantial variation among the SAESs. Nevertheless, the system was quite decentralized, with the researcher being at the hub of a set of influences—operating primarily at the state level—over research problem choice. The most important dynamic was the need for the scientist to balance concerns about career advancement and recognition within scientific organizations with the need to respond to farmers' technical problems.

This decentralized process of research decision making had a number of advantages (see, for example, Ruttan, 1982). The system was flexible with regard to local agroecological and socioeconomic conditions; the farmers of Wisconsin, Maine, and Oregon were not subordinated to a specific national agricultural research policy that might be insensitive to the diversity of agricultural conditions in the U.S. There was "creative duplication of effort," in which research problems would be thoroughly explored within diverse contexts. Most importantly, the system "worked," at least judging by post-World War II productivity trend data (Cochrane, 1979; Ruttan, 1982).

This decentralized system, however, had its limitations. Agricultural research, on the whole, was probably too responsive to farmers' immediate needs, and, as implied by the Pound and Winrock Reports, researchers were given too few incentives to do longer-range research of a "system redesign" nature. Instead, the U.S. public agricultural research system was framed by a productivity paradigm and was largely characterized by the creation of incremental technical solutions to farmers' immediate technical problems. These solutions, given their short-term, incremental nature, more often than not involved chemical solutions—inorganic fertilizers, pesticides, and so forth—rather than input-minimizing or agroecologically-based approaches. USDA played a relatively passive role in agricultural research policy and, in particular, did little to impart a longer time frame to the research process in the agricultural experiment stations. Despite the bitter critiques by Hightower (1973) and others of agribusiness influence on the SAESs, agribusiness industries were in a sense quite passive as well in their influences on agricultural research policy. In part, the passivity of industry was due to the fact that it did not need to actively influence research, given that farmers' demands for short-term results tended to lead to agrochemical solutions (Buttel, 1983).

It was noted earlier that agricultural research has for some time been influenced to a certain degree by the agricultural inputs industries. However, this situation is in the process of being radically changed by biotechnology. Biotechnology, even of a highly applied sort, is quite sophisticated and lies a short distance from fundamental or basic science advances, most of which tend to be made in universities. Moreover, no single private firm can afford to assemble all the basic science researchers and facilities required to provide the new information necessary for its applied research. Agricultural input firms engaging in biotechnology must therefore depend upon a vigorous basic research sector (primarily in universities). In addition, they must ensure that the type of basic research that is done in universities is potentially applicable to the firm's product lines and R&D plans; in general, for the agroinputs industry this would involve an emphasis on plant molecular biology.

It should be emphasized that there are two predominant types of private biotechnology firms which have somewhat different interests in agricultural research policy (see, for example, Kenney *et al.*, 1982; Buttel *et al.*, 1984a). The first is the large integrated agroinputs multinational—generally a chemical, pharmaceutical, oil, or food company—of which there are roughly 15 in the U.S. actively involved in agricultural biotechnology. The second is the small biotechnology start-up firms. Of the roughly 300 start-up firms in the U.S. about 50 have some agriculturally-related research programs and about 20 have some emphasis on plant molecular biology. The agroinputs multinationals have the major advantages of having ample research budgets, the capacity to scale research discoveries up to the production stage, established marketing networks, and a diversity of product lines that facilitates synergies in R&D efforts. The principal advantage enjoyed by start-up firms is their ability to leverage knowledge from universities; in particular, start-up companies are best able to hire university faculty on a part-time basis and to encourage contributions from these scientist-entrepreneurs through stock ownership and other incentives.

The agroinputs multinationals are interested in influencing the public agricultural research system in two major ways: (a) by urging the system to increase its emphasis on basic molecular and cell biology research, and (b) by discouraging the system from producing and making available what are essentially fully developed products (e.g., finished crop varieties) in the public domain, which would provide competition with the companies' product lines. Because the start-up companies generally do not have a line of products, they tend to be less concerned about the land-grant system making public domain products available. Like their multinational counterparts, they are interested in an increased emphasis on basic research in the land-grant universities and, in addition, are especially concerned with maintaining their relationships—often largely invisible—with universities in order to perpetuate the transfer of basic knowledge to the private sector through scientist-entrepreneurs.

A second set of new actors in the agricultural research policy process lies in the Executive Office of the President in the form of science advisory activities and the OSTP. As noted, the apparent demise of the "sunset" industries and the heightened attention to "high-technology" have stimulated unparalleled international competition over technological innovation. While the U.S. was a latecomer to this competitive struggle, the federal government has begun to meet foreign competition by promoting the U.S. competitive position in various high-technologies, including biotechnology (see U.S. Government Interagency Working Group on Competitive and Transfer Aspects of Biotechnology, 1983). The convening of the Winrock workshop and the efforts undertaken to reorient the public agricultural research system to enhance the U.S. competitive situation in biotechnology were one such major effort (Buttel *et al.*, 1983a, 1983b). While most of the recommendations of the Winrock Report have yet to be implemented, it would appear that the White House science policy apparatus has begun to exert unprecedented influence over USDA and its agricultural research programs.

In response, the USDA may itself assume a more activist role in agricultural research policymaking. Shortly after the publication of the Winrock Report, Administrator Terry Kinney of the Agricultural Research Service (ARS) announced that the major thrust of the Winrock recommendations regarding ARS would be implemented in the near future. USDA has not yet, to my knowledge, begun to directly influence land-grant university research in the direction of encouraging more basic research in molecular biology. However, USDA played a major role in pushing for a substantial new competitive grants program in biotechnology with which to fund basic molecular biology research.

Perhaps the most direct influence leading to increased emphasis on biotechnology research in the land-grant universities is coming from deans and experiment station directors. These land-grant officials have become aware of the expectations of external groups—particularly private industry and federal research policy officials—that the land-grant system should place greater emphasis on basic research in general, and biotechnology in particular. A substantial number of land-grant universities have made public announcements and some concrete gestures that they are embracing this new thrust. Most visible are the research agreements signed with private firms, the formation of biotechnology institutes, and the diversion of other research resources to biotechnology.

The deans and experiment station directors of the larger, more prestigious land-grant institutions are thus starting to make important decisions about how their universities and colleges of agriculture should become involved in agricultural applications of molecular biology. But not all land-grant universities are in a position to enter the biotechnological revolution. As noted earlier, perhaps a majority of land-grant universities will have relatively little involvement because of their lack of basic molecular biology programs and facilities. Thus for the deans and directors of the other 25 or 30 land-grant universities, substantially different decisions will need to be made: how to adapt to a new era of biotechnology in which one's university will have little direct role in developing the basic technology. This dilemma will be discussed at greater length below.

A final group of new actors in the public agricultural research policy process has not yet begun to exert influence in the U.S., but may be expected to do so if biotechnology fulfills its proprietary promise. These actors are Third World and Third World-oriented agricultural research officials, many of whom have already begun to express concern that the U.S. public agricultural research system may no longer be a viable source of public domain technologies for application to Third World contexts (Buttel *et al.*, 1984b, 1984d; Kenney and Buttel, 1984; Buttel and Kenney, 1985). Such officials are likely to be directly involved in influencing the U.S. public agricultural research system to develop biotechnologies in the public domain that are are suitable for Third World applications. Put somewhat differently, the international agricultural research centers will find their interests threatened to the degree that the U.S. land-grant system confines its biotechnology research to a basic or fundamental level (or if its applied biotechnology research is substantially proprietary in nature).

## Dilemmas in U.S. Agricultural Biotechnology Research Policy

The previous section suggests four reasons why new biotechnologically-induced structures of research decision making are likely to be more complex and involve far more actors than the traditional system.

*Public Biotechnology Research: How Much, in Place of What, and Where?*

One crucial issue that has already confronted U.S. agricultural research institutions and will continue to do so is the degree to which ARS and the LGUs should shift their resources into biotechnology. Most research policy decision makers clearly recognize that biotechnology will occupy a crucial place in agricultural research, and a quick glance at the employment advertisements in *Science* conveys a strong impression that a substantial share of ARS and LGU resources at the margin are being allocated to biotechnology research (see also NASULCG, 1983). While ARS and LGU embracement of biotechnology will in and of itself generate little opposition, the shift of research resources into biotechnology will inevitably raise the question of what current (or possibly new) programs are being sacrificed in order to pursue biotechnology.

It was noted earlier that not all LGUs will be equally able to engage in biotechnology research. At the time of the rise of commercial biotechnology, only a small handful of LGUs had molecular and cell biology programs of national renown. The majority of LGUs had little or no research activity in molecular and cell biology and very little hope of significant future involvement in this technology. The land-grant system has long had a clear hierarchy of prestige and research accomplishment (Busch and Lacy, 1983). However, there has also long been maintained a myth of the "equality of science" among the LGUs; the smaller, less prestigious stations were not said to be doing inferior or inconsequential research, but rather were doing less research and research more closely targeted to the needs of their states. Biotechnology promises to make the equality of land-grant science an ever more transparent myth. This occurred initially in quite dramatic form in the Winrock Report, which in so many words indicated that federal research funds should be allocated on a competitive basis and be denied to researchers and institutions that are not conducting high quality—which can be interpreted as a euphemism for basic or fundamental—research. Critics of U.S. agricultural research from Winrock and industrial circles recognize clearly that the U.S. public agricultural research system cannot sustain 50 world-class LGUs; even further concentration of research resources in the most sophisticated and prestigious LGUs is seen as the only way to generate fundamental research information of utility to the agroinputs industry.

If we accept that biotechnology and its accompanying political forces will exacerbate the disparities among LGUs, a number of interesting questions are raised. First, will this sharpened hierarchy of land-grant institutions lead to a decline of solidarity among experiment station directors (i.e., in the Experiment Station Committee on Policy) and to unprecedented competition among LGUs for scarce resources? If the majority of LGUs cannot become meaningfully involved in biotechnology research, what can or should be their new roles in the division of labor in public agricultural research? Will the "first-tier" LGUs with strong biotechnology programs, which are essentially being asked to become national-level agricultural research institutions, experience difficulty with state legislators and other state-level groups about the degree to which state funds are being allocated to research which is assumed to benefit the nation as a whole?

### The Division of Labor Between Public and Private Research and Formulation of Research Priorities

It has been widely recognized that a new division of labor between public and private research has been emerging in the U.S. (see, for example, Ruttan, 1982). Industry is performing a greater share of the R&D, and public researchers have entered into closer linkages with industry in order to facilitate commercialization of their research discoveries. Land-grant researchers are becoming more integrated into proprietary research involving trade secrecy, publication delays, and other impediments to the free flow of scientific information. Biotechnology promises to lead to a more rapid elaboration of this emergent division of labor. There are increasingly stronger pressures from industry and White House science policymakers for the LGUs and ARS to focus primarily on basic research, to withdraw from applied research that leads to products in the public domain (especially finished plant varieties), to leave privately profitable applied research to industry, and to strengthen university-industry rela-tionships. While this proposed new division of labor is largely being driven by biotechnology (and the interest that industry has in the new basic science exemplars of molecular and cell biology that are involved), its implementation would transcend biotechnology to encompass the bulk of public agricultural research programs.

This prospective division of labor between public and private research raises a set of ethical and value questions regarding what should be the basic purposes of the public agricultural research system. The federal legislation authorizing public agricultural research suggests that the mass of farmers and rural people should be the principal constituency of the land-grant and ARS systems. Certainly public agricultural researchers are no longer able to deliver new technologies directly to farmers in a manner that they once did. However, the public agricultural research institutions in the U.S. have continued to sustain an ideology of public service to clientele groups within their states. The embracement of large multinational firms as their major constituencies will create rhetorical and political problems in convincing their old constituencies that there needs are being met and that they should support increased state appropriations for agricultural research. At a minimum, the adoption of industry agendas for LGU and ARS biotechnology research will provide new ammunition to Hightower and post-Hightower critics of public agricultural research, thereby creating unsavory publicity for the system at the very time that it is seeking expanded public funding to launch itself into the biotechnology era.

A second dilemma is how and under what conditions the results of basic or fundamental biotechnology research should be transferred to the private sector. Two questions will be of principal importance. First, should ARS and the LGUs deal with biotechnology private sector firms on an individual firm basis or as a collectivity—that is, should the LGUs and ARS work closely with particular firms or make their information available to the industry as a whole? I would argue that most private firms would prefer that university researchers work closely with one particular firm and, in so doing, deny at least some types of information to other firms (and to other scientists). This in turn raises the second question: To what degree will "intellectual property" in biotechnology be controlled by private or public agents? To the degree that public sector agricultural scientists come to work closely with particular private sector biotechnology firms, LGU and ARS laboratories will be dealing with proprietary industry information, and research administrators and scientists will be asked to maintain proprietary secrets and to develop conditions favorable to industry for patenting and licensing of new discoveries. The result could be a truncation of scholarly discourse and further political problems for administrators who will attempt to convince various public interest and clientele groups that their no-longer-quite-so-public research is in the public interest.

It was suggested earlier that the prospective division of labor would involve a substantial shift in the orientation of public sector agricultural research institutions. These institutions, which had long prided themselves on developing technologies for immediate use by their clientele groups, will no doubt be urged to deemphasize applied inquiry and concern themselves with the more fundamental aspects of plant and animal biology. How far should the LGUs and ARS back away from applied research? How strictly should the new division of labor be adhered to— that is, to what degree will ARS and LGUs pursue applied research areas that are simultaneously being explored by private sector firms?

These questions become increasingly difficult to answer, in large part because of the nature of biotechnology itself. While it has long been noted that the distinction between "basic" and "applied" research is often blurred, this is particularly the case in biotechnology-related research, where virtually any area of "applied" research lies relatively close to the frontiers of "basic" knowledge. Thus, the distinction between "basic" and "applied" is becoming more blurred in a scientific sense. On the other hand, it is becoming more distinct in terms of industry expectations of public agricultural research because they increasingly understand "basic" science as "nonproprietary" science (that is, in terms of areas of inquiry in which the results will not have immediate applicability to the development of commercializeable products or which are one input among many in an applied development project).

It should be stressed that the LGUs and ARS will clearly continue to do some applied research (by either definition). The predominant role of state government funding of LGUs ensures that they will have to be responsive to some degree to state-level clientele groups and to allocate some level of resources to problems of immediate, applied importance. But the question will still remain as to what types of applied research will be conducted. On one hand, there will be pressures to sustain old relationships with major commodity groups, which historically led to the types of agricultural technologies that have been the object of criticism on social equity and environmental grounds. However, it may well be the case in the decades to come that land-grant scientists will be constrained in servicing the technical needs of major commodity groups (which will no doubt be the intended customers of private sector biotechnology firms). Will the land-grant system thus be able (or be forced) to seek out new clienteles (e.g., small farmers, "organic" farmers) to shore up their state-level political bases?

The discussion thus far has only briefly touched on the issue of research priorities. It was noted that the private sector will be predominant in the development of products and technologies for use by farmers and that public sector researchers are beginning to experience pressures to withdraw from applied research and place more emphasis on basic research. The public agricultural research system will thus have less control over the ultimate configuration of technologies that will be made available to farmers. In a sense, then, private sector "breeding goals" and research priorities will come to induce those of the public agricultural research sector (rather than vice versa, which was the more predominant pattern for much of the post-World War II period). The extent to which this shift will occur, however, remains an open question.

One way to begin to address this issue is to ask what are the research priorities of private sector biotechnology firms. I would offer a tentative answer to this question: Private sector "breeding" and research goals appear to be characterized by providing solutions to the technical problems of input-intensive producers, because these highly capitalized producers tend to constitute the most attractive markets for new products. Nominally, the following appear to be major private sector agricultural research goals: pesticide- and salt-tolerant plant varieties, nitrogen fixation, growth regulators, and photosynthetic efficiency (National Research Council, 1984). All can be said to be devoted to "patching up" the problems caused by, or to breaking through, current productivity "ceilings" of input-intensive plant agriculture.

While the emphasis of the private biotechnology R&D sector on technologies of greatest utility to input-intensive producers is not surprising, it should also be emphasized that biotechnology is in an important sense a potentially neutral technology. Biotechnology can just as readily be devoted to developing bacterial pesticides as it can to developing pesticide-resistant plant varieties. Biotechnology can be devoted either to developing input-sparing production systems or input-intensive systems (Buttel and Youngberg, 1983).[8] Thus, one of the pivotal policy issues for the public agricultural research system will be the degree to which it, on one hand, chooses to facilitate capital- and input-intensive farming systems or, on the other hand, gives attention to the development of input-minimizing systems. The former is most consistent with the new division of labor envisioned by industry and White House science policymakers. The latter would conflict with the intentions behind the new division of labor, but may allow biotechnology to achieve its greatest promise and allow the public agricultural research system to diversify its clienteles. Input-intensive biotechnologies will be most likely to receive industry support. Pursuit of the input-minimizing trajectory will, on the other hand, require expanded long-term public funding and a commitment by the public agricultural research system to pluralism in its approaches to agricultural problems.

I noted at the outset of the chapter that the basic science exemplars of the agricultural research system are in the midst of a transition from organismic-level biology and inorganic and organic chemistry to molecular and cell biology and biochemistry. Many critics of agricultural research over the past decade have stressed its tendency toward incremental, short-term, reductionistic approaches to production problems—a circumstance that is likely to be exacerbated by an emphasis on cellular and subcellular biology. The era of the new biotechnologies will be one of increased ability to manipulate genetic information. However, it should be emphasized that genetics and genetic information lend themselves to study not only at the molecular level; indeed, some of the most profound breakthroughs in genetics have been occurring at the population and evolutionary levels. More specifically for agricultural research, ecology and systematics (or agroecosystems) offer fruitful approaches, especially with regard to the use of natural processes of plant protection and nutrient provision as substitutes for petrochemical inputs.

Another way of putting the matter is that the way in which biotechnological knowledge will be brought to bear on the development of agricultural technology involves important choices about the time frame over which research is aimed and the decisions as to which inputs should be saved or utilized more intensively. As biotechnology matures, it will no doubt "telescope" the ability of agricultural researchers to provide immediate or short-term solutions to production problems. The result will likely be land-saving technologies (in a country in which agricultural land is abundant) that are capital-intensive (in a country in which the agricultural system is already very capital-intensive). However, there is ample opportunity for biotechnology to become a partner in a longer term, agroecosystems-based inquiry. Just as biotechnology may telescope the ability to develop input-intensive technologies that are of immediate applicability to farmers' needs, biotechnology may also telescope the ability of agricultural researchers to manipulate ecosystem processes and to provide input-minimizing solutions that will benefit farmers and their local communities over a longer time horizon.

## Impacts on Genetic Resources and the Environment

One of the growing concerns about the development of agricultural technology in developed and developing countries has been its impacts on genetic resources. Traditional plant breeding since the 1930s has led to greater uniformity among varieties of particular cultivars, which, when exacerbated by monoculturing, has led to problems such as the corn blight epidemic of the early 1970s. Also, as improved varieties have spread across the globe, *in situ* "collections" of traditional varieties and landraces have slowly disappeared in the "Vavilov Centers" of genetic diversity that are located for the most part in the tropical developing countries. Moreover, it is widely acknowledged that public sector efforts to preserve the genetic material of traditional varieties that are being displaced by "Green Revolution" varieties are inadequate (Jain, 1982; Brown, 1983; Wilkes, 1983).

Biotechnology has two important implications for the status of genetic resources. First, the ability of biotechnological techniques to more directly manipulate genetic information presents the strong possibility of generating even greater genetic uniformity in cultivars. (But it should be mentioned as well that biotechnology may facilitate the tailoring of varieties to specific agroecological zones, thus mitigating genetic uniformity to some degree.) Second, biotechnology, involving as it does the ultimate quest by private firms for the identification and privatization of proprietary molecules (i.e., genetic information), promises to reduce the heretofore free flow of genetic material among private and public plant breeders in developed and developing countries. Private firms will clearly not want to diminish public programs of germplasm preservation, evaluation, and enhancement, as genetic resources are the ultimate and fundamental raw material of their R&D programs. However, private firms will have a growing interest in increasing their control over genetic resources—in particular, by restricting access to their collections of evaluated and enhanced genetic material. This will place more of the burden of germplasm collection and preservation on the public sector at a time when public sector resources are already stretched thin and germplasm preservation facilities are inadequate. It should be noted, however, that biotechnologies will be potentially able to militate against the problem of genetic erosion in *ex situ* collections. Techniques such as cell and tissue culture will be able to increase the speed and efficiency of germplasm evaluation (most germplasm that has been preserved has not yet been fully evaluated), to rescue "wide crosses," and to better generate, identify, and utilize useful mutations. Thus, while biotechnology presents important opportunities to better manage and manipulate *ex situ* genetic information, it will also telescope the existing tendencies of crop improvement programs to diminish the global reservoir of genetic resources. And it should be strongly emphasized as well that biotechnological means of expanding useful genetic resources will do nothing to mitigate the loss of social/cultural knowledge regarding these plants, their communities, cultivation, and cooking (and may give a false sense that *in situ* approaches are less needed).

It was noted earlier that public attention to and debate over biotechnology has been largely confined to matters of biohazards. While there does remain some concern about the health and ecological impacts of genetic modification of microorganisms (Rifkin, 1983), the fear of biohazards has declined significantly among the scientific community and the general public since the heyday of the recombinant DNA controversy in the mid-1970s. That concern about possible toxicological or ecotoxicological impacts of biotechnology has diminished should not, however, imply that there are no human health or ecological risks associated with certain biotechnologies. In particular, there should be vigilance regarding the micro and macroecological implications of biotechnologies. There remain wide segments of the scientific community that see the possibility of genetically modified microorganisms affecting ecosystem processes. At the more macro level, it is useful to keep in mind that biotechnology is increasingly being associated with "neo-cornicopian" views which reflect an assumption that the new biotechnologies will enable humans to drastically curtail their reliance on nonrenewable resources, solve pollution problems, and expand the capacity of the globe to support human life (for contrasting views, see Dahlberg, 1984 and Lakoff, 1984). Biotechnology does have great potential to mitigate environmental problems. Biotechnology is, however, fundamentally based on renewable natural resources (e.g., plant materials as substrates for industrial microbiological production), and the status of the world's renewable natural resource systems has been in steady decline over the past several decades (Brown, 1981; Redclift, 1984). It should thus be recognized that biotechnology can be applied to enhance environmental quality, but that biotechnology is not environmentally benign and should not be viewed as a basis for assuming that the environmental concerns of the 1960s and 1970s will soon be transcended.

*Assessing the Impacts of the New Biotechnologies*

Agricultural policymakers have become keenly aware that the past decade was one of unparalleled questioning of whether the socioeconomic costs of new technologies outweighed the benefits. Stimulated initially by the efforts of public interest groups, such as the Agribusiness Accountability Project, National Rural Center, and Rural America, many social scientists in the land-grant system began to focus their research on understanding the socioeconomic impacts of new agricultural technologies. Much of this research has been conducted for academic (rather than policy) reasons, and the field remains too immature to provide clear guidance for policy purposes. Nevertheless, the implication of much of this research was that publicly developed agricultural technology projects, should they prove to be actually or potentially responsible for undesirable social impacts, could be deleted from the research programs of agricultural research institutions and be replaced by projects that are more socially benign.

Private sector dominance of agricultural biotechnologies will likely undercut much of the policy rationale for assessment of the impacts of agricultural technologies and shift the focus from assessment to regulation. Land-grant and ARS scientists will no longer be so directly "responsible" for the final configuration of agricultural technology products (to the degree that they withdraw from applied and embrace basic research). Moreover, to the degree that technology impact assessment continues to be done in the land-grant system, the logical "policy clienteles" of this research will increasingly be private firms, most of which will be less than excited to hear that their technologies are leading to undesirable socioeconomic impacts. The situation could well be one in which land-grant social scientists, who have only recently begun to gain experience and confidence in generating "social intelligence" on new agricultural technology, will be undercut in their efforts to shape technological change in more beneficial ways. Private sector research policymakers will have no obligation to consider the potential or actual socioeconomic impacts of their technologies in the R&D decision making process. They may even take offense at the fact that the land-grant system is supporting research that reaches a negative verdict on the desirability of private-sector-developed technologies. The result may be a return to the situation of the 1950s when there was little information on and understanding of the impacts of new agricultural technologies. This would be especially tragic with regard to biotechnologies, since there is a strong likelihood that their impacts will be neither neutral nor benign.

### Dilemmas in Biotechnology and International Agricultural Research Policy

Biotechnology generated substantial interest and massive private investments in the developed countries in the late 1970s and early 1980s. But almost coincidentally there emerged a high level of attention to the possibilities of biotechnology for international development, especially in agricultural development. There have been several major conferences on the potential applications of biotechnologies to developing countries (see, for example National Research Council, 1982; International Rice Research Institute, 1984), and biotechnology is now the newest buzzword in international development circles (Daly, 1983; Dixon, 1983). There is wide agreement that biotechnology has enormous possibilities for enhancing agricultural and nonagricultural productivity in the developing countries and for improving the nutritional, health care, and overall economic status of the rural and urban poor in Third World nations. However, as is well known from the uneven and controversial performance of the Green Revolution (compare Griffin, 1974, and Wortman and Cummings, 1978), development problems cannot be solved by biotechnology any more than any technical fix can automatically provide development, growth, and improved living standards.

The application of biotechnology to Third World agriculture involves analagous if not identical social, ethical, and value issues as does agricultural biotechnology in the developed countries. But the implications of biotechnology for the Third World may be even more far-reaching than in the developed countries. This is because the role of the private sector in international agricultural R&D has heretofore been quite limited, especially in the plant improvement area.

The vast bulk of plant improvement R&D for Third World applications has heretofore been conducted within the quasi-public network of the International Agricultural Research Centers (IARCs) or within the national agricultural research institutes of developing countries. The lack of private sector interest in plant improvement for developing countries has been due to several factors. First, crop varieties developed for the temperate zones of the industrialized countries are not directly applicable to Third World conditions as are many plant protection chemicals and synthetic fertilizers. Hence, the development of Third World seed markets requires plant specific breeding investments, which will be undertaken only if there are sufficient market potentials. Second, developing country seed markets have not been highly attractive. The IARCs and national agricultural research institutes have provided formidable competition. Also, seed markets in the major LDC crops (maize, wheat, and rice, which together account for roughly one-half of LDC crop acreage) have been limited for socioeconomic and biological reasons. The market in maize seed has been limited by socioeconomic factors. Interestingly, maize has long been the principal emphasis of developed country seed companies because of its large acreages and because for about 50 years there have been productive (but reproductively unstable) maize hybrids. Most corn production in the Third World, however, is accounted for by semi- or noncommercial peasant smallholders, many of whom intercrop maize with other crops and produce corn largely for household consumption. Rice and wheat have been the most important staple good crops grown by relatively commercial farmers in the LDCs. But there have been major biological barriers to the expansion of markets in wheat and rice seeds—namely, the inability to develop satisfactory, but reproductively unstable hybrids.

Several new factors are leading to rapidly growing interest by seed companies in penetrating Third World seed markets. First, rapid structural changes in the global seed industry have created increased competition and willingness to accept more risk. The principal structural change has been the incorporation of formerly independent seed companies as subsidiaries within chemical, pharmaceutical, petroleum, and food processing multi-national corporations (MNCs). This change, which, as noted earlier, was initially stimulated by the passage by the U.S. Congress of the Plant Variety Protection Act of 1970 and was later given further impetus by the commercial potentials of proprietary biotechnologies, has brought the resources of "deep-pocket" MNCs to bear on private breeding research and seed marketing and led to increased competition. Given the saturated markets for seeds in the First World, seed exports are a logical arena into which this competition will be extended. Second, parallel advances in biotechnology and in the technology of hybridizing rice and wheat have given seed firms far more potential leverage in developing Third World seed markets. Reproductively unstable rice and wheat hybrids can substantially increase agricultural productivity, but will also require farmers to purchase seeds each growing season. Moreover, the reproductive instability of these hybrids will provide "natural" protection—complementing the legal protections of patents and plant breeder's rights—for the proprietary molecules developed through genetic engineering. For example, the fact that farmers growing hybrid rice will not be able to save their own seed will enable a private seed company to incorporate genes for salt-tolerance into rice hybrids without fear that these genes can be duplicated by farmers or competitor firms.

The likelihood of increased involvement of MNCs in LDC-oriented plant improvement R&D and in penetrating developing country seed markets is among the factors that will lead to a fundamentally new institutional structure for international agricultural research. Table 1 indicates that the "Biorevolution" in international agriculture will depart in several major respects from its predecessor, the Green Revolution. Two such differences deserve major emphasis. First, while the major thrust of the Green Revolution was confined to a handful of cereal grains in restricted geographical regions (Griffin, 1974), the Biorevolution has the potential to affect virtually every agricultural region and species—including livestock as well as crops (see NAS, 1984). Second, as indicated above, the course of the Biorevolution, especially with regard to plant improvement, will be influenced to a far greater degree by proprietary considerations than was the Green Revolution.

## LDC Access to Biotechnologies

This emergent structure of international agricultural research has a number of potentially important implications for LDC-oriented agricultural research and LDC agriculture. Two of the most crucial relate to the dominance of MNCs in plant molecular biology R&D and the erosion of the technical superiority of public agricultural research institutions in the developed countries. These considerations suggest two important, interrelated questions: First, will the emergence of agricultural biotechnology serve to exacerbate disparities in technical capacity between First and Third World countries and their agricultural research institutions— particularly because less public expertise will be available? Second, will LDC-oriented public agricultural researchers face significant problems in securing access to the new biotechnologies, many of which will be proprietary? Neither question can be answered at this point with a high degree of certainty. Nevertheless, one can identify several factors that will affect the eventual outcomes.

One such factor will be whether the large number of public sector, LDC-oriented biotechnology research programs that are currently being

**Table 14.1  A Comparison of the Institutional Structures of the Green Revolution and Biorevolution**

| Characteristics | Green Revolution | Biorevolution |
|---|---|---|
| Crops affected | Wheat, rice, maize | Potentially all crops, including vegetables, fruits, agroexport crops (e.g., oil palms, cocao), and specialty crops (e.g., spices, scents) |
| Other products affected | None | Animal products<br>Pharmaceuticals<br>Processed food products<br>Energy |
| Areas affected | Some LDCs; some locations (i.e., if accompanied by irrigation, high quality land, transport availability, etc.) | All areas; all nations, all locations, including marginal lands (characterized by drought, salinity, aluminum toxicity, etc.) |
| Technology development and dissemination | Largely public or quasi-public sector | Largely private sector (multinational corporations and start-up firms, with the former predominating in terms of commercialization) |
| Proprietary considerations | Patents and plant variety protection generally not relevant | Process and products patentable and protectable |
| Capital costs of research | Relatively low | Relatively high |
| Research skills required | Conventional plant breeding and parallel agricultural sciences | Molecular and cell biology expertise, plus conventional plant-breeding skills |
| Crops displaced | None (except the germplasm resources lost along with traditional varieties and landraces) | Potentially any |

*Source:*  Kenney and Buttel (1984).

developed will be able to develop alternatives to—perhaps even pirated copies of—the technologies being developed in private biotechnology firms. There are two major types of LDC-oriented, public sector biotechnology programs. The first consists of international, multilateral quasi-public sector institutions, especially the International Centre for Genetic Engineering and Bio-Technology developed under the auspices of the UN Industrial Development Organization, and the IARCs of the Consultative Group on International Agricultural Research (CGIAR). The former is just now being established and is fully dedicated to biotechnology research, while the latter have been in existence for well over a decade and have as yet only a minor commitment to biotechnology. Nevertheless, both types of quasi-public institutions have begun to embrace biotechnology, at least in part, to ensure that biotechnologies will be available to Third World countries. Moreover, both appear to share the concern that biotechnologies developed in the private sector of developed countries may not be the most appropriate for Third World applications. The second major type of LDC-oriented biotechnology effort consists of several national biotechnology programs. The programs of Brazil, Mexico, China, Cuba, and India appear to be the most adequately financed and most promising, but substantial programs have also been established in the Philippines, Indonesia, Thailand, Korea, and other countries. The motivations behind establishing these national biotechnology programs have largely been threefold: (a) to preempt proprietary technologies that are under development in the industrial countries, (b) to provide the basis for autonomous biotechnology industries (so as, among other things, to prevent the foreign exchange problems that would likely result from massive imports of biotechnology products), and (c) to ensure the development of biotechnologies specifically tailored for LDC needs.

Third World access to biotechnologies is thus a two-edged sword. On one hand, the very fact that LDCs and LDC-oriented research programs are able to become involved in such a "high-technology" activity testifies to a fundamental fact about biotechnology: it is, by comparison with most previous industrial technologies, not highly capital-intensive (Kenney and Buttel, 1985). This technology is within the reach of all but the poorest countries. Biotechnology is, to be sure, more expensive and, in particular, more knowledge- and expertise-intensive than traditional agricultural research methodologies. However, the investments required to establish state-of-the-art biotechnology research and development—and even biotechnology industrial production facilities—are far less than, for example, the cost of a contemporary "turnkey" steel or chemical factory. Moreover, investments in biotechnology R&D offer significant synergies, since a major biotechnology research facility could develop technologies suitable for a wide range of sectors (chemical production, energy production, health care, and sanitation, in addition to agriculture). But on the other hand, there remain a number of formidable barriers to successful LDC involvement in biotechnology. These include infrastructural limitations (e.g., electricity, transportation and accessibility to international airports, lack of information resources); shortages of skilled personnel; fiscal limitations, especially in the current era of global stagnation; and, perhaps above all, the lack of political will. It will likely be the case that a handful of Third World biotechnology programs will prosper while many will fail, and the vast majority of LDCs will not be able to muster even an attempt at establishing a national program. The result will likely be further exacerbation of First World/Third World technical disparities, plus the widening of disparities, *among* the LDCs.

A further factor that will influence LDC access to biotechnologies relates to the security and recognition of patents and other Western institutions, such as Plant Breeder's Rights, for the protection of private intellectual property. Many Third World countries do not have well developed patent systems, and only a small handful recognize Plant Breeder's Rights. Moreover, at the 1983 Conference of the Food and Agriculture Organization, a sizeable majority of Third World countries went on record as opposing Plant Breeder's Rights. Thus, for many LDCs, especially those hoping to establish biotechnology programs of their own, it may be in their interest to decline to recognize Western systems of protecting rights in private intellectual property. However, such an action would involve major risks—for example, introducing the possibility that MNCs, developed country governments, and multilateral development banks will be less willing to transfer other technologies to or underwrite loans for recalcitrant LDCs. Nevertheless, the evolving international political economy of intellectual property will ultimately have a major influence on the degree and conditions of LDC access to the new biotechnologies.

A final factor affecting LDC access to biotechnologies will be the vagaries of market potential as perceived by MNCs. We noted earlier that private sector decision making as to research priorities and product distribution will largely hinge on perceptions of market potential. The Third World, in the aggregate, will quite likely be a very attractive market. However, significant minorities, if not substantial majorities of LDCs and LDC agriculturalists may not be viewed as having sufficiently large markets to justify specialized R&D and marketing infrastructures. The result will be that many countries and agriculturalists will remain unserved or inadequately served by the new biotechnologies. Thus, while it will generally be most advantageous for LDCs to utilize domestically-developed (as opposed to imported) biotechnology products, for many biotechnologies will not be available even in the form of imported products. Biotechnology may thus be more limited in its benefits to the Third World than is implied in many recent enthusiastic pronouncements such as that of Daly (1983).

## The Division of Labor Between Public-Private Research and the Research Agenda

It was noted earlier that LDC-oriented agricultural research in general and plant improvement research in particular have been conducted largely within the IARCs and the LDCs' national agricultural research institutes. This situation is likely to change dramatically due to the institutional structure of biotechnology innovation—in particular, the heightened interest of private biotechnology-seed MNCs in LDC agroinput markets (Buttel *et al.*, 1984c, 1985). But as in the developed countries, the emergent private-sector-led Biorevolution in the Third World will by no means supplant public agricultural research. This will be the case for several reasons. First, there will remain broad areas of biological inquiry (e.g., germplasm preservation, evaluation, and enhancement by the IARCs) that will not be seen as being privately profitable. Next, private firms will continue to depend upon fundamental and nonproprietary knowledge from public agricultural research institutions. Finally, as suggested above, the market-driven nature of private biotechnology R&D for LDC applications will likely lead to an emphasis on large, secure, and relatively capital-intensive production systems. The result will be that sizeable proportions of LDC agriculturalists will be unserved or poorly served by the private sector. Thus, the responsibility for meeting the technical needs of these peasant smallholders will fall ever more clearly and specifically on the IARCs and the national agricultural research institutes of the LDCs (Buttel *et al.*, 1984b).

The prospect of transferring fundamental or applied nonproprietary knowledge from the public to the private sector as well as shifting the emphasis of the IARCs and their national counterparts to the LDC non- or subcommercial smallholder sector while MNCs predominate in commercial crop improvement techniques raises several important questions. One is the degree to which the IARCs will see it as a legitimate role to stress provision of nonproprietary knowledge to private sector firms. The IARCs have historically been willing to do so to some degree, but have long seen their principal clients as being the national agricultural research institutes of LDCs. Another question involves the status of information flows to the IARCs. The CGIAR, the organizational umbrella of the IARCs, was founded with a specific commitment to applied research, and the relatively limited resources of the IARCs simply do not permit the centers to devote substantial resources to fundamental or basic research.

The IARCs are thus highly dependent on the free flow of scientific information, and a major concern for them will be whether they can secure access to biotechnological information, much of which will be proprietary and under the control of private sector firms. A third question, one that long predates but will be made more important because of biotechnological innovation is the degree to, and the means by which the IARCs should stress R&D for the peasant smallholder sector, especially its non- and sub-commercial strata. The debates over the Green Revolution during the 1970s, especially relating to the capital-intensity and, hence, the "landlord-bias" of the initial high-yielding varieties (Griffin, 1974), ultimately led to a stronger and clearer commitment by the IARCs to stress technologies tailored for peasant smallholders. It is not entirely clear, however, how this goal is best pursued. Can this best be accomplished by increasing the research resources devoted to "typical peasant crops" (e.g., crops like cassava which are not generally grown for the market) or by emphasizing low-input systems for the major cereal grains? Should the strategies involve technologies that enable peasant smallholders to become more commercial or those which are premised on preserving the self-provisioning peasantries of the Third World?

The public research policy issues that have been raised thus far have been of a particular character—involving policy options whose outcomes will be shaped largely by factors internal to public research institutions. But as we have argued elsewhere (Buttel *et al.*, 1984b, 1984d), a number of critical issues will face public international research institutions if, as we anticipate, there comes to be direct competition between the public and private sectors. The potential basis for competition is obvious: The crops that have the greatest market potentials for MNC seed-biotechnology companies (wheat, rice, and maize) are also those that have historically received principal emphasis in the IARCs and national agricultural research institutes. In particular, the wheat and rice varieties produced by the national agricultural research institutes from IARC advanced breeding lines and other technologies will represent formidable competition to MNCs. Many LDCs and LDC-oriented public researchers will also likely have reservations about the new private-sector-developed biotechnologies, especially if they take the form of reproductively unstable hybrids. Deployment of these capital-intensive inputs could easily aggravate inequality in agriculture, while rapid growth of seed imports might well exacerbate foreign exchange problems of LDCs (Buttel *et al.*, 1984d; Buttel and Kenney, 1985). Thus, there may be protracted competition between the public and private sectors in international agricultural research. This is in contrast to the U.S., where the land-grant system has steadily withdrawn from competition with the private sector by deemphasizing or terminating the release of finished public domain varieties (Busch *et al.*, 1984).

This is not to suggest that there has already emerged a conflictual situation between developed country biotechnology-seed companies and public international agricultural research organizations (especially the IARCs). The situation now is probably more one of mutual apprehension, with MNCs being concerned about how publicly-subsidized competition will affect private market development, and public international agricultural research institutions becoming increasingly aware that their own access to the new biotechnologies will require cordial relationships with the developed countries' biotechnology firms.

The major harbinger of antagonisms between MNCs and public international agricultural research institutions has thus far not been direct conflict between these organizations, but rather First World-Third World governmental disagreements within international organizations. Many Third World countries have become alarmed about the emergent private sector dominance in, and privatization of, biotechnology knowledge and genetic material. Their governments have expressed these concerns in three principal ways (Buttel et al., 1984d): (a) LDC governments have supported the establishment of ICGEB; (b) they have developed national biotechnology programs; and (c) they have opposed privatization of genetic resources at the last two FAO conferences. Whether what have thus far been North-South conflicts will become public-private conflicts is difficult to anticipate. Nevertheless, the likelihood is that the relative North-South, public-private harmony that has prevailed in the international agricultural research system will be strained by the institutional and technical forces represented by biotechnology.

### Summary:  The Prospect and Challenge of Biotechnology

This chapter began by recounting the brief interlude in the 1970s when a set of "new agenda" issues emerged—for instance, concern about the nature and consequences of changes in farm structure, the ecological impacts of agriculture, the status of farmworkers, the formulation of agricultural research policy, and the impacts of agricultural technologies. Parallel issues emerged in LDC agriculture and agricultural research. A most important reflection of this new agenda era was the expansion of public participation in agricultural research policy and other areas. But the opportunities for public participation have decisively narrowed during the early 1980s for a variety of political and economic reasons. Two relate specifically to biotechnology. The first was the recombinant DNA controversy, which unfortunately probably had the enduring effect of making scientists wary about public participation in research policymaking. The second was the growing pressure on the U.S. land-grant system to concern itself more with embracing biotechnology in service to private industry than with addressing post-Hightower criticisms of public agricultural research. Thus, there is at present little or no broad public participation in research policymaking bearing on biotechnology; public participation has basically been confined to lawsuits (e.g., over release of genetically modified *Pseudomonas syringeae* into the environment in California; see Harl, 1984). The confining of research policymaking to a small circle of land-grant university, ARS, private industry, and government officials may not be a viable strategy over the long term. A combination of setbacks in the courts, "Hightower-like" exposés of industry-university relations in the land-grant system, and conflict of interest embarrassments involving land-grant scientists may be highly damaging and lead to regulation that satisfies neither universities and industry nor their critics. Thus, a system once seen as hegemonic and monolithic may be fragile and threatened.

One key to the future of the land-grant system will be how its scientists and administrators come to deal with the new agenda concerns of the late 1970s as they enter the biotechnology era of the 1980s. It is not implausible that the former critics of the land-grant system may even come to see land-grant scientists as allies in opposition to the dominance of private industry in agricultural R&D. The concerns of the critics can no doubt best be addressed if there remains a viable public agricultural research sector within which there are avenues for public input into research policymaking. While I see more and more examples of land-grant personnel taking the concerns of public interest and "nonmainstream" clientele groups more seriously, the degree to which effective alliances are formed is presently limited by residues of mistrust from the initial confrontations of the 1970s. But land-grant scientists have less to fear from the new agenda activists and the activists less reason to doubt the parallels between their concerns and the interests of land-grant scientists than both groups may realize.

I have thus come to the view that biotechnology will present fundamental challenges, but also substantial opportunities for U.S. public agricultural research institutions. For example, the rise of biotechnology will disrupt the traditional patterns through which public agricultural research institutions have developed research priorities and threaten to subordinate these institutions to the goals of private sector firms. At the same time, the current conjuncture represents an historic opportunity for public research institutions to insulate themselves from commodity group influences and to embrace new agricultural and rural constituencies.

Explicit in the foregoing argument is an assumption that the "new agenda" issues—that is, questions about the ethical and value foundations of research policy—have not been a temporary fad, but rather represent enduring considerations about the role of public agricultural research in society (see Bonnen, 1983).[9] Indeed, I would argue that the pivotal choices to be made about the role of the land-grant system in its approach to biotechnology research will make the ethical and value rationalizations of public sector research even more transparent. I would anticipate that the emergence of biotechnology programs in the land-grant universities will result in unprecedented politicization. For example, there will no doubt be extended debates about whether land-grant universities can serve the public interest by enhancing the biotechnology product lines of a handful of multinational firms.[10] The outcomes of these debates are extremely difficult to forecast at this point. However, the choices that are made will likely be pivotal for the long-term role and future of the public agricultural research system.

## Notes

1. It should be noted and stressed that most biotechnology applications in agriculture will not lead to be dramatic productivity increases (Lewontin, 1984). For example, most crop traits of economic importance are multigenic and therefore will be improved only slowly through recombinant DNA techniques (which are most effective at the single-gene level).

2. It should not be inferred, however, that "routine" (i.e., "maintenance") research is either unnecessary or inherently of inferior quality. There will continue to be a need (and few incentives in ARS or the experiment stations) for maintenance research such as continual monitoring of insect populations and identification of genetic material conveying resistance to insect pests.

3. See OTA (1984:Chapter 13) for data on the public subsidies currently being provided by governments in several advanced industrial countries. The U.S. government is clearly the world's leader in public funding of basic molecular biology research but lags behind several other countries (especially its major biotechnology competitors) in public subsidies to applied biotechnology research.

4. Japan's decision to decline to support ICGEB was based on the straightforward rationale that ICGEB, if successful, would increase competition with Japanese firms over the next several decades. The U.S. decision, while no doubt influenced by similar considerations, was also based on the Reagan Administration's view that it: (a) did not want to add to its present commitments to multilateral institutions (espceially those related to the UN system), (b) prefers bilateral (e.g., U.S. Agency for International Development-sponsored) projects over multilateral ones, and (3) prefers private sector over public sector R&D, if the research is likely to be privately profitable.

5. This is not the case, however, for hybrid seeds—where the performance of the progeny reverts to that of the grandparents.

6. That is, the private sector, recognizing that nonhybridized seeds and other biological inputs could receive neither biological nor legal protection, tended to focus its R&D on machinery, chemicals, and so on, which could be protected through the patent system.

7. Thus, the Congress declined to pass legislation regulating recombinant DNA research (see Krimsky, 1982). Perhaps as importantly, this brief flirtation with public participation in research policy left many molecular biologists in industry and universities feeling threatened by possible federal regulation of biotechnological research. This episode may have substantially diminished the willingness of scientists to welcome public participation in research policymaking in the future.

8. The theoretical neutrality of biotechnologies should not be confused, however, with what are likely to be their impacts on agricultural structures. I would argue that the forces—especially private sector dominance and the market-driven nature of biotechnology R&D—leading to biotechnologies being relatively capital-intensive (and, hence, nonneutral)

are quite strong. These technologies are therefore likely to be most applicable to the farming operations of highly market-oriented and well-capitalized producers. Accordingly, one can anticipate that capital-intensive biotechnologies will be least socially neutral when they are employed in agricultural systems with very unequal distributions of land, credit, and power (see, for example, Griffin, 1974). Thus, the issue of the neutrality of agricultural technology is intimately bound up with the distribution of resources in an agrarian structure, and the pursuit of socially equal and benign technological changes will require "appropriate institutions" as well as "appropriate technologies." I am indebted to Kenneth A. Dahlberg for this point.

9. This is not to suggest that new agenda critics of agricultural research policy always had effective or accurate arguments. See Buttel (1983) for a critique of the views of Hightower (1973) and other new agenda figures.

10. It is curious, given the intensity of mobilization around "new agenda" agricultural research policy issues less than five years ago, why the emergent biotechnology thrust of the U.S. public agricultural research system has received so little scrutiny. The election of the Reagan Administration has, no doubt, been a factor; a good many of the "new agenda" public interest groups were directly or indirectly funded by the federal government, and the funding of such groups was one of the initial casualties of the Administration's fiscal policies. Nevertheless, it is also the case that the national interest overlay of policy discourse over high-technology in general and biotechnology in particular has undercut the development of deeper and more critical perspectives on these technologies. For example, one of the most frequently expressed rationales for taking a more "liberal" view of industry-university arrangements in the biotechnology area is that making these arrangements more attractive to industry is necessary to bolster the U.S. competitive position in biotechnology. More specifically, the argument is often made that if the U.S. does not remain dominant in biotechnology, U.S. agricultural productivity will suffer because of farmers' lack of access to the new biotechnologies. It is unlikely, however, that U.S. agriculturists will be unable to utilize these new technologies even if they are developed in other countries by foreign firms. The U.S. market in general and the U.S. agricultural inputs market in particular are the largest in the world, and virtually all foreign biotechnology MNCs are focusing their industrial strategies around penetrating the U.S. market. Thus, it is very unlikely that U.S. agricultural productivity will be affected by the nominal nationality of the firms that prove to be the most innovative in the agricultural biotechnology area.

# References

Barton, John H. 1984. "Coping with Technological Protectionism." Unpublished manuscript, School of Law, Stanford University.

Bonnen, James T. 1983. "Historical Sources of U.S. Agricultural Productivity: Implications for R&D Policy and Social Science Research." *American Journal of Agricultural Economics* 65:958–966.

Brown, Lester R. 1981. *Building a Sustainable Society.* New York: W. W. Norton.

Brown, William L. 1983. "Genetic Diversity and Genetic Vulnerability—An Appraisal." *Economic Botany* 37:4–12.

Busch, Lawrence; M. Hansen; J. Burkhardt; and W. B. Lacy. 1984. "The Impact of Biotechnology on Public Agricultural Research: The Case of Plant Breeding." Paper presented at the annual meeting of the American Association for the Advancement of Science, New York, May.

Busch, Lawrence, and William B. Lacy. 1983. *Science, Agriculture, and the Politics of Research.* Boulder, Colo.: Westview Press.

Buttel, Frederick H. 1983. "The Land-Grant System: A Sociological Perspective on Value Conflicts and Ethical Issues." In *Agriculture, Change, and Human Values,* ed. Richard Haynes and Ray Lanier, Vol. II, pp. 977–1012. Gainesville: Humanities and Agriculture Program, University of Florida.

Buttel, Frederick H.; J.T. Cowan; M. Kenney; and J. Kloppenburg, Jr. 1984a. "Biotechnology in Agriculture: The Political Economy of Agribusiness Reorganization and Industry-

University Relationships." In *Research in Rural Sociology and Development,* ed. Harry K. Schwartzweller, pp. 315–348. Greenwich, Conn.: JAI Press.

Buttel, Frederick H.; M. Kenney; J. Kloppenburg, Jr.; and J. T. Cowan. 1983a. "Problems and Prospects of Agricultural Research: The Winrock Report." *The Rural Sociologist* 3:67–75.

Buttel, Frederick H.; J. Kloppenburg, Jr.; M. Kenney; and J. T. Cowan. 1983b. "Genetic Engineering and the Restructuring of Agricultural Research." *The Rural Sociologist* 3:132–144.

Buttel, Frederick H.; M. Kenney; and J. Kloppenburg, Jr. 1985. "From Green Revolution to Biorevolution: Some Observations on the Changing Technological Bases of Economic Transformation in the Third World." *Economic Development and Cultural Change,* forthcoming.

_____. 1984b. "The IARCs and the Development and Application of Biotechnologies in Developing Countries." Paper presented at the Inter-Center Seminar on the International Agricultural Research Centers and Biotechnology, International Rice Research Institute, Los Baños, Philippines, April.

_____. 1984c. "Biotechnology and the Third World: Toward a Global Political-Economic Perspective." *Politics and the Life Sciences* 2:160–164.

Buttel, Frederick H.; M. Kenney; J. Kloppenburg, Jr.; and J. T. Cowan. 1984d. "Biotechnology in the World Agricultural System: A New Technological Order for the New Biology?" Paper presented at the annual meeting of the American Association for the Advancement of Science, New York, May.

Buttel, Frederick H., and M. Kenney. 1985. "Biotechnology and International Development: Prospects for Overcoming Dependence in the Information Age." *Policy Studies Journal,* forthcoming.

Buttel, Frederick H., and I. G. Youngberg. 1983. "Implications of Biotechnology for the Development of Sustainable Agricultural Systems." In *Environmentally Sound Agriculture,* ed. W. Lockeretz, pp. 377–400. New York: Praeger.

Cochrane, Willard W. 1979. *The Development of American Agriculture.* Minneapolis: University of Minnesota Press.

Dahlberg, Kenneth A. 1984. "Biotechnology and the Social Sciences: A Critique." *Politics and the Life Sciences* 2:164–167.

Daly, J. 1983. "Biotechnology: Accelerating Development." *Horizons* 2:18–21.

Dixon, B. 1983. "The Third World's Greatest Opportunities." *Bio/Technology* 1:494, 519.

Griffin, Keith. 1974. *The Political Economy of Agrarian Change.* Cambridge, Mass.: Harvard University Press.

Hadwiger, Don F. 1982. *The Politics of Agricultural Research.* Lincoln: University of Nebraska Press.

Harl, Neil E. 1984. "University/Industry Relations—Problems and Promise." Paper presented at the annual meeting of the American Association for the Advancement of Science, New York, May.

Hightower, Jim. 1973. *Hard Tomatoes, Hard Times.* Cambridge, Mass.: Schenkman.

International Rice Research Institute (IRRI). 1984. *The International Agricultural Research Centers and Biotechnology.* Los Baños, Philippines: IRRI, forthcoming.

Jain, H. K. 1982. "Plant Breeders' Rights and Genetic Resources." *The Indian Journal of Genetics and Plant Breeding* 42:121–128.

Kenney, M., and F. H. Buttel. 1984. "Biotechnology: Prospects and Dilemmas for Third World Development." *Development and Change,* forthcoming.

Krimsky, Sheldon. 1982. *Genetic Alchemy.* Cambridge, Mass.: MIT Press.

Lakoff, Sanford. 1984. "Biotechnology and the Developing Countries." *Politics and the Life Sciences* 2:151–159.

Lewontin, Richard C. 1984. "Biotechnology and the Political Ecology of Agricultural Research." Paper presented at the annual meeting of the American Association for the Advancement of Science, New York, May.

Mayer, Alfred, and Jean Mayer. 1974. "Agriculture: The Island Empire." *Daedalus* 103:83–95.

National Academy of Sciences (NAS). 1972. *Report of the Committee on Research Advisory to the U.S. Department of Agriculture.* Washington, D.C.: National Academy of Sciences.

National Academy of Sciences (NAS), National Research Council. 1982. *Priorities in Biotechnology Research for International Development.* Washington, D.C.: National Academy Press.

_____. 1984. *Genetic Engineering of Plants.* Washington, D.C.: National Academy Press.

National Association of State Universities and Land-Grant Colleges (NASULCG), Division of Agriculture, Committee on Biotechnology. 1983. *Emerging Biotechnologies in Agriculture: Issues and Policies—Progress Report II.* National Association of State Universities and Land-Grant Colleges.

Office of Technology Assessment (OTA). 1984. *Commercial Biotechnology.* Washington, D.C.: Office of Technology Assessment.

Redclift, Michael. 1984. *Development and the Environmental Crisis.* London: Methuen.

Rifkin, Jeremy. 1983. *Algeny.* New York: Viking.

Rockefeller Foundation. 1982. *Science for Agriculture.* New York: The Rockefeller Foundation.

Ruttan, Vernon W. 1982. *Agricultural Research Policy.* Minneapolis: University of Minnesota Press.

U.S. Government Interagency Working Group on Competitive and Transfer Aspects of Biotechnology. 1983. *Biobusiness World Data Base.* New York: McGraw-Hill.

Wilkes, Garrison. 1983. "Current Status of Crop Plant Germplasm." *CRC Critical Reviews in Plant Science* 1:133–181.

Wortman, Sterling, and Ralph W. Cummings, Jr. 1978. *To Feed This World.* Baltimore: Johns Hopkins University Press.

# 15

# Value and Ethical Dimensions of Alternative Agricultural Approaches: In Quest of a Regenerative and Just Agriculture

## C. Dean Freudenberger

## Introduction

> In the earliest writings we find that the prophet and scholar alike have lamented the loss of soils and have warned people of the consequences of their wasteful ways. It seems that we have forever talked about land stewardship and the need for a land ethic, and all the while soil destruction continues, in many places at an accelerated pace. Is it possible that we simply lack enough stretch of our ethical potential to evolve a set of values capable of promoting a sustainable agriculture? [Jackson, 1980:7]

These words by Wes Jackson, the Director of the Land Institute at Salina, Kansas, clearly state the historical and contemporary dilemma we face. His question about the possibility of evolving a set of values capable of promoting a sustainable (regenerative) agriculture is the basic one addressed here. As elusive as the subject and definition of values may be, I find that one can indeed identify an emerging set of values in the literature and practices of alternative agriculture which can, at least in a tentative way, answer Jackson's question constructively.[1] The equally fundamental question—Can the political will be generated to implement such values?—is not discussed in this chapter.

For the purpose of developing a working definition, "alternative approaches to agriculture" refers to the multitude of significant efforts evolving across this nation, as well as internationally, which seek to reduce, either completely or partially, dependence upon petro-chemicals (a depleting and non-renewable resource); to reduce the substantial losses of soil, water, animal and plant species; to reduce the negative environmental impact of current approaches; and to promote a freedom from the fear about family, rural community, and financial stress which is so much a part of U.S. agriculture, and world agriculture, today. What unfolds in this brief essay is one practitioner/observer's attempt to make some sense out of a massive array of effort and experimentation, most of which is occurring outside government and state college and university agricultural research and training establishments. My observations and insights are based on thirty-nine years of work and reflection in nearly 60 food-deficit nations of the temperate, tropical and sub-tropical world; in agricultural development schemes; and more recently in the agriculturally-related subject areas of political philosophy, theology, cultural anthropology and social ethics.

The objective of this essay is to help clarify the ethical and value issues and choices which must be considered in the selection of national agricultural research goals. Many of these have been raised or presented in a new light by the critiques and suggested alternatives found in the literature and practices of alternative agriculture. Here I have simply tried to present in outline form the emerging values and the accompanying implementation guidelines found therein. In their quest for a regenerative and just agriculture, those seeking alternatives raise four fundamental questions regarding the values and goals of both agriculture and society:

1. Can social and agricultural systems be developed which stress the importance of responsible freedom in building a responsible society?
2. Can social and agricultural systems be developed which provide meaning in one's work and in one's relationships with society and natural environment?
3. Can social and agricultural systems be developed which recognize the primacy of life and its pattern of sustenance (in a full ecological sense)?
4. Can social and agricultural systems be developed which recognize the need to include the welfare (health, stability, integrity, beauty, harmony) of future generations of both human as well as non-human life forms?

## The Problem Context

### Conventional Perspectives

We all struggle to respond to the crisis of U.S. agriculture. Conventional perspectives can be found in The Agricultural Research Service's publication, *Agricultural Research Service Program Plan,* of January, 1983, which outlines the various physical and economic aspects of this crisis:

> . . . but the rate of increase in agricultural productivity apparently is declining. . . . Erosion, a major problem on nearly one-third of our nation's croplands, not only destroys inherent soil fertility and productivity, but also pollutes water supplies and fills reservoirs and lakes with sediments that are laden with chemicals and nutrients. Of our rangeland, 60 percent is in only poor to fair condition and produces less than half its potential. Groundwater supplies are being depleted in large areas of the Southern Plains and the Southwest. Increased salinity results in costs to both agriculture and municipalities; in the Colorado River basin alone, damages were estimated at 53 million dollars annually by the year 2000 unless salt loading can be controlled. . . . Evidence indicates that air pollution reduces productivity more than previously suspected. . . . About three million acres of farmland, nearly one-third of which is prime land, is diverted to non-agricultural uses each year. [USDA, 1983:17]

Elsewhere, the report stresses that: "A flagging agricultural technology—costly and erratic food supplies and depleted natural resources—is not in the national interest" (USDA, 1983:9). In human terms it is suggested that: "We need to help farmers and ranchers escape their current economic dilemma—net incomes that are comparable to those of the 1930s" (USDA, 1983:15).

The crisis is thus of massive proportions and cuts across the entire social, economic, environmental and resource spectrum of the nation. No aspect of agriculture is unaffected. The crisis demands substantial response. Yet agricultural research programs targeted at the clarification of the causes of, and strategies for dealing with the crisis have involved only 2 percent of the federal research and development budget over the past ten years (U.S. AUB, 1980). Most of the rest went for production-oriented research. Federal allocations fund half of the nation's public sector agricultural research. The Agricultural Research Service of the USDA, which operates a network of over 140 domestic research facilities, had a budget of approximately 460 million dollars for fiscal year 1983. During this same period, the federal government provided about 220 million dollars for the states for agricultural research through several state and federal channels. State appropriations to state agricultural experiment stations amounted to over 500 million dollars in fiscal year 1981. Private sector research expenditures are not known with any degree of accuracy, but estimates are that industry is spending from 750 million to 2.5 billion dollars annually (GAO, 1983). In the case of the private sector, expenditures for research are focused on specific industry-related needs. This represents more than half of all estimated funds available for agricultural research in the United States. Thus, in proportion to the crisis, the response of the nation's agricultural research program is minimal and fragmented.

*Alternative Perspectives*

The response of the various alternative agriculture groups to losses in soil, water, forests, grasslands, fauna, birds, insects, and rural people and their communities has been quite different. Generally, they have sought the historical, ethical, value, and ecological roots of such losses. As one who has lived and worked on the fringes of the growing deserts of six continents, I have become convinced that these deserts are the result, not so much of cyclical climatic changes, but rather of agricultural systems insensitive to the ecological and value foundations upon which regenerative and just agricultural systems are built (see also UN, 1977).

Generally speaking, one can observe that value concerns and relationships about the primacy of the land, the health of the biosphere, and the general health of the human community, are still emerging and are rarely addressed in any systematic fashion. These value concerns and relationships are mentioned in agricultural writings, but not with a priority demanding structured attention and social determination to re-shape social, economic and political structures significantly. It too often seems that all this will be left to be addressed by future societies. Value concerns relating to such intangibles as the beauty, harmony and integrity of the whole biotic community (values which Aldo Leopold [1970] raised in the early years of this century) remain in the background because of the inability of our present commodity orientated society to find ways to address them adequately. When society's value base is in the realm of utility (with hoped-for spinoffs for the human community and biospheric welfare), problems have a way of being defined narrowly, with ensuring narrowly articulated strategies. However, to construct a problem statement and plan of action for agriculture and agricultural research without clarification of value assumptions and identification of the basic and inclusive values involved, is risky business (for a general discussion, see Freudenberger, 1981).

On the positive side of things, and as the central point of this chapter, social and technological structures broaden as values broaden. This is something one can observe amid the efforts of many of those working with alternative approaches in agriculture. As value orientations in agriculture are broadened and articulated to include more ecologically and socially just ways, alternative agriculturalists begin to develop and practice a more intentional concern for the welfare of the whole biotic community of life. In view of what is now known about the magnitude and complexity of the agricultural problem, and given the technological tools at the disposal of the research establishment, they argue that our society must begin to ponder the possibility of achieving a more regenerative and just agriculture (in terms defined below). Whether large-scale systems can achieve this is not clear. However, because agriculture has so much to do with the maintenance of a healthy biosphere and a healthy human community, and because the impact of agriculture is felt in almost every niche of the world, the approach that many alternative agriculturalists are taking is a logical one to pursue, particularly in view of the resource limits and environmental and social stresses we face today and in the coming century.

The search for alternative agricultural systems has had two results. First, a clarifying critique of the weaknesses of prevailing systems has been developed. Second, a challenging conceptualization about the new directions that change can take has emerged.

### Value Questions and Considerations

One of the most significant characteristics of the alternative agricultural literature and experiments is the greater self-awareness those involved have of the underlying values of their approaches. In contrast, discussions of values and goals in the conventional literature tends to be general and rather perfunctory. However, even though the alternative literature is more self-aware, there are many views and many values discussed. The need then is to try to find common themes, questions, concerns, and threads. The four basic questions raised at the outset and discussed below represent one way of seeking and exploring these commonalities.

### Can Social and Agricultural Systems Be Developed Which Stress the Importance of Responsible Freedom in Building a Responsible Society?

The idea of a regenerative (often called sustainable) agriculture emerged in part out of the debate about the nature of a responsible society (see Bock, 1974; and Brown, 1981 for a full discussion). The central question is: "How can a society be judged responsible if it cannot be sustained independently of external and/or non-renewable resources? How can the idea of justice be maintained without a sustainable justice?" Can we entertain for much longer the idea of a free and just society if the resource base of that society becomes eroded? Can a society consider itself to be just if it is sustained at the expense of other societies in other places? The notion that a responsible society has to incorporate long-range time horizons and a clear idea of stability emerged. Among those exploring and developing alternative agricultural systems, one observes a growing awareness that has not been evident in conventional agricultural research. It is that the future is threatened by preoccupations with the immediate goals of production efficiency and economic survival. Generally speaking, good agriculture is currently defined in terms of high yields, inexpensive food for public consumption, and the generation of wealth for a wider range of investments—all understood within relatively limited time horizons. Issues of species decline, climate change, the quality of rural society, the exhaustion of water, soil, vegetative and animal resources, and agricultural land conversion, go largely unaddressed. The paradox of the dysfunctionality of high production yields has become clear in much of the literature on alternative agriculture.

The values which were highlighted in the debate about responsible freedom for achieving a responsible society (something that obviously includes a responsible agriculture) can be seen to underlie deliberations about alternative agricultural systems. Many ideas about the implications of regenerative systems have emerged from this general value context. For example, as the Honorable George E. Brown, Jr. (1981:5) has expressed it: "Agricultural production technologies that are not sustainable imply a violation of inter-generational equity, and therefore a violation of the ethical goal of agriculture."

Clearly, responsible society involves much more than economic viability (as important as this is) measured in short term reference frames and with measuring criteria that exclude other important costs.

*Can Social and Agricultural Systems Be Developed Which Provide Meaning in One's Work and in One's Relationships with Society and Natural Environment?*

Rene Dubos (1980), Aldo Leopold (1970), and others of similar disposition, speak of meaningful relationships as foundational in the search for a more responsible agriculture. Wendell Berry, in *The Unsettling of America* (1977), and *The Gift of Good Land* (1981), stresses the primary importance of values involving relationships and meaningfulness in work. In "People, Land, and Community," Berry (1983:50) articulates the point:

> For human life to continue [in one place] through successive generations requires good use [of the land and soil], good work, all along. For in any agricultural place that will waste or erode—and all will—bad work does not permit "muddling through;" sooner or later it ends human life. Human continuity is virtually synonymous with good farming, and good farming obviously must outlast the life of any good farmer. For it to do this . . . we must have community. Without community, the good work of a single farmer or a single family will not mean much or last long. . . . In its cultural aspect, the community is an order of memories preserved . . . in instructions, songs, and stories, and . . . in ways. A healthy culture holds

> preserving knowledge in place for a long time. . . . The essential wisdom accumulates . . . much as fertility builds in the soil.

These insights raise the issue of the nature of right human relations to the sustaining, ordering, limiting, and creating world. If the well-being of the whole biosphere is considered important, then the question can be asked: "What is the place of human well-being in relation to the well-being of the whole?" In much of the literature of alternative agriculture, the idea is put forth that the welfare of humanity (from the individual to the species) needs to be understood in the context of the welfare of the whole biosphere. This orientation involves a new and more inclusive understanding of relationships, responsibilities, limits, and opportunities. It also clearly challenges the dominant patterns of human technologies operative in the biosphere today. Regarding one of these, agricultural specialization, Richard Harwood (1983:38) observes:

> My own feeling is that the most effective paradigm boundary exists with respect to the desired relationship between our production systems and the natural world. . . . We have been working for decades to free ourselves from the vagaries of nature, to insulate our production systems in every possible way. We sterilize soil and we want to eliminate weeds and all insect life. We, in effect, try as much as possible to grow our own monocrop corn in sterile environments.

The value of meaningful relationships, not only among ourselves as individuals, families, rural societies and the society as a whole, but with the natural world about us, raises the question of whether or not there is a way to proceed into the future which is less threatening to the physical and biological resource base of agriculture. Wendell Berry (1983:51) suggests that there is a critical need for new approaches to thinking about farming systems. For example, he suggests that it would be useful to ponder how to use a piece of land, perhaps a hillside, for hundreds of years. By employing this frame of reference and time horizon, one can more adequately contemplate the full dimensions of agriculture, while also correcting for the narrowness of our reductionistic and utilitarian models. For example, he points out that work on such a hillside farm is never finished. It is continuous, having a past and a future. Meaningful work also requires integrity. To stay on the land requires a good community. It requires a neighborhood of good neighbors who are mutually dependent on each other. It needs the memories, songs, and stories mentioned earlier. This all goes beyond the information and efficiencies of the industrial paradigm of resources, labor management, consumers and government. Recently, I traveled extensively in the southern provinces of France as the guest of the Laboratoire de Socio-economie Agraire et Regionale, under the Ministry of Agriculture. I visited "hillside farms" which have been in existence for more than five centuries. I talked with fourth and fifth generations of farm families. I was thrilled by the quality of the small market towns which help to maintain the quality of life for the farming community. What we so often speculate about as being possible for American agriculture is an exciting reality in other parts of the world—although it may be threatened by industrial paradigms and practices.

*Can Social and Agricultural Systems Be Developed Which Recognize the Primacy of Life and Its Patterns of Sustenance?*

Life, used in an all-inclusive sense, is understood by many in agro-ecology and agricultural and environmental ethics, to be a fundamental value. Proponents of alternative approaches to agriculture emphasize the point that we all share a common origin and common destiny with all life forms in the biosphere. Much of their work draws upon a world view which includes an appreciation of the inter-connectedness and interdependencies of all life. This is to say, different species and habitats help to maintain the health of the whole. All living things are understood to be dependent on essential support systems, many of them critically interdependent (for a full discussion, see Freudenberger, 1984). Within this ecologically orientated frame of reference, agriculture is approached. The idea of a regenerative system for the production of food and fiber to meet human needs unfolds. The challenge raised here is for humans to maintain the integrity of the biotic community, respecting its own value and integrity, while maintaining the productivity of the resource base for agriculture itself.[2]

Interestingly, this emerging view is close to that found in traditional societies. For example, as Chief Seattle, leader of the Suquamish tribe in the Washington territory, pointed out (Woolman, 1971:198):

This we know. The earth does not belong to man; man belongs to the earth. This we know. All things are connected like the blood which unites one family. All things are connected.

Whatever befalls the earth befalls the sons of the earth. Man did not weave the web of life; he is merely a strand in it. Whatever he does to the web, he does to himself.

For almost four decades, I have observed the general consequences of people and their acquired wisdom having been displaced from the land during the many years of colonial occupation to make room for sugar cane, rubber, groundnuts, palm oil, tobacco, cotton, maize and beef cattle. Forests were destroyed in the process. A vast knowledge base was lost. The food base of the tropical forest and savanna was lost. Stating it bluntly for the purpose of clarity, it has become quite obvious to me that humans must choose to be in harmony with natural integrities if they are to survive.  Somehow, tomorrow's farming systems must be built into the pattern of living things—they must become analogues of forests and prairies.  The implications and challenges to agricultural science and the research process are as hopeful as they are awesome.  Since these orientations have not yet attracted wide-spread attention, and because of insufficient work in these areas, it is difficult to imagine the potentials adequately.  But it seems to me that this point about natural integrities is at the heart of the discussion of criteria for selection of national research goals in agricultural research and development.

A powerful and poignant example of the critical importance of these interrelationships struck me in the mid-1950s.  I was working to help develop beef-cattle production in what was then called the Belgian Congo. With the influx of cattle herding activity, and later on as a result of soldiers hunting game with modern weapons, the hippopotamus indigeneous to the local tributaries of the Congo river became extinct.  The result:  a once relatively parasite free community of people became afflicted with shistosomiasis.  Our family baby-sitter died of internal hemorrhaging. Why?  The natural integrities were destroyed.  The hippopotamus functioned to keep the rivers flowing regularly by foraging on the natural plants growing in the rivers.  When the hippopotamus is gone, the grasses grow and slow the normal movement of water.  Thus, in more quiet streams and rivers, the larvae of the Bilharzia snail multiply.  People who for years carried water from these streams, and who bathed along the banks, became infected.  Many died.  Thus, many years ago I learned the lessons which Berry and others are trying to teach today.  Not only must we learn these lessons for our own well-being, but also for the value of contributing to the maintenance of the fragile and wonderous integrity of the planet's ecosystems.

### Can Social and Agricultural Systems Be Developed Which Include The Value of Future Generations and Their Welfare?

The importance of maintaining the resource base of agriculture, and of the health of the whole biosphere itself, is acknowledged in most contemporary agricultural literature.  However, as previously stated, the problem is that this value is too frequently forgotten in the immediacy of the day-to-day struggle for survival, be it at the production or distribution end of the equation.  In seeking to take the welfare of future generations seriously, the literature on alternative agriculture asks such questions as: Does contemporary agriculture really provide guarantees for a healthy environment and a strong resource base for future generations?  Can agricultural research be redirected to adequately feed and employ the generations to come or will it continue the green revolution pattern of buying a little more time until better solutions along more sustainable lines are found? Will contemporary agriculture, with its emphasis on production efficiencies and profit, enable national communities everywhere to restore soil, vegetative cover and animal life, and capture more of the sun's energy? Will the issues of current overproduction remain a basic concern in the western world? To what degree does our western thought and action reflect preoccupations with contemporary issues at the expense of the future? Careful study of the recent Busch and Lacy study (1983) is sobering and provides the reader with significant insights about the present paralysis in agricultural research. Unfortunately, our failure to lay the groundwork of basic research (forgetting the demands of the near future) will take its toll in the coming decades as the returns of traditional applied research diminish (Budiansky, 1984:69).

## Towards a New Paradigm

A paradigm is a basic image, model, or standard through which reality is interpreted and action is guided. Clusters of interrelated propositions arise from a paradigm and they function as a conceptual framework for analyzing, understanding and predicting phenomena. Paradigms are determined by some general consensus among practitioners of a given discipline. Culture and historical factors are inescapable components of such a consensus. Assumptions about relations of humanity to nature underlie them. The general values underlying the four basic questions just discussed contribute to (and grow out of) a paradigm construct somewhere between a model of co-existence to one of a participatory human interaction with the other living communities and patterns of the biosphere. Since values and paradigms are interacting, there is a need for constant re-examination to keep them coherent. It is important to recognize this interrelationship.

New paradigms can help in the search to revitalize political, economic and scientific analysis by pointing to ethical and societal goals that flow from the emerging values underlying the new paradigm. One can see that the search for an alternative agriculture is shaped by, and consistent with, the values of meaningful relationships and work, life and future, as defined in a socio-biological and ecological sense. These values also provide a focal point for criticism of the industrial agricultural model. Some of the literature stresses the losses of soil, water, vegetative, animal, and atmospheric resources and the heavy dependence on oil and the oil derivatives. Other literature criticizes the negative impact of contemporary agriculture upon the health of human communities.

In more positive terms, this new paradigm offers support for a new scientific analysis based on longer-term and more holistic concepts involving people and culture, resources, and environmental enhancement (see, for example, Altieri, 1983). Interdisciplinary thinking is encouraged because of the interdependencies seen in all of these relationships and value orientations. Already, one can see that three main cornerstones have emerged in the alternative systems paradigm which serve to hold together values, practices, and a broadened perspective of the problem and goals of agriculture.

## The Idea of Regenerative Agricultural Science

The word "sustainable" is being more and more replaced by the word "regenerative." For some, the word sustainability does not define time or the quality of the process adequately. For example, it is possible to sustain for quite a long time something that is not good. Our present agricultural system can be sustained for as long as there exists an abundant and relatively inexpensive and reliable source of fossil fuel. The idea of "regeneration" defines the time horizon and processes of production more clearly. A regenerative agriculture is generally conceived as one in which the number of people, the rate of use and regeneration of essential resources, and the rate of waste production are within the capacity of the earth to support and absorb, and where an acceptable quality of human life can be sustained indefinitely. The concept involves new assumptions, and may require new technologies, new uses of existing technology and new social and economic infrastructures. Regenerative agriculture attempts to maintain and improve the organic content of soil, soil microbiological health, moisture capacity and biomass diversity. In other words, it regenerates its own resource base. Essential non-renewable resources are used sparingly. Waste never exceeds the absorption capacity of a given eco-system. Regenerative technologies are site-specific and community, farmer, and farm-family orientated. The regenerative approach tries to respect the intricate regulatory mechanisms of nature involving hundreds of major interrelationships (including the critical but usually neglected matters of maintaining normal radiation patterns of incoming light through the ozone shield, normal flows of oxygen, carbon dioxide, and nitrogen generation and absorption), a healthy soil microbiology, and diversified grasslands and forest complexes, with purity of air, sea and fresh water supplies of the planet (for a thorough consideration of these issues, see UNEP, 1976–81). These concerns form vital building blocks for a new agricultural science.

The concept of regenerative agriculture requires one to look at the problem of American agriculture in a very different light. It suggests that we venture entirely beyond the present system to a much broader and perhaps potentially more valuable one. Research methodologies are suggested which would involve team efforts on the part of the animal and plant population biologists, ecologists, rural sociologists, social ethicists, anthropologists, political philosophers, climatologists, soil physicists and nutritionists, all working for the development of an agro-ecology (for a discussion, see Gabel and Rodale, 1984).

## The Idea of an Ecologically and Socially Based Concept of Justice in Agriculture

A regenerative agriculture cannot survive unless it is socially just. This fact is seen in history. In recent years, growing human populations, the industrial impact upon the earth's ecosystems and the spectacle of desertification on every continent have led to a heightened ecological awareness. In addition, concepts of individual freedom have emerged during the past two decades which begin to acknowledge the obligation of present generations for the welfare of future generations. Individuals and societies are more and more understood as interrelated members of the biosphere; consequently equity and justice must be defined and sought in terms of the value of all life forms (Blackstone, 1980). There is a growing awareness that moral responsibility must be understood in much more inclusive and long-range terms. The concept of justice within the whole environmental/ecological movement is thus developing to include all life. Consequently, the idea of a just society and a just agriculture is redefined to include (and stress) the means by which all share the common heritage of the earth in ways so that all is maintained in health, and a healthy future is guaranteed.

As the interdependencies of the biosphere are better understood, the question of justice among non-human forms of life is raised in some of the literature on alternative approaches to agricultural systems. The question about whether or not it is fair to exhaust a prairie or marshland, is raised. So too are such questions about fairness and responsibility in long-range ecological perspectives with reference to whales, porpoises, elephants, gazelles, buffalo, or the pheasant and quail in fence rows. For reasons of enlightened self-interest, as well as intrinsic value reasons, the question is more and more being raised about how to keep healthy, natural evolutionary parameters.

Consistent with the ideas of regeneration and justice in the ecological sense is the need for the maintenance of a reserve capacity in every agricultural system. This is more and more understood as a necessary step for survival and prevention of sudden catastrophic environmental or natural resource collapse. In the literature on alternative agricultural systems, there is identification of the need for research into biological and environmental limits of the carrying capacity of local, regional, and national agricultural ecosystems. There is recognition of the need to learn to live within these limits. There is a growing recognition that the essential requirements for the health of any organism, be it an earthworm or the whole biosphere, are that non-renewable resources need to be used sparingly and be recycled, that every attempt be made to live within the limits of renewable resource requirements, and that wastes from the process do not exceed the capacity of a given ecosystem to reabsorb.

*Interdisciplinary Approaches*

Throughout the literature on alternative agriculture, one finds examples of approaches to agricultural research that stress agriculture's web of interdependencies. Also, there are calls for environmental protection and enhancement, social and biological resource impact determinations, and the maintenance of soil and water resources. Work in perennial grasses, tree crops and integrated cropping systems (including indigenous animals), is crucial to answering such calls. The question of food security needs to be addressed in all comprehensive research projects. The issue of food security must be understood, not in terms of stockpiles of commodities and storage at strategic locations, but in terms of rehabilitating and expanding the diversity of integrated cropping systems, and in the maintenance of a more secure and talented rural community of farmers and their families operating on an appropriate scale. This issue is one that is presently the object of much research and development in the resource-limited nation of Denmark. Such concerns raise the issue of the need for new criteria in agricultural economics to broaden our understandings of efficiency in production and distribution. The literature about alternative approaches focuses on the need to measure productivity from perspectives of resource use and regeneration. Human/biological justice must also be considered in terms of the maintenance of patterns and the integrities of life. In the field of plant and animal biology, whatever contributes to patterns and integrities can be considered useful. Current specialized approaches, which focus only on livestock and plant breeding, or efficiencies in energy use, or salt tolerance, or disease resistance, without addressing the other aspects of the pattern and problem, typically end up being dysfunctional. From this larger interdisciplinary perspective, the basic question becomes: can ways be found to enable the nation's agricultural education and extension establishment to cope with a whole new agenda?

**Summary**

It is difficult to describe the social dynamics and functions of values and paradigms for agriculture, particularly in a short essay. But, it seems to me that to discount these issues or to suggest that they are outside the scope of modern agricultural research is to prolong the time of recognition of the vital nature of these issues. They are an integral and motive part of both conventional and alternative approaches. The idea of a regenerative and just agriculture is not a throw-back to some kind of a counter-cultural or utopian "Walden Pond" mentality. To the contrary, the idea is consistent with emerging scientific and ethical understandings of our ecological, technological, and social worlds. Together, these new orientations can help greatly in goal conceptualization and problem analysis.

The need for a goal of achieving a socially and ecologically just and regenerative agricultural system must be seen as emerging from our present national and world-wide crisis of degenerating social and ecological systems. A constant theme within the literature of alternative agriculture is that agriculture, to be meaningful and lasting, must rest on a national community of highly skilled farmers who make the commitment to farming as a way of life.

We can understand what it is to work toward the goal, and hence, can have guidelines for choosing new research goals if we subscribe to the values of responsible freedom for responsible society; meaningfulness in relationships and work, life, and sustenance; and the welfare of the future.

A society conducts itself responsibly only if it balances immediate or short-term goals against the long-term goal of perpetuating the conditions which make it viable. Responsible freedom differs from the licentiousness of thinking only of short-term gratifications. A commitment to sustainability is a commitment to responsibility.

Meaningfulness in relationships and work can be achieved only if natural integrities are preserved. Natural integrities preserve the resource base, and it is because the slowly acquired knowledge of local natural integrities accumulated by traditional cultures has been replaced by an insensitive science that we are involved in an agricultural system that destroys its own base. Meaningfulness in relationships and work requires a recognition and experiencing of the human place in the biotic as well as the human community. Community, continuity, and integrity bring short and long-term goals into harmony.

The value of life and sustenance is based on the recognition of the integrity of the biotic community as the support system for all life, and the role that every form of life plays in that community. It is, thereby, the recognition of the value of all life forms. The challenge we face is the reconciliation of preserving the integrity of the biotic community for its own sake and for the sake of maintaining a productive resource base.

The importance of the welfare of future generations requires that we redirect agricultural research so that it addresses the problem of feeding and employing future generations in meaningful work.

The emergence of a new paradigm for understanding the human condition both facilitates the recognition (and adoption) of these values and grows out of them. The recognition that humans are participants in the biotic community rather than mere utilizers of it can function to revitalize political, economic, and scientific analysis, and can lead to the idea of a regenerative agriculture. For such a science to achieve its goals, it must not only utilize interdisciplinary approaches, but must keep in sight the claims that the future is entitled to make on the way we use our resources today.

With this understanding of the underlying values and the new paradigm that is emerging from the alternative agricultural movement, one can identify some ways that U.S. agricultural research goals need to be expanded. Not only must we strive for a regenerative agriculture, we must also recognize that such an idea is dependent upon a secure, prosperous, numerous and highly skilled national community of farmers who are well supported by a sound social (and research) infrastructure and a secure rural society. The implications of a regenerative and just agriculture for the purpose of human community renewal and a rehabilitated and enhanced earth poses an awesome challenge to the nation's research establishment of scientists, program administrators, budget and policy makers, and to the national society at large as it searches for new insights about national security and prioritizes its concerns accordingly.

## Notes

1. In the references and bibliography accompanying this chapter an attempt has been made to include a cross section of the literature describing or promoting the values and practices of alternative agriculture. This was prepared with the assistance of James Riker, a graduate student in Sociology at the University of Kentucky.
2. For a discussion of how a growing recognition of natural-human interdependencies is related to an awareness of the intrinsic value of an increasing variety of natural phenomena, see Whitehead (1966).

## References

Altieri, Miguel A. 1983. *Agroecology: The Scientific Basis of Alternative Agriculture.* Berkeley: University of California, Division of Biological Control.
Bennett, John W. 1977. "Social Theory and the Social Order of the Hutterian Community." *Mennonite Quarterly Review* 51:292–307.
Berry, Wendell. 1977. *The Unsettling of America: Culture and Agriculture.* San Francisco: Sierra Club.
_____. 1981. *The Gift of Good Land.* San Francisco: North Point Press.
_____. 1982. "Ordinary Excellence." *Rain* 9(1):20–21.
_____. 1983. "People, Land and Community." *Sierra* 68(5):48–52.
Blackstone, William T. 1980. "The Search for an Environmental Ethic." In *Matters of Life and Death,* ed. Tom Regan, pp. 299–335. Philadelphia: Temple University Press.
Bock, Paul. 1974. *In Search of a Responsible World Society.* Philadelphia: Westminster Press.
Brown, George E., Jr. 1981. "Stewardship in Agriculture." Address before the Center for the Study of Values, University of Delaware, July 14, 1981.

Brown, Lester. 1981. *Building a Sustainable Society.* New York: W. W. Norton.

Budiansky, Stephen. 1984. "Trouble Amid Plenty." *Atlantic Monthly* 253:65–69.

DeForest, Paul H. 1980. "Technical Choice in the Context of Social Values." In *Appropriate Technology and Social Values: A Critical Appraisal,* ed. Franklin A. Long and Alexandra Oleson, pp. 11–25. Cambridge, Mass.: Ballinger.

Dubos, Rene. 1980. *The Wooing of Earth.* New York: Scribners.

Freudenberger, C. Dean. 1981. *The Gift of Land.* Los Angeles: Franciscan Communication Center.

———. 1984a. *Food for Tomorrow?* Minneapolis: Augsburg.

———. 1984b. "International Implications of U.S. Food Security Programs." In *Food Security in the United States,* ed. Lawrence Busch and William B. Lacy, pp. 343–358. Boulder, Colorado: Westview Press.

Gustafson, James M. 1981. *Ethics from a Theocentric Perspective.* Vol. 1: *Theology and Ethics.* Chicago: University of Chicago Press.

Hadwiger, Don F. 1982. *The Politics of Agricultural Research.* Lincoln: University of Nebraska Press.

Harwood, Richard. 1983. "Why Science Wears Blinders." *New Farm,* 5:38–39.

Jackson, Wes. 1980. *New Roots for Agriculture.* San Francisco: Friends of the Earth.

———. 1983. "Food Security in the United States." In *Science, Agriculture and the Politics of Research,* ed. Lawrence Busch and William B. Lacy. Boulder, Colorado: Westview Press.

Joy, Charles R. 1950. *The Animal World of Albert Schweitzer.* Boston: Beacon Press.

Kuhn, Thomas S. 1970. *The Structure of Scientific Revolutions.* 2nd ed. Chicago: Chicago University Press.

Lacy, William B., and Lawrence Busch, ed. 1983. *Science, Agriculture and the Politics of Research.* Boulder, Colorado: Westview Press.

Leopold, Aldo. 1970. *A Sand County Almanac: With Essays on Conservation from Round River.* San Francisco: Sierra Club.

Long, Franklin A., and Alexandra Oleson, eds. 1980. *Appropriate Technology and Social Values: A Critical Appraisal.* Cambridge, Mass.: Ballinger.

Lowdermilk, W. C. 1978. *The Conquest of the Land Through Seven Thousand Years.* Agriculture Information Bulletin No. 99. Washington, D.C.: U.S. Government Printing Office.

Schumacher, E. F. 1973. *Small is Beautiful.* New York: Harper & Row.

———. 1979. *Good Work.* New York: Harper & Row.

United Nations. Conference on Desertification, Nairobi. 1977. *Desertification: Its Causes and Consequences.* New York: Pergamon Press.

United Nations Environment Program. *United Nations Environment Programme Annual Review,* 1976–1981.

U.S. Department of Agriculture (USDA). 1983. *Agricultural Research Service Program Plan.* Agricultural Research Service. Miscellaneous Publication No. 1429. Washington, D.C.: U.S. Department of Agriculture.

U.S. General Accounting Office (GAO). 1983. *Federal Agricultural Research Funding: Issues and Concerns.* Report. GAO/RCED-84-20. Washington, D.C.: U.S. General Accounting Office.

U.S. National Agricultural Research and Extension Advisory Users Board (U.S. AUB). 1980. "Report to the President and Congress." Washington, D.C.: U.S. Department of Agriculture.

Whitehead, Alfred North. 1966. *Adventure of Ideas.* New York: Macmillan.

## Suggestions for Further Reading

Altieri, Miguel A., et al. 1983. "Developing Sustainable Agroecosystems." *BioScience* 33(1):45–49.

Batie, Sandra S., and R. G. Healy. 1980. *The Future of American Agriculture as a Strategic Resource.* Washington, D.C.: The Conservation Foundation.

Belden, Joe, et al. 1979. "New Directions in Farm, Land and Food Policies." Papers presented at the Conference on Alternative State and Local Policies, Washington, D.C.

Besson, J.M., and Hardy Vogtmann, eds. 1978. *Towards a Sustainable Agriculture.* Oberwil, Switzerland: International Federation of Organic Agriculture Movements.

Boeringa, R., ed. 1980. *Alternative Methods of Agriculture.* Amsterdam, Netherlands: Elsevier.

Buttel, Frederick H., and O. W. Larson, II. 1979. "Farm Size, Structure, and Energy Intensity: An Ecological Analysis of U.S. Agriculture." *Rural Sociology* 44:471–488.

Clawson, Marion. 1982. "Conserving the Soil." *Proceedings of the Academy of Political Science* 34(3):89–98.

Coomer, J., ed. 1981. *Quest for a Sustainable Society.* New York: Pergamon Press.

Douglass, Gordan, ed. 1984. *Agricultural Sustainability in a Changing World Order.* Boulder, Colorado: Westview Press.

Kiley-Worthington, M. 1981. "Ecological Agriculture: What is it and How is Works," *Agriculture and Environment* 6(4):349–381.

Knorr, Dietrich, ed. 1982. *Sustainable Food Systems.* Westport, Conn.: AVI.

Lockeretz, William, ed. 1983. *Environmentally Sound Agriculture.* New York: Praeger.

Lockeretz, William; G. Shearer; and D. H. Kohl. 1981. "Organic Farming in the Farm Belt." *Science* 211:540–546.

Oelhaf, Robert C. 1978. *Organic Agriculture: Economic and Ecological Comparisons with Conventional Methods.* New York: Halsted Press.

Parikh, Kirit, and Ferenc Rabar, ed. 1981. *Food for All in a Sustainable World: The IIASA Food and Agricultural Program.* Laxenburg, Austria: International Institute for Applied Systems Analysis.

Sampson, Neil. 1982. *Farmland or Wasteland? A Time to Choose.* Emmaus, Penn.: Rodale Press.

Stivers, Robert L. 1976. *The Sustainable Society: Ethics and Economic Growth.* Philadelphia, Penn.: Westminster Press.

Stonehouse, B. 1981. *Biological Husbandry: A Scientific Approach to Organic Farming.* London: Butterworth.

Triplett, Glover B., and David M. Van Doren. 1977. "Agriculture without Tillage." *Scientific American* 236:28–33.

U.S. Department of Agriculture (USDA). 1978. *Improving Soils with Organic Wastes.* Report to Congress in Response to Section 1461 of the Food and Agriculture Act of 1977 (P. L. 95–113). Washington, D.C.: U.S. Government Printing Office.

U.S. Department of Agriculture (USDA). 1980. *Report and Recommendations on Organic Farming.* Washington, D.C.: U.S. Government Printing Office.

# Part VI

# Where Do We Go From Here?

# 16

# Research on Farmer Behavior and Social Organization

## John W. Bennett

**Introduction: Agricultural Research in General Terms**

This chapter attempts to assess research on the behavior and social organization of agricultural producers, with special reference to North America. Because the emphasis is on philosophical and methodological issues, the style and format is that of an essay, rather than a review of literature. The underlying question is: What is the utility of behavioral and social science research in a presumably technical field like agricultural production?

The chapter consists of five parts. First, this introduction, which deals with the role of research in agriculture in broad cultural terms. Next, there is a general discussion of agricultural research from a social science viewpoint. Anthropological perspectives tend to be featured here as in the other sections, since anthropology is the writer's principal disciplinary affiliation. The next two parts consist of analyses of key behavior patterns of agricultural producers: those involving the relationship of indigenous knowledge to exogenous expertise; and those involving the making of operating decisions. These two topics have been selected for intensive presentation since they represent the key elements of agricultural production at the farm level. A summary concludes the chapter.

Agriculture as a human activity has existed for at least 6,000 years, while truly scientific research on agriculture has existed for little more than a century—granted arguable exceptions in the form of practical observation or experimentation by farmers, and by specialists in older civilizations like China. These observations and experiences with crops and resources served to establish agricultural systems which provided sustenance for growing populations.  Obviously scientific-style research is not the only way to create an agriculture with survival value.

The emergence of scientific research in agriculture can be attributed, first, to the emergence of science as a profession:  as science came to dominate the knowledge industry, it spread into all forms of human activity. Second, agricultural research designed to increase the yield of food crops became a necessity if food needs were to be met for the rapidly growing world population.  Third, a burgeoning industrial economy demanded agriculturally-produced materials in quantities beyond the capacity of the semi-subsistence smallholder producer to provide.  Fourth, expanding business enterprise found agriculture a profitable market for sales of tools and other materials needed in farming, and hence developed a stake in increased production.  These factors served to create an establishment of professional research and experimentation in basic plant and animal and resource sciences, and in the economic and structural aspects of production and distribution.  In some countries, especially the U.S., this establishment's ability to communicate its results to the farmer was greatly enhanced by distinctive institutions like the land-grant university and its direct feeder lines into farmer communities.

It seems clear that agricultural research is the tip of an iceberg.  That is, it is not concerned solely with the raising of plants and animals, but has evolved into a series of professional fields linked to academic disciplines and major economic and industrial systems.  For example, research in agricultural economics, including both production and marketing, has acquired most of its standards and primary assumptions from professional economic theory, adjusted to the aims of business and industrial enterprise.  That is, agricultural economics, an established social science *within* agriculture, moved away from its origins in practical managerial advice to farmers, toward general models of economic activity relevant for national levels.[1]  This movement also pulled agriculture into larger institutional systems and away from its distinctive rural patterns.  Rural sociology has a similar history:  increasing involvement with general sociology (although there are recent signs of a move away from academic matters).[2]

Agriculture the world over—and again allowing for exceptions—differs from industrial forms of production insofar as the production base consists of relatively small social units:  families, neighborhood or kin groups, and even individuals.  This has meant that if national or regional production targets are to be made more predictable in order to serve society's wider needs, and if the uncertainties created by climate, weather, and markets are to be lessened, the producers themselves need to be made more responsive to approved methods, and to demands for particular output norms.  However, small-scale producers, by their very size and distance from demand-setting institutions, are relatively free to set their own targets and standards, adjusting them to local conditions and constraints as well as to local levels of self-subsistence.

This fluctuating gap between large-scale objectives and small-scale interests and actions has given rise to research initiatives in agronomy and management designed to induce the producer to perform as the larger system wished him to; and, it is hoped, in his own financial interest as well. However, since the two do not always coïncide, any resulting gap obviously becomes one of the causes of the failure of conformity to external demands. Since compulsory production targets are ruled out in democratic societies, a variety of financial incentives, contracts, subsidies and information are substituted in their place. This provides still another reason for the explosion of agricultural research in North America over the past century; much of the research is devoted, directly or indirectly, to the discovery of more efficient incentives to reduce the uncertainty of product deliveries in a system containing a plethora of small-scale producers.

Still, the situation cuts both ways. The small-scale producer has impressive capacity for tolerating uncertainty and risk—risks that large-scale operators or corporate entities, operating on close margins, could not accept. That is, the variability of productive behavior in this population also reflects its relatively high level of adaptive tolerance. Although this contributes to output uncertainties, it is also a major force enabling the larger system to survive without serious production distortions or delays. The variability results, at macroeconomic levels, in a kind of averaging-out of the responses to market needs. This situation has led to an interest on the part of behavioral and social researchers in determining the foundations of these response patterns. This interest has, of course, been more marked with respect to agriculture in Third World countries, since the uncertainties or unpredictabilities there are much greater.[3]

The efflorescence of such research has meant that the practical tasks and knowledge of the farmer have been translated into academic and professional language. This academicization of agriculture has inevitably led to a conceptual dichotomy: the expert vs. the practitioner, or what we will refer to later as indigenous and exogenous knowledge. Since the accumulating expert knowledge was acquired mainly for practical reasons—to increase production or make it more efficient and profitable—academicization led to the feeling that the expert knew more than the farmer, and that therefore the communication flow was from the expert to the practitioner. This situation was ameliorated in North America by the institution of agricultural extension, in which the intermediary or "broker" role is played by a person educated in expertise but also sympathetic to the farmer and his practical knowledge—and, perhaps, in varying degrees, willing to learn from him. Field trials on representative farms, conducted by farmers themselves, have gradually taken over many of the functions of experiment stations and their well-known isolation from real-world farm contexts and conditions.

However, in agrarian development work in the Third World, the indigenous-exogenous dichotomy has been more evident, since great pressure is generated by development programs for rapid change and increased productivity. The expert, called upon to facilitate such change in a short time, may become understandably frustrated by farmers who resist change, and he may develop the attitude that if farmers or "peasants" are expected to increase yield or output, they should accept everything in the program. Thus, anything short of total acceptance can be interpreted as program failure, and hence, the fault of the "beneficiaries." More understanding views have replaced these simplistic conceptions. Research by anthropologists, rural sociologists, and the accumulation of experience on the part of agricultural experts of all kinds, have gradually made us aware of the relative sophistication of the resource practices and farming methods followed by most local farmers, peasants, and tribesmen (e.g., McAndrews and Chia, 1982). Similar awareness has evolved in North America and Europe wherever "traditional" agricultural systems have persisted due to financial difficulties, high risk, and problematic tenure arrangements preventing suitable returns to scale.

The social sciences are not free of blame for the older attitudes which tended to hold agricultural producers responsible for resisting change. Evolutionary and typological conceptions of agricultural sociology and production cling to the margins of Western social sciences: that "peasants" are less "rational" than farmers; that the raising of animals always requires different social organization than the raising of crops; that cultures differ more than they resemble one another; and so on. Assumptions of this kind may not be completely false, but they represent statistical possibilities of differing strength, and in practice, the tendencies may appear in reverse order, as in cases where thoroughgoing commercial motives appear in communities with exotic religions, colorful rituals, or symbolic conceptions of Nature.[4]

That one should avoid assumptions about evolutionary progressions when dealing with specific empirical situations is demonstrated by the "backward bending supply curve" problem in African livestock production. This phenomenon—essentially a tendency for producers not to respond to high prices for animals and to forego market opportunities— was observed during the first round of development-oriented research on African agriculture during the 1960s and '70s. This behavior accounted for much of the failure of ambitious production and marketing schemes in East and Southern Africa which were based on expectations of positive response. Early conclusions were that African livestock herders were "non-rational," or at least not aware of commercial opportunities.

Later research revealed that the tendency was variable, and in other situations, these same herders did respond positively to price incentives. Therefore it became necessary to determine what factors were responsible for apparently contradictory behavior. The problem required social and behavioral research on incentives and risk: pure economic analysis could not provide answers. Eventually it was noted that the size of herds was a key factor: in periods of extreme drought, for example, herders would hold back on sales in order to preserve a basic herd so as to enable rapid expansion when moisture supplies improved. Hedging was also noted: restraints on sales in order to wait for even higher prices. Low (1980) analyzed data from U.S. and Argentinian ranching communities which demonstrated similar varied behavior. Thus, the supposed non-rational or uneconomic behavior of African herders turned out to be as "rational" as similar behavior by modern ranchers.[5]

As data like these have accumulated, the role of research in agricultural management and production has undergone a change. First, the concept of economic rationality has shifted away from concern with utility maximization as the major objective of human productive behavior to more substantive or optimizing concepts. While increase of output remains a major objective of most research programs, more effort is now exerted on determining how increases can be achieved without disruption of the social bases of production, and without abuse of resources.[6] More realistic targets are accepted, with due recognition of the realm of possibility in complex social and geographical contexts.

Second, the topics of research have changed: gene technology is an obvious one, but more relevant to the themes of this paper are experiments in multiple-row and inter-row cropping, small-scale machinery, organic methods of fertilization, and less destructive methods of tillage.[7] Studies of the social components of managerial systems are more frequent than in the past, especially for developing countries. Such changes are all to the good, but in the eyes of the critics of the research establishment, inadequate to the needs.

The basic issue is perhaps not so much a matter of specific topics of research, but how the system of production in particular cases is geared to the economic market, and how this impedes desired changes in the system. The use of environmentally hazardous chemicals is not always a matter of choice, but may be a necessity for farmers who must obtain the largest possible yield in order to stay in business and fulfill financial obligations. Farmers in Western Iowa do not wish to encourage severe soil erosion, but they may have no choice, considering current costs of production and family income demands. Even where a more conservationist approach or a more modest production target is possible, farmers adapted to a high-cost regime may find it difficult to change because of the opportunity costs of such changes in work routine, machinery, and so on.

Such constraints against changes in farming methods and research topics underline the need for different styles of research in the management field. Until recently, the institutional imperatives of high-yield, high-cost mechanized farming were taken for granted and were not a topic for research in themselves. While the abuses attributable to this system were understood, research designed to handle the emerging problems was essentially ameliorative—suggesting incremental repairs within the system, but no radical change. In the view of the radical experimentalists, the need is for research on fundamental alterations in the way modern agriculture is inserted in the national social and economic structure. This has directed attention to small farmers whose operations have generally been less abusive of resources, but whose economy suffers from the excessive costs associated with small scale. In the field of social action, new farm organizations designed to influence political and economic arrangements have proliferated in North America. Agricultural establishments, with their evident stake in the existing system, have had little to do with such movements, nor have they displayed great interest in doing research on them.

The changes taking place in agricultural society, economy, and politics therefore underscore the growing need for a better understanding of the social basis of agricultural production. The existing system in North America evolved as a practical enterprise designed to achieve production goals. The focus was on agronomy and economy; society and behavior were taken as givens or conceived as voluntary means for implementing change and accepting technology. If the desired changes did not materialize, the social-behavioral component was considered to be a constraint in the system, and further inducements to conform were attempted. Research on these social phenomena was performed, but episodically and in the absence of clearly formulated aims, methods, and theory.

In the next section of the chapter we shall define social and behavioral research in agriculture and outline some of its main themes.

### Behavioral and Social Research on Agricultural Producers

By "behavioral research" we mean the study of thoughts and actions of producers as individuals, or individuals taken as exemplifying particular socioeconomic groups.[8] However, even in the latter case, data will be collected on particular individuals since that is the ultimate source of information on social action. The objective is to show how individuals *respond to* certain social and economic stimuli. There is a question as to whether the individuals studied can be taken as representative of aggregates *prior* to the research operation; that is, whether sufficient "background" data exists to permit sampling of such typical individuals as part of the research design. This depends on the context.

By "social research" we mean the study of groups *qua* groups or social categories. Such research is typically generalized at the outset; the method of data collection is generally that of the survey. The data are aggregated; the objectives of the research are to produce statistically generalizable statements about dominant tendencies or patterns. Research on a few individuals may precede social research and serve to establish the problems and hypotheses. However, the individuals are taken as specimens of known data categories: income; land ownership; mode of production; size of family; and so on. When the research is conducted in regions or populations for which considerable information already exists as to conditions which induce variance in behavior or outcome, the prior empirical behavioral step may be eliminated. However, it is the view of the writer that this is always risky, especially in rapidly-changing situations.

While behavioral and social research are often closely linked, the two modalities also have independent functions. Behavioral research on agricultural production is generally concerned with solving particular problems of incentive, motivation, and decision, or of resistance to, or acceptance of techniques and strategies: that is, problems concerned with details of judgement, attitude, awareness, knowledge, and technical actions. Social research, as previously suggested, is more often conducted on populations whose behavior is better understood. The number of unknowns in the research situation is therefore critical: when the producer population is drawn from, say, a Third World "peasant" region whose culture is little known and poorly described in the literature, behavioral-level research may be crucial. If the population consists of, say, North American grain farmers, much can be assumed about their behavior; *i.e.,* the way they make decisions, evaluate results, respond to needs for change. This is because the research population is educated ("socialized") in the commercial market mode of production. To the extent that it is, its "culture" (generalized thought and behavior patterns), can be taken as a given. Even so, there are slip-ups and ambiguities, especially with regard to intangible influences, like national political moods or optimism-pessimism continua that may influence decisions or responses to incentives. There is almost always some need for behavioral-level work in even the most studied farm populations. However, much depends on the nature of the questions asked.

## Behavioral Research

The fundamental limitation of behavioral research in agriculture has to do with the problem of behavior change. There is a paradox here: the purpose of most such research is to facilitate change in the behavior of agricultural producers; hence, if the desired or recommended changes occur, then the research is terminated, its purpose fulfilled. One may argue that there is an infinite regression: there will always be need for change, and hence the need for research. However, the goals of such research must inevitably change; they must be responsive to new needs and new directives. Granted; but if the research is conceived of in terms of the standard "scientific" mode of testable hypotheses which delineate general tendencies or relationships among variables, then flexibility tends to be lost. Once demonstrated, a particular relationship between social organization, human behavior, and agrarian techniques is liable to be taken as fixed, invariant. This view is inherent in the basic social science paradigm of discovery, modeled on the physical sciences, but more specifically, on the conventional concept of culture. In this concept, cultures exist, and once delineated, their characteristics can be used as guides to future outcomes. In contrast to this approach, there is the view that a culture is a time-slice describing general behavior subject to change as circumstances or conditions alter.

In agriculture, the behavioral time-slice consists of a set of techniques and strategies appropriate to particular current conditions of uncertainty and risk. If survival is the ultimate goal of a population engaged in production, then the techniques and strategies will inevitably change as survival conditions are no longer met. There will always be a time lag; in fact, the lag phenomenon is one of the major reasons for conducting research on the need for alternative strategies. Thus, research on agricultural behavior is related to particular sequences and processes of change, and is not, on the whole, an attempt to discover invariant relationships.

An argument on the other side—namely, that there do exist invariant relationships and tendencies which are available for discovery, is based on certain universal aspects of human thought processes, in particular, "rational choice," or the way the human mentality functions in instrumental, or goal-oriented contexts. This view has been elaborated from different perspectives by various scholars; e.g., Herbert Simon (1954) and Mancur Olson (1965). There is no need to question these underlying principles: the fact that agrarian producers everywhere, and at all levels of economic integration and development, think in similar basic categories can be taken as demonstrated. This, however, is not the main issue. While farmers everywhere may think in similar "deep structures," they must also respond to endlessly varying circumstances and influences. Such responses will be shaped by unique experiences, as well as situational values and norms. This variability constitutes the essence of the mandate for research on decision-making.

In development work in Third World countries, the principal goal has been to increase and stabilize production at higher levels of output and efficiency. This is viewed as a survival necessity, at least for the countries taken as national entities. This has meant that the farmers are expected to perform like agricultural producers in developed countries where agriculture is an integral part of the national economy. The producers thus are expected to assimilate the general world-view of these economies, which are based on the idea of maximum output at the least cost, with an appropriate fraction of gain to the producers: that is, the "capitalist" mode of production. ("Capitalist" is put in quotes because the general goals are considered appropriate for all national economic systems: for true capitalists, as well as for existing forms of collectivism.) The producers are expected to demand some sort of reward for their efforts other than the satisfaction of serving national needs. Inherent in this expectation is the idea that people everywhere require such rewards over and above survival necessities or ideological enthusiasm. This, too, represents a recognition of possible behavioral regularities transcending particular cultures.

We have, then, the following: the behavioral substratum of agricultural production (or in general, purposive or instrumental behavior) consists of two principal elements: first, the purposive or "rational" impetus, which is a way of relating means to ends so that the ends sought are reasonably approximated. Second, the "reward" impetus, which relates rewards to immediate needs and definitions of satisfaction, which may or may not correspond to the goals or imperatives of large-scale plans and objectives. Two main conditions establish the need for research. First, there are the circumstances or situations that modify the operations of rational thought in particular cases, and the "cultural" or situational definitions of need and want that influence expectations. Second, there is the temporal lag between changing situations which require behavioral change, and the perception or awareness of the need for altered strategies.

Clearly one of the basic modalities in the latter case is learning. If lag exists, and it almost always does (for good and bad reasons), then the question is how the producers can learn the new techniques required for survival or for satisfaction of whatever level of reward they desire. Little has been done with basic learning processes in agricultural behavior, since the clinical controls associated with research on human learning rarely exist in field situations. However, it is apparent from the two decades of development work in peasant and tribal agriculture that the rate of learning is not fixed, or easily generalized across cultures. It depends on the perception of risk, or the appraisal by the population of possible opportunity costs associated with advocated or needed change. When producers perceive the gains as exceeding the possible costs, they will accept change i.e., learn the new strategies with all deliberate speed. "Tradition" was used in the 1950s as a major explanation of resistance to change, but in the newer knowledge, little causal significance is attributed to this mysterious factor. There is a difference in the instrumental and interpretive modes of culture: instrumental behavior can be changed easily and quickly when advantage or survival is at stake; interpretive modes, such as ritual, are indeed subject to "irrational" resistance due to the important symbolic and social-emotional buttressing of this behavior. However, it is doubtful if reason or rationality is to be considered a significant factor in the context of ritual and symbol, since these modes of behavior are rooted in expressive and kinaesthetic rather than cognitive functions. Still, these interpretive modes of behavior can become embedded in instrumental activities; when they are, one may indeed encounter resistance which increases the lag between needed behavioral change and perception of that change and its relationship to altered strategies. This particular linkage was especially strong in relatively isolated tribal cultures; it was never especially strong in "peasant" populations with an accommodation to markets, taxes, and the need for instrumental rationality.

To restate the central issue: allowing for similar processes of thought, behavioral research in agriculture must be highly situation-specific. Decision behavior is dynamic; while there are basic patterns, these patterns are always subject to situational influence. Once research has shown that the desired change has been accommodated, then the findings are historical, and should not be taken as rigid guidelines for future action in that or a "similar" culture. Behavioral research, like "culture", becomes a descriptive paradigm of particular thought and action modalities characteristic of particular places and times.

*Social Research*

Turning now to social research, we encounter the problem of the relationship of behavior to the generalized frames called social organization or social structure. The anthropologist Raymond Firth (1955) distinguished between the two: by "organization" he referred to the here-and-now, day-by-day response of groups of people to the practical needs of social and economic existence, or what is now usually called "social adaptation." "Structure" on the other hand, was defined as the slow-to-change or invariant sets of expectations associated with such processes as status, prestige, ranking, authority, and power, whether these were expressed in religious or secular terms. The distinction is a useful one, although like all heuristic definitions, is often hard to sustain, since it rests on time: if a pattern of social behavior endures, it is "structure;" if it changes, or fluctuates according to situation, it is "organization." Where does one find the cutting edge? Like other concepts in the sociological field, these assist in clarifying temporal and institutional relations, but are not themselves capable of precisely delineating the phenomena.

If "social organization" is essentially social adaptation (the organized behavior of people involved in coping with ongoing reality), social structure basically concerns the way status positions in an agrarian society affect the rewards obtained from production. This issue has been of minor interest to North American agricultural researchers; there exist only a handful of serious empirical studies of the relationship of status to economic position in American agricultural communities. The anthropologist, Frank Cancian (1967), is the author of one of the best known such studies.

The second dimension of social research in agricultural society concerns the relationships of the farm unit to the community. Rural sociologists have been interested in this for a generation or more, but the rubric, "rural community study,"[9] represents a field of study which transcends any particular discipline: it has been a subject of study for anthropologists, sociologists, historians, writers of *belles lettres* and others. Earlier research was often affected by a nostalgia for rural life. In western civilization, the countryside was felt to be an unspoiled, uncorrupted world, possessing a social system and culture quite different from the urban community. The tradition of ideal types of "folk" and "urban" society, to use Robert Redfield's terms (1941), has a respectable antiquity, extending back at least to the 1840s and typified by Sir Henry Maine's (1864) distinction between societies based on "status" vs. those based on "contract." Such distinctions are seldom used today, being viewed mainly as a literary way of defining general tendencies—something of little use to analytical social science. Moreover, the penetration of "urban" culture into the rural scene has been so pervasive in recent generations that such distinctions have little empirical validity.

More important are attempts to define how the community facilitates, or otherwise influences, the production effort. Here the question becomes one of an analysis of resources—what the community can contribute to the production unit, and how the production unit can obtain these resources and use them to best advantage. The structure of rural society in North America according to the conventional nested box model consists of a series of exchanges or interchanges of resources and services (see Figure 16.1). It is important to remember that these exchanges involve more than material phenomena; they include social relations and symbols. Kinship and friendship networks are vital to the system; they function as channels for needed resources and as organizational nuclei for ritual and

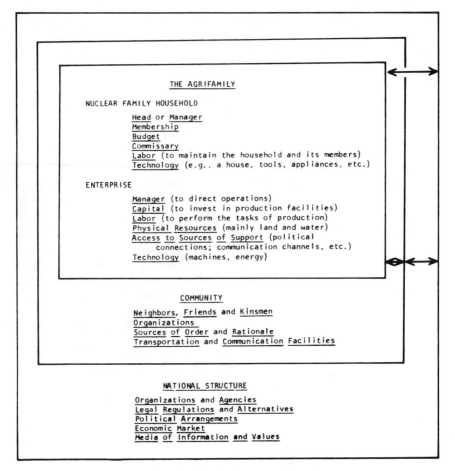

THE AGRIFAMILY

NUCLEAR FAMILY HOUSEHOLD

> Head or Manager
> Membership
> Budget
> Commissary
> Labor (to maintain the household and its members)
> Technology (e.g.. a house, tools, appliances, etc.)

ENTERPRISE

> Manager (to direct operations)
> Capital (to invest in production facilities)
> Labor (to perform the tasks of production)
> Physical Resources (mainly land and water)
> Access to Sources of Support (political
>       connections; communication channels, etc.)
> Technology (machines, energy)

COMMUNITY

> Neighbors, Friends and Kinsmen
> Organizations
> Sources of Order and Rationale
> Transportation and Communication Facilities

NATIONAL STRUCTURE

> Organizations and Agencies
> Legal Regulations and Alternatives
> Political Arrangements
> Economic Market
> Media of Information and Values

Figure 16.1   The Agrifamily System and Its Subsystems

celebration. Interest groups, hobby circles, and social groups, especially through their ceremonial gatherings (church suppers, rodeos, baseball games, women's societies), serve the symbolic needs of the society and serve to organize productive efforts and bring producers into contact with each other. The strictly economic functions of these activities and networks have never been adequately studied, largely because economic and sociocultural phenomena are the prerogatives of different academic disciplines which find it difficult to collaborate. Some of the best studies which do aim at a general synthesis of rural society and economy come from European scholars.[10]

Precisely how is the production function influenced by this complex rural social system? The channeling of resources is obvious, but much more is involved. Since rural society has become an industrial system composed of relatively small units of production, it must rely on the initiative of these producers to obtain the things they need to continue their effort. In recent years the financial aspects of this process have received much attention, but this is nothing new: small production units have difficulties with capital; the fluctuation of prices and costs create a constant problem of cash flow; rising economic values affect the process of transmission of the enterprise to successors, either to kin through inheritance, or to new buyers, since the farm must be refinanced in order to keep up with changing standards of efficiency and output.[11] Farms undergo rhythmic periods of intensive production, and then relaxed effort, as finances reach a plateau of satisfaction or need. There seems to be no significant way to change or eliminate this cyclical pattern. Thus the social structure and organization of rural society almost everywhere contributes to a fluctuation of output, and if this does not become a problem for the nation with respect to a steady supply of agricultural commodities, it is because there is a sufficient number of enterprises so that variations average out.

However, aspects of the production process which interact with the larger community involve the way its social activities and networks affect the mood, or management style of the farm units. Clearly communities have differing preferred styles of action: some emphasize intensive, unremitting productive action in order to obtain and hold status in the community; others frown on such behavior and encourage a more easygoing, or cautious style. (An example will be presented in the next section of the chapter.) Such different styles lead to different modes of production. (For a valuable empirical study of this, see the paper by Smith and Martin [1972] on the "satisficing" approaches to management used by part of North American ranchers. These approaches—based on maximizing satisfaction rather than income—are rooted in symbolic definitions of the good life.)

Another neglected area of research on North American rural society, although one examined by various political historians from their particular perspectives, is collective action. The concept was developed in institutional economics by John R. Commons (1934) in the '20s and '30s, but had little influence in economics since the field moved rapidly in a quantitative direction with neo-classical theory as the base. Applied to the rural scene, the topic concerns the way farmers combine to obtain what they need to continue their production effort. This refers not only to farm movements, always an important phase of North American and European rural life, and becoming more significant in every country, but also to microsocial levels of action, in the context of self-help, exchange of service, commodities, and labor. In dealing with the perennial problems of scale, such combinations have great economic significance, but this has been seldom studied by agricultural researchers. The effects of high technology and high-yield agriculture have tended to reduce the significance of collection action, but with the contemporary farm financial crisis, many of these forms of action are reappearing, as farmers appreciate the need for reducing costs by substituting mutual aid or cooperatives for individual action.

Another aspect of agrarian social organization concerns the relationship of the family or other social group in charge of the farm to the technical institution which is the producing farm itself. More concretely, how does a person who manages an economic enterprise relate to the members of his family and community who provide the labor and skills to run that enterprise? Here again we confront the unique social basis of agriculture as an industry: the small, self-operated production units whose social ties radiate out *via* kinship and friendship lines, through a larger community. In the majority of farming enterprises in North America, the same people both run the business and also live as domestic and kinship groups. In rural sociology and agricultural economics, the business is referred to as the "firm," and the domestic group, the "household." The writer (Bennett, 1982) has called the combined operation the "agrifamily system," and the components, "family household" and "enterprise." Figure 16.1 can be taken as an approximation of the system.

The system has some intriguing sociological features. If the same people are in charge of both components, the resulting system becomes one of conflict resolution, since the needs of the family and those of the enterprise are not always identical. Disposition of the funds available to the units is perhaps the most obvious arena of conflict, since the money available is never sufficient to cover all possible needs of both. In European and North American agricultural society there is a strong alignment of decisions along sex lines: the wife-mother is often the captain of the household finances, while the husband-father is the decision-maker for the farm enterprise.[12] The ability of these two executives to make reasonable allocations of funds is one measure of the success of a farm enterprise. In general, when funds are felt to be inadequate, the historic tendency is for the farm enterprise to receive a greater share than the household members. That is, the relationship is economically asymmetrical because capital investment in the farm firm provides the wherewithal for any subsequent increase in funds available to the family household.

In agrarian societies not fully involved in commercial farming, the allocations will of course differ. That is, priorities other than purely economic ones involving the expansion and development of the enterprise, will tend to be high. Therefore, one microsocial definition of the difference between full-commercial and part-commercial agriculture is the tendency in the latter for allocation decisions to favor the family household (or other social grouping with production functions) rather than the economic activities. Or put in ethnological terms, there is a less clear distinction between the kin group and the farm than there is in full-commercial systems. In the latter, a clear distinction must emerge because of the greater needs for capital investment in the farm firm, as well as general cultural values which favor the distinction. The emergence of this distinction is one mark, then, of the growing "modernization" and "Westernization" of an agricultural society.

While this system of household and enterprise is of global extent and provides a common basis for analysis of perhaps a majority of all agrarian societies, it does not exhaust all the possibilities. Many other social groupings and organizations may be involved in agricultural production at various levels of social integration. Beyond the family household there is the larger kin group, both blood and affinal, which may extend its web out through neighborhoods and regions. Then there are the instrumental labor and exchange networks in all agricultural regions, in which people with generally similar modes of production or enterprise size find ways of helping each other. Cooperatives are another formation: they have become more important in many countries in recent decades. A review of the literature suggests that co-ops can be organized on almost any organizational base: kinship, village commune, caste, and ceremonial organizations are all present. However, there are also some strict limitations on cooperative organization. Perhaps the most important is ownership or at least control of a requisite quantity of productive resources. Cooperation in production and other aspects of agriculture is influential when the members are of comparable size and output, and when they consist of those who can remain in continuous production with little fluctuation (Bennett, 1983). An ideological perspective appears in the criticisms that co-ops are for the wealthier farmers and peasants; the poor are excluded and may become worse off in a community where cooperative production flourishes.

In broader social terms, the basic problem of agriculture throughout history has been diversity of resources and size of enterprise. *No* nation has succeeded in creating an egalitarian agrarian society that endured; *no* nation has succeeded in developing a large agricultural system which even though unequal in rewards, nevertheless provides a reasonable share for all members of its agrarian population. The rural poor are with us, at all levels and degrees of economic development. This is the great unsolved problem of agrarian organization.

Agricultural research needs broadening. The social question in agriculture needs more attention than it gets, especially from the research establishment (although rural sociology in recent years has begun to demonstrate a renewed concern with such issues). But research on such questions has a way of getting lost in the disciplinary maze: the topic often ends up being viewed as not one of "agriculture," but of sociology. The development agencies in some respects show greater willingness to accept larger systems as units of research than students of the domestic scene—hardly surprising, given the considerable confusion and error in early development work.

### Problems of Knowledge

Our topics here are "indigenous" and "exogenous" knowledge. The implication of the latter is that external, non-producing experts, *via* the use of science, can obtain knowledge which is in some way superior to the knowledge accumulated by agrarian producers who have learned by doing. Research is the method used by the expert to acquire his special knowledge. From the expert's perspective, the indigenous person does not perform research; his information comes from observing empirical results or experiencing successes and failures over a period of time. However, since the gathering of knowledge by observing successes and failures is precisely what the research scientist does, the distinction is faulty.

At this point, the argument must shift to another mode: it is not the trial-and-error procedure that distinguishes indigenous-folk from exogenous-expert knowledge, but the way factors influencing outcomes are conceived, defined, and controlled. The researcher, lacking a personal stake in remunerative outcome, is free to attempt to conceive of all factors objectively, whereas the indigenous operator conceives the relevant factors in "folk" ways, and is not free to systematically vary or control many factors because he cannot, or because he is bound by a fear of risking a negative outcome. In this argument, the difference between indigenous and expert knowledge is based on the freedom possessed by the researcher to "play" with the factors affecting outcome because he has no economic or physical survival stake in the results.

Other arguments feature the "traditional" adherence to routines which have proven to be reasonably effective in the past. The indigenous peasant may realize that he is not producing at maximum level, but he has learned (or received information from the past) that if he follows particular methods he can expect a reasonable or steady output or financial reward. "Tradition" thus is defined as the amount of knowledge adequate to produce a particular—possibly modest—quantity of product at a low level of risk of complete failure ("satisficing," in economic terms).

The "binding force of tradition," as it was called by early ethnologists, is thus really production at a standard level of output performed with methods which reduce or stabilize risk. Clearly the knowledge used to realize this type of outcome is adequate to the task, and in the sense of "substantive rationality," it is essentially "expert" knowledge. However, it is also "culturally standardized" expertise. If innovations or changes are introduced, they will be relatively infrequent, and probably incremental, stretched out over a relatively long period of time. That is, "control" of the factors involved may take place, but not in a "scientific" fashion. Trial-and-error, or survival-outcome testing, is the mode of operation.

The distinctions we are laboring over are the consequence of the attempt in modern agriculture to increase output in the shortest possible span of time: that is, to step up the rate and quantity of output over and beyond levels achievable by culturally standardized methods. The objective is to separate the production process from indigenous, culturally-defined standards of output and strategy. This effort has been given close attention in agricultural development programs and projects in Third World countries over the past several decades. However, the effort extends well back into the industrial revolution and the expansion of commercial agriculture in all countries. In general, the effort has been most successful in those countries whose economies and educational systems were already adjusted to commercial enterprise. To the extent that "subsistence" production norms were standard, resistance to the separation of production from cultural definitions could be expected.[13]

To the extent that the production process is separable from cultural constraints, the producers have learned the value of information from sources outside the local community. Hence, "exogenous" knowledge becomes "indigenous." As this occurs, the value of research may change: in various spheres of production, the exogenous, research-derived knowledge may become fully institutionalized. This will mean that at intervals, and in various sectors, the role of the research scientist and the extension agent may become superfluous. However, this will be relative to the particular tasks of production and the factors investigated. Genetic engineering has introduced a new round of research tasks; and hence new information to be transmitted to the producers (see Buttel's chapter in this volume).

However, the separation of production norms and methods from cultural conventions and social constraints is never total, any more than conversion to fully commercial, or income maximizing methods can be total. As knowledge accumulates from whatever source, there is a tendency for it to become part of culturally standardized routines. The producer may be raising crops and livestock for the market, but the tasks of production require adjustments to familial, neighborhood, and community social arrangements and norms. The simplistic polar typology mentioned in the previous section which sharply distinguished "peasants" from "farmers" obscured this pervasive process. Some of this thinking persists, but generally such typologies have given way to analysis of the varying effects of factors and processes such as risk, technology, land tenure, and population/food/labor ratios. The relevant theoretical position stresses the concept of adaptive behavior, the essential idea being that humans everywhere produce what they do on the basis of accumulated knowledge and experience, attempting to ensure a reasonable and stable output. In this view, the peasant is as "rational" as the farmer; the only difference is that he responds to a different set of conditions (Shultz, 1964, represents the pioneer statement). And perhaps most important, his activities are not as completely under the control of economic markets as are those of the farmer.

## The Field of Ethnoscience

A field of study specializing in indigenous knowledge is called ethnoscience, which simply means "folk science"—or the study of a pattern of cognitive information and understandings which have accumulated out of the routines of social existence.[14] Two important behavioral modes are involved: experience (learning by doing) and empirical observation (especially of natural processes). While the cognitive element is stressed by ethnoscience specialists, it should be emphasized that kinesthetic experience plays a large role. Tactile sensation, perceptions of color, odor, concepts of order, symmetry, beauty—all of these are very much involved.[15]

Most of the data collected by the ethnoscientist are linguistic, and in large part, ethnoscience as a field grew up within anthropological linguistics. It did so because nearly all of the published investigations deal with exotic cultural groups. This often has direct significance for development programs, but also has tended to obscure the fact that all agriculturalists, at whatever level of economic development, develop their own folk science. In a developed economy, much of the content of this indigenous knowledge will have been acquired from scientific sources. There is a constant flow of expertise into the ethnoscience of local communities. Often the expert knowledge is transformed in the process, and made more amenable to local conditions. Researchers typically have not shown sufficient awareness of this transformation process, nor have they always appreciated the fact that by transforming the knowledge into indigenous practice and explanation, the research procedure is really being enlarged and extended. However, moves in this direction have been made: the procedure of field trials on working farms is an example.

Since linguistic analysis is crucial in studying indigenous knowledge, and since indigenous knowledge contains many non-technical or symbolic elements, the resulting academic product may seem esoteric and theoretical, and hence irrelevant for practical agricultural specialists. However, the work can be of considerable importance in the effort to understand why farmers do what they do, and how they justify it. The writer is reminded of one of his first published papers, reporting on agricultural practices among farmers in southern Illinois (Passin and Bennett, 1943). Many of these operators tried, whenever possible, to plant and harvest crops in appropriate phases of the moon. "Moon signs" constitute an ancient set of Anglo-Saxon ethnoscientific agricultural knowledge, and it was carried into the Midwest by farmer migrants from the southern mountains in the 19th century. We found the practices surviving in Illinois in the 1940's. Inquiry revealed that the practice was highly variable: while most farmers stated they did it, actual research showed that they used moon signs only when other factors, like weather, were appropriate. Farmers had a carefully-worked out folk theory: that moon signs were not the only factor influencing crops, and that they worked in conjunction with rainfall, temperature, and so on. Moreover, some farmers had what they called a "sperimental" method: they had tried to plant by the signs alone, to see what would happen; and then they combined sign recognition with other factors, fairly systematically, over a period of many years. They had a well-constructed (but unwritten) table of effectiveness of the signs in the presence or absence of other factors. Most of them had concluded that the signs were effective as a kind of "good luck" factor: if you planted and harvested when all the climatic and other variables were appropriate, and also could observe the proper moon signs, good crops were guaranteed. Thus, moon signs had evolved, in their half-science, half-magical ethnoscience, into a form of crop insurance. Underlying this cognitive pattern, of course, was probably the most important factor: following appropriate procedures to the furthest extent possible gave the farmers a feeling of well-being and security.

Explained in this way, ethnoscience is nothing more than folk knowledge, and in agriculture, it can be effective and appropriate. The practical element in the example is the particular strength of the belief in signs: would, for example, a farmer sacrifice some other important precondition of crop welfare in order to observe the signs? A few did, and in the past, more did. But on the whole, we believe that the practice was always subject to this kind of pragmatic testing, and the same has been reported for tribal people. Non-scientific or supernaturalistic beliefs and practices are woven into a dense tapestry of cognitive constructions which work well for the indigenous producer. The trouble starts when the outside expert tries to make them change these practices in order to greatly increase or rationalize output.

Underlying the study of ethnoscience is a concept of essential cultural unity. That is, the basic categories of analysis are virtually the same in every agricultural, tribal, or peasant society studied. C.G. Knight, an ethnoscience specialist working in African agriculture, lists the following:

1. Maintain continuity by following tested procedures. 2. Provide adequate space for food production. 3. Manage a reliable water supply. 4. Provide adequate plant nutrients. 5. Channel solar energy. 6. Control plant succession to protect cultigens. 7. Protect against diseases and pests. 8. Concentrate on the usable portion of the harvest. 9. Transport and distribute food. 10. Store crops and food. 11. Allocate foodstuffs among relevant social units. 12. Convert crops and food into usable forms. 13. Preparation of foods. 14. Make arrangements for proper ingestion of food [paraphrased from Knight, 1980:213–14].

This list defines the process of agriculture as really one phase of the larger "food system"—a concept used by anthropologists working in part- or whole-subsistence societies. However, this is a professional detail. The important aspect of the list is its undeniable universality. While subsistence societies perform many of the tasks by themselves, with local or indigenous knowledge and labor, in developed agricultural systems, many of the tasks are performed by external institutions, or are greatly enhanced by exogenous knowledge and skill. Thus, No. 9 may be a matter of bringing crops from the field to the village in an African tribal-peasant setting, while in North America, it usually means movement of crops by truck or rail to urban points of distribution.

It is apparent therefore that in developed agricultural systems the role of the "primary producer" has indeed become primary, in the sense that the production of crops for external markets reduces the number of tasks that must be performed locally for subsistence purposes. The farmer thus becomes an agent for exogenous institutions; scientific research may preempt much of his experimental knowledge, and his food may come from the supermarket. However, the farmer must continue to adapt and transform expertise into working ethnoscience.

The problem of how ethnoscientific knowledge articulates with scientific knowledge, or expertise, has been tackled by P. Meehan (1980) in a paper designed to suggest how innovation takes place. The result is a combination of both ethnoscience perspectives and communication theory. The key concept is what I would term "message compatibility," which refers to the fact that the information emitted by, e.g. the extension agent is received by the farmer operator only when it is compatible with some symbolic or structural aspect of the latter's ethnoscience perspective. This seems obvious enough, but in development projects, it is rarely observed in practice. When applied, it focuses the extension-education and innovation process on highly specific elements of communication. The procedure has been successfully used (although not necessarily using Meehan's scheme) in some of the work performed at the *Centro Internacional de la Papa* (CIP), in Peru (Rhoades, 1983; and especially Rhoades, 1984b.) Working with the help of high-altitude root-crop farmers in the

Andes, systematic charting of their indigenous concepts of potato cultivation and use were matched to specific messages concerning change and improvement presented by researchers and extension agents. When this was done, farmers were much more inclined to accept the proposed innovations, and in addition, they also were willing to participate in the planning and improvement of the innovations, and to help in educating other farmers. Similar interlocks between indigenous and expert knowledge on pasture and range utilization and improvement in the northern Plains of the U.S. and Canada have been established over the past two generations. The concept of "overgrazing" is an example. Definitions of this deleterious practice on the part of ranchers and experts differ widely, although similar terminology is used. When range specialists began to investigate the nature of the indigenous ranching conceptions of range utilization and abuse, it was found possible to modify the expert concepts of overgrazing to allow for sequential and rhythmic alternation of heavy and light regimes.

In essence, the ethnoscience approach does no more than make explicit something agricultural specialists tend to take for granted: communication. Perhaps a majority of agricultural scientists have received little exposure to the technicalities of language, modes of thought, and forms of expression. If a development specialist working in Guatemala learns that Maya farmers have a set of categories of "hot" and "cold," into which they sort various crops and cultivation techniques (Redfield, 1941, chapter 5), the specialists are likely to ignore it, and assume this is a primitive idea of no significance in agriculture. However, these categories are *symbolically* hot and cold, not *actually*, and they are combined with other factors that influence crop growth—like the Illinois farmers' moon signs. The hot-cold categories are thus important symbols, or grouping concepts, for whole strategies of cultivation, and must be taken seriously.

Ethnoscience need not dwell on production techniques exclusively. Links between indigenous conceptions of the agricultural situation and some of the sociological categories denoted earlier also may be useful in defining aspects of the community culture of production. The writer has investigated farmers' own concepts of production and styles of managing farms in a region of the northern Great Plains (Bennett, 1982). After considerable work, the following paradigm of folk categories of managerial styles emerged (see Figure 16.2).

The terms used in the figure are the most commonly encountered in interviews. The most interesting aspect of the scheme is its four-fold matrix format, based on two categories of judgment: the degree of establishment of the farm firm, and the level of activity of its owner-operator. The most complex cell is the upper right one, which is a graded classification of approved managerial behavior. Least approved were the

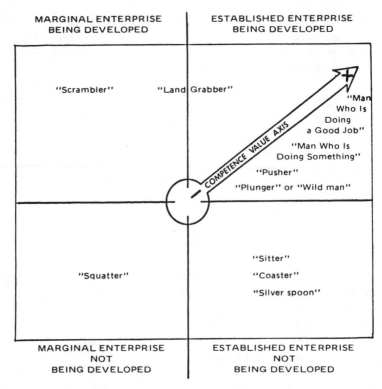

MARGINAL ENTERPRISE
BEING DEVELOPED          ESTABLISHED ENTERPRISE
BEING DEVELOPED

"Scrambler"        "Land Grabber"

COMPETENCE VALUE AXIS

"Man
Who Is
Doing
a Good Job"

"Man Who Is
Doing Something"

"Pusher"

"Plunger" or "Wild man"

"Sitter"

"Coaster"

"Silver spoon"

"Squatter"

MARGINAL ENTERPRISE
NOT
BEING DEVELOPED          ESTABLISHED ENTERPRISE
NOT
BEING DEVELOPED

Figure 16.2   Jasper Categories of Management Style

"plungers" or "pushers," since in this high-risk region, it was assumed that cautious strategies were better in the long run. It is also culturally significant that the most highly approved style was modestly understated: "a man doing a good job," or similar remarks. Fulsome praise was not considered appropriate; working hard but carefully was what any good farmer does, and did not necessarily earn obvious praise.

Finally, we tested these categories against actual economic performance. The results were remarkably consistent, at least for reasonable periods of time (farm managers could change their judgment of their peers over time). That is, farms in the far upper right corner were in fact the most solidly established and continuously productive. The results show that the culturally-based judgments of the operators themselves in this entrepreneurial system were accurate and based on careful observations. Agricultural extension agents—probably unconsciously—also assimilate perspectives of this type as they gain experience and knowledge in a farming community.

## Agricultural Decision-Making

P. Barlett (1980:xiii), in a symposium volume on anthropological research related to decision behavior in agriculture, comments on the larger implications of agricultural decision-making:

> The impacts of farmers' choices in agricultural production can be felt in diverse arenas. Individual farm decisions determine household profits and well being, land use, capital requirements, and the adoption of new technology. They also affect such issues as prestige and leadership in the community and the long-term ecological stability of an area. These choices have implications for what products each nation has to export or to process and use domestically. Also affected are relationships between nations and such vital matters as their balance of payments and their ability to withstand poor weather, rising energy costs, or a rapidly growing population.

This puts a considerable burden on the farmer. Plagued by market uncertainties, weather vagaries, and political confusion, he is also expected to make decisions that affect the national balance of payments. Totalitarian control of agriculture has not worked well anywhere; yet democratic governments are also frustrated when the farmer makes his own, independent choices; hence they seek to persuade him to choose otherwise. (One alternative is an attempt to manipulate macroeconomic conditions so that he gives up his farm to the big companies!)

Research on decision behavior, like other forms of expertise, tends to narrow the field of inquiry; that is, to assume at the outset that farmers really do "make decisions." In general terms they do, but nevertheless such an assumption is based on a rationalistic conception of behavior with its origins mainly in economics. This in turn is based on Western commercial farming experience, where indeed it has been important for farmers to think objectively about production and marketing decisions if they are to make a living. In this context, "decision" becomes an objectified cultural datum, not necessarily a universal behavioral act. Commercial farmers have to think of economic consequences of what they plant and raise; hence this thinking becomes "decision-making." Decisions are objectified when the future must be bound in some fashion.

Of course the potential to think in this manner—that is, to "make decisions"—is present in all members of Homo sapiens, and all farmers do think about the future consequences of their operation. However, there are three important considerations: (a) First, if the farming system retains an important component of self-subsistence, and hence cultural standardization, there is bound to be much routine agricultural activity where farmers need not "make decisions;" they simply do what they have always done. (b) However, since the agrarian context is always marked by considerable uncertainty—in both industrial and tribal-peasant societies—there exists a universal tendency toward objective future-binding forms of thought, since alternatives have to be considered. (c) Still, in no farming system where relatively small kinship or family units control production, will decision-making be purely economic; *i.e.,* devoid of social and cultural constraints. Even where farmers do objectify their operations, they still do so under the influence of factors related to the many domains of social existence.

If this is the case, then theories of agricultural decision-making which assume formal rationality as a major and constant thought and behavioral process are too simple and one-sided. They are potentially accurate only to the extent that the farmer population has assimilated rationalistic thought as a result of mental acculturation in a national culture featuring and requiring such patterns. They remain simplistic to the extent that the farmer continues to operate with a degree of freedom from such modes of thought; or, to the extent that he must modify his decisions in some manner or other in order to cope with various social factors (e.g. a wife who demands a higher income); or a community that looks askance on "pushers." In other words, decision-making is a variable, not a constant, in the instrumental behavior of agriculture.

Has this been demonstrated by anthropologists? Of course, in the sense that anthropologists, by inclination, tend to choose research settings in which economic activities are closely bound to the sociocultural system. Perhaps the term "traditional society" is relevant to social situations in which a maximum internal complexity exists; that is, cases where the concept of "decision" must be used cautiously since the large number of constraints and influences require the producers to develop cautious and routinized strategies.

More useful would be studies of situations in commercial agriculture where despite a need for separation of economic decisions from intervening social factors, farmers nevertheless are clearly influenced by the latter. Such studies by anthropologists are rare; whereas studies of decision-making among commercial farmers by economists and management specialists simply assume rationality and rarely examine the other factors in detail. There is a disciplinary gap in the research that needs filling in.

The writer has attempted to provide a contribution along these lines in his longitudinal study of an agricultural region in southwestern Saskatchewan.[16] It contains an analysis of farming strategies in a large sample of farms over a period of a decade, using quantitative, inspectional, and participative methods. The time study was designed to determine what factors were influential in enterprise-building; or more precisely, to distinguish between people who built or "developed" their farms and those who did not, or did so to a lesser or qualified extent (there were several categories). Criteria for enterprise-building were various: investment, production, income, attitudes, and strategies of operation.

In general, the findings were clear: those who worked hardest in developing or improving their farms and the yield of their crops or livestock were those whose household and kin groups exerted strong demands on the enterprise, and/or those with local status positions to uphold or to acquire. The majority of these people occupied the middle range of farms in terms of resources. The very resource-abundant enterprises, and the very resource-poor farms were alike in that they did the least to improve, change, or otherwise develop their farms and ranches. In addition, evidence was found for the influence of particular cultural styles: ranchers were less inclined to invest in enterprise development than farmers, as a group. Of course these findings are more complex than this summary can render, and there were many factors at work, but the overall results were clear: during the decade of study, the middle-range, middle-class-oriented farmers, lacking the income their families desired, but with sufficient resources to increase the returns to scale assuming that some hard work and money were invested, were those most likely to "do something," in the local parlance. The study simply demonstrates that even in a thoroughly commercial environment, social and behavioral elements are crucial in leading farmers to make decisions to innovate, work harder, or increase the offtake.

This however, does not get at the other question, which is whether the farmers made the decisions for production that government and agribusiness wanted them to. On the whole, the farmers and ranchers followed market opportunities and made choices that were economically appropriate. That is, economic incentives did not supplant social motives, but social demands were on the whole responded to by decisions permitting profitable outcomes, and these outcomes were also, on the whole, those sought by the dominant agricultural interests in the larger society. However, in cases where the resource base was not appropriate to desired profit or production goals, other choices had to be made. It is in this sphere where the agricultural extension agent becomes a crucial figure: he can help the farmer make alternative choices. Our observations suggest that this function is served only in part: farmers are remarkably independent in North America, especially in the West; and extension agents vary greatly in ability, drive, and prestige. In other words, while there is a generalized parallelism or coïncidence between farmer production decisions and national-level economic objectives and/or opportunities, there is less coincidence between appropriate alternative choices and actual alternative choices made by farmers. Obviously, in Third World contexts, the degree of coincidence in both spheres is generally much less.

This is not so much a matter of unruly or unpredictable farmers as it is a measure of their general lack of integration in the whole national socio-economy.

In a study made with linear programming methodology, and based on a very large sample of farmers throughout the Prairie Provinces of Canada in the 1970s (Sahi and Craddock, 1975), it was found that coïncidence between actual production decisions (measured by the planting of particular grain crops in particular quantities, at particular times) and the most desirable decisions (measured by national needs plus profitability to the producer) was high for the major cash crops, but low for specialty crops. Again, in the sphere of alternative decisions, the farmer is likely to experiment and take chances, or use his "own judgment." There are other studies of these processes, but on the whole, it is a relatively neglected aspect of agricultural research (probably due in part to the considerable methodological difficulties and the need for more longitudinal studies.)

Our work with these northern farmers also told us much about the nature of the decision-making process. Many studies of decision-making by economists, sociologists, and anthropologists appear to assume that a decision is something made at one time. We found that in instances of "decision" involving productively-significant activities, change, or investments, it was rarely possible to find a particular point in time when the decision had been made. Instead, we found that decisions "grow on you," to quote one of our farmer participants; they represent an accumulation of many small incremental steps, although in some cases informed by a plan. These plans, however, contain many indeterminate factors: the farmer may proceed to shift from crops to livestock, but he cannot make the change immediately: it may take a decade or more, or be something his successor-son might undertake to complete. And along the way, the "decision" can be reversed if economic fortunes, markets, or resources change. In a sense, there is probably relatively little "decision-making" in the classical stereotyped sense; it is better defined as a *temporal process of adaptive behavior.*

However, the temporal aspect of decision-making *was* contemplated in E. Rogers' innovation-diffusion research (Rogers and Shoemaker, 1971). He called it the "innovation-decision period," and outlined it more or less as follows: step one was the "knowledge function" in which the proposed innovation was discussed with an extension agent; step two was the "persuasion function" which included communication with neighbors and experimental tests of the innovation; step three was the "decision function" in which the innovation, after presumably found to be advisable, was adopted. The fourth and final step was the "confirmation function" in which the innovation was either made a permanent part of the operation, or was discontinued. The time duration of these four stages in the example given in Rogers' text was six years, but presumably this could be either shorter or longer.

In general, this is a realistic scheme, since it acknowledges the time factor, the complexity of innovation and change, and the various behaviors involved: thought, decision, information-gathering, communication, and experimentation. Decisions are only therefore a single element of the entire process of enterprise development. Still, rationalistic conceptions of the behavioral process remain in the Rogers formulation: the process begins when the farmer decides to do something and then goes and gets information. The antecedent factors are neglected: perhaps the farmer had no choice but to change his ways; perhaps someone persuaded him to change; perhaps he had ambition to be a better man; or perhaps his wife pushed him into it. That is, the lead-in phase of the process is, from the sociological viewpoint, the crucial phase, but this is neglected in the tradition of decision-making and innovation research in the agriculture. One may understand why specialists choose to neglect this lead-in activity, since it is not immediately relevant to the carrying out of the innovations or decisions. The social analyst, however, is interested in the whole process of instrumental behavior. Moreover, the innovation-diffusion and decision-making literature is suffused with the proposition that it is good for farmers to accept change. This normative perspective is not false, since the social milieu of developed agriculture includes many of the same values and incentives that appear in professional expertise. However, it is a limited perspective, and particularly misleading when it is applied, without reflection, to all agricultural situations.

Much, if not most, of the work of anthropologists in the decision context has been with "peasant" peoples, and therefore it is this body of research which may have the most to communicate to agricultural specialists. A variety of methods and approaches are in use, as they are in other fields. In most cases, the specific methods used by anthropologists to study decision-making are obtained from these other fields, with the exception of informal or depth interviewing and participation in agricultural routines—which are specialties of anthropological "field work." The most common method is that of the decision tree (a diagram showing how sets of factors led to particular decisions). The trees are constructed as interview and observational data accumulate. The tree, of course, is not necessarily a map of actual thought patterns, but a generalized mode based on data or conclusions of the investigator. Decision trees are always useful, but they tend to become highly specific: separate trees have to be compiled for each activity or domain, and the analysis can become so detailed that the woods are lost for the trees. This microspecificity can be of benefit if the research objective is a narrow practical one, as in the case of C. Gladwin's work in Puebla, where tests needed to be made of a specific development recommendation concerning fertilizing practices (Gladwin, 1980). Gladwin's paper presents many if-then formulations and exceptions to his models, which makes it difficult to obtain a clear picture of the actual course of decision and thought processes.

An alternative method, the "statistical behavior" approach, used by M. Chibnik, involves assembling statistics on various social and economic criteria, like income, or labor time, and running them against patterns of economic choice—in one case, between wage labor and full-time agriculture (Chibnik, 1980). Statistical preponderances of certain factors thus provide plausible evidence of general tendencies or combinations of factors and decisions. This method cuts through the micro-level elements and exceptions noted by Gladwin and others and expresses decision-making in terms of trends or patterns rather than specific causes for specific decisions. (A similar approach, though with different objectives, is used in the writer's own work, cited earlier.) The statistical behavior approach strikes the writer as representing a more realistic rendering of how these complex behavioral processes operate: no two farmers will make identical decisions, at identical times, for identical reasons. This proposition accords well with the anthropological realization that humans have many different potentials and that their behavior is variable, and cannot be explained by simple or single factors.

Methods, however, are simply a matter of finding some appropriate way to examine particular situations. Thus, we can expect that anthropologists, like decision specialists in other fields, will continue to use a variety of approaches. It is more important to examine what it is about agricultural situations which require decision behavior. S. Ortiz (1973, 1980) considers this to be *uncertainty*—and the associated measured risks which derive from uncertainty. We are speaking here of the future: of the way farmers anticipate future events and outcomes.[17] Two modes of anticipation have already been discussed: first, in cases where the agricultural regime is finely tuned to population, climate, and technology, and where exogenous influences which might upset these balances are weak, the future is perceived as resident in present procedures. That is, one follows established routines. This is no doubt an ideal type, but certainly it was closely approximated in tribal contexts until fairly recently. It is no accident that anthropologists were not sensitive to decision-making in their early work: the societies they studied did not really require a heightened awareness of decision-making.

The second mode is simply that in which anticipation of future outcomes becomes vital because various exogenous factors are likely to upset likely outcomes. In other words, to the extent that farmers feel uncertain about outcomes, they will objectify time and events, and seek to avoid, control, or nullify the factors of significance. As we noted earlier, this means that they will be careful about what they do; i.e., they will objectify "decision-making." They will then proceed to devise strategies, which of course take many forms depending on the nature of the uncertainties and the existing precedents for coping with them. And accordingly, the research methods designed to study decision-making must also vary.

There are a great many factors that create uncertainty in agriculture. Anything can modify outcomes: personality, skill, knowledge, weather, taxes, subsidies, markets, costs of machinery, labor supply, community pressures. Since the list is endless, there is no scientific or academic field of study that is not relevant to research on the process. In most of the professional research on uncertainty and decisions in economics and farm management fields, few factors are investigated thoroughly, and generally those are economic and financial. This is in accord with the basic assumptions held by economists about the importance of the utility-maximization process in human behavior. However, since social forces and cultural styles set the stage for economic motivation, research needs to be done on these as well.

Thus, uncertainties are not wholly economic, but also social. One common variety is found in farming societies where the economic scale of production is limited, and where income has to be buttressed by wage labor or some other means, e.g., as in parts of the North American West, with custom labor and machine operation. Here the socioeconomic structure of the community and the demands on income created by consumption standards make it uncertain as to whether the farmers can find the cash, time, and attention to perform necessary tasks. Farmers may know that by working off the farm they are stealing time away from production, and thereby making a good crop or herd less likely, but they may feel they have no choice. They "decide" to work off-farm, in order to get income; or they "decide" not to devote quite as much effort to cultivation as to running harvesters for their neighbors. They are making choices, not decisions.

However, these complex social uncertainties and choices have not been a major target of research by professional agricultural specialists, though sociologists and anthropologists have dealt with them. The more typical economics' study defines its topic as a decision on a particular investment: should the farmer introduce performance-testing in order to improve the performance of his beef herd? Will the cost of this procedure justify the returns? What factors may influence cost-effectiveness in the long run? These questions arise when the farmer entertains such objectives as a result of exogenous factors at work: new standards for beef in the consumer market; rising or falling beef prices; changes in transportation costs—all factors over which the farmer has no direct control, only more or less information. These probably all fall into one very large bag: information uncertainties. And hence, risk: if the farmer's information is incomplete, a particular investment may risk financial loss since there is no certain guarantee that the expected outcome will not be influenced by some factor outside of awareness or knowledge. The farmer may sense this imperfect knowledge, and decide to take the risk of failure anyway—particularly if he thinks he has enough cash reserve to take it, in which case he is self-insured (or he may, of course, seek to buy crop insurance).

The accumulated uncertainties are not simply a matter of decision-making and information-gathering, but are also the foundation for political action. This phase of the process is not usually researched by agricultural specialists or anthropologists for that matter, but by political scientists and historians. Once again we find an academic hiatus in the research function. In North America, the accumulated uncertainties of prices, costs, and marketing led to the Populist movements of the northern Midwest and Great Plains which greatly affected the course of American politics (the 1984 Democratic presidential candidate was an heir of Minnesota Populism). The history of North American agriculture has a pink thread running through it: accumulated uncertainties of production and income experienced by farmers led to collectivist political action at the electoral, legislative, and financial levels.

Uncertainties are thus a micro-level reflection of the great unsolved problem of industrial agriculture: *its social uncertainties often exceed those of subsistence producers.* These uncertainties are not resolvable so long as industrial agriculture remains geared to an economic system that requires fluctuation in order to make profits. Farmers in developed economies thus pay a price for relatively high incomes, favorable positions in the national consumption hierarchy, or access to education, community participation, and political power. The price is, of course, exposure to fluctuating prices and costs which create cyclical movement, which in turn is reflected in psychological frustration and social tension. Farmers lack ultimate control over the economic forces that set the stage for agriculture; they have been engaged in a historical drive to control these forces and the end is by no means in sight. If the present trends in North America continue, there may well be a crisis in agricultural production within the next quarter-century. The rising loss of farm units may or may not be replaced by industrial farming, and even if the volume of production is so replaced, it almost certainly will involve significant ecological and social costs.

## Summary and Reprise

The tradition of agricultural research is grounded in the disciplinary specializations of modern science. Distinctions between agronomy, economics, management, consumption, family life, and community organization are created by the general conception of reality associated with science as it evolved in Western civilization over the past several centuries. This evolution featured a division of effort into disciplines or bodies of knowledge each pursued for its own sake, and more often than not, in isolation from other fields. This separate pursuit was, of course, inevitable given the need to accumulate basic descriptive information on particular topics of interest and complexity. However, the division of reality into these cognitive-based segments rarely conforms to processes of causation and change, which cut across the divisions. It is these aspects of reality that disciplinary segregation cannot easily ascertain. Instead, cause is sought exclusively in the separate segments. For example, the economist may assume that people behave because of "economic" motives, not out of a complex web of emotional, social, political, and economic relations. The philosophy of disciplinary segregation is justified by the several social sciences on the grounds that while multiple causation is taken for granted, there are always major or dominant causal factors. These, however, always seem to be located in the speaker's or writer's discipline!

We have offered a number of examples of the results of disciplinary segregation in agricultural research, so we need not repeat them here. By way of a summary and conclusion, we might attempt a pulling together of the major themes and concepts in agricultural research as it has been practiced by the agricultural establishment over the past generation. The two approaches defined below have been the target of criticism by social-behavior scientists in recent years, for their neglect of social, cultural, and psychological causation.

The first we may call the "scientistic" approach. It is associated mainly with agronomy departments, experiment stations, and the natural-science effort in agriculture generally. It is characterized by faith in science and its handmaiden, technology, as the solutions to all agricultural problems except, of course, those associated with actual production, which are the focus of the second approach. The fundamental credo of the scientistic approach is simply that if something works in one setting, it is very likely to work in all settings. This belief in universal applicability of agronomic knowledge has created numerous difficulties in Third World development work, where procedures created in European or North American laboratories and fields have been transferred to other environments, with very mixed results.

The second, or "economistic," approach is associated mainly with agricultural economics and management science and is informed by the concepts of "utility maximization" and "rational choice" which hold that humans generally seek to improve their lot and try to make the most intelligent and efficient choices to accomplish this end. The emphasis on individual choice coincides with a belief that entrepreneurship is the best way to run an agricultural system. Thus, the economistic approach is closely associated with capitalist agriculture, and in fact does much to explain the behavior of producers embedded in such a system. However, it tends to underplay the significance of collective action, cultural patterns, and variation in individual ability to make choices and act rationally. Above all, the approach undervalues the importance of social networks and atmospheres in guiding and constraining productive behavior.

The professional credo of institutionalized agriculture in North America is an amalgam of these two approaches. They are not in conflict; in fact, they tend to reinforce each other, since they both emanate from the realm of expertise and specialization. They are both professionalized to the extent that the farmer generally has little contact with the specialists; instead, their findings and convictions are communicated to the farmer by a third party, the extension agent. This chain of command may work in North America and parts of Europe, Japan, and a few other countries, where institutions and education have caught up with it, but it has been inappropriate in most of the rest of the world, where tribal-peasant producers lack the education to comprehend the messages, or enough sophistication to be able to take the messages with the appropriate grain of salt.

Both of these approaches neglect social phenomena, and this neglect is as much a matter of disciplines as it is simply of a focus on practical matters of agricultural procedures. There is no doubt that the social dimension of agricultural production was in view in the late 19th and early 20th centuries, when the agriculture-related disciplines were in their infancy, as we pointed out earlier in the chapter. However, as these disciplines became more specialized, they lost sight of the complex activity of agriculture, and came to see it as largely divorced from people and society. The scientists viewed it as plants, animals, soil, and weather; the economists and management specialists saw it as a matter of correct decisions, in the abstract.

The two approaches are not wrong, since they define valid domains. However, they are truncated and over-simplified in their neglect of the complex tissue of agricultural institutions and behavior. It is time they be supplemented by a third approach, which we shall call the "institutional." By this we mean that agriculture is part of society, and it is carried on by members of society with the usual mixture of rules, deviations from the rules, risk-taking, gambling, love, competition, and social relations. The "agricultural systems" or "farming systems" approach, popular in recent years in development work, is an amalgam of the scientistic and rationalistic, focusing on the procedures and not on the human behavior that creates these procedures, tries to apply them, and changes them, and why. Agriculture needs to take its place as a recognized social institution, along with the others; but at the same time, it must be understood that these other institutions—political, social, familial, religious, economic—are also part of agriculture, just as they are part of each other.

## Notes

1. For histories of agricultural economics which explore aspects of this transition, see Case and Williams, 1957; and Salter, 1967. For an appraisal of the relationships of agricultural economics and economic anthropology, see Bennett and Kanel, 1983.

2. I refer here to the current surge of interest among rural sociologists in practical problems of urgency: environmental hazards in agricultural production; equity and income-distribution problems among farmers; social welfare issues; rural crime, and so on. However, the methodological thrust remains academic and disciplinary. For a current review of the state of the discipline, see Friedland, 1982.

3. Expressed almost entirely, however, in the form of research reports, consultant advisories, and the like. As yet, there is no extensive effort to create a combined economic-sociological-behavioral theory of agricultural production. (An early attempt, inspired by the enthusiasm of development, and social scientific participation in programs that took place in the 1950s and '60s, is: Leagans and Loomis, 1971. A more recent statement is Statz and Eicher, 1984, p. 23 esp.)

4. The classic anthropological study in this context is, of course, Sol Tax' *Penny Capitalism* (1953). The issue was also significant for Melanesian enthnology, when the acquisitive and achievement-oriented social organization facilitated a rapid economic modernization after World War II.

5. For a general discussion of some of these issues, and the history of development efforts in livestock production in East Africa, see Bennett, 1984.

6. Heady and Whiting, 1975, represents the first coherent statement of this trend.

7. Adequately dealt with in another paper in this volume.

8. For some position papers on the general topic, see the following: Saint and Coxward, 1977; Almy, 1978; Whyte and Boynton, 1983.

9. The literature on rural community studies is large, but there is some evidence that its vogue has passed. The heyday seems to have been the 1940–60 period, or at least the majority of published studies of North American rural communities (neighborhoods, and towns) seem to have been issued during that 20-year period. Redfield, 1955, is the classic theoretical statement of the mode—at least the anthropological version. Arensberg & Kimball, 1965, present a fine sample of the empirical interests. In the 1970s much of the interest seems to have shifted out of social science into *belles lettres*. The reasons are not hard to find: they are the same factors that have created concern among rural sociologists: the passing of the rural-urban cultural differentiation and the absorption of rural life and society into national frames. (For a classic study of a small town, see Vidich & Bensman, 1958. This can be compared with a contemporary study [Swanson *et. al.*, 1979], to see the changing perspectives on such research. An example of the literary approach to rural community study is Blythe, 1969. In the writer's opinion, the best studies of rural neighborhoods and districts in North America were those produced by the U.S. Dept. of Agriculture's Div. of Farm Population and Rural Welfare in the 1940's: "Rural Life Studies.")

10. Most of whom seem to belong to the disciplines of European historical sociology or history. E.g., Franklin, 1969; Benvenuti, 1962).

11. See Bennett, 1982, chapters 7 and 11 for a detailed analysis.

12. For some studies of sex roles and roles of family members in kin-operated farming enterprises, see the following: Bennett, 1982, chapters 6 and 7 (in cooperation with Seena B. Kohl); Wilkening, 1968 (and other papers by Wilkening). A recent study of family kin roles in relationship to innovation is Calson and Dillman, 1983.

13. All the early work on social-behavioral research in agricultural contexts was informed by this situation. The "resistance" was simply believed, in the First Development Decade of the 1950s, to be against the interests of the indigenous agriculturalists; hence the goal of the social researcher was to provide the development specialist with knowledge which would permit him to overcome this resistance to "modernization." For an example of this approach, see Leagans and Loomis, 1971.

14. This is a new field of study and its literature is not abundant. For surveys in the form of symposium volumes, see: Brokensha and Others, 1980; and Kidd and Colletta, 1980. The literacy issue has a tangential relationship to ethnoscience: see Barnes & Others, 1982; Hauf MS, 1984.

15. The writer recalls a long conversation with an American grain farmer about the strategy of summer fallowing and the highly recommended practice of leaving plant trash on the surface to control wind erosion. The farmer rejected "trash fallow" on strictly aesthetic grounds: "I know it ain't what you're supposed to do, but if I don't leave my fields clean I don't sleep at night!"

16. See Bennett, 1982. Part V of the book is entitled "Management Style," and is an attempt to characterize differences between farm management in terms of social behavioral patterns. Shorter summary versions of the material appears in a paper by Bennett in Barlett, 1980; another summary is Bennett, 1981.

17. The process of anticipation in human behavior is the key to the difficulties of prediction and precise causal analysis in decision behavior, innovation, and the like. Anthropologists used to call it "time binding." Planning should not be confused with this anticipatory function. Plans will change sequentially or sporadically through a temporal span because each subsequent event or development in the project affects the nature of anticipation of future events. The failure to take this into account has led to distortion and failure in the agrarian development process. For a theoretical discussion, see Bennett, 1976.

# References

Almy, Susan, ed. 1978. *Society, Culture, and Agriculture.* A Workshop on Training Programs combining Anthropology and Sociology with the Agricultural Sciences. New York: The Rockefeller Foundation, "Working Papers" series.

Arensberg, Conrad M., and S. T. Kimball. 1965. *Culture and Community.* New York: Harcourt Brace.

Barlett, Peggy, ed. 1980. *Anthropological Decision Making: Anthropological Contributions to Rural Development.* New York: Academic Press.

Barnes, D. F.; F. C. Fliegel; and R. D. Vanneman. 1982. "Rural Literacy and Agricultural Development: Cause or Effect?" *Rural Sociology* 47:251–71.

Bennett, John W. 1976. "Anticipation, Adaptation, and the Concept of Culture in Anthropology." *Science* 192:847–93.

_____. 1980. "Human Ecology as Human Behavior: A Normative Anthropology of Resource Use and Abuse." In *Human Behavior and Environment,* ed. Irwin Altman, Amos Rapoport, and Joachim Wohlwill, Vol. 4, Environment and Culture, pp. 243–277. New York: Plenum Press.

_____. 1981. "Farm Management as Cultural Style: Studies of Adaptive Process in the North American Farm Family." In *Research in Economic Anthropology,* ed. G. Dalton, Vol. 4. Greenwich, Conn.: JAI Press.

_____. 1982. *Of Time and The Enterprise: North American Family Farm Management in a Context of Resource Marginality.* Minneapolis: University of Minnesota Press.

_____. 1983. "Agricultural Cooperatives in the Development Process: Perspectives from Social Science." *Studies in Comparative International Development* 18:3–68.

_____. 1984. *Political Ecology and Development Projects Affecting Pastoralist Peoples in East Africa.* Madison, Wis., Land Tenure Center, University of Wisconsin, Research Paper No. 80.

Bennett, John W., and Don Kanel. 1983. "Agricultural Economics and Economic Anthropology: Confrontation and Accommodation." In *Economic Anthropology: Topics and Theories,* ed. S. Ortiz, Society for Economic Anthropology, Monograph No. 1. Lanhan, Md.: University Press of America.

Benvenuti, Bruno. 1962. *Farming in Cultural Change.* Assen, Netherlands: Van Gorcum.

Blythe, Ronald. 1969. *Akenfield: Portrait of an English Village.* New York: Random House.

Brokensha, David; D. M. Warren; and O. Werner. 1980. *Indigenous Knowledge Systems and Development.* Lanham, Md.: University Press of America.

Campbell, Rex R.; W. D. Heffernan; and J. L. Gilles. 1984. "Farm Operator Cycles and Farm Debts: An Accident of Timing." *Rural Sociologist* 4:404–8.

Cancian, Frank. 1967. "Stratification and Risk-Taking: A Theory Tested on Agricultural Innovation." *American Sociological Review* 32:912–27.

———. 1980. "Risk and Uncertainty in Agricultural Decision Making." In *Agricultural Decision Making: Anthropological Contributions to Rural Development*, ed. Peggy F. Barlett, pp. 161–176. New York: Academic Press.

Carlson, J. E., and D. A. Dillman. 1983. "Influence of Kinship Arrangements on Farmer Innovativeness." *Rural Sociology* 48:183–200.

Case, H. C. M., and D. B. Williams. 1957. *Fifty Years of Farm Management.* Urbana: University of Illinois Press.

Chibnik, Michael. 1980. "The Statistical Behavior Approach: The Choice Between Wage Labor and Cash Cropping in Rural Belize." In *Agricultural Decision Making; Anthropological Contributions to Rural Development*, ed. Peggy F. Barlett, pp. 87–114. New York: Academic Press.

Commons, John R. 1934. *Institutional Economics.* 2 vols. New York: Macmillan.

Firth, Raymond. 1955. "Some Principles of Social Organization." *Journal of the Royal Anthropological Institute* 85:1–20.

Franklin, S. H. 1969. *The European Peasantry: The Final Phase.* London: Methuen.

Friedland, William H. 1982. "The End of Rural Society and the Future of Rural Sociology." *Rural Sociology* 47:589–608.

Gladwin, Christine H. 1980. "A Theory of Real-Life Choice: Applications to Agricultural Decisions." In *Agricultural Decision Making: Anthropological Contributions to Rural Development*, ed. Peggy F. Barlett, pp. 45–86. New York: Academic Press.

Hauf, James. 1984. "Literacy and Innovation: New Evidence from the Study of Oral Cultures." Washington University: Unpublished Paper.

Heady, Earl H., and L. R. Whiting. 1975. *Externalities in the Transformation of Agriculture.* Ames: Iowa State University Press.

Kidd, E., and N. Colletta, ed. 1980. *Tradition for Development: Indigenous Structures and Folk Media in Non-Formal Education.* Berlin: German Foundation for International Development.

Knight, C. Gregory. 1980. "Ethnoscience and the African Farmer: Rationale and Strategy (Tanzania). In *Indigenous Knowledge Systems and Development*, ed. David W. Brokensha, et al., Lanham, Md.: University Press of America.

Leagans, J.P., and Charles P. Loomis. 1971. *Behavioral Change in Agriculture.* Ithaca: Cornell University Press.

Low, Allan. 1980. "The Estimation and Interpretation of Pastoralists' Price Responsiveness." London: Overseas Development Institute, Pastoral Network Paper 10c.

Maine, Sir Henry. 1864. *Ancient Law.* New York: Scribner.

McAndrews, Colin, and Chia Lin Sien ed. 1982. *Too Rapid Rural Development: Perceptions and Perspectives from Southeast Asia.* Athens: Ohio University Press.

Meehan, Peter. 1980. "Science, Ethnoscience, and Agricultural Knowledge Utilization." In *Indigenous Knowledge Systems and Development*, ed. David W. Brokensha, et al., Lanham, Md.: University Press of America.

Olson, Mancur. 1965. *The Logic of Collective Action.* Cambridge: Harvard University Press.

Ortiz, Sutti. 1973. *Uncertainties in Peasant Farming.* New York: Humanities Press.

———. 1980. "Forecasts, Decisions and the Farmer's Response to Uncertain Environments." In *Agricultural Decision Making: Anthropological Contributions to Rural Development*, ed. Peggy F. Barlett, pp. 177–202. New York: Academic Press.

Passin, Herbert, and J.W. Bennett. 1943. "Agricultural Magic in Southern Illinois." *Social Forces* 22:89–106.

Redfield, Robert. 1941. *The Folk Culture of Yucatan.* Chicago: University of Chicago Press.

———. 1955. *The Little Community: Viewpoints for The Study of a Human Whole.* Chicago: University of Chicago Press.

Rhoades, Robert E. 1983. "Tecnicista vs. Campesinista: Praxis and Theory of Farmer Involvement in Agricultural Research." In *Coming Full Circle: Farmers' Participation in the Development of Technology*, ed. P. Matlon et al., pp. 139–150, IDRC-189E. Ottawa: International Development Research Center.

_____. 1984a. "Understanding Small-Scale Farmers in Developing Countries: Sociocultural Perspectives on Agronomic Farm Trials." *Journal of Agronomic Education* 13:64–68.

_____. 1984b. *Anthropology in Agricultural Research: Agricultural Anthropology at the International Potato Center.* Lima, Peru: International Potato Center.

Rogers, Everett M., and F. F. Shoemaker. 1971. *Communication of Innovations: A Cross-cultural Approach.* New York: Free Press.

Sahi, R. K., and W. J. Craddock. 1975. "Estimating Crop Acreages in the Prairie Provinces: Application of Recursive Programming." *Canadian Journal of Agricultural Economics* 23:1–15.

Saint, W. S., and E. W. Coward Jr. 1977. "Agriculture and Behavioral Science: Merging Orientations." *Science* 197:733–36.

Salter, Leonard A. Jr. 1967. *A Critical Review of Research in Land Economics.* Madison: University of Wisconsin Press.

Schultz, Theodore W. 1964. *Transforming Traditional Agriculture.* New Haven: Yale University Press.

_____. 1981. *Investing in People: The Economics of Population Quality.* Berkeley: University of California Press.

Simon, Herbert. 1965. *Administrative Behavior: A Study of Decision-making Processes in Administrative Organization.* New York: Free Press, 1976.

Smith, Arthur H., and W. E. Martin. 1972. "Socioeconomic Behavior of Cattle Ranchers, with Implications for Community Development in the West." *American Journal of Agricultural Economics* 54: 217–25.

Staatz, John M., and C. K. Eicher. 1984. "Agricultural Development Ideas in Historical Perspective." In *Agricultural Development in the Third World,* ed. Carl Eicher and John M. Staatz, pp. 3–32. Baltimore: John Hopkins University Press.

Swanson, Bert E.; R. A. Cohen; and E. P. Swanson. 1979. *Small Towns and Small Towners: A Framework for Survival and Growth.* Beverly Hills: Sage Publications.

Tax, Sol. 1953. *Penny Capitalism: A Guatemalan Indian Economy.* Institute of Social Anthropology, Public. No. 16. Washington: Smithsonian Institution.

Vickers, Brian, ed. 1984. *Occult and Scientific Mentalities in the Renaissance.* New York: Cambridge University Press.

Vidich, Arthur J., and J. Bensman. 1958. *Small Town in Mass Society.* Princeton: Princeton University Press.

Whyte, William. F., and D. Boynton, eds. 1983. *Higher Yielding Human Systems for Agriculture.* Ithaca: Cornell University Press.

Wilkening, Eugene A. 1968. "Aspirations and Task Involvement as Related to Decision-making among Farm Husbands and Wives." *Rural Sociology* 33:30–45.

# 17

# New Directions for Agricultural Research: Summary and Conclusions

## Kenneth A. Dahlberg

## Introduction

One broad goal of the project and this book has been to expand the awareness and horizons of both participants and readers. One major obstacle is the specialized or disciplinary training most of us have received as well as the fact that many of us typically work in specialized departments, agencies, or divisions. From the beginning of the project, there has been a basic conviction on my part that the problems facing modern industrial agriculture cannot effectively be dealt with by relying exclusively on the same sort of specialization that is the source of so many of the problems themselves. Rather, an interdisciplinary and integrative approach was chosen, one involving humanists, social scientists, and natural scientists.

All participants agreed that the interactive process employed in the project and the interdisciplinary nature of the team combined to make each of us more aware of our underlying assumptions and to broaden and clarify our understandings of the larger context of modern agriculture, its neglected dimensions, and emerging alternatives. Here the attempt will be made to summarize the overall findings of the project and to draw out the major implications. It should be emphasized that this effort is that of the editor alone. Obviously, other participants would have somewhat different (or in some cases, quite different) interpretations. More important than my particular interpretation is the integrative and synthesizing effort involved in trying to relate and gain an overview of the various approaches, assumptions, and issues presented in the chapters. It is a process that all readers are encouraged to undertake themselves as well.

First, each chapter's main findings, questions, and implications will be summarized. Additional questions and implications identified by the editor and other reviewers will then be presented. This will be done section by section. Each section's summary will review the main research needs, the corresponding conceptual and data needs, the ethics, values, and goals involved, and the different levels where action or change is needed. A final overview will conclude the book.

## Ethical and Value Issues

The chapter by William H. Aiken, "On Evaluating Agricultural Research," provides us with a valuable "conceptual map" of four views (or more accurately, evaluative perspectives) on how to rank or choose among values and goals. These are the priority view, the trade-off view, the constraint view, and the holistic view. Aiken reviews each, discussing the types of questions that can be raised about each in terms of normative theory. Noting that most people are aware neither of other views nor the view that they themselves hold, Aiken, as befits a philosopher, calls for each of us to become more aware and to engage in a wider and more informed debate about how to apply these different views to policy questions—rather than simply seeking to impose our own view.

He indicates several possible approaches. One is simply to argue for the blanket superiority of one of the approaches. Whether this can be sustained either philosophically or politically is questionable. Next, one can try to combine the four views on the basis of some "supertheory." But this simply removes the basic problems to a higher level of abstraction. Finally, he suggests a more "contextual" approach—where specific policy questions would be examined in light of which view is most appropriate or relevant. Here he notes that the constraint view typically involves matters of health and safety, while the holistic view often relates to environmental and ecosystemic problems. In practice this approach would require an expansion of the decision making process to permit input and debate at the relevant points from representatives of each evaluative perspective.

In his final section, Aiken argues we need more than a "conceptual map"—important as he has demonstrated that to be. He suggests the need to map out the types of issues most typically associated with each evaluative perspective. One clear implication here is a need to map out whether the power configurations associated with different issue areas are related to, or draw upon particular views. For example, one would expect the priority view to be most common where there is a strong "establishment" which can develop consensus and determine and enforce priorities; the priority perspective clearly complements any establishment and aids in providing it with legitimacy. Equally, the trade-off view would appear to be common and reinforcing where there is a pluralistic power structure. In any case, this sort of "mapping" process would complement that called for in my first chapter—where the need to map out the goals and values of different groups and levels was stressed.

Jean Lipman-Blumen's chapter, "Exquisite Decisions in a Global Village," delineates clearly the ethical and value questions facing the First World in its relations with the Third World. Depending upon how one responds to her ten challenges, quite different long-range goals, directions, and priorities are suggested. Substantively, she questions the value of what we have sought as development—primarily economic development through the promotion of industry and the transfer of Western technologies—and the ways we have sought to measure it. National economic indicators tell us little about the actual living conditions of the various groups in a society—especially the weakest, poorest, and hungriest. Women particularly have suffered from the importation of inappropriate technologies and models of development. Such suffering, she argues, derives from fundamental inequalities of power, where " . . . the power relationship between women and men, with differential control over resources, provides the blueprint for all power relationships."

The "ten exquisite decisions" that she discusses bring out fundamental ethical and value issues regarding power, social justice, poverty, and development as they are embodied in our trade and aid policies, as well as how they are facilitated or hindered by actions in other sectors, such as military spending. A re-examination of technology transfer and "knowledge transfer" (the way in which we train and educate Third World students in the U.S.) is called for. Her concluding discussion stresses the need for new types of leadership to address the challenges identified.

One clear implication of this chapter is the need to improve our understanding of global trends and to overcome Western biases. The chapter also demonstrates the need to critically review U.S. foreign policy actions and programs in terms of whether they really advance such stated goals as promoting rural and agricultural development, greater social justice, and general improvement of the lives of the citizens of the Third World. It may well be that the pursuit of national power and national security undermines these goals. If a new goal is added—that of encouraging more sustainable agricultural systems, both at home and abroad—then the interactions with these larger foreign policy questions become even more complex. One emerging alternative viewpoint is that just as the farmer's first priority is to preserve next year's seed corn, a nation's first priority is to develop a sustainable and socially just agriculture and food system and that other domestic or foreign goals are subordinate. In making such judgments, proponents employ both their particular evaluative perspective and their empirical assessment of the degree to which agricultural lands, genetic resources, and rural life are threatened.

While each chapter in the book raises and addresses important ethical and value issues, this section (plus the first chapter) examines such issues in more analytic terms—seeking to describe the major evaluative perspectives, the different values and goals held by different groups, and the types of ethical and value choices involved in the setting of our national priorities. The value of these chapters is to make it quite explicit that ethical and value positions (often unconscious) underlie all aspects of agriculture and agricultural research. The "objectivity" of one level of analysis is framed by the larger value context of the next level. Aiken's point—that the way one evaluates the negative impacts of an enterprise like agriculture largely shapes how one evaluates the larger system—is particularly relevant given that the focus of this book is on neglected dimensions and emerging alternatives.

These initial chapters suggest additional research areas for each major intellectual field. Humanists need to research and discuss the conceptual maps and theories relating to agriculture and evaluations of agriculture; also, there is room for additional clarification of different value, goal, and ethical positions. Social scientists could do much more to map out and describe the different levels of goals and values held by dominant and alternative groups concerned about agriculture. Natural scientists could do much more to make explicit the value assumptions underlying both their professional and individual research activities. A matter for professional ethics as well as a research topic itself is the matter of distributional impacts. As other sections make clear, one cannot simply assume that a given research project or proposal will produce beneficial results. Better knowledge is needed of present and probable future impacts and how they are likely to be distributed through current institutional structures. How one evaluates the actual apportionment of impacts lies at the heart of both social and ethical theories.

**The Global Setting**

Charles F. Cooper's chapter, "American Agriculture and the Global Community," suggests that important as the human community and its growing numbers are, there is a larger community of species upon which we humans are ultimately dependent. We interact with them on a global basis through the larger impacts of our technologies upon the waters, lands, forests, and climatic and atmospheric systems of the biosphere. Cooper goes beyond the typical ecological review of these problems. In citing the new "evolutionary responsibility" we have acquired for the preservation of species and the viability of their habitat, Cooper also points to the fundamental ethical dilemma of how to reconcile this responsibility with the immediate needs of impoverished people in regions of great genetic diversity.

Cooper argues that current agricultural policies and systems are based upon hidden assumptions regarding the biological stability and equilibrium of agro-ecosystems which are outmoded and need to be replaced with newer concepts and understandings of the resilience of ecosystems. Once an ecosystem begins to lose its natural resilience (the ability to return to its current region of stability—typically that which is most favorable for human purposes), it can be prevented from moving to other, less desirable regions of stability only by "increasing external subsidies of energy and resources, increasing knowledge, and increasingly error-free control." Agro-ecosystems are doubly threatened with loss of resilience. Pollution, overuse, and resource degradation threaten natural resilience. Additional pressure and instability is introduced by the dependence of U.S. farmers upon widely fluctuating foreign markets, while these same exports often threaten economically viable and ecologically sound approaches to rural development abroad.

Cooper's chapter offers a good example of the effective incorporation of interdisciplinary concerns within the framework of a scholar's professional training. More than most ecologists, Cooper incorporates both economic and humanistic elements in his chapter. Particularly notable is his constant concern with how various research programs will benefit or harm the small peasant farmer—as exemplified in his discussion of the need to make sure in the design of weather forecasting programs that their benefits will not be captured by governments and large corporations alone. Cooper's chapter demonstrates the need for additional work on the ecological and resource foundations of modern agricultural systems— broadly defined. In addition to alerting us to the need to evaluate the resilience of particular systems and to assess how irreversible genetic losses may reduce that resilience, this new theory clearly implies that social and technological pressures need to be researched as part of any overall assessment of the resilience of a system. Finally, Cooper's review of the internal ecological threats to Third World agriculture, combined with Pimentel and Pimentel's later review of similar threats in the U.S. suggests the need to examine the ecological pressures exerted within each that derive from outside trade, aid, and technology processes.

Alain de Janvry and E. Phillip LeVeen's chapter, "Historical Forces that have Shaped World Agriculture: A Structural Perspective," demonstrates the importance of such a perspective in identifying broad social, institutional, and economic trends that are neglected in most conventional analyses. The long-term process of the commodification of food and agriculture is something associated with the rise of the modern industrial state. The importance of the development of formal markets, the monetization of economies, and the creation of labor markets (with a surplus) all suggest the analytic neglect of the informal sectors of society, especially those in the Third World. The increasing economic dependence of farmers and peasants as they are integrated into national and international agribusiness chains and divisions of labor is highlighted. The internationalization of capital compounds this dependence and threatens local food self-sufficiency in the Third World. First world farmers are threatened with the production "treadmill." Ultimately national economies, especially export-oriented ones like the U.S., are threatened with commodity instabilities which can affect the whole economy.

Neglect of the new actors who shape agricultural policy, but have no direct interest in farming (commodity exporters and their governmental allies) and neglect of the new social relations emerging from the historic trends described also lead, they argue, to a faulty diagnosis of both First and Third World agricultural problems. In the U.S., the family farm cannot be saved, they argue, either by strengthening current policies or seeking reform packages based on a new populism. In the Third World, they argue that except for a few still traditionally structured societies, land reform and rural development programs are inadequate to counter the trend towards an increasingly cornered peasantry. They present no remedies, but their analysis implies the need—one way or another—to moderate or reverse the basic structural trends they identify.

Perhaps closest to the emerging literature on "world systems," this chapter goes beyond many such analyses by focusing on agriculture and rural development and how they have had, and will continue to have profound impacts on industrial society. The analysis itself also illustrates another gap: the tendency to examine agriculture and rural development in capitalist and socialist countries separately—much like the tendency to study separately "modern" and "traditional" (read First and Third world) agriculture. My own interpretation is that many of the trends identified, particularly those related to the formalization of the economy and the state's power over it, are common to all modern industrial states, socialist and capitalist. Both have economic theories assuming control over nature and the substitutability of resources in the pursuit of material and technological progress. Both have difficulty dealing with environmental problems and the systemic issues they raise. Clearly, too, there are significant historic and institutional differences between them as well as differences in the way wealth, income, and other resources are distributed. However, in terms of impacts on Third World agriculture, it is clear that industrial agriculture, as promoted by capitalist approaches and countries, has been by far the most influential.

The chapters in this section clearly portray the analytic and substantive challenges we face in understanding the global setting and its importance. Major needs in conceptual clarification and in data relate to the tendency in Western culture to focus almost exclusively on the formal, rational, economic, and technological aspects of society. The informal, non-rational, ecologic, and social dimensions of our own and other cultures need much more exploration. Substantively, issues of species survival (including our own), evolutionary responsibility, and social justice have been generated by our technological capacities to influence natural and social systems, while new dilemmas emerge from our inability to fully control or regulate such impacts. This gap between our powers and our effective responsibility suggests two broad alternatives. One, widely discussed, is to create some form of world governent. The other, which takes greater account of the "invisible" factors mentioned above, is to restructure and largely (but not fully) decentralize many industrial institutions and infrastructures. These broader challenges go well beyond the more obvious needs to map out the various ways that global and international systems increasingly shape national and local contexts. An underlying question for researchers is whether the largely Western origins and assumptions of their disciplines can be reinterpreted and broadened to a truly global compass.

### The National Setting: Past and Present Goals and Priorities in U.S. Agriculture and Agricultural Research

The first chapter in this section, "Publicly-Sponsored Agricultural Research in the United States from an Historical Perspective," by David B. Danbom, provides a valuable overview of the changing cultural setting of agriculture and the evolution of agricultural research institutions. He traces the different views society has had of farmers, from the Jeffersonian view that farmers were almost intrinsically virtuous, to the late nineteenth century urban view that farmers were virtuous to the degree that they obtained the necessary education and training to serve society. Today, posing as "agribusinessmen," farmers have sought equal recognition with other commercial sectors. Whatever their changes in status, it is notable that with the creation of the land grant colleges and the experiment station system farmers received earlier and more extensive public funding than other economic sectors.

These new institutions were created by Congress in the absence of the expertise, knowledge, and data to make them effective. Many years of experimentation and gradual professionalization were required to give them clear direction and smooth operation (as new needs are identified today, perhaps comparable institutional innovation is needed). The early directions—a professionalism based on the natural science disciplines, a narrow problem-oriented approach with production as the chief goal, and an equation of scientific and technological advance with progress for all in the society—are still largely with us even though there have been several periods of intense external criticism. Danbom indicates that the system has never been able to develop effective internal means of self-criticism. Henry Wallace's attempts in the 1930s to bring in broader perspectives through greater use of social scientists did not last. Overall, alliances between the research establishment and the larger and wealthier farmers and other powerful groups have given it a generally conservative cast.

The question of the responsiveness of the system is an important one, especially today when there are again major external critiques and the system is seen to be undermining one of its own main rationales—the preservation of the family farm. Danbom's analysis suggests major institutional inertia, but some capacity to change. If we seek to place this sort of largely national history in a global perspective, then it would seem that there is a need to examine in more detail the role, not just of wars, but of expanding markets, trade, and aid in shaping research goals, particularly those related to productivity. Also, the issues of shifting control over agricultural policy and research agendas needs to be examined in this light. Finally, by combining our current problem context with Danbom's analysis we can see that neither the earlier Jeffersonian vision nor the later idealism of professional researchers in seeking to help farmers improve society is an adequate vision today. The question of an appropriate vision for the future emerges with force—particularly if one considers an era of declining resource availability as a real possibility.

Dale L. Stansbury's chapter on the context and implications of the 1977 Farm Bill deals with the shorter-term responses of the political system to perceived changes and needs in agriculture. He points out that such perceptions are shaped by the larger national social, economic, and scientific context. After several decades of relative calm, the 1970s brought a wide range of agriculturally related issues before Congress: world hunger, oil shocks, environmental threats, economic pressures, etc. The ensuing debates and conflicts involved basically different approaches to research— those researchers outside of agriculture stressing basic research, competitive grants, and peer review (things that would also give them more access to agricultural research funds) and those inside emphasizing applied research, formula funding, and administrative allocation. Questions of focus—for example, animal research versus crop research—also emerged. For legislators, however, the main issues were the big dollar and constituency issues, things such as commodity and food stamp programs. The research issues (Title XIV) were delegated to staff, where an open process involving all organized groups led from an initial four page draft to a forty-one page laundry list of findings and purposes.

The organizational changes proposed were aimed at: a) developing an "early warning system" to bring out problems perceived by users (through creation of the Users Advisory Board), b) creating a new body, the Joint Council, to coordinate and adjudicate among the issues brought up, and c) setting up a new subcommittee in the executive branch to serve as a policy forum. The political vagaries of institutional change were illustrated when one conferee at the last moment vetoed the planned inclusion of EPA and OSHA on the Joint Council. Even with a difficult and confrontational beginning, Stansbury argues that the new advisory/policy development system has brought important issues into the open, has generated dialogue, and has helped to broaden the research agenda somewhat. He warns against both a despotism of tradition (attempts to maintain the *status quo* in departments, disciplines, and budgets) and elitist take-overs by those outside agriculture who think they know both what is good for it and how to manage it better. An important short-term question raised by this chapter is: given all the changes since 1977, how will research issues and funding be handled in the 1985 Farm Bill? A longer-term question also emerges: Is our political process able to anticipate new or neglected issues (such as those analyzed in this book) and address them politically, or can it only respond to those broad and burning issues brought to it by currently powerful and vocal groups?

The chapter by John Patrick Jordan, Paul O'Connell, and Roland Robinson, "Historical Evolution of the State Experiment Station System," offers a concise overview of the system from within. The early roots and major pieces of legislation establishing the system are described along with a review of some of the early debates over whether the Land Grant schools should conduct research, and if so, what kind. The shifting definitions of state and federal responsibilities and funding are then traced through their various legislative embodiments. The organizational and procedural innovations contained in the 1977 and 1981 Farm Bills are described and figures are given on the current program emphasis within the State Agricultural Experiment Station (SAES) system in terms of scientist years per program goal.

The chapter then reviews the characteristics of the SAES system—its decentralized nature; its research, teaching, and extension functions; its diverse funding sources; and how it is organized on the basis of academic disciplines (in contrast to other USDA research programs which are organized on the basis of problem areas). Various accomplishments of the agricultural sciences are reviewed in light of the longer term shifts from hand power to horse power to mechanical power to "science power." The accomplishments highlighted are the development of hybrid corn, changes in the broiler industry since the 1950s, and improvements in farm management.

An extensive list of the future challenges facing the SAES system is presented. These revolve around several perceived needs: a) to improve the science base of agricultural research (especially in the biotechnology field), b) to improve the competitive position of U.S. agricultural exports, c) to improve the efficiency of plant and animal production through a variety of techniques; and d) to encourage more interaction between nutritionists and agriculturalists. Areas of concern which are identified include: preserving the availability of the natural resource base, developing better ways to evaluate and monitor food safety, making the best use of forest and range land, and encouraging exchanges of germplasm. The concluding remarks stress the positive benefits of the system to taxpayers and the need to go beyond technological advances alone in the search for greater efficiency, productivity, and resource maintenance.

This chapter offers a good presentation of how those involved in administering one of the major components of the agricultural research system understand it. As such, it should be of use to both observers of, and participants in, the system. It reflects a continuing emphasis on production, productivity, and efficiency as the major goals of the system, although the concerns of a number of critics are acknowledged. The description of the legislative history of the system includes much more discussion of the specific research topics mentioned than the larger social goals and purposes provided by Congress to guide and evaluate the direction of such research. Accomplishments tend to be highlighted much more than problems, both in emphasis and in interpretation. A good example of this can be seen in the view of the broiler industry presented here—which stresses the increases in productivity and efficiency—as contrasted to that presented by Heffernan (see below)—which stresses the social costs and the risks of concentration. More generally, the chapter does not address the challenges of the emerging bi-modal structure of agriculture nor the need to incorporate into current research assessments of environmental, social, and technological impacts.

This section makes clear the way in which conceptions of agriculture and rural life have changed as we have become more industrialized. From a broad socio-economic conception at the founding of the Republic, where farming was seen as a way of life with intrinsic value, today we find the "official" view to be that of farming as a business and agriculture as an economic sector just like any other. In part, this can be seen to be a result of the narrow professionalization and production-orientation that Danbom documents; in part, it can be seen as an attempt by farmers and their "defenders" to compensate for their declining status and political power by seeking to portray their activities in the currency of those with higher status and prestige in the society. The new concerns and criticisms discussed in this book and elsewhere—regarding the environmental, health, and structural problems of agriculture and the concerns of the larger society with nutrition, food safety, unemployment, etc.—all suggest that once again a re-conceptualization of agriculture may be needed. One that would see that moving towards greater ecological integrity and sustainability, rural revitalization, and a more equitable and diverse agriculture and food system may well require an understanding of agriculture and rural life as being more fundamental than other sectors.

## Assessing Neglected Dimensions: Evaluative Concepts and Indices in Agricultural Research

Molly Joel Coye's chapter on "The Health Effects of Agricultural Production" offers perhaps the most striking example of an area of major neglect—an "externality" little explored by any of the many disciplines within the agricultural research establishment. Unfortunately, the urban origins of the public health field and the general exclusion of farmers and agricultural workers from most major federal health and safety legislation have meant that there has been relatively little attention given from that side either, except in such major agricultural states as California and Florida. Her review of the state of knowledge of the effects of current production systems upon the health of agricultural workers and farmers reveals huge data gaps, serious problems with the quality of what data there is, lack of sufficient review by regulatory agencies, and legal and proprietary constraints taking precedence over health considerations. An additional problem is that regulatory policies for protecting the general public (for example, those setting pesticide residue limits) are often based on theoretical models and averaging techniques which ignore significant ethnic differences in the consumption of various foods and ignore the higher susceptibility of particular groups such as children, pregnant women, etc. Sampling and monitoring efforts are typically sporadic, underfunded, and directed at the most acute and short-term problems. Very little is done to monitor longer-term effects.

Even with these difficulties and a clear underreporting of accidents and problems, agricultural workers register the third highest injury rate of any industry; illness rates are also high. General rural health is poor, especially in terms of mental health. Aggregated statistics and the lack of common reporting procedures (or even a common format for death certificates among states) make it difficult to assess the health of farmers and their families as compared to the general rural population. Coye stresses the need for better data, more surveys, and more research. However, she argues that structural changes may also be needed—for example, shifting the burden of proof regarding the presumed harmlessness of new chemicals. Finally, she stresses the need for the agricultural research community to move away from narrow definitions of agriculture and to include public health concerns and processes (involving agricultural workers, farmers, and the rural population) as a major research priority.

Coye's chapter reinforces Danbom's observations regarding the momentum of public agencies, once their direction is established. One of the major questions here is how one goes about encouraging two groups—the agricultural research establishment and the public health agencies—each to move in new directions and to learn to cooperate in the process. The ethical implications of the neglect of health issues are also significant. It is morally questionable to make major decisions involving agricultural health matters when one is in the dark regarding their immediate, much less potential intergenerational consequences. Yet, how does one overcome the political fear of "finding more trouble" if new light on negative health effects is generated through better surveys, data, and research? Perhaps most inequitable is the fact that it is the poorest, weakest, and least organized groups in our society who bear the greatest risks and costs of an agricultural production system that could well afford to offer them better protection. Fundamental issues of social justice, political, corporate, and consumer responsibility are raised here.

William D. Heffernan's "Review and Evaluation of Social Externalities" examines the reasons for, and the consequences of, neglecting the social costs and benefits of agriculture. The general abundance of agricultural resources and food (plus a strong tradition of decentralization) have meant that the U.S. has never developed a national food policy. Also, there has been strong political opposition by key Congressmen to the USDA developing any internal capacity for assessing and criticizing the social consequences of agricultural policies or technologies—witness the elimination of the Bureau of Agricultural Economics which Henry Wallace had created and which had raised such questions. Finally, the narrow problem- and production-orientation of a research system based on an equally narrow efficiency paradigm led to a situation where there was virtually no encouragement for researchers to ask about the social consequences of their work, while at the same time there was strong political and administrative discouragement for so doing. Heffernan asks why this paradigm, which stresses the saving of labor and to a lesser extent reducing crop acreages, still is largely unquestioned at a time when approaches which make more efficient use of, or which save energy, water, soil, and especially capital would make more sense.

Heffernan reviews the general social consequences of the two thrusts of agricultural research: those reducing the need for labor, and those increasing output per non-human unit of input. Labor has been "transferred" out of agriculture (with corresponding increases in urban problems relating to schools, welfare, crime, etc.), while those remaining on the farm have been increasingly placed on a "production treadmill" where they have to produce more and more with less and less of a profit margin. As urban capital has flowed into rural areas to meet the needs of of capital intensive approaches, control over agriculture has shifted to urban centers. Heffernan presents a striking analysis of farms as "rural assembly plants" which add little value to agricultural inputs produced elsewhere (with farmers thus circulating only the return to their labor—perhaps 10 percent of total input costs—in their rural communities). This analysis suggests the need for different conceptual and data maps. Equally challenging is his case study of the development of the broiler industry over the past 30 years. What was once one of the most decentralized, competitive, and farmer-managed production fields is now among the most geographically concentrated, oligopolistic, and centrally managed industries.

While Heffernan does not argue that agricultural research caused these changes, it certainly facilitated them—particularly since there was virtually no questioning of the social consequences of research innovations. Besides calling for a re-examination of the efficiency paradigm and encouraging social assessments of research innovations, Heffernan's chapter also implies the need to examine systematically the social consequences of economic and tax policies—since they are no more neutral in their distributional impacts than technologies. Beyond that, new approaches, concepts, and data are needed to try to evaluate and incorporate into research policy making a wide range of non-measurable goals and values—such as freedom and human dignity—as well as probable production effects; for example, those on health, safety, environmental integrity, and sustainability, which are not easy to measure and which include intergenerational dimensions.

Patrick Madden's chapter, "Beyond Conventional Economics—An Examination of the Values Implicit in the Neoclassical Economic Paradigm as Applied to the Evaluation of Agricultural Research," goes far to explain why there has been so little questioning by economists of the social impacts of agricultural research and technologies. First, he reviews the different schools of economic thought, stressing the dominant neoclassical school—which blends a liberal Lockean tradition with positivistic understandings of modern math and science. Among the assumptions which Madden examines for their implicit values are those of "harmlessness," which is based on Pareto and Hicks-Kaldor criteria which tend to give preference to existing institutions, distributions of property rights, and income; "consumer sovereignty," which he argues is ultimately based on greed and which fails to distinguish between wants and needs; and "intergenerational equity," where the serious technical and philosophical difficulties of discount rates are reviewed.

Madden then analyzes in detail the value assumptions underlying the three major approaches used in the economic evaluation of agricultural research. All three are built upon often weak and uneven data bases—a fact that should raise basic questions about the construction of elaborate models upon them. The consumer and producer surplus approach depends heavily upon the previously criticized discounting assumptions. Also, this approach includes little on the distribution of costs and benefits, nor are externalities even estimated. Regression studies avoid discounting problems, but haven't addressed externalities or future generations. Also, in those few studies where research budgets and efforts are disaggregated, it is shown that there are higher rates of return where research is linked with extension and farmers. An area of needed research is on public-private research interactions. Mathematical programming approaches offer considerable promise in evaluating technological choices at the farm level, and can even include some environmental factors (where they are known). Overall, Madden concludes that since the vast majority of agri-cultural research is conducted in the private sector, the social responsibil-ity of those in the public sector is that much greater, and that a prerequi-site for economists assuming their share is for them to become much more aware of the value assumptions within and surrounding their discipline.

Becoming aware of one's assumptions and moving beyond them are two different things, particularly if an organized group is involved. Works like Madden's will hopefully encourage economists to become more aware of the full implications of the tendency to reduce all values to monetary values and to enshrine consumer sovereignty; however, how does one then go beyond that to effectively assess and evaluate non-economic and non-monetary phenomena and values? Does one do better to seek a re-conceptualization of economics to include principles based on ecology and ethics—or does one start with one of the other two fields? Each has its own venerable traditions and sources of legitimacy. Each would have its own advantages in serving as a starting point for more holistic approaches. However, it would appear that economics faces one serious difficulty the others do not. Given the power of the neoclassical view as a rationale for dominant institutions and vested interests—as well as the important role that economists have played as policy advisers—it is unlikely that major transformations in the discipline will occur, even in the face of new problems.

The chapter "Energy and Other Natural Resources Used by Agriculture and Society" by David Pimentel and Susan Pimentel reviews many of these new problems as well as their historical roots. Pointing to the ways in which current high levels of crop production have caused the gradual degradation of soils and the rapid depletion of water and energy resources, they argue the need for an agricultural policy based upon ecological principles. Using an historical analysis of changing energy flows in crop production, they show that from 1700 to the present, U.S. energy inputs to corn have been increased fifteen times to increase production three and one half times. Even so, fossil fuels provide only seven percent of the total energy input for corn, the other 93 percent coming from solar energy. Using an analysis based on energy flows, they show clearly the interdependence of resources and how high fossil fuel inputs have affected labor, soil, and water resources.

Besides the "invisibility" of solar energy, conventional analyses also neglect the massive and crucial role of various natural biota in maintaining and regenerating the natural ecosystems upon which agriculture depends. They fix almost half again as much nitrogen as is provided by fertilizers; pollination by insects is crucial and no substitutes exist; waste degradation, water purification, and oxygen renewal are "free" services which depend upon maintaining the viability of the many species involved. Important beginnings are being made to identify and employ both ecological principles and natural biota in alternative fertilization, pest control, and soil erosion control programs. These all require new knowledge and techniques, plus localized approaches to application. These approaches need to be combined with others—such as legislative approaches seeking land and soil preservation—to work out a more holistic and ecologically based approach to resource management, one that includes energy costs and efficiencies, geographic factors, and population distributions.

The broad historical review of energy use in U.S. crop production clearly suggests the need to develop longer term strategies and policies to become less dependent upon non-renewable fossil fuels, while at the same time avoiding the overuse of renewable systems. Equally, the chapter highlights the "invisible" natural services and systems which economic and technological analyses typically ignore or neglect. Clearly, much more research needs to be done here—as it is not even clear what the key data and conceptual gaps are, especially in regard to the role of natural biota. Finally, there is the question of how to integrate into this type of natural science based analysis, human resources, goals, and social factors.

This section on neglected dimensions demonstrates the momentum of institutions, fields, and disciplines—each of which has its own set of priorities, value assumptions, and history. It also makes clear that we have few conceptual means, much less the necessary data sets to assess either the general societal benefits or costs of agriculture and agricultural research. To do this we need far greater research into health, safety, social, environmental, and resource externalities. Also, more research is needed on structural trends towards greater economic concentration and their effect upon rural and ecological diversity. Finally, these chapters alert us to the importance of processes which are "invisible" in conventional analyses. Making these more visible, plus addressing the many ethical questions involved in the use and misuse of partial data relating to them cannot but have a significant impact upon the way we evaluate the needs, accomplishments, goals, and priorities of agriculture and agricultural research.

### Emerging Alternatives and Their Implications

This section attempts to anticipate the problems and potentials of the major alternatives to conventional agriculture: those involving major commitments to biotechnological approaches and techniques, and those stressing sustainability, structural change, and organic farming. Generally, the latter are referred to as "alternative agriculture," while the former are usually seen as an elaboration of current approaches. However, as Buttel points out in his chapter, biotechnological approaches may transform agriculture and agricultural research institutions in fundamental ways.

William Lockeretz's chapter, "Alternative Agriculture," is important, not only because of the questions it raises, but because it represents an attempt to critically reflect on the directions and potential problems of alternative agriculture. As Danbom pointed out earlier, such critical reflection has been largely lacking within the agricultural research establishment. Thus, the types of questions Lockeretz raises should be seen to apply equally, if not more so, to conventional agriculture.

Lockeretz begins with the important point that "alternative agriculture" is a broad term which is interpreted differently by different groups. Some stress organic farming as the core; others the need to reduce dependence on the larger industrial economy; others the need for greater decentralization and self-reliance; others long-term sustainability; others rural revitalization and small-scale farming; and others healthier foods. The basic questions are whether the goals of these various groups are compatible, how they can best pursue them, and what policies and trade-offs are involved. Since these groups are seeking significant changes, there is the question—common to all groups seeking major changes—of whether pragmatic approaches involving compromise are best or whether goals should be sought in their pure form.

Lockeretz then applies these various questions to organic agriculture. Is it a matter of proper techniques or of larger goals? What are the proper and best ways of marketing in terms of identification, certification, premium prices, etc.? What about consumer and government support? Should it be sought and if so, on what basis? Turning to energy questions, Lockeretz stresses the need to analyze the trade-offs involved in terms of the total systems involved—to make sure that "savings" in one sector are not "lost" in others. Finally, he addresses the goal of localized food production. After discussing the pros and cons of our current national food distribution system, he raises questions about how one defines "local" if one is advocating localized systems. What is the extent? What about storage problems? And perhaps most fundamentally, is the underlying goal to strengthen local agriculture and farmers (which may involve their producing "exports") or to provide local citizens with food while reducing their dependence on external systems?

The conclusions Lockeretz draws apply to both alternative and conventional agriculture: there is a need for explicitly stating goals and examining trade-offs within a systems' perspective. More fundamentally, there is a need for conventional agriculture to develop the same sort of self-correcting and critical questioning that Lockeretz demonstrates here in regard to alternative agriculture. Going beyond Lockeretz's analysis, it should be noted that alternative agriculture can be seen as a reservoir of practical experience and experimentation which is available for wider adoption should economic and/or social conditions change. This is particularly true of local gardening and other forms of production for household use within urban areas—a neglected dimension that even Lockeretz does not discuss. Also, since alternative agriculture stresses the need to adapt to local and regional conditions through the use of ecosystemic approaches, it represents a model with more resilience. Finally, the diversity of the groups involved (even though they largely share a common paradigm) suggests the need to understand the questions raised not in stark "either-or" terms, but more in terms of balancing dynamically related factors.

Frederick H. Buttel's chapter, "Biotechnology and Agricultural Research Policy: Emergent Issues," raises quite a different set of questions—all relating to the potential impacts of biotechnologies upon current systems. After sketching the various critiques of the agricultural research establishment from the early 1970s onward, Buttel describes today's context as including a new set of actors and pressures which have emerged from the development of biotechnologies. He sees these as both a fundamental challenge and an opportunity for the research establishment to re-examine its role and goals. Many of the new actors involve the biotechnology firms, whether the large, integrated agroinput multinationals or the small start-up firms. In addition, there is the interest of the Office of Science and Technology Policy (OSTP) in the White House as evidenced in the 1982 Winrock Report. The latter essentially argues the need for agricultural research to focus on biotechnology primarily as a tool of national power in international economic and technological competition. This view reflects little concern for its potential impact on farmers.

The dilemmas and probable impacts Buttel examines include growing disparities among the land grant universities and a shifting division of labor between public and private research. He suggests the strong possibility that private research goals and agendas will have increasing influence upon publicly funded research and points out that basic questions regarding its public purposes are thereby raised. In addition, the whole area may become politicized because it will be difficult to argue that the public interest is served by public research institutions increasingly co-opted by large private firms and interests. One alternative would be for publicly funded research to develop new client groups—small farmers, urban gardeners, etc.—and to work on areas which will be neglected by the private sector. Buttel also examines the ways in which biotechnological approaches may further threaten genetic resources by extending the use of monocultural practices. Internationally there is already quite a bit of politicization—deriving from the fears of the Third World that they will be left out of the coming "biorevolution" and will become increasingly dependent upon large foreign suppliers. Here again, the publicly funded sector—the international agricultural research centers—are placed in a very difficult position. Should they seek to develop biotechnological expertise in the crops they have traditionally dealt with (wheat, rice, and maize)? Or should they seek to expand their work with small peasant farmers and various subsistence groups? The former risks their co-optation by the large multinationals, while the latter may carry less glamor and weight with governments and funding agencies.

While Buttel's chapter makes very clear the need for careful and wide-ranging assessments of the potential impacts of biotechnology, it also suggests that greater private sector research will undercut the rationale for such assessments and perhaps make them politically more difficult. One of the fundamental ethical and political questions that emerges from his chapter is: To what degree does government have a legitimate role in protecting vital non-economic goals (such as genetic conservation, equity, free scientific inquiry, environmental integrity, etc.) from reduction to the purely economic goals of the private sector, even though the latter may possibly promote national economic interests in the short term. The chapter also brings out one of the potential risks of viewing agriculture only in larger national and international economic terms. That is, that in pursuing national economic goals, agriculture comes to be seen simply as another "tool." One clear implication of this book is that in terms of developing more sustainable and resilient agricultural systems, the farmer is one of the central and critical elements and that all larger systems need to be designed with his basic needs and motivations—economic, social, and moral—in mind.

C. Dean Freudenberger's chapter, "Value and Ethical Dimensions of Alternative Agricultural Approaches: In Quest of a Regenerative and Just Agriculture," seeks to clarify these dimensions by examining four basic questions raised by practitioners and proponents of alternative agriculture. He begins by contrasting conventional and alternative perspectives on what exactly are the problems facing agriculture. The conventional view largely addresses a range of physical and biological problems, with occasional mention of social aspects. The alternative perspective includes these, but places them in a larger global context including problems of hunger, social justice, and genetic diversity.

In discussing the four basic questions raised by the alternative critique *and* vision, he shows the many linkages between the ideas of a regenerative and of a socially just agriculture. His discussion of responsibility links questions of intergenerational responsibility and equity with the responsibility to sustain the biosphere's ecological heritage. In reviewing discussions of the presence or absence of meaning in relationships and work, he focuses on the interactions over time of place, community, and work. The fundamental value of life in all its varied forms and interconnectedness leads to the idea of the need to respect the "natural integrities" upon which we all depend. Each of these points suggests the need to include the welfare of future generations—human and non-human—in our vision of the future and in the  agricultural research agenda that flows from it.

Just as current approaches are based on a particular paradigm which emphasizes production and economic values, these alternative approaches suggest an emerging paradigm. The main characteristics Freudenberger sees involve the concept of a regenerative agriculture wedded to ecologically and socially based concepts of justice. Interdisciplinary approaches are required to develop and promote such concepts as are new research agendas. Freudenberger's exploratory review—with its larger compass—combines well with Lockeretz's more policy oriented approach. However, as shown in the Buttel, Heffernan, and de Janvry and LeVeen chapters, there is also a need to include the distribution and impact of political and economic power—a point that simply reinforces Freudenberger's observation regarding the importance of interdisciplinary approaches.

The chapters in this section suggest that U.S. agriculture and agricultural research may well be at a turning point—whether this is realized by most researchers or not. If this is the case, then it is vital that the underlying assumptions of the conventional paradigm be brought to light, discussed, and evaluated in terms of both the larger trends outlined earlier and the various alternatives outlined in this section. Wide-ranging and open discussion of genuine alternatives is needed, both to provide for a critical review of current programs, policies, and priorities and to clarify the underlying choices and responsibilities facing us in the future. The increasing importance of private sector research—especially in the biotechnology field—suggests new kinds of responsibilities for publicly funded agricultural research. These would appear to include: more research on the neglected areas described in this book; more emphasis on making environmental and social impact assessments of both public and privately funded research and development; greater attention to examining and perhaps even developing regulatory arrangements to address anticipated (as well as current) impacts; and the need to respond to, and protect the interests of a much wider range of groups than has been the case to date.

**Where Do We Go from Here?**

This section contains two different chapters. The first is that of a long-time researcher of human ecology and its agricultural manifestations. His research has been conducted outside the agricultural research establishment and represents a model of interdisciplinary work. The second is this chapter.

John Bennett's chapter, "Research on Farmer Behavior and Social Organization," argues that most agricultural research focuses on general and macro processes and neglects the critical importance of the micro behavior of farmers, peasants, and their ecosystems. Agricultural research is new—having an existence of only about 150 years—as compared to the 12,000 years of agriculture, and has grown out of the dominance of the scientific professions. The latter have operated upon assumptions of the superiority of "expert" or exogenous knowledge over "practitioner" or indogenous knowledge. Recent anthropological and sociological research has helped to correct the view that Third World peasants act differently, or "irrationally" as compared to farmers in industrial countries. Such research suggests the importance of approaches which seek to include symbols, values, social structures, and the various motives of farmers in their mapping out of micro-macro interactions.

Bennett argues that the assumed superiority of expert knowledge, the narrowness of disciplilnary specialization, and the lack of careful and integrated micro studies have combined to seriously limit our knowledge of farmer behavior and especially their decision processes. He argues that the field of ethnoscience offers a useful approach to address the cultural dimensions of farmer behavior. The need for much longer time horizons in examining "the temporal process of adaptive behavior" of farmers is stressed. From his own longitudinal studies of North American plains agriculture, Bennett points out that—as one farmer explained—decisions "grow on you;" that is, they are part of a process involving social pressures, environmental constraints, and a range of risks and uncertainties.

Problems of understanding the environment are analogous. They need to be understood both in terms of the ecosystemic dynamics and the institutional patterns (both micro and macro) which influence resource utilization and conservation. When one combines all these factors in an examination of specific farm systems, one sees that they are embodied in locally adapted socio-cultural systems. For example, Bennett argues that we must understand the "family farm" as the "agrifamily system," where there is a combination of economic and social systems changing and adapting over time. Equally, at the macro level we must all try to seek better understandings of why rural poverty persists in all societies.

Bennett's conclusion that the agricultural research agenda needs broadening is very different in substance than other similar conclusions. This is because he is arguing that current disciplines and university structures grew up in simpler times and that they no longer represent nor can adequately capture the complexity and interdependence of human activities. At the same time he is fully aware of the difficulty of bringing change to these "quasi-political institutions." He asks us how we are "to attain larger visions of human complexity in a fragmented knowledge industry?" Clearly, his own work, as well as the chapters on alternatives suggest that academics and researchers need to examine the full complexity of farmer behavior—ecological, social, and managerial—as well as carefully reviewing what those seeking alternatives outside the comfortable confines of academia are doing and saying. Expanding our awareness of the full dimensions of current practices as well as of genuine possibilities and alternatives is one of the prerequisites for attaining the larger visions Bennett calls for.

## Conclusions

Four main themes emerge from the chapters: a) that the basic context of agriculture is changing in fundamental ways in terms of resource, socio-economic, and technological trends (the magnitude of perceived change often being related to the degree of awareness one has of the other three themes); b) that there are a number of largely "invisible" externalities that need to be brought into our evaluations of the real costs and benefits of current agricultural production modes; c) that a wide range of alternative approaches and conceptions are emerging which need to be considered seriously and carefully by all concerned about the future of agriculture; and d) that the choices in and between conventional and alternative approaches to agriculture require us all to clarify our personal and societal goals and priorities and their underlying values. Let us examine each of these in turn.

*Changing Contexts*

The changing context of agriculture is recognized by all analysts. What is at dispute is how best to understand the changes, their causes, and their implications. The broad outlines of this changing context and some of the causes were presented in Chaper 1. At the symposium which was held as part of this project, a number of specific public policy issues, trade-offs, and implications emerged in the wide-ranging discussions that occurred. Differences within and between conventional and alternative perspectives also emerged. These were nicely captured in a series of questions which John W. Bennett saw running through the discussions and debates. A representative cross section included the following:

> Should we protect ecosystems at the cost of lowering agricultural income? Can we feed the world and maintain the profits of international business? Can we create national goals for agriculture when the system generates huge profits or politial gains through manipulation of instabilities—instabilities accentuated by dependence on export markets? Can we create goals for agriculture more respecting of the environment and at the same time more rewarding for farmers? Can we continue to discharge rural population into cities and also maintain employment for urban populations? Can we increase the return on investment for farmers and still maintain relatively low prices for farm products to the consumer? Why continue to push productivity per acre and low labor costs when we need to maintain a rural population? Can we continue to treat farm labor as a peonage when all other industrial labor has protection over its working conditions? Do we regulate against pollution, etc. or do we improve farming systems? Can we change our economistic thinking about market prices and regard them as normative approximations subject to change depending upon the social policies involved—that is, change resulting from actual negotiations? Can we replace monitary definitions of value with other values—posterity, equity, truth, beauty? Can we reduce energy inputs and still maintin high crop yields? Can we support alternative agriculture as an institution and as a movement and at the same time avoid co-opting it into the system? Should we give biotechnology to private or public research empires? How much difference is there from one empire to another? Must alternative agriculture live up to the same standards of productivity and profit as conventional agriculture? Should the U.S. spend more on agricultural development in the Third World, or do we let the world market system determine outcomes?

Bennett saw a number of dilemmas underlying these questions— dilemmas relating to the fundamental problems of modern pluralism, shifting balances of power between groups, as well as the 5,000 year long tradition of "cheap food" policies that arose as part of civilization. Whether or not one agrees with Bennett, two conclusions can be drawn. First, that as soon as one moves towards spelling out the policy implications of either conventional or alternative perspectives, a host of trade-off and priority questions emerge—which, as stressed below, need much greater analytic and ethical clarification. Second, that major efforts are needed to map out and better evaluate the longer-term structural, resource, and technological sources of the changes so dramatically affecting agriculture. This can be done more at the global level, as Cooper, and de Janvry and LeVeen have done, or more at the national level, as Buttel, and Pimentel and Pimentel have done. The conceptual, data, and methodological requirements are great, but the risks of misreading or simply missing the implications of macro changes and trends are greater. Institutional inertia and political resistance can be expected. Even so, there appears to be some openness on the part of the agricultural research establishment to the need for broad-range assessments.

*Externalities*

While the chapters have made important contributions towards our better understanding the extent and significance of externalities (particularly those relating to environmental, social, and rural health matters), it is in regard to tracing the various cultural, institutional, and political reasons for their neglect that it breaks the most new ground. These have been analyzed at the international, national, and sectoral levels, although not in a fully systematic manner—for we have few theories or approaches that can integrate these dimensions. Over the past 50 years agriculture and agricultural research priorities have become increasingly dominated by narrow conceptions and models—particularly those based on production goals and neo-classical economic models. Madden has shown the limitations of these, even in their own terms. When one then places them in larger national and international contexts—where the informal sectors of society are larger and where environmental, resource, and population problems are more diverse—it becomes clear that broader, more inclusive, and more self-aware approaches are needed.

Two broad implications flow from the above. First, if we are going to be able to clearly describe and map the distributional impacts of the various externalities identified, much more effort will need to be devoted to developing the concepts, data, and research teams required. The chapters on environmental, resource, social, and rural health externalities suggest the magnitude of effort required. Also, they suggest a fundamental conceptual shift: from research on agriculture as a sectoral and largely economic activity to research on agriculture as only one form of food production, one embedded in larger and interacting resource, technological, and social systems on the one hand, and dependent upon complex family, community, and local environmental conditions on the other. This is not to suggest the abandonment of conventional sectoral and economic research; rather that it can become a more valuable analytic tool to the degree that its limitations in dealing with other levels (both macro and micro) and with systemic dimensions are recognized.

The second implication is that our understandings of agriculture and its positive and negative results can be expected to become very different as we actually incorporate "external" costs, benefits, and trends—and their actual distribution among different groups and levels—into our research on, and evaluations of agriculture. Our "pictures" of the relative scale efficiencies of different size farms can be expected to change as the high energy, social, health, and resource costs of large-scale and intensive approaches become more visible. Equally, evaluations of how economic (in the broadest sense) conventional and alternative approaches are can also be expected to change. Similarly, current calculations of the cost effectiveness of investments in public agricultural research can be expected to change, probably showing less dramatic returns. However, given the strength of the cultural roots supporting current conceptions, the momentum of institutional patterns, and the power of the various vested interests that benefit from the current distribution of costs and benefits, it must be recognized that efforts to develop and especially to incorporate these various externalities into our evaluations of agriculture will be a difficult and challenging task.

## Emerging Alternatives

The range of emerging alternatives—both practical and conceptual—suggests that a number of people are worried enough about the direction of current approaches to make the considerable efforts involved in seeking alternatives. These alternatives are based not only on a recognition of the larger resource, structural, and technological trends, but upon a cluster of values and goals which stress the need for a more resilient, regenerative, and socially just agriculture. The range is impressive, including a) attempts to transform current practices and conceptions through such alternatives as integrated pest management or farming systems approaches; b) attempts to develop new systems, such as those based on organic approaches, localized food systems, or greater urban food production; c) research on bioregionally adapted systems (perennial polycultures and permacultures); and d) research on agro-ecological and agro-forestry approaches, whether through the examination of traditional peoples or the employment of systems models.

Each of these approaches tends to reject narrow professional, disciplinary, or sectoral definitions of agriculture. Systems approaches and interdisciplinary work are stressed. There are a number of implications that derive from these alternatives. In one sense, they represent an external response to the historic lack of self-criticism agriculture and the research establishment have had of their own activities. In another sense, they represent a fundamental conceptual shift from agricultural research to research on food and fibre systems—research which draws upon ecologically-based resource models and concerns for social justice. This involves a shift from an emphasis on production *per se* to an analysis of what sorts of food and fibre are needed for what specific purposes—a shift analogous to the development of end-use analysis in the energy field. Such food and fibre systems approaches also can include informal as well as formal dimensions; nutritional, waste disposal, and recycling aspects as well as input and production factors; urban as well as rural systems; and the interrelationships of different levels, goals, and priorities.

These alternative approaches—diverse as they are and often only in early and incomplete stages of development—suggest the need for a much greater self-questioning by the research establishment. First, as to why these approaches developed largely outside of it; next, as to the different models and assumptions which are used. However, for the research establishment to evaluate these models and assumptions, it will have to become more self-aware of its own models and assumptions. Equally, it will need to examine how effective these are in practice in achieving the larger goals it claims to be pursuing as well as how these goals themselves compare to the larger goals of the various alternative approaches. Finally, it will need to try to counter typical academic and institutional inertia and the tendency to identify with the *status quo.*

### Goals, Values, and Priorities

It is not only the need to evaluate and choose within and between the relative merits and costs of conventional and alternative approaches to agriculture that requires a much greater clarification of goals, values, and priorities. There is also the rise of new movements and actors—consumer groups, hunger action groups, animal rights groups, urban food cooperatives, environmentalists, nutritionists, and so on—that have concerns, values, and goals that relate more to food systems than to agriculture per se. Finally, there are shifts in the ethics, values, and goals of the larger society as we face great national and global uncertainties about nuclear war, environmental threats to the biosphere, increasing population, and increasing pressure on resources.

Of all the neglected dimensions examined in this book, ethics, values, goals, and priorities are most neglected in terms of serious analysis. There are, of course, regular, but very general and often rhetorical references to the important goals and values they are pursuing found in the literature of both conventional and alternative approaches. For serious analysis and clarification to occur, however, several of the major problem areas identified in the book must be addressed together. There must be a much clearer and detailed description of the full range of costs and benefits of agricultural systems (and how they are distributed)—including the many externalities and informal dimensions that have been brought out. That is, there must be a more complete and accurate picture of how agricultural and food systems operate within their larger context if we are to make reasonable evaluations and choices. There must be a better understanding of the various groups involved with both conventional and alternative approaches, what their professed and operative values, goals, and priorities are, and at what level each is relevant. That is, rather than assuming that behavior is motivated simply by utility maximization (the rational economic man), we must examine the complex interaction of goals, symbols, values, environmental and economic pressures, etc., that are involved in actual decision processes. Bennett's chapter describes this fully. Finally, there is the need for all to become more aware of the evaluative standards or models they and others employ—as is so clearly articulated by Aiken.

Important as better analysis and clarification of values, goals, and priorities is, we must keep in mind that this is really only part of a larger set of needs. Individual researchers, the various disciplines and professions, the different old and new groups concerned about agriculture, and the society at large all need to try to understand the transformations occurring in agriculture (and the society more generally) and to ask what their own hopes and responsibilities for the future are. Equally, all must recognize (as with war), that agriculture is too important to leave only to those directly involved in planning and conducting it. Much greater discussion and public participation is needed within and between the groups mentioned above if we as a society are going to develop a clearer and more concrete vision of the kind of food systems we want to strive for in the future, systems which are more resilient, regenerative, and socially just.

By raising fundamental questions regarding current directions in agriculture and agricultural research, bringing out a number of neglected dimensions, and discussing some of the emerging alternatives, it is hoped that this volume will contribute to a broadening and deepening of both professional and public discussions and debates regarding the future of agriculture.

# Index

# Contributors

Kenneth A. Dahlberg is Professor of Political Science at Western Michigan University, Kalamazoo. He has been the principal investigator for this NSF/NEH project. His book *Beyond the Green Revolution* was awarded the 1981 Harold and Margaret Sprout Award of the International Studies Association. He has served on several scientific advisory panels and has published on global environmental and biological diversity issues.

William H. Aiken is Associate Professor of Philosophy at Chatham College, Pittsburgh. In addition to various articles, he co-edited *World Hunger and Moral Obligation*. His research interests include individual rights, distributive justice, and environmental ethics as they apply to agriculture.

John W. Bennett is Professor of Anthropology at Washington University, St. Louis. His most recent books include *The Ecological Transition* and *Of Time and the Enterprise: North American Family Farm Management in a Context of Resource Marginality*. He is co-director of a recently funded three year binational project to examine the development of culture history and agricultural development in the Northern Plains.

Frederick H. Buttel is Associate Professor of Rural Sociology at Cornell University, Ithaca. His publications include various articles on the political economy of agriculture, rural structures, and bio-technological issues. He has co-edited several books, including *The Rural Sociology of the Advanced Societies: Critical Perspectives*.

Charles F. Cooper is Professor of Biology at San Diego State University and former Director of their Center for Regional Environmental Studies. In addition to serving on a number of national and international scientific advisory panels, he has published many articles on ecosystem-climate relationships, computer simulation of ecological processes, and ecology in relation to public policy.

Molly Joel Coye was a medical investigative officer for Region IX of the National Institute of Occupational Safety and Health from 1980 to 1985 as well as chief of the Occupational Health Clinic, San Francisco General Hospital. She has written numerous articles on occupational health problems, the ethical issues of research in occupational medicine, and on the health risks facing agricultural workers.

David B. Danbom is Associate Professor of History at North Dakota State University, Fargo. His research interests involve the nature of rural America and the ways it has changed, particularly during the Progressive Era. This, and his interest in the ways science has been institutionalized in agriculture are combined in his book, *The Resisted Revolution: Urban America and the Industrialization of Agriculture, 1900–1930.*

Alain de Janvry is Professor of Agricultural and Resource Economics at the University of California, Berkeley. He has served as consultant for several foundations and international agencies. His research interests in political economy, the peasantry, and rural development are blended in his book *The Agrarian Question and Reformism in Latin America,* as well as in numerous articles.

C. Dean Freudenberger is Professor of International Development Studies and Missions at the School of Theology, Claremont, California. Over the past 30 years, he has served in over 100 countries as an advisor on food policy and food production. His most recent books are *The Gift of Land* and *Food for Tomorrow?*

William D. Heffernan is Professor of Rural Sociology at the University of Missouri, Columbia. His research interests in rural affairs and small scale farming are reflected in his many articles and through his service on the Boards of such diverse groups as the Council of Agricultural Science and Technology and the National Sharecroppers/Rural Advancement Fund.

John Patrick Jordan is administrator of the Cooperative State Research Service, USDA. Previously, he served as director of the Agricultural Experiment Station and Cooperative Extension Service at Colorado State University, Fort Collins. Trained as a biochemist, his research interests include metabolic processes in both natural and artificial environments.

E. Phillip LeVeen is director of Public Interest Economics–West, Berkeley, California. Earlier, he taught at the University of California, Berkeley. In addition to extensive consulting activities, his publications have focused on the social and economic consequences of federal and California water resource development and the environmental and resource impacts of agricultural technologies.

Jean Lipman-Blumen is the Thornton F. Bradshaw Professor of Public Policy and Organizational Behavior at the Claremont Graduate School, Claremont, California. In addition to many national and international consultancies, she has written extensively in three fields: gender roles, education, and agriculture. She was co-principal investigator for the recent USDA publication *The Paradox of Success.* Her most recent book is *Gender Roles and Power.*

William Lockeretz is Research Associate Professor at the School of Nutrition, Tufts University, Bedford, Massachusetts. He has done extensive research on the energy efficiency of different agricultural production systems. In addition to his many articles, he has edited three books, most recently *Environmentally Sound Agriculture.* He is currently engaged in a research project on developing closer ties between farmers and urban consumers.

Patrick Madden is Professor of Agricultural Economics, The Pennsylvania State University, University Park. He has done extensive research on issues of farm size, rural development, the evaluation of nutrition programs, and the diffusion of agricultural technologies. His many articles reflect these concerns, plus a growing interest in the economic and social barriers to more regenerative farming systems.

Paul F. O'Connell is special assistant to the Assistant Secretary for Science & Education, USDA. He has several publications in natural resource economics, primarily concerned with multiple use management on western National Forests. He recently led a team that prepared the mandated reports called for in the 1981 farm bill—*Needs Assessment, Five Year Plan,* and *Priorities Report.*

David Pimentel is Professor of Insect Ecology and Agricultural Sciences, Cornell University, Ithaca. He has served on scientific advisory panels for the National Academy of Sciences, the Department of Energy, and other agencies. His research interests include the ecological and economic aspects of pest control, energy use in the food system, and natural resources management. He has written numerous scientific papers and books, including *Food, Energy, and Society.*

Susan Pimentel serves in a policy-making role as special counsel to a Maryland State representative. She has particular interest in environmental issues and has published several articles on natural resource use and food policy.

Roland R. Robinson is Principal Agricultural Economist, Cooperative State Research Service, USDA. In addition to preparing many reports for CSRS, he has had research interests in science management and the institutional history of CSRS and the SAES.

Dale L. Stansbury is Director, Federal Relations, Agriculture and Natural Resources, for the National Association of State Universities and Land Grant Colleges. He previously served as chief economist for the Senate Committee on Agriculture, Nutrition, and Forestry. Trained as an agricultural economist, he currently is emphasizing the development of public policies for the support of science.